P9-EKB-901

D0013964

Arizona, New Mexico & the Grand Canyon

TRIPS

58 THEMED ITINERARIES **1005** LOCAL PLACES TO SEE

Becca Blond,
Aaron Anderson, Sara Benson, Jennifer Denniston, Lisa Dunford,
Josh Krist, Wendy Yanagihara

ARIZONA, NEW MEXICO & THE GRAND CANYON TRIPS

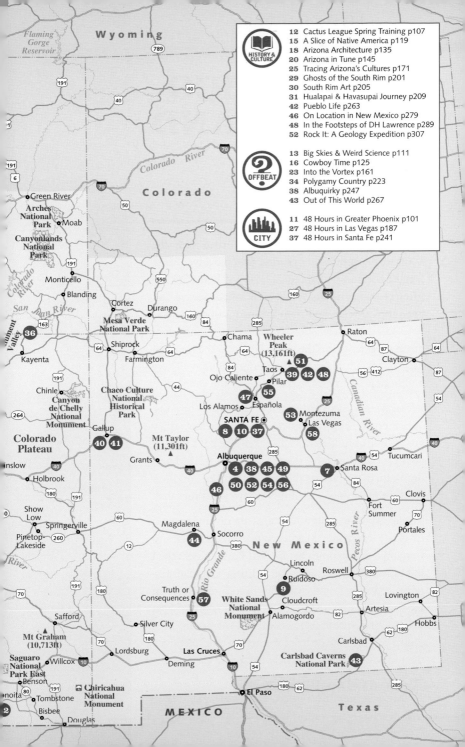

ARIZONA, NEW MEXICO & THE GRAND CANYON TRIPS

From stargazing retreats to Route 66 road trips, the Southwest is a breeding ground for epic adventures. But the trickiest part about vacationing here isn't figuring out what to do, it's deciding what to leave out. Even those of us who live in this magically lit land of sage-scented desert, snow-capped mountains, giant green succulents and the wildest cities in the west, get flustered when planning the perfect holiday. There are more ways to escape than days in the year.

We're here to help you narrow down the options. Whether you're on a quest for margaritas, spicy green chile or hidden hot springs, we've got a trip for you. Our authors have driven, paddled, walked and drank their way across the region to bring you their 58 favorite ways of reaching Southwestern nirvana.

These easy-to-execute adventures are diverse enough to excite everyone. Maybe you've seen the Grand Canyon a dozen times before. But have you checked out its wedding-cake layers on a rim-to-rim hike? Experienced it in fast-forward motion, bucking down the Colorado's rapids? From thematic to epic, offbeat to outdoorsy, historical to downright wacky, our trips dump you into the heart of the action and introduce the old Southwest from a new perspective.

⊕ **HIKING THE NORTH RIM** p213
Outstanding views of the Grand Canyon from Tuweep, Arizona

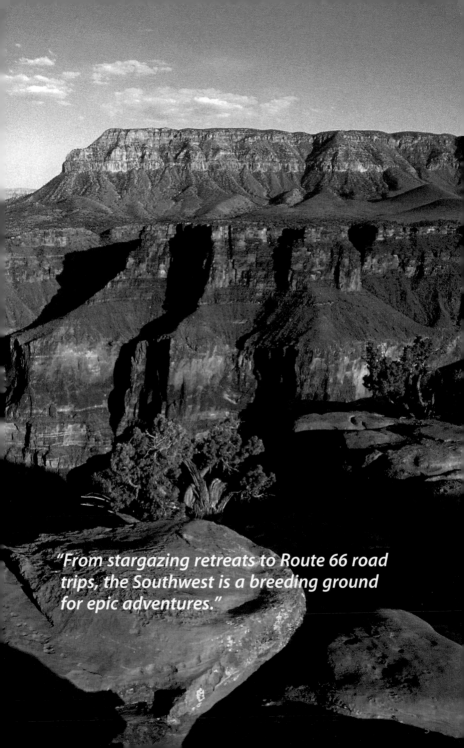

"From stargazing retreats to Route 66 road trips, the Southwest is a breeding ground for epic adventures."

CRUISING THE MOTHER ROAD

Drive America's original highway, Route 66, across the belly of New Mexico and Arizona, passing tumbleweeds, 1950s billboards, greasy-spoon diners and half a century's worth of nostalgia in the small towns along the way.

PHOTOGRAPHING MONUMENT VALLEY p129
Navajo tour guide in Antelope Canyon, Arizona

MOTORING THE MOTHER ROAD: ROUTE 66 p45
Iconic car outside the Wigwam Motel, Route 66, Arizona

SOUTHERN DESERT WANDERINGS p149
Cacti at sunset, Saguaro National Park, Arizona

LAZING ON LAKE POWELL p219
Horseshoe Bend on the Colorado River near Page, Arizona

Iconic Trips

Welcome to epic America, the luscious backdrop to Hollywood blockbusters and the red-rock land of limitless horizons – where Native American ruins and **Wild West legends** (p89) hark back to distant eras, and quirky art houses sit next to saguaro cacti on rural routes. From **Gunfighters & Gold Miners** (p73) and ghost towns to **Rafting the Colorado's** (p55) monster rapids, these 10 iconic adventures represent the best road-, river- and train-tripping west of the Mississippi.

"...these 10 iconic adventures represent the best road-, river- and train-tripping west of the Mississippi."

ONE BIG DROP

The single biggest single drop on the Colorado River in the Grand Canyon is at Lava Falls – here the river plummets 37 stomach-churning feet in 300 yards.

RIM-TO-RIM CANYON HIKE p67
Hikers on the Bright Angel Trail, Grand Canyon National Park, Arizona

FOUR CORNERS CRUISE p35
Arches National Park, Utah

GUNFIGHTERS & GOLD MINERS p73
Dilapidated shack and truck from another era, Jerome, Arizona

"...invest in a killer car stereo and spend as much time as possible road tripping the Southwest USA ..."

Routes

Somewhere between Dr Seussian red-rock formation number 59 and yet another psychedelic sunset you realize you haven't only witnessed five-star beauty, you've also formulated a five-year plan: invest in a killer car stereo and spend as much time as possible road tripping the Southwest USA, a place invented for such meanderings. Whether you are searching for handicrafts on the **Fiber Arts Trail** (p271), checking out **Ice Caves & Wolf Dens on Hwy 53** (p255), New Mexico's most eccentric scenic drive, or going on a **Fantastic Canyon Voyage** (p193) from Phoenix, you can't go wrong on these seven routes. Set to a backdrop of jagged peaks and crumbling adobe, Native American ruins and small towns, they are the most memorable drives in the west.

BEST SHORT DRIVE: THE LAS VEGAS STRIP

It's only 4.5 miles long, but it's also one of America's most legendary drives. For the ultimate Strip cruise, rent a convertible, dress up as Elvis and drive (slowly) after dark.

 # Food & Drink

From organic vegan to cowboy campfire, eating in the Southwest is as eclectic and diverse as the region's culture and landscape. And our six adventures in eating and drinking let you experience it all. Hunt for the best cut of beef on our **Steak-Lovers' Arizona** (p115) trip, or treat yourself to small-batch beer tasting on New Mexico's **Brewpub Crawl** (p251) and Arizona's **Grapes & Hops in the Desert** (p155). Margaritas are New Mexico's unofficial state drink, and our **Margarita Marathon** (p299) gives you the tangy sweet scoop on scoring the tequila concoctions. If you feel toxic after too much booze and beef, take our expert's advice and catch a healthy buzz on the **Farm to Table: Organic New Mexico** (p275) trip.

GREEN CHILE IN THE FAST LANE

New Mexico harvests more than 30,000 acres of chiles annually, predominantly in the Southwestern town of Hatch, where just about every restaurant (including McDonald's) offers green chile as a side.

Outdoors

When it comes to the great outdoors, the Southwest is one giant playground. And our 14 outdoor-oriented trips serve an all-you-can eat buffet of both adrenalin-pumping and relaxing natural adventures. Water rats can devote days to **Rafting & Fishing the Rio Grande** (p319) or getting a sun tan while **Lazing on Lake Powell** (p219). To fly down sick single track, head to western New Mexico and ride trails described in our **Mountain Biking Gallup** (p259) adventure. If you want mind-blowing scenery and minimal exercise, try **Photographing Monument Valley** (p129) or discovering new natural soaking pools in **Hot Springs & Swimming Holes** (p311). Wannabe astronomers won't want to miss our **Stargazing New Mexico** (p335) trip, one of the most unusual trips around.

" *When it comes to the great outdoors, the Southwest is one giant playground.*"

WATER, WATER, EVERYWHERE

Lake Powell contains about 8.5 trillion gallons of water and has 1960 miles of coastline, more than the coastline from Seattle to San Diego.

CALLING WANNABE MOVIE STARS...

Have you ever wanted to play dead (or breath the same air as Brad Pitt) in a movie? Then check out www.nmfilm.com for info on "extras" casting calls in New Mexico.

"The legend of the Wild West has always been America's grandest tale..."

History & Culture

The legend of the Wild West has always been America's grandest tale, capturing the imagination of writers, photographers, singers, filmmakers and travelers the world over. Individuality is the cultural idiom of the Southwest and the focus of our 12 cultural and historical trips. We strive to take the stuffiness out of the history lesson, and bring the region to life through experiences. Follow baseball's spring training trail with our **Cactus League Spring Training** (p107) trip, go **On Location in New Mexico** (p279), checking out movie locations, unearth your inner rock hunter on **Rock It: A Geology Expedition** (p307), and seek out ancient cultures on our **A Slice of Native America** (p119) trip.

Offbeat

Home to UFO fanatics, vortex junkies, New Age artists and environmental warriors, the Southwest is like nowhere else in the USA. Whether you want to sip an Atomic Ale in the birthplace of nuclear fission or swap tales of conspiracy theories and UFO sightings in the birthplace of alien mania, our offbeat adventures take you **Out of This World** (p267) and way off the mainstream grid. For a different kind of religious experience, step **Into the Vortex** (p161) and realign your chakras in red-rock energy fields. From lava tubes and lunar landscapes in **Big Skies & Weird Science** (p111) to **Albuquirky** (p247), these six trips explore the best of the kitsch, occult and downright weird Southwest.

BIG SKIES & WEIRD SCIENCE p111
Exhibit inside the Titan Missile Museum, Arizona

ALBUQUIRKY p247
International Balloon Fiesta Mass Ascension, Albuquerque, New Mexico

OUT OF THIS WORLD p267
Aliens at an Alien Festival, Roswell, New Mexico

DRIVING WITH ALIENS

Between Carlsbad and Roswell, New Mexico Hwy 285 is dubbed the "extraterrestrial highway." It's a high-traffic route: the alien headquarters town of Roswell attracts thousands of human visitors each year.

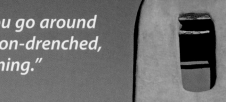

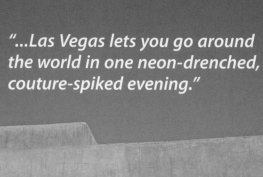

"...Las Vegas lets you go around the world in one neon-drenched, couture-spiked evening."

Cities

From the world's most famous art alley to serious-bling shopping, five-star eating and posh hotels, the Southwest's gateway cities serve cake and let you eat it too. When it comes to fantasies, Las Vegas, Santa Fe and Phoenix are all about indulging. Our **48 Hours in Las Vegas** (p187) trip lets you go around the world in one neon-drenched, couture-spiked evening. Spend **48 Hours in Santa Fe** (p241), the USA's oldest existing capital and top art destination, home to an eclectic lot of retired filmmakers, acclaimed sculptors and adobe architecture. Arizona's biggest metropolis may resemble one squirming strip mall from above, but after **48 Hours in Phoenix** (p101), you'll have discovered the best spas, swimming pools and golf resorts in the country.

BEST TRIPS

WRITTEN IN STONE: UTAH'S NATIONAL PARKS p227
The Narrows, Zion National Park, Utah

TINY TOWNS OF RIM COUNTRY p139
Lost Dutchman State Park, Arizona

Contents

GRAND CANYON REGION TRIPS 185

NEW MEXICO TRIPS 239

Trips by Theme

CITIES

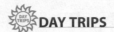
DAY TRIPS

Trips by Season

SPRING

SUMMER

FALL

WINTER

YEAR-ROUND

Expert-Recommended Trips

The Authors

BECCA BLOND
Becca has written 32 travel guides for Lonely Planet since 2003, including the last two editions of Lonely Planet's *Southwest USA*. When in Santa Fe, be sure to visit the Loretto Chapel, where she married the love of her life and writing partner, Aaron Anderson, on October 18, 2008.

SARA BENSON
Sara has contributed to dozens of Lonely Planet titles, including *Las Vegas* and *Encounter Las Vegas*. Her travel writing has featured in magazines and newspapers, both in print and online, including the *Los Angeles Times* and *Las Vegas Review-Journal*.

AARON ANDERSON
Aaron began his professional career making beer, not books, working as a microbrewer before becoming a travel writer. He's since contributed to seven Lonely Planet guides, including *Cycling in Britain*, *Thailand* and *Madagascar & Comoros*.

JENNIFER DENNISTON
Since 1991 Jennifer has traveled the back roads and trails of northern New Mexico, falling in love with the region's distinct landscape and culture, especially its green chile and acequias, and the smell of burning piñon in a kiva fireplace. As New Mexican folksinger Bill Hearne sang, "If I ain't happy here, I ain't happy nowhere."

LISA DUNFORD
It was slot canyons and slickrock, ancient American ruins and rock art that first attracted Lisa to Utah. But tripping around talking about her great-great-great-grandfather Brigham Young turned out to be just as intriguing. Lisa is the author of the Utah chapter of Lonely Planet's *Southwest USA* guide.

JOSH KRIST
In Arizona, Josh Krist grew up; went to university; camped alone in the desert for three days when he was 14; worked on a firefighting airplane; rode rickety motorcycles; and reported for a few of the daily newspapers. He's written about Mexico, Thailand, Vietnam and the Caribbean for Lonely Planet.

WENDY YANAGIHARA
Though her first experience of the Grand Canyon was typical – a family road trip, Dad posing for a photo pretending to fall over the edge (don't do it!) – Wendy has since hiked from rim to rim, rafted the Colorado, and only begun to explore the wonders of the canyon.

LONELY PLANET AUTHORS
Why is our travel information the best in the world? It's simple: our authors are independent, dedicated travelers. They don't research using just the internet or phone, and they don't take freebies, so you can rely on their advice being well researched and impartial. They travel widely, to all the popular spots and off the beaten track. They personally visit thousands of hotels, restaurants, cafés, bars, galleries, palaces, museums and more – and they take pride in getting all the details right, and telling it how it is. Think you can do it? Find out how at lonelyplanet.com.

CONTRIBUTING EXPERTS

Dr Yemane Asmerom Yemane Asmerom directs the radiogenic isotope lab in the University of New Mexico's department of Earth and Planetary Sciences and studies subjects ranging from Rio Grande Rift volcanics to Carlsbad Caverns stalagmites. He lends his expertise to Rock It: A Geology Expedition p307.

Edward Borins and Nancy Rutland Edward Borins has been a bookseller since 1973. In 1979, he and his wife Eva opened Edwards Books & Art in downtown Toronto, and it soon grew to five stores. After moving to Santa Fe in 1997, they purchased Garcia Street Books, which has been consistently voted Santa Fe's best independent bookstore. Nancy Rutland opened Bookworks in 1984 after receiving an MA in English from the University of Virginia. She lives in Corrales, and, when not reading, she enjoys walks along the Rio Grande with her husband and dogs. She can be reached at nancyr@bkwrks.com. They provided knowledgeable guidance on the In the Footsteps of DH Lawrence trip p289.

Blair Carl Blair Carl is an 11-year Sedona resident and tour guide (www.blairsedona.net) to some of the best spiritual spots in the area. He lent his expertise to the mind-bending Into the Vortex trip p161.

Ted Flicker Ted Flicker is the writer and director of the 1967 comedic classic *The President's Analyst,* and the creator of the popular 1970s TV show *Barney Miller,* which gave him the getaway money to leave Hollywood, move to Santa Fe and learn to sculpt. To find out more, visit www.tedflicker.com. He shares insider knowledge in On Location in New Mexico p279.

Richard Harris Richard Harris, a gourmet cook, has written 36 travel and history books, including many on the American West, and is president of the New Mexico Book Association. He lives in Santa Fe and provided valuable guidance on the Farm to Table: Organic New Mexico trip p275.

Fran Lightly Fran Lightly, Sonoita Vineyards' winemaker, worked for 10 years in California's Livermore Valley before touring the country's up-and-coming wine regions. Southern Arizona wines knocked his socks off, so he stayed. For a sip of his expertise take the Grapes & Hops in the Desert trip p155.

Cliff Ochser Cliff Ochser, founder of Evening Sky Tours, was instrumental in helping Lowell Observatory build the Discovery Channel Telescope, under construction in Happy Jack. He lent his stellar insights to the Big Skies & Weird Science trip p111.

Shipherd Reed Shipherd Reed hauls a copperplated trailer around Arizona and New Mexico to record the stories of underground miners – a vanishing breed – for the University of Arizona's Miners Story Project (www.minersstory.org). He shared his insights in the Gunfighters & Gold Miners trip p73.

William Reese Ranger William Reese has lived and worked on both rims of the Grand Canyon for more than 10 years and logged hundreds of canyon miles; he shares some favorite hikes in Hiking the North Rim p213.

ARIZONA, NEW MEXICO & THE GRAND CANYON ICONIC TRIPS

ICONIC
TRIPS

Road trips were invented for the Southwest. The birthplace of atomic energy, alien mania and sin (city) has long served as the luscious backdrop for Hollywood movies and magazine photo shoots with good reason. The blockbuster scenery is of the crimson rock, pumpkin mesa, big blue sky and golden light persuasion. Not only is the Southwest blessed with iconic good looks, she offers a healthy dose of history, adrenalin-pumping activities and tarmac worthy of a convertible.

In this chapter we take you on epic road, river and train trips. Drive deep into the heart of the Wild West, revisiting cowboy and Indian culture in ghost towns where the scent of last century's tobacco mingles with the grease of yesterday's cheeseburgers at the saloon where Billy the Kid knocked down a few cold ones back in 1882. Cruise the nostalgia highway on our Route 66 road trip, passing tumbleweeds, 1950s billboards and greasy spoon diners along the way. Or snap a photo with a hand and foot in four states on our Four Corners loop. Adrenalin junkies will find their speed while dam diving New Mexico's astonishingly clear, almost tropically warm Blue Hole or rafting the Grand Canyon's monster rapids. Whether you're soul-searching at a quirky rural highway art-house next to a giant saguaro cacti or dancing your heart out on the Strip, these are the trips of your lifetime.

PLAYLIST 🎵 Everyone has their own idea of the ultimate road-trip mix. Below are a few tunes we find ourselves singing along to while cruising America's most iconic scenery and down her most famous stretches of pavement.

- "Take it Easy," The Eagles
- "Route 66," Nat King Cole
- "Route 666," Brian Berdan
- "Arizona," Kings of Leon
- "Yuma, AZ," Damien Jurado
- "Taos, New Mexico," Waylon Jennings
- "Santa Fe," Bob Dylan
- "Viva Las Vegas," Elvis Presley

BEST ICONIC TRIPS

ARIZONA, NEW MEXICO & THE GRAND CANYON ICONIC TRIPS

Four Corners Cruise

WHY GO From the neon chaos of Las Vegas to the solitude of the Grand Canyon, the scenery on this epic 3000-mile road trip across five states is ripped straight from the silver screen. Throw in a Wild West back-story, neo-Hippie art colonies, giant cacti and UFOs and get ready for one grand Jack Kerouac–style adventure.

TIME
2 – 3 weeks

DISTANCE
3000 miles

BEST TIME TO GO
Year-round

START
Las Vegas, NV

END
Las Vegas, NV

ALSO GOOD FOR

Your iconic journey starts in ❶ Las Vegas, America's most scintillating adult playground. Seedy yet decadent, Sin City is a puzzling paradox where fate is decided by the spin of a roulette wheel and time seems irrelevant. Here the sight of the Great Pyramids of Egypt, the Eiffel Tower, the Italian lake country and the Brooklyn Bridge in the same mile, leave you feeling like you've stumbled into someone else's acid trip. Is that really a bible-toting Elvis kissing a giddy young couple that's just pledged eternity in the Chapel of Love? A Gucci-garbed porn star hawking her hip-hop demo amid the chaos of clanking slots and flashing neon? The answer is more than likely yes.

All that glitters is likely gold in this high-octane desert oasis, where the poor feel rich and the rich lose thousands. At the opulent ❷ Bellagio, glamour's sweet stench is thicker than the cigarette smoke of the blue-haired grandmother feeding quarters into the nickel slots. Inspired by the beauty of lakeside Italy, the casino resort is the city's original Euro pimp pleasure palace. Check out the ceiling in the hotel lobby. It's made from a vibrantly colored bouquet of 2000 handblown glass flowers.

Las Vegas tempts you to lose your inhibitions and indulge your naughtiest fantasies. And what better place to loosen up than Sin City's guiltiest new pleasure, the ❸ Pussycat Dolls Lounge? Lingerie-clad ladies do a little aerial swinging, play rub-a-dub-dub in a tub and flaunt their bodies during sexy song-and-dance numbers at this burlesque lounge

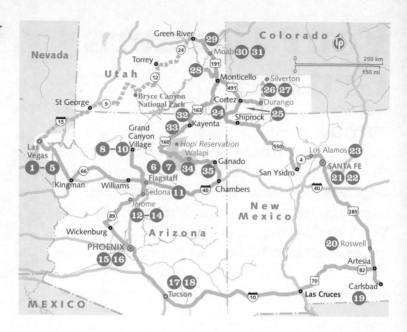

inside Caesar's Palace. When the club opened, Busta Rhymes got so excited he jumped on stage and inadvertently started a tradition. Eva Longaria Parker, Nicole Kidman and Jessica Simpson are just a few of the celebrities who have performed impromptu with the Dolls since.

High-drama and neon drenched, the ❹ Palms casino hotel is just off the strip and caters to the Hollywood crowd. Paris Hilton and her pals like to play in exclusive sci-fi inspired ❺ ghostbar on the 55th floor. It has amazing 360° panoramic views of the famous Las Vegas Strip. When you can't keep your eyes open, move the party to your room. We hear the Hugh Hefner suite – with a round bed, and a glass-enclosed infinity pool on the porch – is the sexiest room in town.

After a couple days in Las Vegas, make a run for the border. The Arizona border, that is. It's about 250 miles from Sin City to Arizona's favorite crunchy college-meets-ski town, ❻ Flagstaff, your destination for the night. The drive itself is attractive, linking up Route 66 in Kingman and following an old stretch of the "Mother Road" east over empty umber hills and tumbleweeds before climbing into the gentle mountains outside Flagstaff. You'll be feeling road worn and weary by this point, so check into the ❼ Hotel Monte Vista, once the inn of choice for film stars like Humphrey Bogart, Clark Gable and Jane Russell. As befits a place with such a pedigree, it is said to be haunted (but only by friendly ghosts, the proprietors proclaim).

It's just under 80 beautiful, winding miles from Flagstaff to America's most iconic natural attraction, the **⑧ Grand Canyon**. Although many people (and tour buses) see little more of the park than the South Rim viewing center, to do so would be a shame. To make the most out of this national park, you need to devote at least three days to the region. Whether you get to the bottom via mule or foot power is not important, but spending the night at **⑨ Phantom Ranch** on the canyon floor is paramount. Catch a Grand Canyon sunset, an amazing play of light and shadow, from the porch of the **⑩ El Tovar** on your last night. Albert Einstein and Teddy Roosevelt have both slumbered at this rambling 1905 wooden lodge, and so should you. The place hasn't lost a lick of its genteel historic patina.

Loop south from the Grand Canyon and drive through 110 miles of Arizona's red rock country to **⑪ Sedona**. With spindly towers, grand buttes and flat-topped mesas carved in crimson sandstone the town can easily hold its own against national parks when it comes to breathtaking beauty. Memorialized in countless Western flicks, the scenery has provided a jaw-dropping back-drop for those riding tall in the saddle. Though Sedona was founded in the 19th century, the discovery of energy vortices here in the 1980s turned this once modest settlement into a bustling New Age destination – many believe this area is the center of vortices that radiate the Earth's power. Follow Hwy 89A south from Sedona. The first part of the drive winds through the best of red rock country – when the light hits these massive rocks at the right angle they glow tomato, pumpkin and gold. It then climbs the crumbling ridge of the Mogollon Rim to **⑫ Jerome**, our favorite ghost-gone-gallery town in the Southwest. Wedged into steep Cleopatra Hill, Jerome resembles those higgledy-piggledy Mediterranean hamlets clinging to a rocky hillside. Well, at least from afar. Close-ups reveal a history solidly rooted in the Old West. Jerome was home of the unimaginably fertile United Verde Mine, nicknamed the "Billion Dollar Copper Camp." It was also the wickedest town in the West, teeming with brothels, saloons and opium dens. When the mines petered out, the remaining residents looked to tourism as the new gold. Spend the night at the **⑬ Mile High Inn**. Once a bordello and then a hardware store, today it's a snug, but haunted, B&B. Reserve the Lariat & Lace Room for the best chance of seeing a ghost; the former madam supposedly still hangs out here. The **⑭ Asylum Restaurant**, in the Jerome Grand Hotel, has the best views and food in town. The venerable dining room is decorated with deep-red walls, lazily twirling fans and gilded artwork.

"As befits a place with such a pedigree, Hotel Monte Vista is said to be haunted ..."

A conglomeration of some 20 cities zippered together by freeways, **⑮ Phoenix**, 120 miles south, resembles one giant (and not particularly pretty) strip mall upon first look. But there's much more here than seen on the initial glance.

Phoenix is an excellent place to get pampered in a ritzy spa at a five-star resort, dine on juicy steaks and practice your golf game – there are more than 230 courses in the metropolis. Try staying at the **16** **Boulders Resort**, where tensions evaporate the moment you arrive. It's a desert oasis blending nearly imperceptibly into a landscape of natural rock formations that is home to the ultra-posh Golden Door Spa and an 18-hole Jay Morris–designed championship golf course.

ASK A LOCAL

"What so special about Santa Fe? The light. The atmosphere. It is like not being in America, and yet I am still here. There is no place else in the country with architecture like here. One of the great things about Santa Fe is it's the classic American small town. I go to restaurants and always run into people I know. I even run into them on the sidewalk. And it's not pretentious. That's part of why I moved here."

Ted Flicker, Santa Fe sculptor

It's just a short hop from Phoenix south to the bustling college town of **17** **Tucson**. Less intimidating than her big sister, Tucson is Arizona's second largest city, but feels like a small town. This is a town rich in Hispanic heritage (more than 20% of the population is of Mexican or Central American descent), so Spanish slides easily off most tongues and high-quality Mexican restaurants abound. The eclectic shops toting vintage garb, scores of funky restaurants and dive bars don't let you forget Tucson is a college town at heart, home turf to the 37,000-strong University of Arizona (U of A). Right in the thick of things downtown, infamous bank robber John Dillinger and his gang were captured at the **18** **Hotel Congress** during their 1934 stay after a fire forced them out of their guestroom. Today this bohemian vintage beauty remains a hot spot to slumber. Don't miss one of Tucson's best live music venues, Club Congress, which is in the same building.

Get a good night's rest in Tucson, because your next destination is 475 miles (eight hours) away in southeastern New Mexico. It's a long haul across from Tucson to **19** **Carlsbad Caverns National Park**, but this stretch of pavement is made for road tripping. Pump up the stereo and sing at the top of your lungs as you whiz past fields of giant cacti, huge skies and pancake-flat desert on your way to this enchanted underground wonderland. Musty-smelling limestone and fluttering free tail bats (the population is 250,000 strong) add to the creepiness as you descend 800ft into the strange underground world of one of the planet's greatest cave systems. Ranger-led tours take you into the dripping heart of the 75-sq-mile network of some 100 caves. Emerge before sunset. You don't want to miss the cartoon-like spectacle of thousands of bats flying from the mouths of the caves, cutting black lines through the crimson sky as they circle overhead, looking for a buggy dinner.

Move from bats to extraterrestrials by following Hwy 285 north to **20** **Roswell**, the alien capital of the world. Sure this town is about as cheesy as it gets for most of us, but conspiracy theorists and *X-Files* fanatics journey here in the utmost seriousness. Whether or not you believe a flying saucer crashed here in July 1947, Roswell merits a visit if only to experience America's alien obsession. While in town, make sure to pay a visit to the International UFO Museum & Research Center. It just might make a believer out of you...

Spunky **21** Santa Fe is the next tick on your list. The USA's oldest capital is also the country's top art destination. Home to retired cityfolk and with world-class galleries and adobe everywhere, it's the heart and soul of New Mexico. Food is just another form of art in Santa Fe, and it's always a toss-up whether the city boasts more quality restaurants or galleries. Either way, you can't go wrong at **22** Shed, a low-key restaurant right on the historic plaza. Sink your teeth into a fresh squeezed lime margarita, creamy guacamole and a spicy green chile–drenched enchilada and you'll think you've died and gone to Southwest foodie heaven. Cut northwest from Santa Fe, through the nuclear town of **23** Los Alamos, and into Indian country. The wild northern corner of the state has long been the domain of the Navajo, Pueblo, Zuni, Apache and Laguna people.

New Mexico, Arizona, Utah and Colorado meet at the **24** Four Corners Navajo Tribal Park. Plant a foot in each state – this is the only spot in America where four states touch in one corner – and take a silly picture. Then cross into southwestern Colorado. With striking scenery, wild history and cool mountain towns, this part of the state looks like it belongs in a John Denver music video. There is a mystery without a conclusion in the ruins of **25** Mesa Verde National Park, your first stop in Colorado. In AD 1300 an entire civilization of Ancestral Puebloans vanished without a trace. Their disappearance has proven so intriguing that eight centuries later, historians and tourists flock to the cliffside empires in search of

DETOUR Climb aboard the steam-driven **Durango & Silverton Narrow Gauge Railway** (www.durangotrain.com) for the train ride of the summer. The train, running between Durango and Silverton, has been in continuous operation for 123 years, and the scenic 45-mile journey north to Silverton – the entire town is a National Historic Landmark – takes 3½ hours each way. The voyage costs $75 for adults and $45 for children. It is most glorious in late September or early October when the trees put on a magnificent color show.

puzzle-solving clues. The largest, and most impressive, cliff dwellings are around Wetherhill and Chapin Mesas. Wear sturdy shoes – hiking here involves scrambling up ancient wooden ladders and down narrow holes.

After you gathered all your clues, head east on Hwy 160 for 65 miles to **26** Durango, your destination for the night. It's one of those archetypal old Colorado mining towns filled with graceful old hotels and Victorian-era saloons; a place seemingly frozen in time. The waitress slinging drinks at the scarred wooden bar is dressed straight out of the early 19th century. The antique-laden inn and the musician pounding ragtime on worn ivory keys add to the surrealism. It usually takes stepping into a classy store or modern restaurant to break the spell of yesteryear, and realize it's still the new '00s, and you haven't really traveled back two centuries to 1898. There's a dining option poised to charm the most critical of palates and a store for any desire, from outdoor apparel to fancy jewelry or funky retro garb. Durango's lovely old-world **27** **Strater Hotel** is the best place to sleep. The museum-worthy interior features a Stradivarius violin and gold-plated commemorative Winchester in the lobby.

"... you may hear spontaneous popping noises in distant rocks – the sound of arches forming."

Head west to eastern Utah when you are finished exploring Durango. Nicknamed Canyon Country, this desolate corner of Utah is home to soaring snow-blanketed peaks towering over plunging red-rock river canyons. The terrain is so inhospitable that it was the last region to be mapped on continental US. Utah's largest and wildest park is **28** **Canyonlands National Park**. Over 65 million years, water carved serpentine, sheer-walled gorges along the course of the Colorado and Green Rivers, which now define the park's three districts. Arches, bridges, needles, spires, craters, mesas, buttes – wherever you look there is evidence of crumbling, decaying beauty and a vision of ancient earth here. Hike, raft and 4WD (Cataract Canyon offers some of the wildest white water in the West), but be sure that you have plenty of gas, food and water before leaving the hub town of Moab. Difficult terrain and lack of water render this the least developed and visited of the major Southwestern national parks. The Island in the Sky district, 32 miles south of Moab off Hwy 191 and Hwy 313, is the easiest area to visit.

It's about 50 miles from the Island in the Sky District to **29** **Arches National Park**. Northeast of Moab, the park is home to the most crimson arches in the world. Consider a moonlight exploration, when it's cooler and the rocks feel truly ghostly. Many arches are easily reached by paved roads and relatively short hiking trails. Highlights include Balanced Rock, the oft-photographed Delicate Arch (best captured in the late afternoon) and the spectacularly elongated Landscape Arch. As you casually stroll beneath these monuments to nature's power, listen carefully, especially in winter, and you may hear spontaneous popping noises in distant rocks – the sound of arches forming.

Encircled by stunning orange rocks and the snow-capped La Sal Mountains, **30** **Moab** lies between the two parks and is Utah's adrenalin-junkie destination. In this active and outdoorsy town with legendary slickrock mountains, it seems as though every pedestrian clutches a Nalgene water bottle and every car totes a few dusty mountain bikes. Moab bills itself as Utah's recreation capital, and it delivers. Get some rest at the **31** Gonzo Inn, a fun and funky boutique with a gecko theme. Check out retro color splashes in the spacious rooms and suites, which also boast kitchenettes and cool patios.

Follow Hwy 191 south from Moab (it eventually becomes Hwy 163) for about 150 miles, dipping back into Arizona to see drop dead gorgeous Monument Valley. Home of western America's most visceral landscape, it's nearly impossible to visit this sacred place without feeling a serious sense of déjà vu. That's because the flaming-red buttes and impossibly slender spires bursting to the heavens have starred in countless Hollywood Westerns. Great views of the rock formations are found all along Hwy 163, but to get up close and personal follow the signs to **32** Monument Valley Navajo Tribal Park. From the visitor center, a rough and unpaved road goes through 17 miles of stunning valley views. Continuing south on Hwy 160 from Monument Valley, you'll cross through the vast lands of the Navajo Reservation. The evidence of hard times is everywhere here, from the rusting tumbledown trailers to social services buildings in small nowhere towns. Still, gorgeous sites are peppered throughout.

Nine miles off Hwy 160, **33** Navajo National Monument is one of the lesser-visited cliff dwellings in the region. Hike to the sublimely well preserved Ancestral Puebloan cliff dwellings of Betatkin and Keet Seel. Accessible only by foot, there's something truly magical about approaching these ancient stone villages in relative solitude. You can also walk a half-mile from the visitor center to catch a glimpse of Betatkin.

The nearby Hopi Reservation is also worth exploring. Don't miss the village of **34** Walapi on First Hopi Mesa – the reservation stretches across three mesa tops. The most dramatic of the Hopi enclaves, Walapi dates back to AD 1200 and clings like an aerie

DETOUR An alternative way to reach Las Vegas from the Moab area takes you along Utah's most scenically orgasmic byway, Hwy 12, stopping along along the way to gawk at magnificent **Bryce Canyon National Park**. The road eventually merges with Hwy 15 south to Las Vegas. Make sure to take advantage of the byway's pull-offs to watch this amazing hued landscape slide from slickrock desert to red rock canyon to wooded high plateau.

onto the mesa's narrow end – the mostly empty old sandstone-colored stone houses seem to organically sprout from the cliffs. The Hopi are best known for their ceremonial dances, although many, especially the super sacred Kachina Dances, are Hopi-only affairs. These are serious, holy ceremonies not meant for photo-snapping or gawking tourists. Each village decides which dances it allows the public to attend, but your best shot is between late August and November, when the Social and Butterfly Dances take place.

It's a grueling 370-mile drive northeast (take Hwy 264 east from the Hopi Reservation) to **35** **Canyon de Chelly National Monument** on the outskirts of Ganado, but the remote and beautiful park is worth the nearly eight hour drive. A National Park Service–maintained site on private Navajo land, multi-pronged Canyon de Chelly (pronounced 'd-SHAY') is far removed from time and space and modern civilization. It shelters prehistoric rock art and 1000-year-old Ancestral Puebloan dwellings built into water resistant alcoves.

NAVAJO CRAFTS

The Navajo rely on the tourist economy to survive; help keep their heritage alive by purchasing their renowned crafts – you'll see stalls and gift shops throughout the Navajo Nation, the reservation that is also home to Monument Valley's legendary scenery. The Navajo are best known for their intricately carved animal fetishes like turquoise bears, coyotes, bison and other animal talismans.

Follow Hwy 191 south across the psychedelic painted desert – this is another magnificent bit of pavement – until it links up with I-40 in Chambers. From here retrace your footsteps west to Las Vegas. Plan a few celebratory nights in Vegas at the end of your trip. You will have completed nearly 3000 miles around the most iconic attractions in the West, so treat yourself to some bubbly, a massage and room service at a dazzling hotel in the country and century of your choice.

Becca Blond

TRIP INFORMATION

GETTING THERE
Las Vegas is 573 miles west of Albuquerque and 300 miles northwest of Phoenix on Hwy 15.

DO

Arches National Park
5 miles north of Moab, it features the world's largest concentration of sandstone arches. ☎ 435-719-2299; www.nps.gov/arch; Hwy 191, UT; per vehicle $20; ☽ visitors center 7:30am-6:30pm Apr-Oct, 8am-4:30pm Nov-Mar

Bellagio
The original opulent Las Vegas pleasure palazzo. Casino guests are first dazzled by the choreographed dancing fountain show every 15 to 30 minutes during the afternoon and evening. ☎ 702-693-7111; www.bellagio .com; 3600 Las Vegas Blvd S, Las Vegas, NV; ☽ 24 hr

Canyonlands National Park
Covering 527 sq miles this is Utah's largest and wildest national park. The most accessible entrance is 32 miles south of Moab. ☎ 435-719-2313; www.nps.gov/cany; per vehicle $20; Hwy 313, UT; ☽ visitors center 8am-4:30pm

Carlsbad Caverns National Park
The entrance to this giant cave system is 23 miles southwest of Carlsbad town. ☎ 800-967-2283; www.nps.gov/cave; 3225 National Parks Hwy, NM; admission from $6; ☽ 8am-5pm, to 7pm late May–mid-Aug; ⅁

Mesa Verde National Park
It's about 21 miles to the visitors center from the park entrance. ☎ 800-449-2288; www .nps.gov/meve; US 160, CO; 7-day park entry per vehicle $15, cyclists, hikers & motorcyclists $8; ☽ 8am-4:30pm Mon-Fri

Monument Valley Navajo Tribal Park
The visitors center has a blissfully cold water fountain and a restaurant. The road into the park is accessed from Hwy 163. ☎ 435-727-5870; Monument Valley Rd, AZ; admission

per person $5; ☽ 6am-9pm May-Sep, 8am-5pm Oct-Apr

EAT & DRINK

Asylum Restaurant
Amazing views and equally good food inside the Jerome Grand Hotel. The wine list is long. ☎ 928-639-3197; 200 Hill St, Jerome, AZ; dinner mains $18-29; ☽ 11am-10pm

ghost bar
A clubby crowd, often thick with celebs, packs this sky-high ultra lounge. DJs spin pop and hip-hop mash-ups. ☎ 702-942-7777; 55th fl, Palms, 4321 W Flamingo Rd, Las Vegas, NV; cover $10-20; ☽ 8pm-4am

Pussycat Dolls Lounge
Lingerie-clad ladies do a little aerial swinging and flaunt sexy song-and-dance numbers at this SoCal import. ☎ 702-731-7873; 3570 Las Vegas Blvd S, Las Vegas, NV; cover $10-30; ☽ 8pm-4am Tue-Sat

Shed
This family-run, James Beard Award–winning, restaurant has been serving New Mexican fare in an atmospheric 1692 adobe since 1953. ☎ 505-982-9030; 113½ E Palace Ave, Santa Fe, NM; lunch $8-10, dinner $9-20; ☽ 11am-2:30pm & 5:30-9pm Mon-Sat; ⅁

SLEEP

Boulders Resort
Relaxation is paramount at this world-class resort with a posh spa and equally fabulous golf course. ☎ 480-488-9009, 866-397-6520; www.theboulders.com; 34531 N Tom Darlington Dr, Phoenix, AZ; casitas $400-800, villas from $600

El Tovar
Standard rooms are on the small side, so those in need of elbow room should go for the deluxe rooms. Both offer casual luxury and high standards of comfort. ☎ 888-297-2757; www.grandcanyonlodges.com; Grand Canyon Village, AZ; r $166-256, ste $306-406

Gonzo Inn
The ample suites can comfortably sleep four. Amenities include wi-fi and a swimming pool; rates include breakfast. ☎ 435-259-2515, 800-791-4044; www.gonzoinn.com; 100 W 200 South, Moab, UT; r $145-315

Hotel Congress
Many rooms at this beautifully restored 1919 hotel have period furnishings; ask for one at the end of the hall away from the thumping Club Congress. ☎ 520-622-8848, 800-722-8848; 311 E Congress St, Tucson, AZ; r $70-120; ✆

Hotel Monte Vista
The 50 rooms and suites have been restored to their 1920s glory, and are old-fashioned but comfortable. Wi-fi is available. ☎ 928-779-6971; www.hotelmontevista.com; 100 N San Francisco St, Flagstaff, AZ; r $70-170

Mile High Inn
Seven newly remodeled rooms have such unusual furnishings as a tandem chair and a lodge pole bed. Breakfast is served until a hangover-friendly noon. ☎ 928-634-5094; www.jeromemilehighinn.com; 309 Main St, Jerome, AZ; r $85-125

Palms
Standard rooms are generous, as are tech-savvy amenities. Request an upper floor to score a Strip view. ☎ 702-942-7777, 866-942-7770; www.palms.com; 4321 W Flamingo Rd, Las Vegas, NV; r $109-459, ste from $209

Phantom Ranch
There are six cozy cabins sleeping four to 10 and single-sex dorms outfitted for 10 people. It ain't luxury, but after a day on the trail, even a bunk is likely to feel heavenly. ☎ 888-297-2757; www.grandcanyonlodges.com; Bottom of the Grand Canyon, AZ; per bunk $37

Strater Hotel
Romantic rooms feature antiques, crystal and lace. Beds are super comfortable with impeccable linens. Prices are slashed by more than 50% in winter. ☎ 970-247-4431; www.strater.com; 699 Main St, Durango, CO; r $200

USEFUL WEBSITES
www.americansouthwest.net
www.notesfromtheroad.com

LINK YOUR TRIP
www.lonelyplanet.com/trip-planner

Motoring the Mother Road: Route 66

WHY GO Blast the oldies mix, roll down the roof and relive the golden days of road tripping kicking it down Route 66, the Mother Road of motoring. From kitsch to scuba, tumbleweeds to mom-and-pop milkshake shops, driving Route 66 across Arizona and New Mexico is a safari into nostalgic Americana's heart and soul.

Never has a road been so symbolic as Route 66. Snaking across the belly of America, linking Chicago and Los Angeles, it is the original highway of dreams leading to the Promised Land and was constructed in 1926. Along the route are old motor-court hotels that haven't changed a bit since the country's 1950s motoring heyday. First called the "Mother Road" in John Steinbeck's novel *The Grapes of Wrath,* over the last 80-odd years the road has become the subject of countless novels, books, songs and photographs.

Route 66 came into its own during the Depression years, when hundreds of thousands of migrants escaping the Dust Bowl slogged west in beat-up jalopies painted with "California or bust" signs. Meanwhile unemployed young men were hired to pave the final stretches of muddy road. They completed the job, as it turns out, just in time for WWII. Hitchhiking soldiers and factory workers rode the road next. Then, amid the jubilant postwar boom, Americans took their newfound optimism and wealth on the road, essentially inventing the modern driving vacation. And so the era of "getting your kicks on Route 66" was born. Traffic flowed busily in both directions. But just as the Mother Road hit her stride, President Dwight Eisenhower, inspired by the German autobahn, proposed a new interstate system for the USA. Slowly but surely, each of Route 66's 2200 miles was bypassed. Towns became ghosts and traffic ground nearly to a halt. By 1984, the road was history.

TIME
10 days

DISTANCE
700 miles

BEST TIME TO GO
Apr – Jun

START
Arizona/ California border

END
Las Vegas, NM

ALSO GOOD FOR

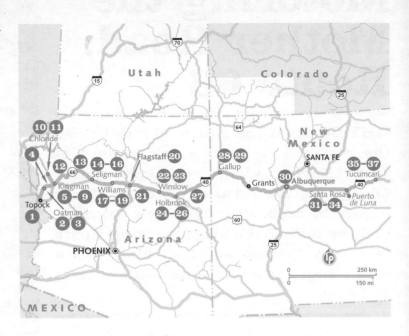

Heading east from California, Route 66 enters Arizona near the 20-mile **1 Topock Gorge**, a dramatic walled canyon that's one of the prettiest sections of the Colorado River. Continue north through Golden Shores, where you can refuel before the rugged 20-mile trip to the terrifically crusty former gold mining town of **2 Oatman** cupped by pinnacles and craggy hills. Since the veins of ore ran dry in 1942, the little settlement has re-invented itself as a movie set and unapologetic Wild West tourist trap, complete with staged gun fights (daily at noon) and gift stores named Fast Fanny's Place and the Classy Ass. And speaking of asses, there are plenty of them (the four-legged kind, that is) roaming the streets and shamelessly begging for carrots (sold at $1 per bag). Stupid and endearing, they're descendents from pack animals left behind by the early miners.

SAVE THE MOTHER ROAD!

A movement for preservation of the Mother Road resulted in the **National Historic Route 66 Association** (www.national66.com), a nonprofit alliance of federal, state and private interests. Every year another landmark goes up for sale, but more are rescued from ruin.

Squeezed among the shops is the 1902 **3 Oatman Hotel**, a surprisingly modest shack where Clark Gable and Carole Lombard spent their wedding night in 1939. Clark apparently returned quite frequently to play cards with the miners in the downstairs saloon, which is awash in one-dollar bills (some $40,000 worth, by the barmaid's estimate). You can no longer stay the night, but you can still grab a couple tacos and a beer in the musky old saloon smelling of yesteryear's sweat, grease and cigarettes. Look for it on the first floor.

Leaving Oatman keep your wits about you as the road twists and turns past tumbleweeds, saguaro cacti and falling rocks as it travels over ❹ Sitgreaves Pass (3523ft) then corkscrews into the rugged Black Mountains and through a claustrophobic canyon before dropping you in ❺ Kingman, your destination for the night. Founded in the heady 1880s railway days, Kingman is a quiet place today. Check out the former Methodist church at 5th and Spring St where Clark Gable and Carole Lombard tied the knot. Or learn about hometown hero Andy Devine, who had his Hollywood breakthrough as the perpetually befuddled driver of the eponymous Stagecoach in John Ford's Oscar-winning 1939 movie. At the western end of Kingman, in a 1907 powerhouse, is the ❻ Route 66 Museum, with a charmingly put-together collection of memorabilia. Admission here also gets you into the ❼ Mohave Museum of History & Arts, a warren of rooms filled with extraordinarily eclectic stuff. It's old-fashioned, sure, but heck, they're making the most of meager funds, so give 'em a break. Kids get to clamber around a 1923 wooden caboose, while grown-ups may well be enthralled by the documentary on Route 66. The ❽ Hotel Brunswick delivers a winning cocktail of historic grandeur, modern amenities and upbeat young owners, Jen and Jason. The hotel dates to 1909 and is supposedly haunted. Have dinner at ❾ Mr D'z Route 66 Diner. Order a cheeseburger with onion rings and a root-beer float. If you're craving over-easy eggs and toast before bed, breakfast is served all day.

"…grab a beer in the musky, old saloon smelling of yesteryear's sweat, grease and cigarettes…"

The hills surrounding the town of ❿ Chloride, situated some 20 miles northwest of Kingman, once spewed forth tons of silver, gold, copper and turquoise from as many as 75 mines. These days, this peaceful semi-ghost town is inhabited by quirky locals who create bizarre junk sculptures and proudly display them outside their ramshackle homes. You can post a letter in Arizona's oldest continually operating post office – it's been around since 1862 – or snap a picture of yourself behind bars at the crumbling jail. Up in the hills, reached via a super-rough 1.5-mile dirt road, are Roy Purcell's psychedelic rock murals. If you don't have a 4WD, hike up or risk a busted axle. Two gun-fighting troupes stage rip-roaring shoot'em-ups each Saturday at high noon. When the sun goes down and the stars come out, you'll feel the true Wild West spirit. Spend a night under the velvet sky, at Bonnie and John's simple place, ⓫ Sheps Miners Inn & Yesterday's. It offers plain, but cozy, adobe-walled rooms with squeaking mattresses behind the onsite restaurant and Western saloon. Even if you don't stay the night, Yesterday's is worth a visit for hearty American grub, international beers

and toe-tapping live music nightly in a creaky wooden floor, vintage gas pumps and hand-painted mural environment. It's Route 66 at its bohemian Wild West best.

From Chloride backtrack to Kingman. Here the Mother Road arcs northeast away from I-40 for 115 miles of old-school Route 66 motoring. Teensy Hackberry is one of the few still kicking settlements on this segment of the Mother Road's original alignment. History comes alive inside an eccentrically remodeled gas station housing the ⑫ **Old Route 66 Visitor Center.** The life's work of highway memorialist Robert Waldmire, the building started as a general store in 1934, and is a great place to stop for an ice-cold Coke and Mother Road memorabilia. Check out the vintage petrol pumps, cars faded by decades of hot desert light, old toilet seats and rusted-out ironwork adorning this quirky roadside attraction. After a drive through a few more blink-and-miss-them towns, you arrive in the Hualapai Reservation tribal capital, Peach Springs. Nine miles after passing tiny Peach Springs, look for a plaster dinosaur welcoming you to the ⑬ **Grand Canyon Caverns & Inn**, a cool subterranean retreat from the summer heat. An elevator drops 210ft underground to artificially lit limestone caverns and the skeletal remains of a prehistoric ground sloth.

Slice through rolling hills for 23 miles to ⑭ **Seligman**, a town that takes its Route 66 heritage seriously – you can still grab a burger at a mom-and-pop shop or refuel at a full-service gas station. This is thanks to the Delgadillo brothers, who for decades have been the Mother Road's biggest boosters. Juan sadly passed away in 2004, but octogenarian Angel and his wife Vilma still run ⑮ **Angel & Vilma Delgadillo's Route 66 Gift Shop**, where you can poke around for souvenirs and admire license plates sent in by fans from all over the world. If Angel is around, he's usually happy to regale you with stories about the Dust Bowl era. He's seen it all. Angel's madcap brother Juan used to rule prankishly supreme

ROUTE 66'S ANGEL

Angel Delgadillo, the barber of Seligman, remembers exactly where he was when shiny new I-40 replaced Route 66 as the USA's primary east–west vein at 2pm on September 22, 1978: standing in front of his house, watching the town he had grown up in start to die. Angel made it his mission to stop Seligman from becoming another Route 66 ghost-town. Aside from transforming his barbershop into a tourist-attracting gift store, in 1987 he successfully lobbied state legislature to preserve Arizona's section of the highway.

over the ⑯ **Snow Cap Drive-In**, a Route 66 burger joint that's been frying beef patties since before I-40 made traffic along the Mother Road nearly extinct. It's now kept going by Juan's sons Bob and John. The crazy decor is only the beginning. Wait 'til you see the menu featuring cheeseburgers with cheese and "dead chicken"!

The railroad town of ⑰ Williams has all the charm and authenticity of "Main Street America." Route 66 slices through the town's historic center, which is a pastiche of Victorian-era brick houses harking back to a proud but bawdy frontier past and 1950s motels from the Route 66 heyday, some still sporting original neon signs. In a 1930s gas station, ⑱ Cruiser's Café 66, you'll find Chevy fins dangling above racing-car red and inky black booths, while the ceiling is sheathed in shiny tin. Dogs are allowed at the outdoor tables. Have a drink at the ⑲ World Famous Sultana Bar. Back during Prohibition, boozers on a mission would steal down to the basement for bootleg liquor and gambling.

Route 66 runs concurrently with I-40 when it barrels into spirited ⑳ Flagstaff, a cultured college town that still bleeds Old West at its heart.

ROUTE 66 READS

John Steinbeck's *Grapes of Wrath* is the classic novel of travel on the Mother Road during the Dust Bowl era. Woody Guthrie's *Bound for Glory* is the road trip autobiography of a folk singer during the Depression. Several museums and bookshops along Route 66 stock Native American, Old West and pioneer writing with ties to the old highway.

East of here mountain views soon flatten into relentlessly featureless prairie. Fortunately, there are a number of worthwhile spots to break the monotony of the journey. First up is ㉑ Meteor Crater, located about 35 miles east of Flagstaff. The wooly mammoths and ground sloths that slouched around northern Arizona 50,000 years ago must have got quite a nasty surprise when a fiery meteor crashed into their neighborhood, blasting a hole some 550ft deep and nearly a mile across. Today the privately owned property is a major tourist attraction with exhibits about meteorites, crater geology and the Apollo astronauts who used its lunarlike surface to train for their moon missions.

"Well, I'm standing on a corner in Winslow, Arizona…" Sound familiar? Thanks to The Eagles' 1972 tune *Take It Easy* (written by Jackson Browne and Glenn Frey), lonesome little ㉒ Winslow is now a popular stop on the tourist track. Pose with the life-sized bronze statue of a hitchhiker backed by a charmingly hokey trompe l'oeil mural of that famous "girl – oh Lord! – in a flatbed Ford" at the corner of 2nd St and Kinsley Ave. Up above, a painted eagle poignantly keeps an eye on the action, and sometimes a red antique Ford parks next to the scene. Spend the night at the oh so fine ㉓ La Posada Hotel. The Mary Colter–designed 1930s hacienda features elaborate tile work, glass-and-tin chandeliers, Navajo rugs and other details that accent its rustic Western-style elegance. Grab modern Southwestern fare at the excellent hotel restaurant.

Wild West fans will love ㉔ Holbrook. Once one of Arizona's most wicked towns, it had a reputation as being "too tough for women or churches. – or so the town's tourism posters claim. Visit the ㉕ **Navajo County Histori-cal Museum** inside the 1898 county courthouse, a gracefully aging heap of bricks whose Perry Mason–era courtroom still hosts hearings. Downstairs, curator Steve and his Chihuahua named Peewee preside over an amiably eclectic collection of Wild West memorabilia. A creepy highlight is the old county jail whose windowless cells were still in use until 1976. Devotees of Route 66 schlockabilia will love to snooze in one of the 15 concrete teepees at ㉖ **Wigwam Motel**. Each room is outfitted with restored 1950s hickory log-pole furniture and retro TVs.

About 25 miles east of Holbrook (the turnoff is at mile marker 311), just before the New Mexican border, is one of the most bizarre attractions just off the highway. The ㉗ **Petrified Forest National Park** is filled with fragmented, fossilized 225-million-year-old logs scattered over a vast area of semidesert grassland. Many logs are huge – up to 6ft in diameter – and at least one spans a ravine to form a natural bridge. The trees arrived via major floods, only to be buried beneath silica-rich volcanic ash before they could decompose. Groundwater dissolved the silica, carried it through the logs and crystallized into solid, sparkly quartz mashed up with iron, carbon, manganese and other minerals. Uplift and erosion eventually exposed the logs.

STRETCH YOUR LEGS: GALLUP MURAL WALK

Take a walk around Gallup – begin at City Hall on the corner of W Aztec Ave and S 2nd St – and experience her 126-year-old story through art. Many buildings around this old Route 66 town double as canvases, sporting giant murals, both abstract and realist, that memorialize special events in Gallup's roller-coaster history. The city's mural painting tradition started in the 1930s as part of President Franklin D Roosevelt's Great Depression Work Projects Administration (WPA) program.

Cross the state line and stop in ㉘ **Gallup**, the mother town on New Mexico's portion of the Mother Road. Settled in the 1881 railway days, Gallup had her heyday during the road-tripping 1950s, a decade she never seems to have left. Even today many of the dilapidated old hotels, pawn shops and billboards mixed in with today's galleries and Native American handicraft stores have not changed since the Eisenhower administration. Just outside the Navajo Nation, modern day Gallup is an interesting mix of Anglos and Native Americans. And it's not unusual to hear people speaking Navajo on their cell phones while buying groceries at the local Walmart. All roads in downtown Gallup dead-end onto Route 66, which runs uninterrupted through town. The historic district is lined with about 20 renovated light red sandstone buildings, including the beautifully restored ㉙ **El Morro Theater**. Completed in 1926 – the same year as the highway – it is a grand old Spanish Colonial–style theater hosting Saturday movies, children's programs and live theatre and dance.

Route 66 gallops across the Continental Divide (7275ft) east of Gallup, then hauls itself across 140 miles of big country space to ㉚ **Albuquerque**. If you need to catch up on time, this is a good stretch to do it. The speed limit here is 80 mph, making it easy to cover a lot of ground quickly. Spend the night in Albuquerque and head out early the next morning. Route 66 through the eastern half of New Mexico is much more exciting than the western portion. Tiny ㉛ **Santa Rosa**, 120 miles east of Albuquerque, is home to one of the USA's top 10 dive spots, as in scuba. How can that be? It's thanks to the bell-shaped, 81ft-deep ㉜ **Blue Hole**. Fed by a natural spring flowing at 3000 gallons a minute, the water in the 81ft hole is both very clear and relatively warm (it stays a constant 64°F year-round). Platforms for diving are suspended about 25ft down. You can rent equipment, but diving here is strictly do-it-yourself (no tours). You will need to show proof of PADI or NAUI certification to get the required diving permit – sold next to the hole.

 **DETOUR**

Nine miles south of Santa Rosa along Hwy 91, tiny **Puerto de Luna** was founded in the 1860s and is one of the oldest settlements in New Mexico. The drive there is pretty, winding through arroyos surrounded by eroded sandstone mesas. In town you'll find an old county courthouse, a village church and a bunch of weathered adobe buildings. It's all quite charming, as long as you're not in a hurry to do something else.

The ㉝ **Route 66 Auto Museum** is also here. It boasts upwards of 35 cars in its exhibit hall, from the 1920s through the 1960s, all in beautiful condition, and lots of 1950s memorabilia. It's a fun place; enjoy a milkshake at the '50s-style snack shack. Santa Rosa is home to nine long-established family-owned diners and roadside cafés, all with historic allure. Our pick is ㉞ **Joseph's Bar & Grill**. Route 66 nostalgia lines the walls of this place. Many of the bountiful Mexican and American recipes have been handed down through the generations and are used to good effect. Joseph's also mixes the best margaritas on Route 66.

A ranching and farming town sandwiched between the mesas and the plains, ㉟ **Tucumcari** is your final destination. For a Route 66 farewell, drive Tucumcari's main street after the sun goes down and dozens of Old Western neon signs cast a crazy rainbow colored glow. The bright, flashing signs are relics of Tucumcari's Route 66 heyday: business owners installed them as part of a crafty marketing campaign to attract weary travelers – basically the concept was the bigger and brighter the sign, the better the chance of convincing motorists to stop at your motel. Tucumcari's Route 66 motoring legacy is recorded on 23 life-size murals around town. The pieces of art, which adorn buildings on and just north and south of Route 66, are the life work of local painters Doug and Sharon Quarles. Taking the town's mural walk is a great way to stretch your legs and experience Tucumcari's all-American history.

Popular in these here parts for its menu of Mexican and American classic diner fare, **36 Del's Restaurant** offers burgers and burritos, as well as a hearty salad bar and lots of soup choices. End your Route 66 odyssey in one of the most beautifully restored motor-court motels on the highway. The centuries melt away at the **37 Blue Swallow Motel**, which is listed on the State and National Registers of Historic Places. The motel's classic neon sign has been featured in many Route 66 articles and boasts Blue Swallow offers a "100% refrigerated bar."

Becca Blond

TRIP INFORMATION

GETTING THERE
This trip starts in Topock Gorge, AZ, 15 miles east of the California line. The trip ends in Tucumcari, NM, 170 miles east of Albuquerque.

DO

Angel & Vilma Delgadillo's Route 66 Gift Shop
The mother of Mother Road gift shops is run by an affable octogenarian named Angel, who is one of Route 66's biggest fans. ☎ 928-422-3352; www.route66giftshop.com; 217 E Rte 66, Seligman, AZ; 🕒 9am-5pm

Blue Hole/Santa Rosa Dive Center
Visit this shop right next to the hole to rent equipment and buy a Blue Hole dive permit – you must show proof of certification. ☎ 505-472-3370; www.santarosanm.org; Hwy 40/US66, Santa Rosa, NM; weekly dive permit $8; 🕒 9am-dusk Sat & Sun, appt only Mon-Fri

El Morro Theater
Downtown Gallup's centerpiece was beautifully restored in 2006; it hosts movies, theater and dance performances. ☎ 505-726-0050; 207 West Coal St, Gallup, NM; 🕒 call for hours; ♿

Grand Canyon Caverns & Inn
Besides the caverns, the complex has a motel, campsites and a restaurant serving burgers and fried food (mains $5 to $15). ☎ 928-422-3223; www.grandcanyoncaverns.com; Route 66 at Mile 115, AZ; 1hr tour adult/child $15/10; r $85, campsites $15-30; 🕒 8am-6pm May-Sep, 10am-4pm Oct-Apr; ♿

Meteor Crater
You're not allowed to go into the crater, but guided one-hour rim walking tours take you around the circumference. ☎ 928-289-2362; www.meteorcrater.com; adult/child/senior $15/7/13; Route 66, AZ; 🕒 7am-7pm Jun–mid-Sep, 8am-5pm mid-Sep–May

Mohave Museum of History & Arts
All sorts of regional topics are dealt with; admission free with Route 66 Museum ticket. ☎ 928-753-3195; www.mohavemuseum.org; 400 W Beale St, Kingman, AZ; adult/child/senior $4/free/3; 🕒 9am-5pm Mon-Fri, 1-5pm Sat; ♿

Navajo County Historical Museum
Holbrook's wild history is told at this museum that doubles as the town visitor center and courthouse. ☎ 928-524-6558; Holbrook, AZ; donations appreciated; 🕒 8am-5pm Mon-Fri, 8am-4pm Sat & Sun

Old Route 66 Visitor Center
One man's living shrine to all things Mother Road, this is the coolest visitor center in Arizona. ☎ 928-769-2605; Route 66, Hackberry, AZ; admission free; 🕒 call for hours

Route 66 Auto Museum
Desperate to motor down Route 66 in a restored 1950s Chevelle? Buy one at this museum doubling as an antique car dealer. ☎ 505-472-1966; www.route66automuseum.com; 2766 Rte 66, Santa Rosa, NM; adult/child under 12 $5/free; 🕒 7:30am-7pm May-Aug, to 5pm Sep-Apr

Route 66 Museum
The museum is also home to Kingman's excellent Power House Visitor Center. ☎ 928-753-6106, 866-427-7866; www.kingmantourism.org; 120 W Andy Devine Ave, Kingman, NM; adult/child/senior $4/free/3; 🕒 9am-6pm Mar-Oct, 8am-5pm Nov-Feb; ♿

EAT & DRINK

Cruiser's Café 66
This Americana diner plays up the roadster theme big time. Grab a cheeseburger, fries and thick vanilla shake. ☎ 928-635-2445; 233 W Route 66, Williams, AZ; dishes $7-16; 🕒 11am-9pm; 🍽

Del's Restaurant
Try Del's take-away service if you'd rather dine from the comfort of your motel bed. ☎ 505-461-1740; 1202 E Tucumcari Blvd, Tucumcari, AZ; mains $5-15; 🕒 7.30am-9pm Mon-Sat

Joseph's Bar & Grill
A popular local hang-out, Joseph's serves burgers, steaks and lots of green chile.

☎ 505-472-3361; 865 Will Rogers Dr, Santa Rosa, NM; mains $6-12; ✆ breakfast, lunch and dinner

Mr D'z Route 66 Diner
Get your *American Graffiti* fix at this modern-vintage diner with its hot-pink and turquoise color scheme and cool memorabilia. ☎ 928-718-0066; 105 E Andy Devine Ave, Kingman, AZ; dishes $4-13; ✆ 7am-9pm

Oatman Hotel
The hotel is no longer taking guests, but you can still order a couple of tacos and beers at this old-fashioned saloon on the first floor. ☎ 928-768-4408; 181 Main St, Oatman, AZ; ✆ call for hours

Snow Cap Drive-In
Cheeseburgers with cheese and "dead chicken" are menu staples at this classic Route 66 drive-in. ☎ 928-422-3291; 301 E Rte 66, Seligman, AZ; mains $4-8; ✆ Mar-Nov

World Famous Sultana Bar
Play pool, have a beer and mingle with colorful locals at this bar that used to sell moonshine during Prohibition days. Sometimes there's live music. ☎ 928-635-2028; 301 W Rte 66, Williams, AZ; ✆ 10am-2am

SLEEP

Blue Swallow Motel
Spend the night in this beautifully restored motel and feel time slide in reverse. The place has a great lobby, friendly owners and vintage, uniquely decorated rooms. Wi-fi available. ☎ 505-461-9849; www.blue swallowmotel.com; 815 E Tucumcari Blvd, Tucumcari, NM; r from $59

Hotel Brunswick
Cash-strapped solo travelers can shack up in the 12 super-basic cowboy/girl singles with shared baths. Breakfast and wi-fi included. ☎ 928-718-1800; www.hotel -brunswick.com; 315 E Andy Devine Ave, Kingman; r $35-95

La Posada Hotel
Gracious Southwestern style in an exquisite 1930s Harvey House, the hotel has hosted everyone from Einstein to John Wayne. ☎ 928-289-4366; www.laposada.org; 303 E 2nd St, Winslow, AZ; r from $100

Sheps Miners Inn & Yesterday's
A friendly Western guesthouse with simple rooms and the most lively saloon for miles. ☎ 928-565-4251; 9827 2nd St, Chloride, AZ; r $35-65, mains $7-20

Wigwam Motel
Comfy enough on the inside, with plenty of retro touches, the exterior of the faux wigwams are fine examples of roadside kitsch. ☎ 928-524-3048; www.galerie-kokopelli .com/wigwam; 811 W Hopi Dr, Holbrook, AZ; r $48-58

USEFUL WEBSITES
www.azrt66.com
www.rt66nm.org

LINK YOUR TRIP

www.lonelyplanet.com/trip-planner

Rafting the Colorado

WHY GO There's a reason they call it the trip of a lifetime. Rafting the Colorado River is truly awesome, not only for its monster rapids, but also for the ever-changing beauty of canyon walls, and the solitude of sleeping under the stars in the inner-gorge wilderness.

So you've scored a river permit, gathered your buddies, and hired an outfitter to supply your crew with cookstoves and ammo cans. Or maybe you've booked a week on a commercial trip and can leave the planning to a pro. Either way, you're about to experience one of the most mind-blowing rivers you'll ever have the privilege of running. All told, the layers of canyon geology through which you'll travel represent at least two *billion* years, and if that doesn't get your rocks off, the white water will. With so many notable rapids, beautiful side hikes, camping beaches and put-in and take out points, this trip's route should be viewed as a necessarily exclusive selection of highlights.

Slap on the sunscreen, keep your camera handy (but safely zipped into a plastic bag), and get ready to head down 87, 187 or maybe all 279 river miles of the mighty Colorado. You're slashing your connection to the outside world for the duration of your trip.

Take a virgin dip into the frigid river at ❶ Lees Ferry and then put in. Take a look at the low-lying cliffs of the Moenkopi Formation atop darker red Kaibab Limestone rising around you, the top layers of Grand Canyon strata. Then glide onto the Colorado and muse on the depth – literal and figurative – of this venerable canyon you're rafting. As you gently float away from Lees Ferry, you'll enter Grand Canyon National Park after several miles of smooth water and riffles. But after some fun first-day rapids like ❷ Badger Creek and Soap Creek, you'll

TIME
7 – 14 days

DISTANCE
187 river miles

BEST TIME TO GO
May – Oct

START
Lees Ferry, AZ

END
Whitmore Wash, AZ

ALSO GOOD FOR

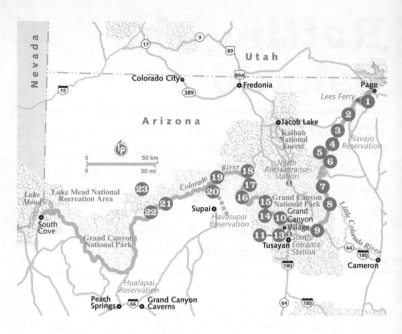

get the hang of the Colorado River rating system, which classifies rapids from Class 1 to 10 (rather than the standard I to V).

After your first day on the river, you'll also get into the groove of using those regulation ammo cans (wilderness toilets) within the privacy of tamarisk stands – giving guilty thanks for invasive flora – and sleeping on still beaches along the river. Waking on that first morning is magical, with the light slowly sliding down canyon walls and revealing the rich color of rock and river.

"... the only place you'll ever ride mini-rapids with a personal flotation device strapped to your bum."

On your second day, stop at ③ North Canyon for the hike through this side canyon leading to a small, seashell-like grotto. Depending on the weather, there may be a reflective pool here filled with tadpoles or a running tributary with little waterfalls to negotiate along the way. The curves, ridges and slabs of this side canyon give a tantalizing first taste of what you'll explore on stops along the river. Once you return to the river, you'll quickly bounce into the ④ Roaring Twenties, a series of smallish but not insignificant rapids along mile markers 20 through 29.

Day three you'll drift by the verdant cliffside oasis of ⑤ Vasey's Paradise, kept green by the water springing directly out of the wall, before rounding a bend and spying the wide mouth of ⑥ Redwall Cavern. As you approach, the scale of this enormous cave will surprise you. The cool sand inside may bear the tracks of ravens, frogs or kangaroo mice, but you'll want to add your own when you stop here for a snack and some Frisbee tossing. Camping isn't allowed in the cavern, but if you happen to have brought your cello, the acoustics in here are fantastic.

Though the fourth day brings hours of drifting between a few good rapids, highlights include a hike up to ancient **7 Puebloan granaries** at Nankoweap, where ancient Native Americans stored corn for lean times. Hiking the steep trail to the granaries affords spectacular views of river and canyon from high above. Downriver, marvel at the intensely saturated purple, blue and green layers of Bright Angel Shale before stopping at the confluence of the incongruously warm, turquoise-hued **8 Little Colorado River**. This may be the only place you'll ever ride mini-rapids with a personal flotation device strapped to your bum.

Big-time whitewater is on tap for day five, with monster rapids like Unkar, Nevills, **9 Hance** (rated as Class 7 or 8), Sockdolager and Grapevine Rapids socking you with some of that cold Colorado water and a fat adrenaline rush. *This* is what it's about. Between exhilarating drops, catch your breath and check out the oldest rock layer in the canyon, which now appears at river level. The smooth, black Vishnu schist shot through with pink Zoroaster granite is some of the oldest exposed rock on the planet, and it marks your arrival to **10 Phantom Ranch**.

ASK A LOCAL "Rafting the canyon is like a chess game, in that there are so many moves you can make – the only difference is, you never lose. As in chess, every move affects the rest of the game, but on the river you could do 20 miles every day doing short hikes, or maybe 45 miles in a day, camp there for two nights and spend all day hiking. But whatever moves you do make, you can't ever lose."

Matt Fahey, Flagstaff

If you're just stopping off here, sip some cold lemonade in the canteen (keep your cup for cheap refills) and scratch out some postcards from the bottom of the canyon. This is also the only place on the river where you'll find a pay phone. If you're spending the night at Phantom, claim a comfy bunk in your air-conditioned cabin, hop in the shower, and take in a ranger talk before dinner. No one goes hungry here, and vegetarians can look forward to some killer chili.

Pre-hydrate the night before your hike out, and be sure to get started at (or before) first light to avoid hiking in the heat of midday. At the end of your six- to nine-hour haul up the **11 Bright Angel Trail**, reward yourself with a soul-soothing chocolate ice cream at the South Rim's **12 Bright Angel Fountain**, sitting on the low, circular stone bench on the rim as you rest your legs. After your (heavenly) shower, sup on half a citrus-glazed roast

duck, sip a prickly-pear margarita on the back deck and lie down for a very sound sleep at the historic ⓭ **El Tovar**.

If, lucky you, your river time flows on, you'll continue floating under the suspension bridges near Phantom Ranch to hit several serious rapids, beginning with Horn Creek, with the challenge of Granite soon thereafter, and finishing with the famously burly ⓮ **Hermit Rapid**. After punching through the waves and holes of these beasts, you'll be elated, exhausted and ready to spend a calm night between the soaring schist walls of the Upper Granite Gorge.

RIVER PERMITS

On commercial river trips, the operator takes care of your permit. If you plan a private trip, you must apply for your own through the **Grand Canyon River Permits Office** (☎ 928-638-7843, 800-959-9164; https://npspermits.us). Entering your name in the weighted lottery system requires an application fee of $25, and if you win a spot, you'll automatically be charged a nonrefundable $400 deposit (which goes toward the cost of the $100-per-person permit). See www .nps.gov/grca/planyourvisit/whitewater-rafting .htm for more detailed information.

By day six, you're well into river mode, relishing the prospect of slamming through big whitewater like the 'gems' – starting with the biggest, ⓯ **Crystal Rapid**, and followed by the midsized Sapphire, Turquoise, Ruby and Serpentine Rapids. A series of smaller rapids are strung out below these, after which some floating brings you to ⓰ **Elves Chasm**. Hiking up this narrow canyon leads to a lush little grotto fed by small waterfalls, at the bottom of which lies an inviting pool amid moss and maidenhair ferns.

You may be on day seven or eight by the time you hit the churn of ⓱ **Deubendorff Rapid** and make a beeline for ⓲ **Tapeats Creek**, one of the absolute best hikes in the canyon. Even better, when made into a 10-mile loop connecting with Deer Creek, the hike takes in waterfalls, pools laced with scarlet monkeyflowers and watercress, narrows carved through Tapeats sandstone and well-preserved petroglyphs. The source of Thunder River lies along this hike, an incredible waterfall shooting out of the base of a cliff into Tapeats Creek.

You'll bypass Granite Narrows, the narrowest point (76 feet) in the canyon, if you take the Deer Creek loop, continuing down about a dozen river miles to another favorite hike at ⓳ **Matkatamiba Canyon**. Matkat's beautifully curvaceous narrows with striated, rippling walls require a little stemming and scrambling to stay above the water at the bottom of the canyon, but it's an easy hike that opens out onto a pavilion edged in green.

If you manage not to go ass over teakettle in Upset Rapid, the river will bring you to ⑳ **Havasu Canyon** on the next day, where another hike beckons. Leading up to the famous travertine canyon and blue-green pools of the Havasupai Reservation, Havasu Creek meets the Colorado with warm, turquoise waters that beg for a swim.

Around day thirteen, a day of gentle drifting allows you to steel yourself for infamous Lava. As you approach, the terrifyingly thrilling maelstrom of ㉑ **Lava Falls Rapid** will reveal itself with a roar before giving you the ride of your life – this is a crucial one to scout. After Lava, you can breathe easy. Take-outs at ㉒ **Whitmore Wash** – the wash at river mile 187, where a trail leads up to the North Rim – will have you boarding a helicopter bound for the rim. Instead of jettisoning your river serenity into oblivion with an immediate return to Las Vegas, transition with a steak dinner and a down-home stay at slightly kitschy ㉓ **Bar 10 Ranch**. You can while away a few days on the ranch, skeet shootin', horseback riding and dancing before braving "civilization" again.

Wendy Yanagihara

ICONIC
TRIPS

TRIP INFORMATION

GETTING THERE
Rafting trips on the upper half of the Colorado put in at Lees Ferry, north of Flagstaff.

DO
River Outfitters
Grand Canyon River Outfitters Association (www.gcroa.org) is a good starting point, with listings for all 16 river concessionaires certified to run the Grand Canyon. Because prices for commercial trips vary significantly depending on the length of the trip, we haven't listed prices; outfitters' rates tend to be competitive.

Arizona Raft Adventures
Has run paddle, oar and motorized trips since 1965; offers trips of six to 16 days. ☎ 928-526-8200, 800-786-7238; www.azraft.com; 4050 E Huntington Dr, Flagstaff, AZ 86004

Canyon Explorations & Canyon Expeditions
Family-run, established in 1987, this business offers trips of six to 16 days on the river. ☎ 928-774-4559, 800-654-0723; www.canyonexplorations.com; PO Box 310, Flagstaff, AZ 86002

Canyoneers
Descended from the company originally founded by Norm Nevills, who led the first paying passengers down the Colorado. ☎ 928-526-0924, 800-525-0924; www.canyon eers.com; PO Box 2997, Flagstaff, AZ 86004

Grand Canyon Dories
One of the only companies running trips in traditional wooden dories, with trips from five to 19 days. ☎ 209-736-0805, 800-877-3679; www.oars.com/grandcanyon/dories .html; PO Box 216, Altaville, CA 95221

Hatch River Expeditions
Best known for its river-running family pedigree, Hatch is now most visible for its motorized raft trips. ☎ 928-355-2241, 800-856-8966; www.hatchriverexpeditions.com; HC 67 Box 35, Marble Canyon, AZ 86036

OARS
With trips from five to 15 days, this outfit is one of the most distinguished. ☎ 209-736-4677, 800-346-6277; www.oars.com; PO Box 67, Angels Camp, CA 95222

Outdoors Unlimited
Well respected and experienced, this company offers oar and paddle trips of five to 15 days. ☎ 928-526-2852, 800-637-7238; www.outdoorsunlimited.com; 6900 Townsend Winona Rd, Flagstaff, AZ 86004

EAT & SLEEP
Bright Angel Fountain
Should be your first stop after slogging up to the South Rim, for a well-earned, frosty chocolate milkshake. ☎ 928-638-2631; www.grandcanyonlodges.com; Grand Canyon Village, AZ; mains $5-10; ⊗ 8am-8pm; ♿

El Tovar Dining Room
A meal here or cocktail on the back porch is *de rigueur*. Rooms at the historic lodge are the best on the rim. ☎ 928-638-2631; www.grand canyonlodges.com; Grand Canyon Village, AZ; lunch from $11, dinner $21-35; ⊗ 6:30-11am, 11:30am-2pm & 5-10pm; ♿

Bar 10 Ranch
The place to stay when you put in or take out at Whitmore Wash. ☎ 435-628-4010, 800-582-4139; www.bar10.com; Whitmore Wash, AZ; per person $100; ♿

Phantom Ranch
The six-person dorm-cabins are air-conditioned, which feels wildly decadent after hiking into the scorching canyon. ☎ 928-638-2631; www .grandcanyonlodges.com;dm $36; ♿

USEFUL WEBSITES
https://npspermits.us

www.gcroa.org

www.lonelyplanet.com/trip-planner

LINK YOUR TRIP
TRIP

A Green Chile Adventure

WHY GO Nothing says New Mexico more than green chile. Come in the fall, during harvest season, when the cottonwoods along the Rio Grande yellow, the smell of roasting chiles and piñon fires permeate the air, and hot-air balloons dot the skies around Albuquerque.

TIME
3 – 4 days

DISTANCE
140 miles

BEST TIME TO GO
Aug – Oct

START
Albuquerque, NM

END
Taos, NM

ALSO GOOD FOR

New Mexicans love their chile. Welcome signs on the interstates feature huge red and green chiles, red ristras hang from adobe homes north to south, and even McDonald's offers green chile on its burgers. Chop and scramble it in eggs, stir-fry it fresh with pork for an Asian twist, add it along with lettuce and tomato on a turkey sandwich. You can't get away from the stuff, and while some visitors never do develop a taste for its fire, others soon acquire a discerning palate that drives an obsessive search for the perfect chile. This one's too hot, that one's too gelatinous, this one has no flavor at all, and soon you're talking about chile as much as farmers around here talk about rain. To get a sampling of the state's best, from sauces loaded with chopped veggies to the perfect green-chile cheeseburger, this fiery green trail of chile hot spots takes you to local favorites.

For a tasty cup of java and the hottest green in ① Albuquerque, head to the decidedly crunchy ② Java Joe's. Hidden in a residential neighborhood off old Route 66, this tiny spot looks, at first glance, like the usual granola and herbal tea hang-out. Local art hangs on the walls and half-read newspapers sit on the tables. You can grind your own coffee to take home, or grab a mug to enjoy with a homemade cranberry scone. But don't be deceived – the chile on its chicken burrito packs more punch than a triple espresso, and the black beans are as good as any you'll find in a fancy restaurant. A few miles down the road, past the 1954 Indian art stores and dance clubs along downtown Albuquerque's Central Ave and into student haunts around the

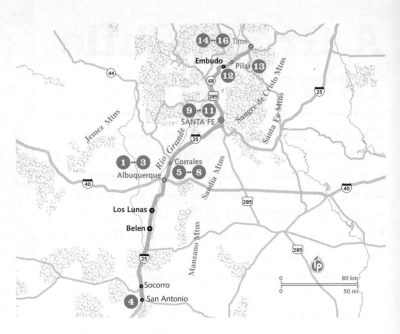

University of New Mexico, is ❸ **El Patio**. A couple blocks from the campus on Harvard St, this under-the-radar stand-by for simple, fresh and tasty fare is easy to miss – look for the vintage neon sign and the blue fence around the tiny patio. Sitting outside with a Dos Equis, a plate of green chile enchiladas and a basket of hot *sopapillas* just might be the closest thing to nirvana this side of the Mississippi. It doesn't take cash, but there's an ATM in the back.

"...it's the green chile that reigns supreme in the fall."

If you still haven't found your idea of chile perfection, consider cruising about an hour south on I-25 to blink-and-you-miss-it San Antonio. Here, the dark lil' ❹ **Owl Bar** serves up no-frills chile that's the subject of statewide debate. Some folks drive miles for its green-chile cheeseburger, while others gripe that the reputation is undeserved. The best in New Mexico? You decide.

To fully appreciate New Mexican green chile, visit in the late summer or fall, when acres upon acres of chile fields throughout the state begin to ripen and farmers don straw hats to protect their faces from the still burning desert sun and spread into the fields to hand-pick the fragile pods before they turn red. Despite the Albuquerque sprawl, it's surprisingly easy to find your way to rural pockets of orchards, chile fields and pastures. From I-40 take the Rio Grande Blvd exit (about a mile west of I-25) and head north, past fields and stables, sheep and llamas, rambling ranches and palatial estates, to the farming community of ⑤ Corrales. Here, old Hispanic farming families mingle with organic-inclined newcomers, tiny homes with thick adobe walls sit beside multimillion dollar haciendas, and dirt roads twist and wind through the cottonwoods.

Once allowed to ripen to red, the flavor of the green chile changes distinctly, and just about every New Mexican prefers one to the other. Both green and red can be used to make sauces for the ubiquitous burrito and enchiladas, but it's the green chile that reigns supreme in the fall. Green-chile stands pop up along country and city roads all over the state, farmers bring overflowing pick-up trucks to grower markets, and New Mexicans get busy preparing the chiles for the upcoming year. In Albuquerque, folks head to ⑥ Wagner Farm, a seasonal farm stand that sells produce grown in their fields throughout Corrales. They bring their coolers or garbage bags, select a bushel for roasting at the cylinder roasters on site, and drag home bags of the blackened pods. Enjoy a fresh-made peach turnover, watch 'em roast the chiles, and pick up a gallon of apple cider.

"The smell of rain mingles with that of roasting chiles, and the Sandia Mountains glow red with the setting sun..."

Just down Dixon Rd from the farm stand is the friendly and simple ⑦ Nora Dixon Place. Take some time to sit in the courtyard, watching the hummingbirds and lizards, enjoying the roses and wisteria. If you're lucky, a passing evening monsoon will settle the dust. The smell of New Mexican rain mingles with that of roasting chiles, and the Sandia Mountains glow red with the setting sun (in fact, Sandia means "watermelon" in Spanish). During the annual balloon fiesta in early October, the skies fill with bright hot-air balloons every morning. Pull on a fleece, pour a mug of coffee and ask for your green-chile eggs outside so you can watch the balloons float in the shadow of the Sandia Mountains. They drift silently above the trees, so close that you can hear the rumble of propane burners, and it's not unusual to see them land in the fields throughout town.

The ⑧ Rio Grande Bosque, home to porcupines, muskrats, birds and

GREEN CHILE BY MAIL

Several companies cater to green chile addicts, FedEx-ing fresh and frozen green chile anywhere in the US, from California to Maine, Texas to North Dakota.

- **www.hatchnmgreenchile.com** Fresh Hatch green chiles in 10lb to 25lb bushels, and nothin' smaller.
- **www.hotchile.com** Order 8lb to 24lb in 2lb bags of roasted, peeled, diced and frozen green chile.
- **www.chileshop.com** All things chile, from salsas to jams.

more, is about a half-mile walk down Dixon Rd. Here, a wide red dirt path, popular for horseback riding, biking and walking, hugs the irrigation ditch, and several trails cut over to the Rio Grande. Standing next to the willows by the river, looking at the mountains and listening to the distinct caw of the migrating Sandhill Cranes and the wind in the wizened trees, you'd never know downtown Albuquerque is only a 20-minute drive away. Grab a burrito to go from Wagners to enjoy on your walk.

The autumn ritual of preparing green chile continues in the kitchen, as it takes hours to peel the chiles, scrape the seeds and package them into ziplocks for the freezer. Some go right into the pot, mixed up with family secrets to cook up piquant sauces of green to use year-round on heuvos rancheros, tacos and just about anything else. And some gets diced up, thrown into a pot of beans with a little garlic and salt, and left to simmer all day. Unfortunately, if you're like most visitors to New Mexico, you'll hesitate to buy any chiles because, to the average cook, they're mysteriously alien. No worries. Drive up I-25 to ⑨ **Santa Fe**, swing by Santa Fe train depot to pick up some extra-hot green at the year-round Saturday and Tuesday morning farmers market, and take an afternoon class at the ⑩ **Santa Fe School of Cooking**. Classes are offered just about daily, and they have an excellent collection of Southwest cookbooks and green-chile products, like green-chile pistachios, jelly and mustard. You can try out those recipes in the kitchen of an historic casita at ⑪ **Dunshees**. Hidden in a quiet stretch of old adobes and desert gardens, this beautifully furnished nest is within walking distance of galleries and shops along Canyon Rd. With a kiva fireplace and private patio, it makes a delightful place to hunker down with a bottle of wine, a piñon fire, and a bowl of your own green-chile stew.

FOOD FESTIVALS

Feast on green chile, piñon and tortillas at these annual celebrations of New Mexico food.

- **Hatch Chile Festival** The sleepy town of Hatch celebrates its most famous export.
- **Santa Fe Wine & Chile Fiesta** Santa Fe chefs pair Southwest dishes with wines from New Mexico and beyond.
- **Whole Enchilada Festival** The state's biggest enchilada and plenty of chile.
- **Lincoln County Cowboy Symposium** Cowboy food New Mexico–style.
- **New Mexico Food & Dance Festival** Historic adobe buildings and chile fields at Rancho de la Golondrinas.

From Santa Fe, it's an easy hour and a half drive along the Rio Grande River to Taos. Stop at ⑫ **Embudo Station** for a green-chile stew with a kick – you could spend hours under the shade of a cottonwood not doing much of anything at all. Continuing north, the road passes ⑬ **Pilar**. Detour a mile or two west on State Rd 570, past several campgrounds, to digest your meal at the bridge over the river. This popular raft launch for white-water trips down the Rio Grande makes a pleasant spot to splash around before returning to Hwy 68 for the final 20-minute stretch to ⑭ **Taos**.

Pedestrian-friendly downtown Taos boasts excellent art galleries and fantastic hiking trails wind through the aspen and ponderosa of the surrounding mountains. End the day with a pint of green-chile beer and a green-chile smothered burrito at ⑮ **Eske's Brew Pub & Eatery**. The vegetarian chile, with huge chunks of carrots, zucchini and other goodies, is unusual even in this vegetarian-friendly town, and just the smell of the beer is ecstasy to a green-chile addict. It's an acquired taste, so ask for a sample before ordering a pint. On weekends, it features live music from country to folk to rock.

From Eske's, drive a few miles out of town to ⑯ **Old Taos Guesthouse**, historic bed and breakfast, with Southwestern furnishing and viga (wood beamed) ceilings, set on 8 acres of grass and orchards. Views from the courtyard stretch across the volcano-dotted Taos Plateau into the flatness of the horizon.

In the morning, owner Tim will share his favorite hiking trails over a homemadebreakfast of fruit, muffins and, you guessed it, green-chile casserole.
Jennifer Denniston

> **ASK A LOCAL**
>
> "Once you've had green chile, you become an addict. And anytime you're anywhere away from it, you're a fiend to get it. I go to Hatch for my chile. I have my favorite vendor I go to. I bring my big ol' cooler and they roast 'em and I bring 'em home. The road that cuts southwest from Hatch to Demming goes through chile fields and ranch country. It's beautiful. "
> *Angela LeQuieu, Rio Rancho, NM*

TRIP INFORMATION

GETTING THERE
Albuquerque lies 63 miles south of Santa Fe on I-25.

DO
Santa Fe School of Cooking
Regular classes on New Mexican cuisine and an excellent selection of cookbooks and green-chile condiments. ☎ 505-983-4511; www.santafeschoolofcooking.com; 116 W San Francisco St, Santa Fe, NM; ☼ varied

Wagner Farm
Locally grown chile in farming village outside Albuquerque. ☎ 505-898-3903; 5000 Corrales Rd, Corrales, NM; ☼ Jul-Nov; ♿

EAT
El Patio
University of New Mexico hang-out with the city's best green-chile enchiladas. ☎ 505-268-4245; 142 Harvard Dr SE, Albuquerque, NM; mains $5-10; ☼ 11am-9:30pm Mon-Sat; ♿

Embudo Station
Old narrow-gauge railroad station along the Rio Grande River, with cottonwoods, outdoor seating and chile with a kick. ☎ 505-852-4707; Hwy 67, Embudo, NM; mains $8-15; ☼ Mar-Oct, hours vary; ♿

Eske's Brew Pub & Eatery
Drink the chile with a pint of aromatic Taos Green Chile Beer. ☎ 575-758-1517; 106 Des Georges Lane, Taos, NM; mains $5-12; ☼ 12:30pm-9pm Sun-Thu & to 10pm Fri-Sat, seasonal variations

Java Joe's
Comfy coffeeshop with black beans and some of the hottest chile in town. ☎ 505-765-1514; 906 Park Ave SW, Albuquerque; mains $5-12; ☼ 6:30am-3:30pm; ♿ ✽

Owl Bar
Nothing can beat the simple green-chile cheeseburger at this hole-in-the-wall south of Albuquerque. ☎ 505-835-9946; 77 Hwy 380, San Antonio, NM; mains $4-7; ☼ 11:30am-9pm Tue-Sun Mar-Oct

SLEEP
Dunshees
Beautifully appointed suite or casita with kiva fireplaces, private patios, and gardens. ☎ 505-982-0988; www.dunshees.com; 986 Acequia Madre, Santa Fe, NM; suites $125-140; ♿ ✽

Nora Dixon Place
Friendly B&B in a rural village outside of Albuquerque. Ask for the Bosque Room, with a kiva fireplace and Mexican tiles. ☎ 505-898-3662; www.noradixon.com; 312 Dixon Rd, Corrales, NM; r $102-124; ♿

Old Taos Guesthouse
This 200-year-old former farm sits on 8 acres of grass and cottonwoods. ☎ 575-758-5448; www.oldtaos.com; 1028 Witt Rd, Taos, NM; r $90-175; ♿ ✽

USEFUL WEBSITES
www.chilepepperinstitute.com
www.greenchile.com

SUGGESTED READS
- *Red or Green? New Mexican Cuisine*, Clyde Casey
- *Artisan Farming: Lessons, Lore and Recipes*, Richard Harris

LINK YOUR TRIP www.lonelyplanet.com/trip-planner

Rim-to-Rim Canyon Hike

WHY GO Views from the canyon's scenic overlooks are breathtaking, it's true, but to fully appreciate the immensity and essential wildness of the Big Ditch, below the rim is where it's at. And hiking the canyon rim-to-rim is the ultimate way to immerse yourself in its depth and magnificent beauty.

If the Grand Canyon's enormity doesn't quite hit you as you crunch down your first few North Kaibab switchbacks in the misty morning light, it will once you've passed through Supai Tunnel and look below upon the trail slashed along the rugged contours of sheer cliff walls. You have taken the plunge.

Most hikers going rim-to-rim make the journey in two or three days, depending on which trails and in which direction they're hiking. This route covers one popular hike spanning two to three days (North Rim to South Rim), but you could easily reverse the direction and/or add a day or two as you please.

It's possible to link any number of North Rim trails to South Rim trails. For the experienced canyon hiker, multiday backcountry trips in the inner gorge are nearly solitary experiences on primitive trails and backcountry campsites. But first-time canyon hikers should start on well-traveled corridor trails to get a feel for the very unique conditions of the Grand Canyon – it's easy to underestimate the elevation change, the intense, scorching heat and the amount of water you'll need, or to get psyched out by the dynamic of descending into the gorge and ascending (seemingly interminably) out.

Turn your expectations upside down by starting your hike from the serene North Rim – this is the stripped-down rim of the Grand Canyon,

TIME
3 – 5 days

DISTANCE
25 miles

BEST TIME TO GO
May – Oct

START
North Rim, AZ

END
South Rim, AZ

ALSO GOOD FOR

ICONIC TRIPS

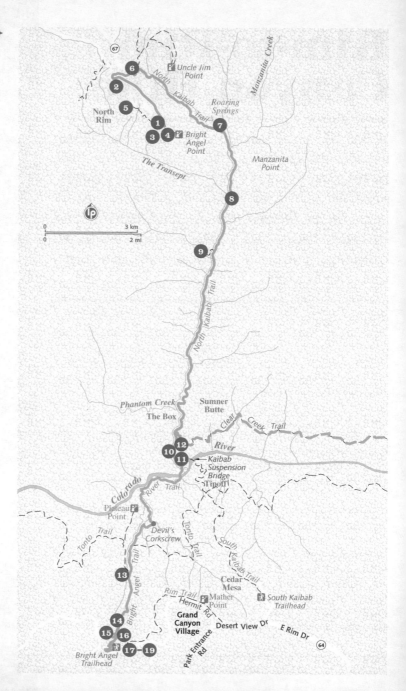

without crowds or commotion. On your drive to the national park, you'll wind through the northern section of Kaibab National Forest, with its vast stands of ponderosa and sections of burned-out trees from the 40,000-acre wildland Warm Fire in 2006. Once you've arrived at the park's North Rim, make a lunch stop at ❶ **Deli in the Pines** for a cold pasta salad and a soda before heading over to the ❷ **North Rim Backcountry Information Center**. Here, you can get a permit for camping below the rim and find out what current conditions are in the inner gorge. It can snow on the North Rim even during the summer, while temperatures at the bottom of the canyon can shoot beyond 110° F in the shade. Save your energy for the big hike, but if you have a few hours, take the flat, 2-mile Cape Final trail to one of the most phenomenal overlooks on either rim.

While you're waiting for a table at ❸ **Grand Canyon Lodge Dining Room**, give Brighty (the burro statue in the sunroom) a rub on the nose for good luck. Then get yourself a beer at ❹ **Roughrider Saloon**, take it out to the terrace, and gulp it in slow swigs as you absorb the wide-angle view of the canyon. (But don't forget you're at altitude and it sucks hiking with a hangover.) Carb load, gourmet-style, with pasta at the lodge – though you can't go wrong with wild-caught salmon and roasted squash – and then bed down in one of the comfy little cabins at the lodge, or head back to your tent at ❺ **North Rim Campground**, where quiet campsites nestle beneath the ponderosa pines.

In the morning, pack up, be sure your toenails are trimmed (ignore them at your peril), and catch the hiker shuttle from Grand Canyon Lodge (purchase tickets in advance at the lodge) to the ❻ **North Kaibab Trailhead** (8250ft) to start down the 14 miles you have ahead of you. It may be all downhill, but it can be tough on your joints, and the temperature typically rises from 3°F to 2°F for every 1000ft you descend.

The trail begins with steep switchbacks through pines and aspens before opening out to the canyon. Almost 2 miles down are pit toilets and drinking water, just before Supai Tunnel, which was blasted out of the Esplanade sandstone when the trail was built. The edge of the trail drops off dramatically on its descent to Redwall Bridge, which crosses Roaring Springs

SAFE TREKS

A few tips for safe hiking in the canyon:

- Avoid dehydration and hyponatremia (dangerously low sodium level in the blood) by sipping water frequently and having a salty snack while you're at it.

- It's tempting to try hiking to the river and back in a day – not recommended at any time of year, but particularly ill-considered in summer.

- Rule of thumb: it generally takes twice as long to hike up as it does hiking down.

Canyon. About 4½ miles from the trailhead is a spur trail leading to the waterfalls of ❼ **Roaring Springs** (5200ft), a lovely place to soak your feet and rest in the shade of cottonwoods.

A short way beyond is the pumphouse, where there's another faucet for filling your water bottle before you cross Bright Angel Creek and hike another mile and a half to ⑧ **Cottonwood Campground** (4080ft). You could break up the descent by staying the night here, or continue along the trail, which by now has leveled off to a gentler decline. From here on down to the river, the trail meanders along Bright Angel Creek. The soundtrack of the creek will only whet your appetite for hiking the spur trail to ⑨ **Ribbon Falls** (3720ft), a short, sweet reprieve from the main trail's exposed desert scrub. Stand in the mist of the falls and soak it up like the maidenhair fern thriving in this cool oasis.

ANT OR GRASSHOPPER?

Some of us plan ahead, some don't. If you can commit to specific dates, your best bet for planning a rim-to-rim hike is to book 13 months ahead for Phantom Ranch and rim accommodations, or four months in advance for a backcountry permit.

If your life is less predictable, a limited number of backcountry permits are reserved for walk-ins, and last-minute accommodation cancellations happen. If you have wiggle room with dates, you can often luck out at the last minute.

Three miles farther down the trail, which has passed through open canyon, it's now a matter of getting through The Box – so called because it's a walled-in canyon within the canyon, and as oppressively hot as it sounds. From Ribbon Falls to Phantom Ranch, it's just under 4 miles with walls rising sharply from the sides of the trail and creek before The Box widens back up and you spy the shady cottonwoods of ⑩ **Phantom Ranch** (2546ft). Open the creaky door, lean on the counter and order a lemonade as you check in (or before you pitch your tent at ⑪ **Bright Angel Campground**). If you've reserved a dinner at ⑫ **Phantom Ranch Canteen**, show up on time for your dinner seating or you'll be locked out (!) and pick up a sack lunch for tomorrow on your way out.

"…the next leg of the hike leads to ominously-named Jacob's Ladder, a seemingly never-ending series of switchbacks through Redwall Limestone."

You'll want to avoid hiking in midday desert heat, especially during the summer, so wake in the wee hours (as in 4am or 5am) and don your headlamp. Nibble on your bagel as you stumble through the Phantom Ranch homestead to the Kaibab Suspension Bridge across the Colorado. It's a steady climb up the switchbacks of Devil's Corkscrew, but as the light throws dramatic morning shadows onto the buttes and cliffs, you can look forward to even more beautiful scenery on your hike up.

Splash your face and soak your hat or bandana in Garden Creek when you make one of the shallow crossings along the trail, and continue on to ⑬ **Indian Garden** (3800ft), about 4½ miles up from the river. There's water, pit toilets and a campground here, all under the welcoming shade of rustling cottonwoods. If you aren't camping here, it's a good place to put your feet up and dig into your sack lunch, since the next leg of the hike leads to ominously-named Jacob's Ladder, a seemingly never-ending series of switchbacks through Redwall Limestone. Leaving Indian Garden, the landscape rolls out ahead of you in a transitional zone between riparian lushness and piñon-and-juniper scrub.

It's a bit of a haul, and you may tire of mule trains kicking up dust as you pull alongside the wall to let them pass, but it's inherently satisfying to look down at all the zigzagging switchbacks you've already climbed. *You kick ass!* The next resting point is ⑭ **Three-Mile Resthouse** (4920ft), where you'll find more water and a small shelter. Take advantage of the stop to check out the view from the point beyond the resthouse, and see if you can spot some wheeling California condors catching updrafts.

Keep on trucking a mile up from here to Two-Mile Corner - a couple hundred yards beyond, look for the ⑮ **petroglyphs** painted on the underside of a boulder above the trail. It's now just half a mile to ⑯ **Mile-and-a-Half Resthouse** (5720ft), where toilets, a shelter and drinking water await. Stop awhile, or continue hiking through the two tunnels, when you'll be smiling beatifically at the fresh-faced souls on their way down the trail. When you've reached the rim, don't stop until you arrive at the ⑰ **Bright Angel Fountain**, where the milkshakes are topped

> **DETOUR**
>
> The **Clear Creek Trail** is an excellent out-and-back hike that starts a quarter-mile north of Phantom. It's an exposed, 9.2-mile backcountry hike with no water until you reach Clear Creek, but the views of temples and gorges within the canyon are worth planning for. Or do it as a day hike, as there are two logical overlooks that mark good turnaround points.

with a metric ton of whipped cream and will give you the best brain-freeze of your life. Enjoy this treat on the low stone benches outside the bustling lobby of ⑱ **Bright Angel Lodge & Cabins**, then check in, have a shower and tuck into a well-deserved dinner in the ever-so-dignified ⑲ **El Tovar Dining Room**, because you have rocked the rim-to-rim.

Wendy Yanagihara

TRIP INFORMATION

GETTING THERE
The South Rim is 92 miles north of Flagstaff, AZ; the North Rim is 264 miles south of Las Vegas, NV.

DO
South Rim Backcountry Information Center
Unless you apply in advance for a backcountry permit, expect to be waitlisted before receiving a permit during the summer. ☎ 928-638-7875; www.nps.gov/grca/planyourvisit/backcountry-permit.htm; PO Box 129, Grand Canyon Village, AZ; ☽ 8am-5pm

North Rim Backcountry Information Center
Since it's less crowded, you might have less of a wait for a backcountry permit. ☎ 928-638-7868; www.nps.gov/grca/planyourvisit/backcountry-permit.htm; North Rim, AZ; ☽ 8am-noon & 1-5pm mid-May–mid-Oct

EAT & DRINK
Bright Angel Fountain
The first place to hit for ice cream and hot dogs after hiking up to the Bright Angel Trailhead. ☎ 928-638-2631; www.grandcanyonlodges.com; Grand Canyon Village, AZ; mains $5-10; ☽ 8am-8pm; ♿

Deli in the Pines
Eat here or get fresh salads, pizza and sandwiches to take on your North Rim hikes. ☎ 928-638-2611, 928-645-6865; www.grandcanyonforever.com; North Rim, AZ; mains $5-10; ☽ 7am-9pm May-Oct; ♿

El Tovar Dining Room
The best place to treat yourself to an upscale dinner on the South Rim. ☎ 928-638-2631; www.grandcanyonlodges.com; Grand Canyon Village, AZ; lunch $11-12, dinner $21-35; ☽ 6:30-11am, 11:30am-2pm & 5-10pm; ♿

Grand Canyon Lodge Dining Room
This venerable wood and stone lodge gracefully complements the landscape of the North Rim. Elegant meals are available when the lodge is open, from May through October. ☎ 877-386-4383; www.grandcanyonforever.com; North Rim, AZ; r $107, cabin $111-156; ♿ 🐾

Phantom Ranch Canteen
Steak dinners are served at 5pm, hiker's stew and vegetarian chili at 6:30pm. ☎ 928-638-2631; www.grandcanyonlodges.com; Phantom Ranch, AZ; sack lunches $11, dinner $25-39; ☽ 8am-4pm & 8-10pm Apr-Oct, from 8:30am Nov-Mar; ♿

Roughrider Saloon
The saloon has some quality microbrews on tap, a full bar and even espresso drinks. ☎ 928-638-2611, 928-645-6865; www.grandcanyonforever.com; North Rim, AZ; ☽ 11:30am-11pm May-Oct

SLEEP
Bright Angel Lodge & Cabins
While the cabins are loaded with character, they're adjacent to the Rim Trail and can be a bit noisy. ☎ 928-638-2631; www.grandcanyonlodges.com; Grand Canyon Village, AZ; r $79-90, cabin $111-159, ste $138-333; ♿

Phantom Ranch
The best – and, well, only – accommodations at the bottom of the canyon. ☎ 928-638-2631; www.grandcanyonlodges.com; Phantom Ranch, AZ; dm $36; ♿

North Rim Campground
With general store, gas station, shower facilities and coin-operated laundry, this lovely campground has sites scattered beneath ponderosa pines. ☎ 800-365-2267; http://reservations.nps.gov; North Rim, AZ; r $79-90, cabin $111-159, ste $138-333; ♿

USEFUL WEBSITES
www.trans-canyonshuttle.com

www.lonelyplanet.com/trip-planner

LINK YOUR TRIP
TRIP

Gunfighters & Gold Miners

WHY GO Gold, copper and silver mining was big business in the late 1800s, and it drew a motley crew to Arizona. These men settled disputes over poker games and saloon girls with a quick-draw six-shooter. As Shipherd Reed from the Miners Story Project will show you, their legacy remains in the old mining towns that dot the state.

TIME
4 days

DISTANCE
720 miles

BEST TIME TO GO
Oct – Mar

START
Jerome, AZ

END
Phoenix, AZ

ALSO GOOD FOR

Men who've plunged deep into the earth for copper, gold and other metals tell Tucson resident Shipherd Reed their tales. But he has to work fast – the bold breed is quickly disappearing. "The impetus for this project was the realization that there is no underground mining anymore in Arizona – it's all strip-mining now. This way of life, this culture of underground mining, was a huge part of Arizona for more than a century," he explains.

Start the journey into Arizona's rugged past in ❶ Jerome, an old mining town perched precariously on a hillside 115 miles northwest of Phoenix. Strut into the ❷ Spirit Room, an old gunslingers' saloon, and practice your 12oz quick draw. Modern outlaws, aka bikers, still hang out here. Indeed, groups of bikers rumble into Jerome almost daily, with weekends being especially crazy. And if you get a little too spirited with the Spirit Room crowd, the ultrafriendly ❸ Connor Hotel is attached for lodging.

For a more gentrified experience, drink and dine at the ❹ Asylum Restaurant in the ❺ Jerome Grand Hotel. Once a miners' hospital, it has morphed into Jerome's top address with the views to prove it.

Before leaving town, Reed recommends stopping by the ❻ Mine Museum across from the Spirit Room. The best exhibits are at the

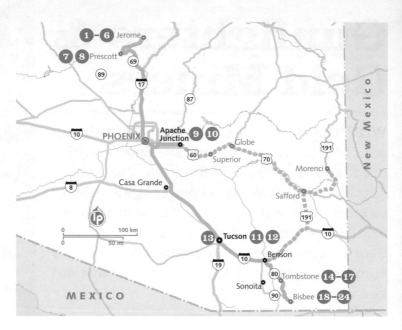

back of the gift shop, detailing early Jerome's ethnic diversity and its thriving red-light district.

In **7** Prescott, situated 35 miles southwest of Jerome, it's obligatory to swagger through the swinging doors of a saloon at least once. The **8** Palace Saloon, on Whiskey Row, is the perfect place to give it a go. Imagine you're greeting Doc Holliday or Wyatt Earp – both former patrons – as you belly up at Arizona's oldest frontier bar.

> "A disagreement over 1 cubic yard of land often put a miner 6ft under it."

After lunch at the Palace, head south and watch the scenery turn from scrubby rolling hills to towering rock formations around **9** Superstition Mountain Museum in Apache Junction, 135 miles south of Prescott. Inside you'll learn about the Lost Dutchman Gold Mine, a fabled mother lode that still draws treasure hunters. Feel the fever? You can look for fat nuggets yourself at **10** Lost Dutchman State Park.

Ease 130 miles down I-10 to Tucson and watch the desert get as flat as a board. Timewarp into yesteryear at the **11** Hotel Congress, with its radio-only rooms and Sam Spade movie set decor. Speaking of drama, bank robber John Dillinger spent a night on the 3rd floor here, until a fire drove him out and, soon enough, into the cuffs of lawmen.

The next morning, stop by the **12** **University of Arizona Mineral Museum** to listen to Reed's miner interviews and ogle mondo crystals. If you're traveling with kids, you'll appreciate **13** **Old Tucson**, which provides a G-rated picture of Arizona's outlaw days. Originally built as a film set, it's now a sort of Wild West theme park set in a huge patch of gorgeous cacti. It's a few miles southeast of the Arizona-Sonora Desert Museum, off Hwy 86.

Seventy-five miles southeast of Tucson, **14** **Tombstone** is billed as "the town too tough to die." Underneath the sometimes-hokey facade lurks an intriguing Wild West history. Visitors can see a reenactment of the shoot out at the **15** **OK Corral** at 2pm daily, with an additional show at 3:30pm on busy days.

Tombstone's one-stop sin shop in the 1880s was the **16** **Bird Cage Theater** – a saloon, dance hall, gambling parlor and home for 'negotiable affections.' Today it's filled with dusty artifacts like Doc Holliday's old card table. Employees report ghost sightings on a regular basis.

Reed says that mining and gun fighting often came as a pair because back when the West was young, claim borders were often in dispute. A disagreement over 1 cubic yard of land – if that land happened to hold the mother lode – often put a miner 6ft under it. Lots of miners lost their lives in such fights. The **17** **Boothill Graveyard**, off Hwy 80 about a quarter-mile north of town, is where they take their final nap. The OK Corral's unlucky threesome are buried in row 2.

Twenty-five miles south of Tombstone on Hwy 80 is **18** **Bisbee** – the number one pick for a mining tour, according to Reed, "not just because it's very picturesque, but because they've done a great job of preserving the history there." People who have

> **DETOUR** To see a modern mining boom town, head to **Safford**, 135 miles north of Bisbee, and the nearby **Graham County Museum** (www.visitgraham county.com). An hour east of Safford, the **Morenci Mine Tour** (☎877-646-8687) takes visitors to an open-pit mine in a huge truck. Heading back to Phoenix, pass through **Globe**, another modern mine town, and **Superior**, where there's talk of opening the **Resolution Copper Mine** (www.resolutioncopper.com), a proposed 7000ft-deep shaft that will rely on robotic equipment.

visited San Francisco might have a déjà vu moment: Bisbee's Victorian buildings are set on rolling hills and the mile-high city is surprisingly cool.

"The parallels between those two cities have always fascinated me," Reed says. "It's fitting that a lot of the people who kept this place from turning into a ghost town were part of the whole Haight-Ashbury scene and came here when that broke up. Now Bisbee is a pretty, artsy place and there is no shortage of characters."

Besides hipness, Bisbee is all about copper. The ⑲ **Copper Queen Hotel** was built in 1902 to give visiting fat cats a place to spend the night. Cut right to the crux of the matter – literally –with ⑳ **Queen Mine Tours** and delve a quarter-mile straight into the cold earth on a small rail car. Retired miners with firsthand stories of the place serve as guides. Dress as if you're going into a refrigerator; you'll receive a safety jacket, hat, and light as accessories.

Dedicate at least two hours to the ㉑ **Bisbee Mining & Historical Museum**, a Smithsonian affiliate. It's housed in the 1897 former headquarters of the Phelps Dodge Copper Mining Co and does an excellent job documenting the town's past and the changing face of mining. You even get to "drive" an industrial mining shovel with a dipper larger than most living rooms.

GEORGE WARREN

He may be credited with discovering Bisbee's mega-rich Queen Mine, but George Warren's tale is a hard-luck one. He was sent to investigate a promising deposit spotted by two other prospectors, and ended up filing the mining claim in his own name. So far, so good. Warren then downed a few drinks at the local pub, boasted that he could outrun a horse, bet his new mine claim on the stunt…and lost. Soon after, Queen Mine started producing a fortune. Warren's consolation prize? Artists modeled the miner on the state seal after him.

If you're lucky, the person collecting admission fees that day will be La Verne Williams, "The Hugging Mayor." The name doesn't lie – she really was Bisbee's mayor at one time, and indeed gives a serious embrace to surprised out-of-towners.

To learn more about Bisbee's unique architecture and modern-day renaissance, take the ㉒ **Historic Walking Tour**. Led by the affable Michael London – in full gunslinger get-up – he's one of the many former San Franciscans who moved to Bisbee in the early 1970s. With historic photographs, he shows how mining irrevocably changed the city over the years.

A high-proof taste of Bisbee's yesteryear swirls in the glasses at the ㉓ **Stock Exchange Saloon**. The original stock boards from 1919 still grace the walls, and these days it's a good place to meet locals and hear live music. For a glimpse of new, sophisticated Bisbee, peek behind the steel art nouveau door at ㉔ **Cafe Roka**. Modern American cuisine fills the plates here; reservations are essential.

Now that you're no longer a "dandy," or newcomer, in the slang of miners, head back to Phoenix. Take the long way (see detour box) to see what modern mining towns look like today.

Josh Krist

TRIP INFORMATION

GETTING THERE

From Phoenix, Jerome is 110 miles northwest via I-17 and Hwy 89A. Bisbee is 210 miles southwest via I-10 and Hwy 80..

DO

Bird Cage Theater

A gaggle of ghosts haunt Tombstone's old sin pit, now transformed into a funky museum. ☎ 520-457-3421; 517 E Allen St, Tombstone, AZ; adult/child/senior $10/7/9; ☽ 8am-6pm

Bisbee Mining & Historical Museum

Bisbee's riotous heyday comes to life through old photos and interactive exhibits. ☎ 520-432-7071; www.bisbeemuseum.org; 5 Copper Queen Plaza, Bisbee, AZ; adult/child/senior $7.50/3/6.50; ☽ 10am-4pm

Boothill Graveyard

Gunfighters' headstones fill this old grave-yard. The most poetic reads: "Here lies Lester Moore, four slugs from a 44, no less, no more." Enter via the gift shop. ☎ 520-457-9344; Hwy 80, Tombstone, AZ; admission free, ☽ 7.30am-6pm

Historic Walking Tour

Dig deep into Bisbee's past on this one-hour walkabout. It leaves every hour on the hour. ☎ 520-432-3554; www.discoverbisbee.com; 2 Copper Canyon Plaza, Bisbee, AZ; tour $10; ☽ 9am-5pm Mon-Fri, 10am-4pm Sat & Sun

Lost Dutchman State Park

Search for the legendary Lost Dutchman Gold Mine. Or just hike the abundant trails; bring lots of water. ☎ 480-982-4485; 6109 N Apache Trail, Apache Junction, AZ; ☽ sun-rise-10pm

Mine Museum

See the Colt pistol used by a local marshal to gun down vigilantes on Main St back in the day. ☎ 928-634-5477; 200 Main St, Jerome, AZ; adult/child/senior $2/free/1; ☽ 9am-4:30pm

OK Corral

Site of the famous gunfight (reenacted daily) and now the historic heart of Tombstone. ☎ 520-457-3456; www.ok-corral.com; Allen St btwn 3rd & 4th Sts, Tombstone, AZ; admission $7.50, without gunfight $5.50; ☽ 9am-5pm

Old Tucson

Built in 1939 as the set for the film *Arizona*, these days it's a silly-fun family theme park. ☎ 520-883-0100; www.oldtucson.com; 201 S Kinney Rd, Tucson, AZ; adult/child 4-11 yr $17/11; ☽ 10am-4pm; ☝

Queen Mine Tours

Dress warmly and prepare to go deep into the hillside for a clamber around the hard places miners worked. ☎ 520-432-2071; www.queenminetour.com; 119 Arizona St, Bisbee, AZ; adult/child $12/5; ☽ 9am-3:30pm

Superstition Mountain Museum

Yes, it's known for its Lost Dutchman Gold Mine exhibit, but there's also the Elvis Presley Memorial Chapel. ☎ 480-983-4888; www.superstitionmountainmuseum.org; 4087 N Apache Trail, Apache Junction, AZ; adult/child/senior $5/2/4; ☽ 9am-4pm

University of Arizona Mineral Museum

Miners' oral histories and lots of rocks sit below Flandrau Science Center on the university campus. ☎ 520-621-7827; www.uamineralmuseum.org; 1601 E University Blvd, Tucson, AZ; adult/child under four $5/free; ☽ 9am-3pm & 6-9pm Thu & Fri, noon-9pm Sat, noon-5pm Sun

EAT & DRINK

Asylum Restaurant

The fantastic views and wine list make Asy-lum the most upscale place in town. Just ask the ghosts who haunt it. ☎ 928-639-3197; 200 Hill St, Jerome, AZ; dinner mains $18-29; ☽ lunch & dinner

Cafe Roka

Four-course dining is the rule at this sophisti-cated restaurant, so prep those taste buds for dishes like the signature roast duck. Reservations essential. ☎ 520-432-5153; 35 Main St, Bisbee, AZ; dinner mains $15-25; ☺ dinner Thu-Sat

Palace Saloon
Arizona's oldest frontier bar comes complete with a swinging saloon door, framed photos and Old West memorabilia, including antique gambling machines. ☎ 928-541-1996; www.historicpalace.com; 120 S Montezuma St, Prescott, AZ; mains $8-20; ☺ lunch & dinner

Spirit Room
A dark, old-time saloon with a pool table and bordello scene mural. Live music every Saturday and Sunday afternoon and some weeknights. ☎ 928-634-8809; 166 Main St, Jerome, AZ; ☺ 10am-2am

Stock Exchange Saloon
Keeping the legacy of historic Bisbee alive one drink at a time, the long bar is a prime place to meet local characters. ☎ 520-432-9924; 15 Brewery Ave, Bisbee, AZ; ☺ 11am-1:30am

SLEEP

Connor Hotel
Rooms waft old-school flair while staying spiffy and comfy. Rooms 1 to 4 get most of the noise from the Spirit Room bar, below. ☎ 928-634-5006, 800-523-3554; www.connorhotel.com; 164 Main St, Jerome, AZ; r $90-165

Copper Queen Hotel
The Copper Queen combines late-19th-century elegance with modern amenities. Its downstairs restaurant and patio bar draw locals and tourists alike. ☎ 520-432-2216; www.copperqueen.com; 11 Howell Ave, Bisbee, AZ; r $90-180

Hotel Congress
A historic property where old-fashioned radios are the in-room entertainment. Opt for a room at the hotel's far end if you're noise sensitive. ☎ 520-622-8848; www.hotel congress.com; 311 E Congress St, Tucson, AZ; r $70-120; ☺

Jerome Grand Hotel
Get a third-floor balcony room for other-worldly views of the valley below. It's a 10-minute uphill walk from the main strip. ☎ 928-634-8200; www.jeromegrand hotel.com; 200 Hill St, Jerome, AZ; r $120-460

USEFUL WEBSITES
www.azjerome.com
www.discoverbisbee.com

LINK YOUR TRIP
www.lonelyplanet.com/trip-planner

Dam Diving

WHY GO The Southwestern states haven't let a lack of ocean-front property deter them from introducing scuba diving to their activities rosters: they simply moved the sport to the lake. Saying you've gone "dam diving in the desert" is damn cool, but the fact that it's eco-friendly makes this backyard scuba experience even better.

The Southwest USA has always been a bit of a rebel. This is cowboy and Indian country after all. Home to the Wild West of lore. So it's no surprise that when locals and researchers decided they wanted to scuba dive in New Mexico, Arizona and Nevada, these states figured out a way to make it happen. Despite being more than a thousand miles from the nearest ocean. How? Enter the National Park Service's Submerged Resources Center (SRC), an elite group of underwater archaeologists based in Santa Fe. The SRC team dives in dams around the region. Why? The region's dams are filled with all sorts of archaeological wonders, from a crashed B-29 bomber to sandstone towers and ancient cliff dwellings. All of which have been covered up by the harnessing of nearly all the Southwest's water supplies by dams.

All this historical junk at the bottom of the river and lake beds is interesting not just to scientists and archaeologists who descend in the name of cataloging the artifacts, it's also interesting to scuba enthusiasts looking for an off-the-grid green diving experience. Although the number of dive shops offering organized tours is still limited, anyone with PADI or NAUI certification and their own equipment can take the plunge. If you're looking for a dive experience that goes beyond the usual submerged chambers and tropical fish, and is also not harmful to the environment, then this is the trip for you. Diving here means exploring some of the USA's least visited sites in its least expected

TIME
4 days

DISTANCE
700 miles

BEST TIME TO GO
Jun – Aug

START
Santa Rosa, NM

END
Las Vegas, NV

ALSO GOOD FOR

environment – the landlocked desert. Plus the dive community tends to be based around small mom-and-pop shops located in small towns, and the surge in diving popularity has helped sustain their sagging economies. By diving in an artificial setting – ie not on a living reef – you're taking the most ecofriendly option. You can't do much damage by accidentally slapping your fin against an abandoned old bomber, but you can kill a number of living organisms in a reef with just one swipe.

"Santa Rosa is a hole-in-the-wall town best known for its amazing Blue Hole."

Complete the Southwest scuba trifecta by diving all three spots in one trip – please note you need to be an experienced diver to do this trip. However, less experienced divers can dip their toe in the Colorado River. Start in ❶ Santa Rosa, in eastern New Mexico off historic Route 66 (also called I-40 here) about 1½ hours from Albuquerque. Santa Rosa is a hole-in-the-wall town best known for its amazing Blue Hole. On first drive through the town doesn't look like much – just a dusty road with a smattering of fading neon-lit restaurants and curio shops left over from the Route 66 glory days. But once you reach the packed parking lot of the premier scuba spot in the Southwest, you'll have a new appreciation for this little middle-of-nowhere town. Appropriately called the ❷ Blue Hole, the lake is a crystal clear 81ft-deep artesian well that attracts scuba enthusiasts, researchers and college classes from across the country. Located in semi-arid ranch country, where the great plains meet red mesas, the bell-shaped hole surrounded by a rock wall is a geological phenomenon: a constant 3000-gallon-a-minute flow of fresh water keeps it crystal clear and a comfortable 64° F year-round, even when it's snowing. Look up from underwater to see trees and buildings on the shore reflected in the mirrorlike surface. You have to be PADI or NAUI certified, and comfortable diving without an instructor, to scuba here. If you have your own equipment, all you need to do is pick up a permit from the ❸ Santa Rosa City Hall and head to the hole. If you need to rent tanks or have yours refilled, head to the ❹ Santa Rosa Dive Center, located right next to the hole. The center is currently under construction, with a new building set to open in August 2009, but is still operating. You can also get permits here. Please note that there is no organized scuba excursions at Blue Hole, it is a do-it-yourself activity. Once you are underwater check out the 131ft-long submerged cavern in the lake: it's quite a sight.

Blue Hole is just one of a dozen lakes fed by underground mineral springs around Santa Rosa. If you just want to swim, head to ❺ Park Lake, the Southwest's largest natural swimming pool, located smack in the middle of downtown Santa Rosa. There's a long twisty waterslide tube that drops you into the lake. And should you tire of propelling yourself through the water, you can fish from the shore. Santa Rosa is a classic pitstop on Route 66 – the road's original alignment is now the tree-lined path leading to Blue Hole – and home to nine long-stablished family-owned diners and roadside cafes, all with historic allure. Try ❻ Comet II Drive-in for dinner. The classic drive-up joint is run by Johnny and Alice Martinez, and serves delicious Mexican fare with a Southwestern flair. Try the *carne adobada* and green-chile enchiladas: both are delicious. Join the locals at the ❼ Silver Moon for a plate of bacon and eggs and a steaming cup of coffee in the morning. A trademark Route 66 eatery that first opened its doors in 1959, Silver Moon is a long-standing favorite of travelers following the historic highway's old road-house trail. We don't

DETOUR Nine miles south of Santa Rosa on Hwy 91, tiny **Puerto de Luna** was founded in the 1860s and is one of the oldest settlements in New Mexico. The drive there is pretty, winding through arroyos surrounded by eroded sandstone mesas. In town you'll find an old county courthouse, a village church and a bunch of weathered adobe buildings. Visit the **Grezlachowski Territorial House**, where Billy the Kid ate his last Christmas dinner in 1880 with one of the town's most colorful citizens, a retired Civil War chaplain known simply as Grezla. The town is also known for its "PDL Chile," a unique spicy chile pepper cultivated here for more than 100 years.

usually advocate sleeping in chains, but in Santa Rosa the ❽ La Quinta Inn simply is the best place to sleep. Sitting atop Santa Rosa's highest point, it offers great city views. Plus it has a heated indoor swimming pool, giant Jacuzzi and welcomes Fido.

Okay, so it's kind of a long-haul – just shy of 700 miles long – drive from Santa Rosa in eastern New Mexico all the way across Arizona into Nevada and the capital of sin, **9 Las Vegas**, which serves as the base for the next two dives. But this is an iconic trip, so we had to add a little road tripping in… Plus you're getting to scuba dive and go to Vegas, so what's 700 measly miles really? Everyone knows some of the best memories are made on the open road, bonding with your driving buddy over Red Bull, Taco Bell and cheesy '80s ballads. The Colorado River and Lake Mead, straddling the Arizona and Nevada state lines, are where your next dives happen. But your operator, small and friendly **10 Sin City Scuba,** is based just down the road in Las Vegas. The company operates a 10-person boat captained by a former member of the US Coast Guard. Do its **11 Colorado River Dive** first. The shore-entry dive starts just south of Hoover Dam and is appropriate for novices. It follows the swift moving current downstream through water up to 70ft deep. Be on the lookout for rare humpback suckerfish. It's a fun trip, one that's different enough to keep experienced divers as excited as the beginners – technically you can swim the entire route with half your body in Arizona and the other half in Nevada, as the Colorado River is the state dividing line. How many of your friends can brag they've dived in two states simultaneously? If that thought doesn't sweeten the 10-hour drive, then checking into the **12 Hard Rock Casino Hotel**, just east of the Strip, should. As you're already on a water kick, stay at the hotel with the best pool in town: music is pumped in through underwater speakers, there is seasonal swim-up blackjack and Tahitian-style cabanas for rent at the ultra hip Beach Club. The summer Rehab pool parties are legendary, attracting a sex-charged crowd flush with celebrities. The Hard Rock is also home to one of the world's most impressive collections of rock 'n' roll memorabilia, including Jim Morrison's handwritten lyrics. Skip the Hard Rock's overpriced meals, and head to nearby **13 Firefly** for dinner. Always hopping, the restaurant serves traditional Spanish tapas. Wash your meal down with sangria or a flavor-infused mojitos.

DIY DIVING

Red-rock canyons, yawning arches and sheer sandstone cliffs dip into the Colorado River at Lake Powell, the second largest manmade lake in the US. If you have your own scuba equipment, and can get your hands on a house-boat, diving Lake Powell is a real treat. The beauty hidden beneath the lake's tropical sea–colored surface is phenomenal, and includes underground canyons and schools of hungry fish. Top dive spots include **Bullfrog Area** and **Iceberg Canyon**. Visit www.utahdiving.com/powell.htm.

Dive **14 Lake Mead** the following morning. You will need to present expert technical diving certification to participate. If you have the right card, however, this is one of the most amazing dives in America. Above the dam at Lake Mead, divers can explore the fuselage of a mostly intact B-29 bomber that crash-landed into Lake Mead in 1948, but was only located in 2001. The honor doesn't come cheap – it's nearly $500 – but it's a once-in-a-lifetime opportunity to relive this region's Cold War history. Plus, diving here is one of those ecofriendly scuba experiences we told you about earlier. The site can only be dived through Sin City, and only on specific dates during the year as it is protected as a National Park Service preserved site.

After diving the dam, learn about its history with a visit to the ⑮ **Boulder City/Hoover Dam Museum** in Boulder City, a small town just west of Lake Mead. The small but engagingly hands-on museum has exhibits focusing on Depression-era America and the tough living conditions endured by the people who came to build the dam. A 20-minute film features historic footage of the project. Before heading back to your Las Vegas hotel room, rehash your dive trip over dinner at ⑯ **Milo's**. The wine bar has sidewalk tables and serves delicious fresh sandwiches and gourmet cheese plates. If you don't feel like drinking wine, there are five flavors of ice-tea to choose from along with 50 different beers from all over the world. The wine list is long and includes lots of by-the-glass options.

Becca Blond

TRIP INFORMATION

GETTING THERE
Santa Rosa is 118 miles east of Albuquerque on I-40/Route 66.

DO

Boulder City/Hoover Dam Museum
This hands-on museum is upstairs at the historic Boulder Dam Hotel, where Bette Davis, FDR and Howard Hughes once slept. ☎ 702-294-1988; www.bcmha.org; 1305 Arizona St, Boulder City, NV; adult/senior & child $2/1; ☷ 10am-5pm Mon-Sat, noon-5pm Sun; ☗

Santa Rosa City Hall
Diving permits are sold here. Make sure to bring your PADI or NAUI card. ☎ 505-472-3763; www.santarosanm.org; 486 Route 66, Santa Rosa, NM; weekly/annual permit $8/25; ☷ 8am-5pm Mon-Fri

Santa Rosa Dive Center
Refills oxygen tanks, rents equipment and sells permits. If you need to visit during the week, call to arrange an appointment. ☎ 505-472-3370; www.santarosanm .com; Hwy 40/US66, Blue Hole, Santa Rosa, NM; ☷ 8am-dusk Sat & Sun, by appt only Mon-Fri

Park Lake
Free waterslide and swimming in the center of Santa Rosa. ☎ 505-472-3763; www.santa rosanm.org; cnr Lake Dr & Route 66, Santa Rosa, NM; paddle boat rental per 1½hr $1; ☷ dawn-dusk Jun–mid-Sep; ☗

Sin City Scuba
Organizes Colorado River dives ($150) below Hoover Dam, and expert-only scuba trips to a sunken B-29 bomber in Lake Mead ($465). Operates out of Las Vegas. ☎ 702-558-5361; www.sincityscuba.com; 3540 W Sahara 553, Las Vegas, NV

SLEEP & EAT

Comet II Drive-In
A classic drive-in restaurant offering more than the usual burger-and-fries menu. ☎ 505-472-3663; 239 Parker Ave, Santa Rosa, NM; dishes $5-10; ☷ 11am-9pm Tue-Sun

Firefly
East of the Strip, this popular restaurant serves Spanish tapas; DJs spin some nights. ☎ 702-369-3971; Citibank Plaza, 3900 Paradise Rd, Las Vegas, NV; small dishes $4-10 large dishes $11-20; ☷ 11:30am-2am Sun-Fri, 5pm-2am Sat

Hard Rock Casino Hotel
A hip boutique hotel popular with the Hollywood crowd. Bright colored Euro-minimalist rooms feature wi-fi access and plasma-screen TVs. ☎ 702-693-5000; www.hardrockhotel .com; 4455 Paradise Rd, LAs Vegas, NV; r $110-450

La Quinta Inn
Rooms are big, sunny and clean, if a little bland. Free wi-fi is a perk. ☎ 505-472-4800; www.lq.com; 1701 Will Rogers Dr, Santa Rosa, NM; r from $59; ☗

Milo's
Soups, salads, sandwiches and gourmet cheese plates are featured at this wine bar. ☎ 702-293-9540; 538 Nevada Way, Las Vegas, NV; dishes $4-18; ☷ 11am-10pm Sun-Thu, 11am-midnight Fri-Sat

Silver Moon
Silver Moon serves fantastic homemade *chile rellenos* and other tasty diner grub dressed up with a New Mexican twist. ☎ 505-472-3162; Will Rogers Dr, Santa Rosa, NM; mains $5-15; ☷ 7am-9pm.

USEFUL WEBSITES
www.geocities.com/Yosemite/Trails/8215

www.lonelyplanet.com/trip-planner

LINK YOUR TRIP

In Search of Georgia O'Keeffe

WHY GO "I am going West," Georgia O'Keeffe wrote. "...the country seems to call one in a way that one has to answer it." Yes, O'Keeffe's West, its desert cut by the Chama River, its silence, its lavender and sage, does indeed call.

A notorious recluse and iconic American artist, Georgia O'Keeffe found her lifeblood in the arid landscapes, endless nothingness and brilliant colors of northern New Mexico. Come into her West, explore its valleys and rocky outcrops, in this search for Georgia O'Keeffe.

Any visit to O'Keeffe country must begin with a stop at the ❶ Georgia O'Keeffe Museum, home to more than 1000 of O'Keeffe's paintings, drawings and sculptures dating from 1901 to 1984. After a bite at the museum's upscale café, head north from Santa Fe on Hwy 285. The state's tourist face fades in Española before shifting again into the river valley farms of acequias, cottonwoods and verdant fields of O'Keeffe's hometown of ❷ Abiquiu, 49 miles northwest of Santa Fe. Settled in 1754 through a Spanish land grant, the tiny town has a few galleries and a lovely church, but O'Keeffe's Abiquiu is less a centralized town than a landscape.

After the death of her photographer husband Alfred Steiglitz, O'Keeffe moved to Abiquiu permanently from New York City. One of her two homes, purchased in 1940 and open to the public by tour only through ❸ Georgia O'Keeffe Home & Studio Tour, sits on the hillside just up the road from the post office. Enclosed by an adobe wall, this classic adobe hacienda blends seamlessly into the landscape and remains much as it did when O'Keeffe lived here. Across Hwy 285 is ❹ Bode's General Merchandise, the best place around for breakfast or a deli sandwich. Pick up a cold drink for a hike through the white rock spirals of ❺ White City, one of the most surreal landscapes in O'Keeffe country. The ❻ Dar al Islam Mosque, whose members

TIME
3 days

DISTANCE
190 miles

BEST TIME TO GO
May – Oct

START
Santa Fe, NM

END
Abiquiu, NM

ALSO GOOD FOR

HISTORY &
CULTURE

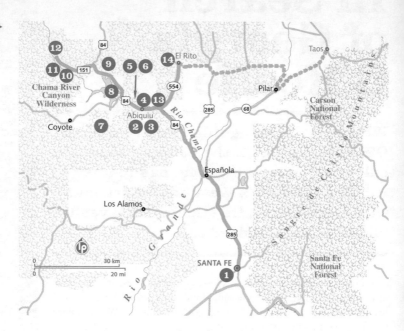

own 1357-acres that include White City, welcomes visitors to their North African–styled mosque. A dirt road leads about a half-mile from the entrance, marked by a discrete arch on the north side of County Rd 155, left to the mosque and right to an unmarked parking lot at the trailhead.

O'Keeffe once called the flat-topped ❼ **Pedernal**, visible from just about anywhere in Abiquiu, her private mountain. "It belongs to me," she said. "God told me if I painted it enough, I could have it." And paint it she did, again and again and again. One of the best views is from ❽ **Abiquiu Reservoir**, a deservedly popular swimming spot, with cold, clear waters and sandstone shores that lies about five minutes north of Abiquiu town.

O'KEEFFE ON FILM

The 1977 documentary *Georgia O'Keeffe* features spectacular footage of Abiquiu landscape and a rare opportunity to hear O'Keeffe herself talk about her life, her vision, and her art. Produced near the end of her life, with little outside narration, this one-hour documentary inspires even those who know very little about the artist to find their way to her Abiquiu.

Some of O'Keeffe's most celebrated works were inspired by the stark and dramatic surrounds of ❾ **Ghost Ranch**. She visited the ranch for the first time in 1934, and in 1940 she purchased a house there. Though this home is closed to the public, the ranch offers one-hour guided tours of the buttes and mesas memorialized in her work, and several hiking trails traverse the grounds.

Forest Service Rd 151, a dirt road impassable in wet weather, cuts south from Hwy 84 into the unspeakably beautiful ❿ **Chama River Canyon Wilderness**. The Chama River flows through the ponderosa pine, willows and cottonwoods of the red-rock canyon, and several campsites and day-use pull-offs rest along its bank. One of the best, with several sites directly on the river, is ⓫ **Rio Chama Campground**.

"…you'll notice that the sound of your voice offends the silence."

After 14 miles, the road dead-ends at ⓬ **Monastery of Christ in the Desert**. As you pull in and climb out of the car, you'll notice that the sound of your voice offends the silence. Tip-toe through the lavender and sage, past cross after cross lining the stone path, toward the Japanese–New Mexican inspired monastery that emerges gently from the cliffs. The Chama River, which plays prominently in O'Keeffe's work, flows alongside, and the monastery offers accommodation for folks of all religions. So set down your easel or your sketchpad, just as O'Keeffe might have done, and stay awhile. Only one room has a private bath, and guests join the monks for a communal silent breakfast. If you'd prefer more traditional lodging, a Southwest-style room or bosque-view casita at ⓭ **Abiquiu Inn** is the perfect end to a day exploring O'Keeffe country.

While there's a restaurant at Abiquiu Inn and down the road you'll find a tiny pizza joint, it's worth a 15-minute drive for one of the best meals in the region. Just north of Abiquiu, in the tiny oasis of El Rito, is the kind of restaurant that everybody hopes to stumble upon. Housed in a small adobe with a long portal overlooking an orchard, ⓮ **Walter's Place** serves home-cooked meals, including cheese made from its own goats' milk, and green chile and piñon meatloaf. As the story goes, Walter Chappel, an art photographer, lived in the house with his partner who worked for O'Keeffe.

> **DETOUR** While O'Keeffe called Abiquiu home, she often traveled to Taos, home to numerous writers and artists. Her paintings of the **Taos Pueblo** and the **Rancho de Pueblo Church** are some of her most famous images. Take Hwy 554 past El Rito, slice down and cross the Rio Grande, and continue to Taos on Hwy 68.

Walter made his lunches, and one day O'Keeffe asked for a taste. She loved it, so Walter occasionally cooked for O'Keeffe and her friends in his home. Walter died in 2000, but his house was purchased, restored, and opened as a restaurant. So bring a bottle of wine and sit in the courtyard, much as O'Keeffe herself did not so very long ago.

Jennifer Denniston

TRIP INFORMATION

GETTING THERE
Santa Fe lies 63 miles north of Albuquerque on I-25.

DO
Dar al Islam Mosque
A traditional Islamic community welcomes visitors to its spectacular hillside mosque on weekdays. Call in advance to confirm. ☎ 505-685-4515; 342 County Rd 155, Abiquiu, NM; ⏱ varied; ♿

Georgia O'Keeffe Home & Studio Tour
The home and studio remain untouched since her death in 1986. Make reservations well in advance, or check for cancellations at the tour office. ☎ 505-685-4539; shuttle from Abiquiu Inn, Abiquiu, NM; 1hr tour $35-50; ⏱ varied

Georgia O'Keeffe Museum
Dusty desert walls and natural light showcase O'Keeffe's desert landscapes, abstract flowers and brilliant use of color. ☎ 505-946-1000; www.okeeffemuseum.org; 217 Johnson St, Santa Fe, NM; adult/child/NM resident $8/free/4; ⏱ 10am-5pm Sat-Thu, to 8pm Fri; ♿

Ghost Ranch
Site of O'Keeffe's home, this 21,000-acre ranch offers two museums, hiking trails, guided tours of O'Keeffe landscape and workshops, as well as a variety of accommodations. ☎ 505-685-4333; www.ghostranch.org; Hwy 84, btwn Mile 225 & 226, Abiquiu, NM; 1hr tour $25; ⏱ varied, closed Dec; ♿ 🐾

EAT
Bode's General Merchandise
Everyone from artists to cowboys, farmers to tourists, stop for deli sandwiches, burritos, organic veggies, wine and more. ☎ 505-685-4422; Hwy 84, Mile 212, Abiquiu, NM; mains $12-17; ⏱ 7am-7pm, with seasonal variations; ♿

Walter's Place
Tiny home with chickens and goats in the back, outdoor seating and eclectic home-cooking. Bring your own wine or beer. ☎ 505-581-4498; El Rito, NM; mains $12-17; ⏱ 5-10pm Fri & Sat; ♿

SLEEP
Abiquiu Inn
Handsome rooms surround a central courtyard and roomy casitas offer bosque views. ☎ 505-685-4378; www.abiquiuinn.com; 21120 Hwy 84, Abiquiu, NM; r $79-140, casitas $140-195; ♿ 🐾

Monastery of Christ in the Desert
Working monastery offers simple brick and white rooms and surreal silence. ☎ 505-545-8567; www.christdesert.org; 14 miles south on FR 151, NM; r $90-145; ♿

Rio Chama Campground
Riverside camping with nine tent-only site surrounded by brilliant colored cliffs, birds and the silence of the Chama River Canyon Wilderness. 12 miles south on FR 151, NM; tent site free; ⏱ May-Nov 15; ♿ 🐾

USEFUL WEBSITES
www.publiclands.org
www.santafe.org.com

LINK YOUR TRIP
www.lonelyplanet.com/trip-planner

Billy the Kid Byway

WHY GO America's legendary bad boy, Billy the Kid, may have blazed this trail in a rain of bullets, but he isn't the only headliner on his byway. He shares pavement with America's most beloved bear, Smokey, who also hails from this region of brilliant light, bucolic emerald woods and a distinct cowboy culture.

From grassy plains to cool mountains to million-acre forest in between, the Billy the Kid Byway follows the outlaw's blood-stained footsteps around 87 miles of stunning southeastern New Mexican scenery. Although drivable year-round, this route is most magnificent during the short fall foliage season – usually mid-September – when the trees in the Lincoln Forest appear as a blazing fire of orange, crimson and canary. Those in search of quirky regional festivals will enjoy driving this byway between May and October when everyone from Billy to Smokey is given a celebration somewhere.

So who was this Billy the Kid anyway? The truth is no one totally knows. So much speculation swirls. Even the most basic information about Billy the Kid tends to cast a shadow larger than the outlaw himself. Here's what we do know. The Kid didn't start out as a murderer. His first known childhood crimes included stealing laundry. All that changed after 1878, when a wild teenager named Henry McCarty, alias William Bonney, aka Billy the Kid arrived in Lincoln about the time the town erupted into all-out war over control of the dry-goods business.

Tangled up in the thick of the action the Kid was captured or cornered a number of times but managed brazen and lucky escapes before finally being shot by Sheriff Pat Garrett near Fort Sumner in 1881, where he lies in a grave in a barren yard. Maybe. Enough controversy still dangles over whether Billy conspired with Sheriff Garrett to fake

TIME
4 days

DISTANCE
87 miles

BEST TIME TO GO
Jul – Oct

START
Ruidoso, NM

END
Ruidoso, NM

ALSO GOOD FOR

ROUTE

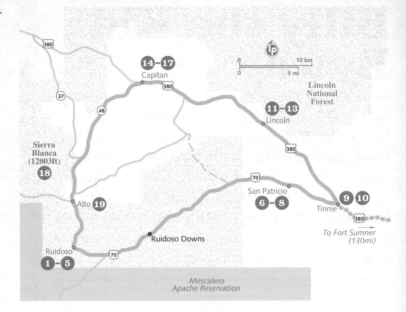

his death that there is a movement afoot to exhume the body and do a little DNA testing. Visit during the first full weekend of August and you'll experience this town of 70 residents' biggest show of the year, Old Lincoln Days.

"...a supposed favorite haunt of the outlaw teenager, although it's unlikely he visited for baking supplies."

Now in its sixth decade, the two-day festival features musicians and mountain men, doctors and desperadoes wander the streets in period costume, and there are demonstrations of spinning, blacksmithing and other common frontier skills. In the evening there is the folk pageant, "The Last Escape of Billy the Kid."

This trip starts in ritzy **①** **Ruidoso**. A favorite with the Texan crowd who come for skiing on New Mexico's highest peak – nearby Sierra Blanca which tops out 3ft shy of 12,000 feet – and for the horseracing in the summer. Plus the town – its name means "noisy" in Spanish (referring to the lovely bubbling of the small Rio Ruidoso creek running through town) – has a fabulous climate thanks to its lofty location in the Sacramento Mountains at the edge of the Lincoln Forest. The **②** **Billy the Kid Interpretive Center** features a mini-tour of the byway, and is a good place to get your bearings for the road trip ahead. Look down, there's a very colorful map painted on the gallery floor! The visitor center is located just east of Ruidoso in Ruidoso Downs (where the racetrack also is). Mosey across the street when you are done and stop in at the excellent **③** **Hubbard Museum of the American West**. It displays more than 10,000 Western-related items including Old West stagecoaches and Native American pottery, and works by Frederic Remington and Charles M Russell. An impressive collection of horse-related displays, including a collection of saddles and the Racehorse Hall of Fame, lures horse-lovers. Head west into Ruidoso proper and look for the plain red fading adobe structure with a big 20ft waterwheel attached. This is ④ Dowlin's Mill, one of the only remaining buildings on Ruidoso's main street that actually dates back to Billy the Kid's time. It was a supposed favorite haunt of the outlaw teenager, although it's unlikely he visited for baking supplies. The proprietor was also known for selling moonshine and throwing wild dance parties. The mill still functions today; and its flour is sold at the onsite gift shop.

Grab a bite at ⑤ Casa Blanca, home of to-die-for *chile rellenos* and the best margaritas in town. If you're not in the mood for Mexican, there are burgers and perfectly crisped chicken fried steak. After lunch take an easy 20-mile cruise through bucolic countryside on Hwy 70 east to ⑥ San Patricio. The tranquil country village in the Hondo Valley boasts the kind of golden glow and gentle scenery that's been drawing artists to New Mexico for more than a century now. Check into the ⑦ Hurd la Rinconada Gallery & Guest Ranch. The 2500-acre property is your destination for the night. Owned and run by artist Peter Hurd, the gallery portion showcases Hurd's own work, along with that of his relatives NC and Andrew Wyeth, his mother Henriette Wyeth and his father Michael Hurd. The six casitas are stylish with original art and modern conveniences. Pets can stay for $20 per visit. Also visit the well respected ⑧ Benson Fine Art Gallery inside an impressive 130-year-old adobe building. The gallery showcases contemporary sculpture and paintings, along with less usual findings like jewelry, pottery and even a few pieces of antique furniture. Drive a few miles down the highway to ⑨ Tinnie, a tiny town at the junction of US 70 and US 380, for dinner. The ⑩ Tinnie Silver Dollar Steakhouse & Saloon is so good that folks come all the way from Ruidoso to eat here. Enjoy an old-fashioned fancy night out and a big juicy cut of steak at this one-time general store that's been converted into a rather posh steakhouse. Check out the German stained-glass windows from the 1950s and the shiny hardwood bar transported from Chicago. If you drink one too many whiskeys there are two guestrooms set up for romance with hot tubs and big, sink-into-me beds.

RACING RUIDOSO DOWNS

Dedicated nearly entirely to quarter horse races (most tracks cater to the more delicate thoroughbred), Ruidoso Downs, on I-70 just outside Ruidoso, is one of the region's biggest racing venues. The season begins in May and runs through Labor Day weekend, when the big event takes place. The All American Futurity draws nearly 20,000 people, and is known as the world's richest quarter horse race – it offers a $1 million purse to the winner of the 21-second sprint.

More of a museum than a town, ⑪ Lincoln is the most famous stop on the Billy the Kid Byway. This is where the gun battle that turned Billy the Kid into a legend took place. Favoring authentic over Hollywood, Lincoln is about as close to 19th-century reality as it gets. Some say it's the best preserved Wild West town in America. Modern influences, such as souvenir stands, are not allowed in town, and the main street has been designated the ⑫ Lincoln State Monument. It's a pretty cool place to get away from this century for an afternoon. Start at the ⑬ Anderson Freeman Visitor Center & Museum, where exhibits on the Buffalo soldiers, Apaches and the Lincoln County War explain the town's history. The admission price includes entry to the Tunstall Store (with a remarkable display of late-19th-century merchandise), the courthouse where the Kid escaped imprisonment, and Dr Wood's house, an intact turn-of-the-century doctor's home and office. The Tunstall Store and Dr Wood's house are closed from March to November.

> *"...did you know that Smokey the Bear was a real, live black bear cub..."*

When you've explored Lincoln (it doesn't take more than a few hours to wander around the museums), continue 12 miles west to ⑭ Capitan. This small town on the edge of the million-acre Lincoln Forest proves the Byway isn't all about Billy, even if it does bear his name. Fame is shared with another of America's most famous legends, a black bear named Smokey. You've seen his likeness in state and national forests everywhere around the region. But did you know that Smokey the Bear was a real, live black bear cub, and not just a sketch summoned from some designer's imagination? Once upon a time, he was found clinging to a tree, paws charred from a 17,000-acre forest fire in the Capitan Mountains. Smokey's burns healed, and he moved to Washington, DC. Working from his new home at the National Zoo, Smokey became the poster bear for fire protection. After his death, Smokey's body was returned to the New Mexican mountains. You can see the famous bear's grave at the 3-acre ⑮ Smokey Bear Historical State Park. The Smokey the Bear Stampede takes place every 4th of July and features a parade, a rodeo, cookouts and other festivities. The place also goes wild during Smokey the Bear Days, celebrated the first weekend in May. That festival includes a street dance, woodcarving contest, craft and antique car shows. Spend the night at the ⑯ Smokey Bear Motel. The place offers tidy rooms with handmade

DETOUR

If you're driving the byway solely for Billy, then you will want to make the 156-mile trek northeast from Ruidoso to **Fort Sumner** to visit the Kid's grave. The **Fort Sumner State Monument** is 4 miles southeast of town and the place where Sheriff Pat Garret shot and killed Billy the Kid on July 14, 1881. The outlaw was just 21 years old. Billy's grave is behind the **Old Fort Sumner Museum** in town. His tombstone is protected by an iron cage to keep 'souvenir hunters' from stealing it.

wood furniture including rocking chairs. The motel has a restaurant, but when it's open the **⑰ Greenhouse Café** is the best bet in town. The café, which attracts people living around the region, grows all its own herbs and lettuce, and does a fabulous steak smothered in mushrooms and garlic. Complete the loop back to Ruidoso on Hwy 48, which skirts the eastern edge of the million-acre Lincoln National Forest – this is the part of the drive that really rocks in fall when the leaves put on a spectacular color show. The Sacramento Mountain range to the west of the highway adds to the scenic allure. Keep an eye out for New Mexico's highest peak, **⑱ Sierra Blanca** (11,997ft). There is an especially clear view from the highway around tiny **⑲ Alto**, 11 miles north of Ruidoso.

Becca Blond

ICONIC
TRIPS

TRIP INFORMATION

GETTING THERE
Ruidoso is 185 miles southeast of Albu-querque. Take I-25 south to Hwy 380 E, which runs straight through Ruidoso.

DO

Anderson Freeman Visitor Center & Museum
Focuses on Native American history and the fa-mous Lincoln County War in which Billy the Kid made his name. ☎ 575-653-4025; Hwy 380, Lincoln; admission $6; ☽ 8:30am-4:30pm

Benson Fine Art Gallery
No matter the medium – the gallery features everything from jewelry to sculpture – all the art has a Southwestern bent. ☎ 575-653-4081; www.bensonfineart.biz; Rte 13, San Patricio, NM; ☽ call for hours

Billy the Kid Interpretive Center
Dig up the dirt on Billy the Kid, and the byway named for him at this visitor center/museum next to the Hubbard Museum in Ruidoso Downs. ☎ 575-378-5318; US 70, Ruidoso Downs, NM; admission free; ☽ 10am-5pm Thu-Tue

Dowlin's Mill
According to legend, Billy the Kid once hid out in a flour barrel at this working water mill, whether that's myth or reality remains a mystery. ☎ 505-257-2811; 641 Sudderth Dr, Ruidoso, NM; admission free; ☽ call for hours

Hubbard Museum of the American West
Displays more than 10,000 Western artifacts, many paying homage to the working horse. ☎ 575-378-4142; www.hubbardmuseum .org; 841 Hwy 70 W, Ruidoso, NM; admission $6; ☽ 9am-5pm

Smokey Bear Historical State Park
Pay your respects to America's firefight-ing bear crusader in his final resting place.

☎ 575-354-2748; www.smokeybearpark. com; 118 Smokey Bear Blvd, NM; per day $2; ☽ 9am-5pm

EAT

Casa Blanca
Dine on Southwestern cuisine and delish margaritas from a table on the pleasant patio or inside the renovated Spanish-style house. ☎ 575-257-2495; 501 Mechem Dr, Ruidoso, NM; mains $6-20; ☽ 11am-9pm

Greenhouse Café
Call for reservations, this restaurant, spe-cializing in home-grown ingredients, is very popular with residents from around the region. ☎ 575-354-0373; 103 Lincoln St, Capitan, NM; mains $12; ☽ 11am-2pm & 5-9pm Wed-Sat & 10am-2pm Sun May–mid-Sep

Tinnie Silver Dollar Steakhouse & Saloon
A well-respected steakhouse that also does a fancy brunch. ☎ 575-653-4425; www.tinnie silverdollar.com; Tinnie, NM; mains $20-35; ☽ 4-10pm Mon-Sat, 10am-3pm Sun

SLEEP

Hurd la Rinconada Gallery & Guest Ranch
Stylish casitas on a 2500-acre art ranch. The biggest unit sleeps six. ☎ 575-653-4331; www.wyethartists.com; 105 La Rinconada, San Patricio, NM; casitas $125-250

Smokey Bear Motel
It may not offer the most original, or luxuri-ous, rooms in the region, but it is very good value. ☎ 575-354-2253; www.smokey bearmotel.com; 315 Smokey Bear Blvd, Capitan, NM; r $50-65

USEFUL WEBSITES
www.billybyway.com

www.lonelyplanet.com/trip-planner

LINK YOUR TRIP
TRIP

Southwest by Train

WHY GO Stare blankly out your window at the plaintive desert of New Mexico and Arizona, stroll downtown Santa Fe and Flagstaff, bed down in historic hotels, and choo-choo up to the canyon on a vintage train. In an age of rising fuel costs and city sprawl, riding the rails can be easy and economical.

TIME
5 days

DISTANCE
470 miles

BEST TIME TO GO
Sep – Jun

START
Santa Fe, NM

END
Grand Canyon South Rim, AZ

ALSO GOOD FOR

Following the completion of the Transcontinental Railroad in 1869, travelers rode steam trains to the Wild West. Stories of Kit Carson, photographs by Edward Curtis and paintings by Thomas Moran fueled the imagination, and Americans eagerly voyaged across the country to see the mountains and the canyons. They were, after all, young America's cathedrals, billed as grander than the Swiss Alps and more stunning than the Sistine Chapel. While today the interstates, fast food joints and ubiquitous chain motels give easy access to the West, they take something away as well. This train trip brings back a little bit of that something.

Begin with a few days exploring Santa Fe's historic landmarks, museums and galleries, most within walking distance of ❶ La Fonda. Built in 1922, the hotel was purchased by the Atchison, Topeka & Santa Fe Railroad in 1925 and leased to Fred Harvey. Nicknamed "the civilizer of the West," Harvey had exclusive rights to hotels and restaurants along the rail-line west of the Mississippi, and his elegant "Harvey Hotels" played an integral role in developing tourism in the Southwest. Today, La Fonda drips Southwestern charm, Fred Harvey–style. For a less expensive option, try the ❷ El Rey Inn, a short cab ride from downtown Santa Fe.

The westbound ❸ Amtrak departs Lamy, 20 minutes south of Santa Fe and accessible via a prearranged Amtrak shuttle from your hotel, daily at 2:24pm. One-and-a-half hours later, the train arrives

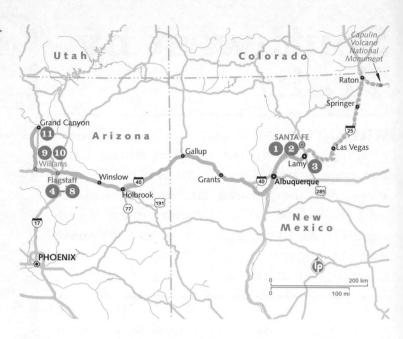

in Albuquerque, where vendors sell turquoise jewelry and Navajo-style blankets from the platform and new passengers board. You sit with a glass of wine as the train pulls away from the city's outskirts, and stare out at the massive red-rock mesas and plateaus of Navajo country, your book lying open and unread in your lap. The train rolls on, through the flat desert plains of western Arizona, and, in about five hours, up into the Ponderosa surrounds of ❹ **Flagstaff**.

"...sit with a glass of wine, and stare out at the massive red-rock mesas... "

Gather your bags and hop onto the platform. It's colder here, and even in the summer you will pull on your fleece before heading to a room for the night. The streets of this welcoming college town are busy as you walk to the ❺ **Weatherford Hotel**. Rooms here, decorated with lace curtains, period antiques and claw-foot cast-iron tubs, take you back to the 1930s. The wrap-around 2nd floor porch off the bar is a great place to kick back with a cold beer after the train ride.

Wake up for tofu scrambles and coffee at ❻ **Macy's European Coffee House**, a popular local hang-out. Students tap away on computers and parents sit with the crossword puzzle while kids nurse giant mugs of hot chocolate and vegan apple turnovers. If you're feeling ambitious, rent a bike and pick up a bike-trail map at ❼ **Absolute Bikes**. Head west on Route 66 from the shop and follow it for about 3 miles to S Woody Mountain Rd; take a left and ride 4 miles through pines and meadows to the **8** Arboretum at Flagstaff. Walk through and read about the landscape you've been watching from the train window. Trails wind around gardens with more than 2300 species of plants; it's a beautiful spot for a picnic.

Jump on the 8:57pm Amtrak or the 3.45pm Amtrak bus shuttle to Williams, a tiny tourist town 35 miles west of Flagstaff, and sleep at the **9** Lodge, an updated Route 66 classic (or stay in Flagstaff and take a shuttle or cab in the morning). The **10** Grand Canyon Railway departs from Williams. Catch the predeparture Wild West Show at 9:30am, with

DETOUR Riding Amtrak from Colorado, consider jumping off for a day in **Raton**. While there's not much to recommend in this tiny town, rent a car and head to **Capulin Volcano National Monument** (www.nps.gov/cavo/). You can drive to the rim of this beautiful cinder cone volcano, formed 60,000 years ago, and take in the 360-degree views; there are also several short hikes. Stay a few blocks from the train station at **El Portal** (☎575-445-3631), built in 1905. Simple rooms hark back to 1930s America.

goofy cowboys wearing spurs, silly banter and an Old West façade, before boarding the vintage train for the two-and-a-half-hour ride to the canyon.

As the train slowly chugs north, out of town and down in elevation into the shrubbery of the desert, the mountains softly arch in the distance, nothing but shaded silhouettes, and the coolness of morning fades. The train lulls you along, passing landscape void of cars and buildings, and with few other hints of the 21st century. Cowboy singers pass through the train, plucking Johnny Cash, and someone walks down the aisle with bottles of soda and water. Folks exchange stories and talk politics until the train pulls into the station at **11** Grand Canyon National Park, a short walk from the canyon rim.

Americans resist the train, thinking that they need the flexibility of a car, and perhaps feeling anchorless without it. But this trip is easy, with no middle-of-the-night departures. No,

ABOUT TICKETS & SEATS

While Amtrak offers private sleeping cars, the eight-hour stretch heading west from Santa Fe, NM to Williams, AZ is covered during the day. To get off the train along the way, book each leg separately; ask about an Amtrak Rail Pass. The best seats on the Grand Canyon Railway are the ultra-basic Coach with wood-framed windows that slide up, or the luxury car, with cushioned leather armchairs, champagne and access to the train's open-air rear platform. First-class seats lack historic charm.

you don't have the same freedom you have in your own car, but it offers a different kind of freedom. You don't have any choice but to slow down and enjoy the ride.
Jennifer Denniston

TRIP INFORMATION

GETTING THERE

Santa Fe lies 63 miles north of Albuquerque. There is a regular shuttle service between Albuquerque Sunport airport and Santa Fe.

DO

Absolute Bikes
Rent a bike, perfect for exploring the museums and parks of Flagstaff. ☎ 928-779-5969; www.absolutebikes.net; 200 E Route 66, Flagstaff, AZ; per day $35-70; ⊙ 9am-7pm Mon-Fri, 9am-6pm Sat, 10am-4pm Sun; ♿

Amtrak
Amtrak's *Southwest Chief* stops daily in Lamy, NM (with shuttle service to Santa Fe), Albuquerque, NM, Flagstaff, AZ and Williams, AZ on its route from Chicago, IL to Los Angeles, CA. It departs Albuquerque, NM at 4:45pm and arrives Flagstaff at 8:51pm. ☎ 800-872-7245; www.amtrak.com; 1-way Santa Fe to Flagstaff $79-136; ⊙ daily; ♿

Arboretum at Flagstaff
Cacti, wildflowers, a butterfly garden and more. Live birds of prey shows daily at noon and 2pm. ☎ 928-774-1442; www.thearb.org; 4001 S Woody Mountain Rd, Flagstaff, AZ; adult $6/6-17yr $3/under 6yr free; ⊙ 9am-5pm Apr-Oct; ♿

Grand Canyon Railway
Vintage train to the South Rim, with hotel and meal packages, and guided tours designed to fit the train schedule. ☎ 800-843-8724; www.thetrain.com; Train Depot, Williams, AZ; roundtrip adult $65-170, child $35-100; ⊙ depart Williams 10am, Grand Canyon 4pm; ♿

Grand Canyon National Park
Make advanced reservations for lunch at the canyon's El Tovar lodge, overnight accommodation, tours and mule rides. **advanced reservations** ☎ 888-297-2757, **same-day reservations** ☎ 928-638-2631; www.gov/grca/; ♿

EAT & SLEEP

Macy's European Coffee House
Decidedly crunchy coffee shop one-half block from the train depot. ☎ 928-774-2243; 14 S Beaver St, Flagstaff, AZ; ⊙ 6am-10pm, kitchen closes at 4pm; ♿

El Rey Inn
Route 66 motel with gardened grounds. Some suites have a kiva fireplace. ☎ 800-521-1349; www.elreyinnsantafe.com; 1862 Cerrillos Rd, Santa Fe, NM; r & ste $99-220; ♿

La Fonda
Elegant historic hotel. Catch folk singer Bill Hearne, a Santa Fe institution, at the bar on Wednesday nights. ☎ 505-982-5511; www.lafonda.com; Williams Depot, Santa Fe, NM; r $319-539; ♿

Lodge
Adobe-style roadside motel with updated rooms and friendly service; request the Lodge building. ☎ 877-563-4366; www.thelodgeonroute66.com; 200 E Route 66, Williams, AZ; r & ste $90-150; ♿ 🐾

Weatherford Hotel
Serving travelers to the Grand Canyon since 1900. Look for the wrap-around 2nd floor porch. ☎ 928-779-1919; www.weatherfordhotel.com; 23 N Leroux St, Flagstaff, AZ; r $60-175; ♿

USEFUL WEBSITES
www.flagstaffarizona.org
www.santafe.org

SUGGESTED READS
- *Inventing the Southwest: The Fred Harvey Company and Native American Art*, Kathleen Howard
- *Nothing Like It In the World: The Men Who Build the Transcontinental Railroad 1863-1869*, Stephen Ambrose

www.lonelyplanet.com/trip-planner

LINK YOUR TRIP

ARIZONA TRIPS

Arizonans are proud to be the Grand Canyon's home state but we'll tell you there is much more to the place than a giant hole in the ground. Plus the weather here is just about perfect – how can you beat nearly a full year's worth of sunshine and big blue skies?

Still, although you may know there's much more to Arizona than golf and the Grand Canyon, it's not always easy to pinpoint exactly which hidden treasures you wish to show your visiting mother-in-law or your best friend from Tennessee. Don't worry, that's where we come in. We'll have you drinking wine in the desert, discovering vortexes and New Age crystal shops in the beautiful red rocks around Sedona, following the Cactus League spring training trail or hunting for ghosts in Wild West Jerome. These 16 Arizona trips give you the knowledge to plan the ultimate insider trip, capable of blowing your in-laws out of the water. Forget about the Grand Canyon for now – we agree it's a fabulous hole, which is why we devote an entire chapter to the region. These trips are all about Arizona's unique attitude, and get to the heart of her cowboy chic meets old fashioned Wild West vibe.

PLAYLIST ♫♫

Cacti and cowboys meet progressive '90s punk: Arizona music is as varied as the Grand Canyon state's desert meets mountain meets major metropolis landscape. Here we've given you a mix that gets your feet thumping as you clock miles over tumbleweeds on Route 66, negotiate a maze of concrete freeways in Phoenix and roll through a bizarre Saguaro cacti–strewn desertscape.

- "By the Time I Get to Phoenix," Glen Campbell
- "Leather & Lace," Stevie Nicks
- "The Middle," Jimmy Eat World
- "Hey Jealousy," The Gin Blossoms
- "You're No Good," Linda Ronstadt
- "Rhinestone Cowboy," Glen Campbell
- "No Air," Jordin Sparks
- "Lake of Fire," Meat Puppets

BEST ARIZONA TRIPS

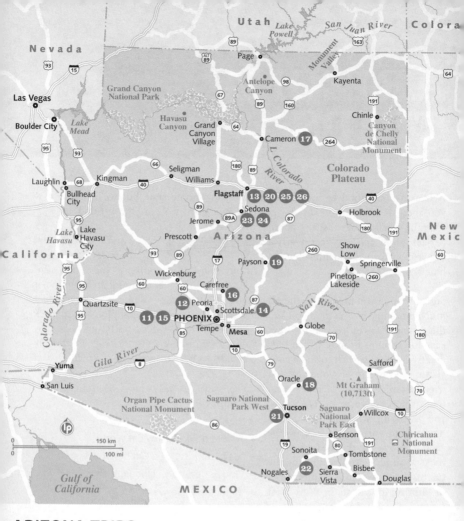

ARIZONA TRIPS

FOOD & DRINK

14 Steak-Lovers' Arizona p115
22 Grapes & Hops in the Desert p155

HISTORY & CULTURE

12 Cactus League Spring Training p107
15 A Slice of Native America p119
18 Arizona Architecture p135
20 Arizona in Tune p145
25 Tracing Arizona's Cultures p171

OUTDOORS

17 Photographing Monument Valley p129
19 Tiny Towns of Rim Country p139
21 Southern Desert Wanderings p149
24 Sedona Red Rock Adventure p165
26 Flagstaff's Northern Playground p175

OFFBEAT

13 Big Skies & Weird Science p111
16 Cowboy Time p125
23 Into the Vortex p161

CITY

11 48 Hours in Greater Phoenix p101

48 Hours in Greater Phoenix

WHY GO Call it what you will – a desert escape, a sprawl of suburbs, or a mythical bird rising from its own ashes – Phoenix is a force to be reckoned with. Leave your coat behind and prepare for two days of top-notch museums, desert oddities, steak and martinis, and most of all, glorious sun.

TIME
2 days

BEST TIME TO GO
Oct – Mar

START
Central Phoenix , AZ

END
Downtown Scottsdale, AZ

When you fly into the Valley of the Sun at night, the lights of the city below are indistinguishable from the stars above. You have to wonder if some pilot, somewhere, has ever confused up and down. In any case, you've arrived at an enormous city in the middle of the desert, and you'll be very busy the next two days.

Start at the corner of Central Ave and McDowell St to satisfy your appetite for the finer things at the ❶ **Phoenix Art Museum.** A treasure of paintings and sculptures that span the ages, visitors new to Southwestern art will heart the Georgia O'Keeffe piece and her many imitators. Check out work from the art world's most famous dysfunctional couple – Frida Kahlo and Diego Rivera. Kahlo's piece is especially stark and disturbing, so lighten up with the Monet or take the kids to the ingeniously crafted miniature period-sets in the Thorne Rooms.

Fine art deserves a pairing of fine sandwiches and salads at the museum's ❷ **Arcadia Farms Café**, where all the food is organic and sure to please. Continue the museum touring at the nearby ❸ **Heard Museum** – a treasure of Native American art and artifacts (39,000 pieces, including kachina dolls, pottery and jewelry). Run by the Arcadia Farms group, ❹ **City Bakery at Arizona Science Center** is a tasty excuse for dessert and a visit to the attached ❺ **Arizona Science Center**. Full of hands-on science exhibits, the center has a planetarium so stunning it makes agoraphobics squirm.

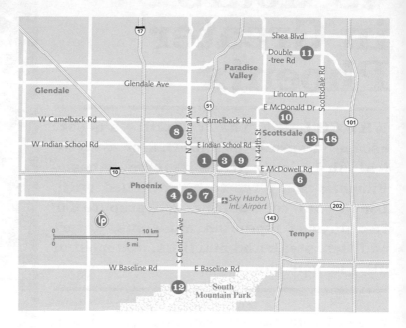

From here, head to the **6** **Desert Botanical Gardens** for the beauty of the untamed desert where the ocotillo plants reach their long arms toward the sky like so many green fountains. It's the place to reconnect with nature on walking paths that wind through 50 acres of desert life; from modest shrubs that bloom bright flowers in the spring to every shape of cactus. The place hosts solstice celebrations, night flashlight tours from May 1 through August, and special exhibits like pieces from glass artist Dale Chihuly integrated into the desert.

The star example of downtown's revitalization – or at least the tastiest – is **7** **Pizzeria Bianco**, set in a former exposed-brick machine shop at 6th and Adams Sts. Hard to believe that pizza can be that good? The ultimate demanding guest, Martha Stewart, ate here with friends and gave it a thumb's up. The secret: fresh, local ingredients and homemade mozzarella. It doesn't take reservations, so come early or prepare for a wait. If you can't snag one of the 42 seats, console yourself with a meal sometime at **8** **Pane Bianco** and taste the mozzarella goodness that put the pizzeria on the map. For liquid indulgence, try a post-supper cocktail at **9** **Durant's**, a martini and steak place with overstuffed leather booths and red-velvet wallpaper that was started long ago by Jack Durant, a man with underworld connections. To this day, powerbrokers do their deals here.

Watch the sun set red over Phoenix from the huge windows of the coolly elegant Jade bar at the **10** **Sanctuary Camelback Mountain Resort & Spa**.

Perched on the side of the mountain, it really does look like a huge resting camel contentedly looking over the valley. If there's a wildfire somewhere in the state or it's been a windy day (which kicks up dust and pushes out pollution), prepare for a dazzling show of red and yellow and blue in the sky. Sanctuary is a boutique resort; the service is first rate and the rooms draw the sort of celebrities that prefer peace, quiet and comfort over the glare and pop of the paparazzo's flash. If one of the 98 mountain or spa casitas doesn't do it for you – and if they don't, we really live in different worlds – they have private homes for rent on the mountain that are great for groups.

The next morning, hike Camelback Mountain – if you dare. It's a steep 1200ft climb from the base of Echo Canyon to the "head" of the camel. You might see locals loaded with colorful ropes and nylon webbing hiking up the first part of the trail – they're going to the rock formation known as the Praying Monk (look at it from a distance and you can make out the monk shape) to do an 80ft climb up the monk's back.

ART ATTACK

Every Thursday evening more than 100 of Scottsdale's galleries keep their doors open until 9pm for **Art Walk** (www.scottsdalegalleries.com), centered on Marshall Way and Main St. On the first Friday evening of every month, downtown Phoenix kicks up the gritty and fun factor a few notches for **First Fridays** (www.artlinkphoenix.com). In addition to cruising the funky art galleries downtown and a glimpse of the city's intelligentsia, expect music and the occasional poetry slam.

Before leaving this corner of the Valley, pay ⑪ Cosanti a visit. This unusual complex of cast-concrete structures is the home and studio of Frank Lloyd Wright student Paolo Soleri, and where Soleri's signature bronze and ceramic bells are crafted. For more wacky architecture, call ahead to make sure ⑫ Mystery Castle is open. Imagine a life-size sand castle built by someone while they listened to Jimi Hendrix and you'll have an inkling of what this home – made mainly of found materials – looks like.

If you're not staying at the Sanctuary, head to downtown Scottsdale and check into the ⑬ Hotel Valley Ho for a taste of the good life, Rat Pack–style. Midcentury modern gets a 21st-century twist at this jazzy joint that

URBAN WILDERNESS

If you have the extra time, spend half a day at **South Mountain Regional Park** (http://phoenix.gov/parks/hikesoth.html). Even though it's in Phoenix, the 16,000 acres offer plenty of trails to hike or bike where civilization feels thousands of miles away. Drive to the top along small, crazy-curving roads and you're rewarded with a view of the valley below. Horseback riding is available, and check for Silent Sundays – when roads are closed to motorized vehicles.

once bedded Bing Crosby, Natalie Wood and Janet Leigh. The mood works well in the balconied rooms, and the pool and poolside bar make it easy to do a whole lot of nothing. The VH Spa is good enough reason to stay in all day.

For the young or the restless, from here it's an easy walk around Scottsdale's compact downtown – where the Arts District juts against the historic Old Town – studded with galleries, little shops, plenty of good eating, and drinking places that span the range from the Budweiser crowd to the Bordeaux set. Satisfy a sweet tooth at the **14** **Sugar Bowl** candy shop. An Arizona institution, the sticky-sweet concoctions have bribed children into good behavior since the 1950s.

If renewing the wardrobe is key to your mental renewal – looking good is feeling good – nearby Scottsdale Fashion Sq is a temple of sophisticated consumerism. Or, let the public art and neat restaurants around the **15** **Scottsdale Museum of Contemporary Art** work some magic. The museum showcases global art, architecture and design, including James Turrell's otherworldly *Skyspace* in the sculpture garden. The museum is part of the local performing arts center along with the **16** **Orange Table** café, a decidedly unpretentious, lively place that specializes in mean mimosas.

"An Arizona institution, the sticky-sweet concoctions have bribed children into good behavior since the 1950s."

No matter how you decide to spend the rest of your day, make reservations for **17** **Digestif**, serving, as they put it, "Cal-Ital food for the soul." Set in the SouthBridge area of downtown Scottsdale (there are plans for a Soleri-designed pedestrian bridge nearby), it has an absinthe happy hour every day between 5pm and 6pm. Check out the listening booths on the way to the bathrooms – the owners showcase local bands.

Downtown Scottsdale has no shortage of things to do at night – and there's no shame in staying in to soak up more of the Hotel Valley Ho's decadent martinis, er, vibe. But, if it's a Thursday or Sunday night the karaoke at **18** **BS West,** a gay bar, is how fun-seeking locals, of whatever persuasion, have been reeling in the years for quite some time now.

All good things must come to an end, but don't you feel better? Like the fiery Phoenix rising from its own ashes, hopefully you feel new again.
Josh Krist

TRIP INFORMATION

GETTING THERE

Phoenix is about 150 miles south of Flagstaff and 115 miles north of Tucson.

DO

Arizona Science Center

Play with 300-odd hands-on exhibits, watch live demonstrations, or take in the mysteries of our universe at the planetarium. ☎ 602-716-2000; www.azscience.org; 600 E Washington St, Phoenix; adult/concession $9/7; ◷ 10am-5pm

Cosanti

Show up in the morning to watch the signature bells poured into molds. ☎ 480-948-6145; www.arcosanti.org; 6433 E Doubletree Ranch Rd, Scottsdale; donation appreciated; ◷ 9am-5pm Mon-Sat, 11am-5pm Sun

Desert Botanical Gardens

During December's nighttime *luminarias,* the plants are draped in miles of lights. Check for solstice celebrations. ☎ 480-941-1225; 1201 N Galvin Pkwy, Phoenix; adult/child/student/senior $10/4/5/9; ◷ 8am-8pm, seasonal variations

Heard Museum

A fascinating museum, be sure to check out the busy events schedule and the superb gift shop. ☎ 602-252-8848; www.heard.org; 2301 N Central Ave, Phoenix; adult/child/student/senior $10/3/5/9; ◷ 9:30am-5pm

Mystery Castle

Just be sure to call ahead to make sure tours are still being offered. ☎ 602-268-1581; 800 E Mineral Rd, Phoenix; adult/child $5/3; ◷ 11am-4pm Thu-Sun Oct-May or by appointment

Phoenix Art Museum

Free guided tours at 1pm and 2pm; kids love the miniature period rooms. ☎ 602-257-1880; www.phxart.org; 1625 N Central Ave, Phoenix; adult/child/$10/4; ◷ 10am-9pm Tue, 10am-5pm Wed-Sun

Scottsdale Museum of Contemporary Art

Anchors an area full of public art and standout restaurants. ☎ 480-874-4666; www.smoca.org; 7374 E 2nd St, Scottsdale; adult/child $7/free; ◷ 10am-5pm Tue-Wed & Fri-Sat, 10am-8pm Thu, noon-5pm Sun

EAT

Arcadia Farms Café

Try the gourmet sandwiches or the crispy crab cakes; it's all seasonal and organic-only. ☎ 602-257-2191; www.arcadiafarmscafe.com; 1625 N Central Ave, Phoenix; mains $11-15; ◷ 10am-5pm Tue-Sun

City Bakery at Arizona Science Center

It's not necessary to buy science-center admission to eat at this place, run by the same group that does Arcadia Farms Café. ☎ 602-257-8860; www.azscience.org/city_bakery.php; 600 E Washington St, Phoenix; mains from $9; ◷ 10am-5pm

Digestif

Try the From Farm to Table: sunchokes, fava beans, oyster mushrooms, pecorino and saba served with truffled mushroom tea. ☎ 480-425-9463; www.digestifscottsdale; 7114 E Stetson Dr, Scottsdale; dinner $18-28; ◷ 11am-midnight

Orange Table

This jazzy joint tucked behind the Scottsdale Performing Arts Center has more than three dozen wholesome sandwiches on the menu. ☎ 480-424-6819; 7373 E Scottsdale Mall, Scottsdale; dishes $4.50-12.50; ◷ 7am-10pm Tue-Sat, 7am-3pm Sun & Mon

Pane Bianco

A café from the Pizzeria Bianco group, taste the homemade mozzarella in a salad or sandwich without the pizzeria wait. ☎ 602-234-2100; www.pizzeriabianco.com/pane; 4404 N Central Ave, Phoenix; mains $8; ◷ 11am-3pm Tue-Sat

Pizzeria Bianco
James Beard–winner Chris Bianco makes the best pizza in town and maybe even all of America. ☎ 602-258-8300; www.pizzeria bianco.com; 623 E Adams St, Phoenix; pizza $10-14; ⊙ dinner Tue-Sat

Sugar Bowl
This pink-and-white place has been cooling sun-baked citizens since the '50s. Sandwiches and salads, too. ☎ 480-946-0051; 4005 N Scotts-dale Rd, Scottsdale; dishes $4-9; ⊙ 11am-10pm Sun-Thu, 11am-midnight Fri & Sat

DRINK

BS West
A gay bar and dance club in the Old Town; has pool tables, a small dance floor and kara-oke some nights. ☎ 480-945-9028; www .bswest.com; 7125 E 5th Ave, Scottsdale; ⊙ 2pm-2am

Durant's
With red-velvet wallpaper and overstuffed red-leather booths, the steaks are as sumptu-ous as the decor. ☎ 602-264-5967; www .durantsaz.com; 2611 N Central Ave, Phoe-nix; mains from $20; ⊙ 11am-10pm Mon-Thu, 11am-11pm Fri & Sat, 4:30-10pm Sun

SLEEP

Hotel Valley Ho
A centrally located and fun place to stay with a great spa and a Trader Vic's restaurant on site. ☎ 480-248-2000; www.hotelvalleyho.com; 6850 E Main St, Scottsdale; r $99-600

Sanctuary Camelback Mountain Resort & Spa
The location is second to none; steep dis-counts during hottest months. ☎ 480-948-2100; www.sanctuaryoncamelback.com; 5700 E McDonald Dr, Paradise Valley; r $415-750, private home from $3000

USEFUL WEBSITES
www.scottsdalecvb.com
www.visitphoenix.com

LINK YOUR TRIP
www.lonelyplanet.com/trip-planner

Cactus League Spring Training

HISTORY & CULTURE

WHY GO The crack of a bat, the sweet smell of corn dogs and the warm days of an Arizona spring – come see the best baseball clubs in the country duke it out in pre-season play. In March, the biggest conundrum a baseball fan faces is which of the 12 Cactus League teams to see.

TIME
2 days

DISTANCE
150 miles

BEST TIME TO GO
late Feb – Mar

START
Phoenix, AZ

END
Tucson, AZ

ALSO GOOD FOR

CITY

You know spring training has started when Japanese TV news crews are camped out front of ❶ **Peoria Sports Complex**, talking to the camera about Japanese-born Seattle Mariners sensations Ichiro Suzuki and Kazuhiro Sasaki.

The stadium, set in the northwestern Phoenix suburb of Peoria, is home to both the Mariners' and the San Diego Padres' spring training – fans with an affinity for West Coast sluggers should definitely pay the spiffy sports complex a visit. Notice how many people avoid walking in front of the TV cameras. Any local will tell you that sports fans call in sick a lot this time of year and spring training crowds are unusually camera-shy. The players, however, aren't shy at all. Between innings most of them are open to talking to fans and signing autographs – maybe it's the smaller venues or maybe it's because they know that spring training brings out the truest fans.

Spring training brings alive the baseball of a bygone era, when juicing is what mom did to oranges in the morning. The historic ❷ **Phoenix Municipal Stadium** is the spring training home of the Oakland A's and a good place to relive the sport's golden days: Willie Mays hit the first spring training home run in 1964 here. Look across third base for great views of the wind-carved rock formations that look like scoops of melting ice cream at Papago Park. The old-timey stadium isn't flashy, but it's comfortable enough after its revamp, and with only 7800 seats, there's not a bad place to cop a squat in the house.

HISTORY & CULTURE

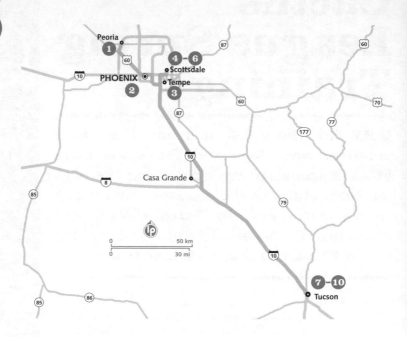

Head to **3** **Four Peaks Brewing Company** for some post-game brews. Just 4 miles away from "Phoenix Muni," as locals call it, the tall brews are ice-cold, and now is the best time of year to make the most of the outdoor patio.

Set in the toniest town in the Valley of the Sun and also 4 miles from Phoenix Muni, **4** **Scottsdale Stadium** is the home of the San Francisco Giants. Designed by the same people who did Camden Yards in Baltimore, it's one of the nicest city stadiums in Arizona – good food, fancy beers on tap, pretty people as well as art and baseball memorabilia dotted throughout. For all of these reasons, spring training tickets sell out fast. Bring lots of sunscreen or wear a sombrero – shade is minimal.

"...the bases are loaded with baseball history here."

After the game, it's a quick walk or free trolley ride to downtown Scottsdale's bevy of food and drink. For the ultimate post-game spot, saddle up at **5** **Pink Pony Steakhouse,** near Indian School and Scottsdale Rds. *The* place for league officials and players to gather ever since Scottsdale Stadium was built in 1956, the bases are loaded with baseball history here.

Just a mile away from Scottsdale Stadium, **6** **Hotel Valley Ho** is the place where celebrities hung out in the days when luxury was not a dirty word.

With an outdoor pool complete with a bar and spa service, people who don't like baseball are happy to work on their tan and down a few daiquiris during the day here.

It takes about two hours to drive the 115 miles south to Tucson – if you're going to rent a car, be sure to spring for one with satellite radio. Thankfully, spring training games both here and in Florida – the other spring training state – are broadcast live. The family-friendly ❼ **Windmill Inn at St Philips Plaza** is a good place to hang out between games – there are restaurants and a day spa in the attached plaza.

Spring training came to Arizona in 1946 when Bill Veeck, owner of the Cleveland Indians, was none too happy that Larry Doby, the American League's first black player, had to stay in a different hotel than the white players during spring training in Florida. Veeck brought his team to Tucson's ❽ **Hi Corbett Field** and convinced the head of the New York Giants to bring his team to Phoenix Municipal Stadium. On March 8, 1946, the Indians beat the Giants 3-1 here and the Cactus League was born.

Set in the Reid Park complex, nowadays the field is where the Colorado Rockies come to dust off the snow – they've trained here prior to every season in franchise history. Like at all the spring training spots, there's a platoon of kids and adults with mitts hoping to catch a foul ball. The oldest park in the league, the 1937-built stadium still charms with its nod to Spanish colonial architecture and quiet setting.

Teams that train at ❾ **Tucson Electric Park** must have their voltage meter cranked to 11 – Arizona's own Diamondbacks and the Chicago White Sox both train here and they've both won World Series pennants. With the Santa Catalina Mountains in the background, the sunsets alone are worth the price of admission.

TICKET SCORE

Ticket prices range anywhere from $3 to $20 and at most stadiums it's easy enough just to show up and get in. Spring sees a lot of snow birds: people who come from places like Chicago to enjoy a warm winter. That means it can be hard to get tickets for teams that are big in colder climes, like the Chicago White Sox. Scalping is legal in Arizona, fortunately, or you can buy tix online ahead of time.

Before leaving Tucson be sure to eat at ❿ **El Charro Café**, a local institution that's been serving *carne seca* and other Sonora-Mexican treats since before Hi Corbett Field existed. If you need to end the trip, so be it. But remember, to Cactus League like a local means calling in sick to extend the fun by a day or two. Stripped of all the glitz and glamour, baseball here is simple and good, just like mom's apple pie.

Josh Krist

HISTORY & CULTURE

TRIP INFORMATION

GETTING THERE
Phoenix is 115 miles north of Tucson, and Scottsdale and Phoenix share a border.

DO
Hi Corbett Field
Set in the Reid Park Complex – next to a zoo and two golf courses, it's the springtime home of the Colorado Rockies and the oldest stadium in the Cactus League. ☎ 520-327-9467; http://rockies.mlb.com/spring_training; 3400 E Camino Campestre, Tucson

Peoria Sports Complex
Home of the San Diego Padres and Seattle Mariners; whole rows of chain hotels and restaurants line the nearby streets. ☎ 623-773-8700; www.peoriaaz.gov/sports complex; 16101 N 83rd Ave, Peoria

Phoenix Municipal Stadium
A 7800-seat stadium that's the spring training home of the Oakland A's; it's just a stone's throw away from both the Tempe and Scottsdale borders. ☎ 602-392-0074; http://athletics.mlb.com/spring_training; 5999 E Van Buren St, Phoenix

Scottsdale Stadium
Home of the San Francisco Giants and within a walk or trolley ride of Scottsdale bars and eateries. ☎ 480-312-2586; www.scottsdaleaz.gov/stadium; 7408 E Osborn Rd, Scottsdale

Tucson Electric Park
Awesome views of the mountains and home of the Arizona Diamondbacks and the Chicago White Sox – both World Series champions. ☎ 520-434-1000; www.pima.gov/tep; 2500 E Ajo Way, Tucson

EAT & DRINK
El Charro Café
Where locals take out-of-towners every chance they get. *Carne seca* is meat that's been dried and then rehydrated; super delicious. ☎ 520-622-1922; 311 N Court Ave, Tucson; mains $8-18; ☺ lunch & dinner

Four Peaks Brewing Company
A quintessential neighborhood brewpub set in a Mission Revival–style building. Enjoy that patio before it gets too hot. ☎ 480-303-9967; www.fourpeaks.com; 1340 E 8th St, Tempe; ☺ 11am-2am

Pink Pony Steakhouse
Full of memorabilia, it's the best place in the state for post-game suds and grub. ☎ 480-945-6697; 3831 N Scottsdale Rd, Scottsdale; ☺ 10am-10:30pm Mon-Fri, 4-10pm Sat-Sun; mains $15-25

SLEEP
Hotel Valley Ho
A mile away from Scottsdale Municipal Stadium and a great place for non-fans to while away the day. ☎ 480-248-2000; www.hotelvalleyho.com; 6850 E Main St, Scottsdale; r $320-610

Windmill Inn at St Philips Plaza
The two-room suites feel big as half a ballpark. Kids under 18 and pets stay free. Free bike rentals, too. ☎ 520-577-0007; www.windmillinns.com; 4250 N Campbell Ave, Tucson; r $80-220; ☺ ☺

USEFUL WEBSITES
www.cactusleague.com

LINK YOUR TRIP
TRIP
www.lonelyplanet.com/trip-planner

Big Skies & Weird Science

WHY GO Whether it's seeing the bright rings of Saturn or standing in the room where two men could have plunged the world into a nuclear winter, prepare for a mental blast off. Even people who think they don't like astronomy or science will have a few "wow" moments on this trip with professional stargazer Cliff Ochser.

Long-time fixture in Arizona astronomy and stargazing guide Cliff Ochser says, "Arizona's great for astronomy because we have more research telescopes than any other state and we have 300 days a year of clear skies." Ochser suggests starting at the ❶ **Lowell Observatory** in Flagstaff. At 7000ft of elevation, Flagstaff isn't just closer to the stars than any other big city in Arizona, it's the first International Dark Sky city in the world. Stars here shine like diamonds sprinkled on black felt.

Experience the nightly stargazing during the week. Weekends can get crowded and long waits to look through a telescope are common – and seeing the bright rings of Saturn are worth the wait. The privately built observatory (in operation since 1894) is where Pluto, the celestial body formerly known as a planet, was discovered in 1930. "A day tour is still worthwhile at Lowell," says Ochser. "It's really about the history there and they have some good films and great exhibits."

Two miles from Lowell Observatory, ❷ **Comfi Cottages** gives families and those in need of privacy a base of operations in Flagstaff. Perks include a fridge stocked with breakfast foods, a barbecue and bikes.

After a starry night in Flagstaff head 40 miles east on I-40 to ❸ **Meteor Crater**. To some, it's just a 550ft-deep hole in the desert nearly a mile across. To others, especially kids who can easily imagine the blazing meteor screaming down in a fiery ball, it's an awesome sight – and one of the best-preserved impact craters in the world.

TIME
3 days

DISTANCE
425 miles

BEST TIME TO GO
Oct – Mar

START
Flagstaff, AZ

END
Tucson, AZ

ALSO GOOD FOR

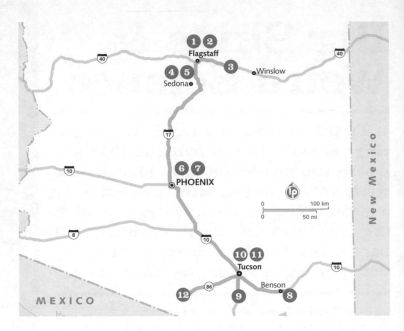

Get ready for more awesome sights in red rock–studded Sedona. Ochser, former director of development at Lowell Observatory, says that during his time there he realized that the best way for newbies to see the stars would be in small groups with a high astronomer-to-visitor ratio. So, he started ④ **Evening Sky Tours**. The astronomer-guides are friendly and knowledgeable and, best of all, they bring plenty of blankets. Like at all Arizona star parties, the recommended attire is a thick coat and hat. On good nights the stars look so close against the towering rocks of Sedona that seeing a big-eyed alien step out of a star onto a big rock wouldn't be a huge surprise. "Sedona really does have some of the best skies in Arizona. We throw off very little light pollution here," says Ochser.

> *"Aliens float through the space as Mr Spock and Obi-Wan Kenobi look on approvingly."*

For out-of-this-world eats after the tour, go to the '50s-themed ⑤ **Red Planet Diner**. Aliens float through the space as busts of Mr Spock and Obi-Wan Kenobi look on approvingly.

The next morning, ponder that at light speed it would take less than a second to drive to Tucson. A 230-mile drive, the ⑥ **Arizona Science Center** in Phoenix is a good halfway point and the center will get restless kids worn out to a manageable level with its ever-popular "Grossology" exhibition, featuring oversized noses and other larger-than-life icky places. Afterwards, grab a gourmet salad or sandwich at the attached ⑦ **City Bakery at Arizona Science Center** – if the Grossology exhibit didn't kill your appetite.

② OFFBEAT

Enjoy the brief stretch of desert and the odd pecan grove on the way to Tucson. About 50 miles east of Tucson off the I-10, gaze lovingly at the ❽ **Astronomer's Inn**. The home of the Vega-Bray Observatory, there are four themed rooms here (one is outer space–themed) and guests can participate in nightly star viewings. The next morning, enjoy the third rock from the sun by splashing around on a small boat at the B&B's private lake.

The next morning, head to the ❾ **Titan Missile Museum**, 24 miles south of Tucson. It's an original Titan II missile site where a crew of two stood at the ready to launch a nuclear warhead within seconds of receiving a presidential order. Walking through several 3-ton blast doors, you enter the control room where you experience a simulated launch.

EX-GUV SPOTS ALIENS

Fife Symington, ex-governor of Arizona, down-played the March 1997 sightings of mysterious lights floating around the state. At a news conference he announced that he had found the culprit, and brought out one of his underlings dressed in an alien costume. Symington, who was under investigation for fraud at the time, admitted years later that he too saw the lights and is sure he saw an alien craft. He said he was afraid to start a panic.

On the way back to the Astronomer's Inn visit the ❿ **Pima Air & Space Museum**; walk down the steps of JFK's Air Force One and wave like a president. Give yourself at least two hours to wander through the 275 aircraft on display.

Serious plane-spotters will enjoy the one-hour bus tour of the nearby 309th ⓫ **Aerospace Maintenance & Regeneration Center** – aka the "boneyard" – where some 5000 aircraft are mothballed in the dry desert air. Because the tour is on an active military base, you need to make reservations at least one hour in advance and will have to show photo ID before getting on the bus. Tours depart from the Pima Air & Space Museum.

Finally, drive the winding road to ⓬ **Kitt Peak National Observatory**. Near Sells, 56 miles southwest of Tucson, this 6875ft-high mountain top is a perfect site for one of the world's largest observatories. It's equipped with two radio and 23 optical telescopes, including one boasting a diameter of 12ft.

Guided one-hour tours go inside the building housing the telescopes but you don't get to look through any of them. To get a peek at the cosmic eye candy, sign up well in advance for the Nightly Observing Program, a three-hour session starting at sunset and limited to 20 people.

Tucson, the final frontier (of this trip, at least) is the place to end your stellar journey. Think about it: you've seen the most popular attractions in the universe and never left the state.

Josh Krist

TRIP INFORMATION

GETTING THERE
It's a 265-mile drive between Flagstaff and Tucson, the two main cities for this trip.

DO

Aerospace Maintenance & Regeneration Center
One-hour bus tours depart from the Pima Air & Space Museum. Reserve at least one hour and board 30 minutes before. **Amarg;** ☎ 520-574-0462; Tucson; adult/child $6/3; ☽ 9am-5pm Mon-Fri, last tour 4pm

Arizona Science Center
Play with 300-odd hands-on exhibits, watch live demonstrations, or take in the mysteries of our universe at the planetarium. ☎ 602-716-2000; www.azscience.org; 600 E Washington St, Phoenix; adult/concession $9/7; ☽ 10am-5pm

Evening Sky Tours
Small groups, warm blankets and comfy chairs between telescope viewings – cold nights never looked so good. ☎ 928-203-0006; www.eveningskytours.com; Sedona; adult/child $60/$20; ☽ after sunset

Kitt Peak National Observatory
Book two to four weeks in advance for the worthwhile nightly observing program. ☎ 520-318-8726; www.noao.edu/kpno; Hwy 86, Sells; daytime admission by donation, observing program adult/student/senior $41/36/36; ☽ Sep–mid-Jul

Lowell Observatory
Nightly stargazing. During the day 30-minute tours offered hourly between 1:15pm and 4:15pm. ☎ 928-233-3211; www.lowell.edu; 1400 W Mars Hill Rd, Flagstaff; adult/child/student/senior $6/3/4/4; ☽ 9am-5pm, 5:30-10pm, seasonal variations

Meteor Crater
Tours into the crater depart from 9:15am to 2:15pm daily (free with admission). ☎ 928-

289-2362; www.meteorcrater.com; I-40 exit 233; adult/child/senior $15/7/13; ☽ 7am-7pm Jun–mid-Sep, seasonal variations

Pima Air & Space Museum
Combination tickets available for Titan Missile Museum and Amarg. ☎ 520-574-0462; www.pimaair.org; 6000 E Valencia Rd, Tucson; Jun-Oct adult/child $11.75/8, Nov-May $13.50/9; ☽ 9am-5pm, last admission 4pm

Titan Missile Museum
Look into combo tickets for Pima Air & Space Museum. ☎ 520-574-9658; www.titanmissilemuseum.org; 1580 W Duval Mine Rd, Sahuarita; adult/child/senior $8.50/5/7.50; ☽ 9am-4:30pm (last tour), seasonal variations

EAT

City Bakery at Arizona Science Center
It's not necessary to buy science-center admission to eat here. ☎ 602-257-8860; www.azscience.org/city_bakery.php; 600 E Washington St, Phoenix; mains from $9; ☽ 10am-5pm

Red Planet Diner
Grill food, including a fair number of vegetarian choices, in a space-age environment. ☎ 928-282-6070; 1655 W Hwy 89A, Sedona; dishes $9-14; ☽ 10am-11pm

SLEEP

Astronomer's Inn
A self-guided tour for guests is $45 and a four-hour session on a 20-inch scope is $160. ☎ 520-586-7906; www.astronomersinn.com; 1311 S Astronomers Rd, Benson; r $105-210; ☽ Oct 15-May 1

Comfi Cottages
Some weekends and holidays may require a minimum stay. ☎ 928-774-0731; www.comficottages.com; 1612 N Aztec St, Flagstaff; cottages $135-280; ☽

USEFUL WEBSITES
www.astronomycast.com
www.darksky.org
www.lonelyplanet.com/trip-planner

LINK YOUR TRIP

Steak-Lovers' Arizona

WHY GO Cattle, cotton and copper: the three Cs that Arizona was built on, but only one of them tastes good over a wood-fired grill. Get ready for beef and lots of it, at the best steak houses in the state. Better yet, out here in the West, the drinks are as strong as the day is long.

TIME
5 days

DISTANCE
450 miles

BEST TIME TO GO
Year-round

START
Scottsdale, AZ

END
Tuscon, AZ

ALSO GOOD FOR

You don't need to drive here like you just stole some baby diapers and are on the run, but, fans of the film *Raising Arizona* might have an odd sense of déjà vu when pulling up to Scottsdale's ❶ Reata Pass Steakhouse – the Old West steakhouse appeared in some episodes of *Bonanza* as well. Opened in 1882 as a stagecoach stop, the star attraction these days is the beef, from cuts of New York strip to tenderloin to dishes like filet mignon. After dinner, make like it's still the good old days and kick up your heels at the sister bar next door, ❷ Greasewood Flat. The outdoor drinking joint attracts locals of all stripes looking to let loose under the stars.

Afterwards, rest up at ❸ Hermosa Inn, a Scottsdale boutique hotel that began as the private home and studio of cowboy artist Lon Megargee. Today, the 35 rooms and casitas give off soothing vibes thanks to Spanish-Colonial decor that makes nice use of color and proportion, just like Megargee's paintings. There's an excellent restaurant, but no pool to work off those calories. And yes, the on-site eatery serves steak.

Sharpen the steak knives and brush up on cowboy slang, because 10 miles south of Central Phoenix is ❹ Rawhide Western Town & Steakhouse, a 1880s frontier-town theme park set on the Gila River Indian Reservation. The steakhouse has rattlesnake and Rocky Mountain oysters (bull testicles) for adventurous eaters and mesquite-grilled slabs of beef for everyone else, usually accompanied by music and entertainment. Consider a sundown cookout, which includes

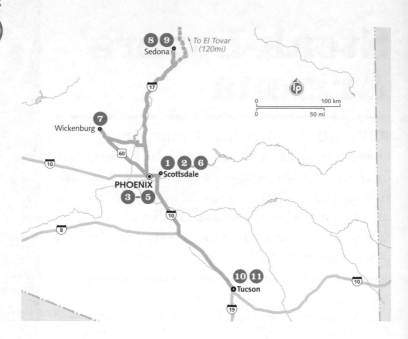

a hayride and Western dancing for even more silly fun. The food at the Rawhide Steakhouse is solid but not top of the line; the ambience makes up for it.

After another night at the casita, head to Central Phoenix for a night of classy sips and steaks at **5** **Durant's**, bedecked with red-leather booths and red-velvet wallpaper. The martinis at Durant's are like small swimming pools, and when you enter through the back door the kitchen staff shouts out a welcome over the clatter of chopping knives and the low roar of a wood fire that's grilling steaks to perfection. But the steak's Durant's thing. On that count, this joint is the cow's moo. Anything is good, but the filet mignon is butta'. If you're watching your red-meat intake, there's also seafood on offer. Come during lunch to save a few bucks and see the lawyer and legislator types doing deals.

> *"Steak with a coffee rub? Oh yeah, it's good."*

If you really don't want to slide off of Scottsdale's luxurious lap, check out where steakhouse meets piano bar at **6** **Mastro's City Hall Steakhouse.** Its sides and appetizer menu has more choices than most, and the tinkling of the piano keys in the background makes the first-rate service feel that much more special. The yummy porterhouse comes in a 3lb slab of goodness made for sharing between two people. The martinis are an oasis and the wine list is the who's who of top-notch vino.

For a few days away from the city – and to experience firsthand how the cowboys wrangle steers – check out **7** **Flying E Ranch**, in the scrubby cowboy country of Wickenburg, 65 miles northwest of Phoenix. This down-home working cattle ranch in the Hassayampa Valley is a big hit with families and gets plenty of repeaters. Guests can chow down after a hayride to the chuck wagon.

From here, head 120 miles north to Sedona for more fresh air and, of course, another great meal. Decadence is queen at **8** **Enchantment Resort**; so close to the red rocks you can almost hear the vortex humming. Seriously, a stray ball from the tennis court will smack the nearby cliffs, and reflected rock formations loom large in the pool. Don't forget sumptuous Mii Amo spa; Enchantment Resort has won more awards and accolades than a five-star general.

For dinner head out to **9** **Cowboy Club**. The usual meaty suspects take a wild turn with the addition of buffalo and game meats like elk. Signature dishes include french-fried cactus and rattlesnake bits on a stick. The restaurant's Silver Saddle Room is the adults-only zone.

Be sure to sleep well before taking the 230-mile trip down to Tucson – a journey that starts in mountains full of ponderosa pines and ends in rolling desert full of saguaro cactus and mesquite trees. The trip is worth it for **10** **Janos**. French-trained James Beard Award winner Janos Wilder is a culinary maestro, and teases flavors out of meat that you didn't know existed. It's probably the most creative take on steak in the state. Steak with a coffee rub? Oh yeah, it's good. His dining room at the Westin La Paloma overlooks the desert valley and is perfect for big, long, romantic meals.

If you've ever wanted to know what it would feel like to have a super-luxurious house far away from the travails of civilization, sleep off dinner at **11** **La Zarzuela B&B**, where fantasies of escaping to a remote artsy enclave come true. Imagine a mansion in the middle of sandy hills carpeted with desert trees and bushes. Set in the foothills of Tucson and only for adult guests, there are five spacious casitas here.

DETOUR It's a long way to go for a steak, no matter how grand, but what really seals the deal are the views – without a doubt the most magnificent of any restaurant in Arizona, if not the country. Set on the South Rim of the Grand Canyon, the **El Tovar Hotel Dining Room** has big picture windows seemingly set on the very edge of the canyon. The filets are almost as good as the views. Reservations (☎ 928-638-2631) are required for dinner.

Once the trip has ended, rest assured: Dr Atkins would be proud.
Josh Krist

TRIP INFORMATION

GETTING THERE
Phoenix is about 150 miles south of Flagstaff and 115 miles north of Tucson. Phoenix and Scottsdale share a border.

DO & EAT

Cowboy Club
Try a beef or buffalo filet mignon or the elk tenderloin. Or just enjoy the rattlesnake skewer. ☎ 928-282-4200; www.cowboyclub .com; 241 N Hwy 89A, Sedona; mains lunch $9-16, dinner $15-25; ☾ lunch & dinner

Durant's
With red-velvet wallpaper and overstuffed red-leather booths, the steaks are as sumptuous as the decor. ☎ 602-264-5967; www .durantsaz.com; 2611 N Central Ave, Phoenix; mains from $20; ☾ 11am-10pm Mon-Thu, 11am-11pm Fri & Sat, 4:30-10pm Sun

Greasewood Flat
Cash only at this outdoor bar, next to Reata Pass Steakhouse. On cold nights they blaze up the fire pits. ☎ 480-585-9430; 27375 N Alma School Pkwy, Scottsdale; ☾ 11am-11pm

Janos
Try the New York strip steak rubbed with coffee, molasses and Mexican chocolate. The attached J Bar is good for an after-steak drink. ☎ 520-615-6100; www.janos.com; 3770 E Sunrise Dr, Tucson; mains $28-50, tasting menu $85; ☾ dinner Mon-Sat

Mastro's City Hall Steakhouse
Seasoned servers, good steaks and an upscale setting that strives for comfort more than pretense. ☎ 480-941-4700; www.mastros restaurants.com; 6991 E Camelback Rd, Phoenix; ☾ 5-10pm Sun-Thu, 5-11pm Fri & Sat

Rawhide Steakhouse
Good steaks in a 1880s frontier-town theme park. Check ahead for sundown cookout times. ☎ 480-502-5600; www.rawhide.com; 5700 W N Loop Rd, Chandler; admission free, per attraction $4, day pass $15, adult/child cookout $45/19; ☾ 5:30-9pm Wed-Thu

Reata Pass Steakhouse
Reservations are recommended. Try the 24oz porterhouse and you'll see why. ☎ 480-585-7277; www.reatapass.com; 27500 N Alma School Pkwy, Scottsdale; mains from $15; ☾ 11am-9pm Tue-Thu, 11am-11pm Fri & Sat, noon-9pm Sun

SLEEP

Enchantment Resort
A country club–style resort tucked into beautiful Boynton Canyon. Sometimes even ostentatious names accurately describe the feeling you get at a place. ☎ 928-282-2900; www.enchantmentresort.com; 525 Boynton Canyon Rd, Sedona; r from $450

Flying E Ranch
The place to try your luck penning a steer. There's no bar, so BYOB. Rates include activities and meals. ☎ 928-684-2690; www .flyingeranch.com; 2801 W Wickenburg Way, Wickenburg; r $310-390 minimum, seasonal; ☾ Nov-Apr; ⚒

Hermosa Inn
The best place in the world to enjoy a food coma, thanks to the soothing Spanish-Colonial decor. ☎ 602-955-8614; www.hermosainn .com; 5532 N Palo Cristi Rd, Scottsdale; r incl breakfast $140-460, villa $310-700

La Zarzuela B&B
An adult-only mansion with five colorful casitas for guests. Set in the middle of acres of virgin desert; quiet and luxury abound. ☎ 520-884-4824; www.zarzuela-az.com; 455 N Camino de Oeste, Tucson; r $275-300; ☾ closed mid-Jun–mid-Sep

USEFUL WEBSITES
www.arizonabeef.com
www.atkins.com

www.lonelyplanet.com/trip-planner

LINK YOUR TRIP

A Slice of Native America

WHY GO Apart from the rich culture you can experience on the major reservations to the north, the museums and archaeological sites near Arizona's three biggest cities tell a fascinating tale of societies that rose, created thriving cities and then disappeared for no apparent reason.

In the saguaro-studded desert just south of Phoenix, **1** Sheraton Wild Horse Pass Resort & Spa is hands down the best spot to start a tour of Arizona's easy to reach Native American sights. Owned by the Gila River tribe and set on their reservation, this 500-room resort is an impressive mix of luxury and tradition. Tribal elders relate ancient legends around the fire pit and wild horses really do run free outside the hotel.

No property in Arizona can compare with the Sheraton Wild Horse Pass on Native American bona fides – built and run by Native Americans – but Scottsdale's **2** Hyatt Regency Scottsdale Resort & Spa has a more central location. It has a small but quite good Native American education center and the hotel occasionally hosts traditional craft demonstrations and dances.

Wherever you stay, tear yourself away for a day to head to Phoenix's palm- and skyscraper-fringed Central Ave for a visit to the **3** Heard Museum. A trip to these artifact-packed halls should count for college credit you learn so much. And, because the museum designers know their stuff, the past springs to life in vivid colors and heartbreaking tales. The 'Boarding School Experience' gallery is about the controversial federal policy of removing Native American children from their families and sending them to remote boarding schools in order to 'Americanize' them. The corner of Central and Indian School Rds, now occupied by Steele Indian School Park, used to have just such a school.

TIME
5 days

DISTANCE
500 miles

BEST TIME TO GO
Year-round

START
Phoenix, AZ

END
Tuscon, AZ

ALSO GOOD FOR

OUTDOORS

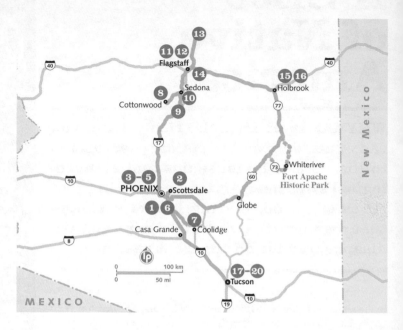

Whet your appetite with lunch at ❹ **Fry Bread House**, a long-time local favorite. This is *the* place for the traditional Native American treat of Navajo tacos – deep-fried bread topped with beans, meat or whatever else. Think of it kind of like an oversized taco-meets-pita. Businesspeople and Native Americans in search of comfort food mingle here during any given lunch rush.

> *"The 1000-year-old Sinagua city carved into a cliff face looks like a rough-hewn castle in the air."*

From the Heard Museum, cruise 2 miles north on Central and make a left at Indian School Rd. Steele Indian School Park will be on your right. Continue to 7th Ave.

Learn about the Hohokam at the ❺ **Pueblo Grande Museum & Archaeology Park**. For the most scenic route head 8 miles southeast – Central Ave to Washington St through old neighborhoods. Inside the museum, you'll learn all about the Hohokam ruins of a Pueblo Grande village located right outside the door. Famous for building such a well-engineered 1000-mile network of irrigation canals that some modern canals simply follow their paths, the civilization simply disappeared in about AD 1500.

No matter where you're sleeping, make dinner reservations at ❻ **Kai**, at Sheraton Wild Horse Pass Resort & Spa. Kai takes Native American to a new level with traditional crops grown along the Gila River and a fine wine list. A sunset dinner on the patio overlooking the virgin desert while horses gallop in the distance: priceless.

Dedicate time for the 100-mile round-trip through housing developments and cotton fields to **7** **Casa Grande Ruins National Monument**. The Casa Grande (big house) is a sort of ancient apartment complex. It's one of the country's largest remaining Hohokam buildings, with 11 rooms spread across four floors. The Pima and Tohono O'odham are probably the modern descendants of the Hohokam, but scientists are still debating what happened to the tribe.

After another night in the Phoenix area, watch the megalopolis ever so slowly peel away as you head north on I-17 towards **8** **Tuzigoot National Monument**. The 40-mile round-trip from I-17 on Hwy 260/279 is time well spent for the seriously obsessed. (Those who are short on time may want to skip it.) Featuring stone-walled dwellings set on a pueblo, Tuzigoot lets visitors get close to the homes of the ancient Sinagua – another lost tribe. At its peak, as many as 225 people lived in the 110 rooms here.

Where I-17 starts turning into a scenic (albeit high-speed) drive through blasted mountains, about 100 miles north of Phoenix, stands **9** **Montezuma Castle National Monument**, the ultimate must-see. The 1000-year-old Sinagua city carved into a cliff face looks like a rough-hewn castle in the air. Take the time to really let it sink in and imagine a thriving community up there.

Break on through to the other side with a **10** **Crossing Worlds** tour to Hopi, Navajo and other Native American sacred sites in Sedona. Now more commonly known as a center of New Age, Native American tribes knew long ago that Sedona's landscape is spiritually charged. The red-rock towers here glow in the sunset and look like they're about to blast off – a stop in Sedona humbles even the skeptics.

Cross back into the world of highways and finding a good radio station and

ASK A LOCAL

"What's cool is that right in the middle of the desert, this inhospitable place, they [the Hohokams] had a whole system of canals and agriculture and were able to do so much. We know they had trade routes all the way down to Mexico. Why do I think they left? Martians (laughs)."

Brandon Protas, former Pueblo Grande Museum volunteer

continue on to Flagstaff, a fun college town set at about 7000ft. The nights are frosty here, but the beds are big and warm at **11** **Inn at 410**. A few of the 10 rooms here have a Southwestern theme.

Power up on coffee the next morning in downtown Flagstaff for a visit to **12** **Museum of Northern Arizona**. Three miles north of downtown, it's in a stone building set in a pretty little pine grove. Don't miss the collections of Hopi kachina dolls, native basketry and ceramics, and Navajo textiles.

From the museum, head back towards the center of Flagstaff to hit Hwy 89 north. Take that for 12 miles and turn right at the sign for Sunset Crater

Volcano–Wupatki National Monuments. The visitor center for **13** **Wupatki National Monument** is 21 miles from this junction, on a winding paved road that runs through rolling fields of wild grass. Some people are bored to tears by this drive, while others love it. Once here, though, you're treated to the sight of freestanding pueblos that were built after Sunset Crater blew its top in the 11th century. With the snowcapped San Francisco Peaks looming behind the ancient dwellings, this is the most photogenic spot on the trip.

Next, head to Holbrook, 90 miles southeast of Flagstaff on the super-straight and none-too-exciting I-40 (and Route 66). On the way there, take in the wonder of **14** **Walnut Canyon**, just outside of Flagstaff. Assuming the trail is open, you can get close-ups of 25 of the rooms carved into vertical limestone walls where the Sinagua people lived more than 900 years ago.

> **DETOUR**
>
> When driving through the White Mountain Apache Reservation it's worth a stop at **Fort Apache Historic Park** (www.wmat.nsn.us/fortapachepark .htm), just 4 miles south of Whiteriver. Walking tours, the Apache cultural center and museum, and exhibits on the soldiers who were stationed here during the "Apache Wars" bring alive the turbulent history of Arizona's original tenants.

Holbrook's **15** **Navajo County Historical Museum** is set inside the 1898 county courthouse, a charming heap of bricks with a still-working courtroom. The building doubles as the visitors center and hosts free Native American dances at 7pm in summer. Stay at the **16** **Wigwam Motel**, a collection of faux teepees made of concrete that look straight out of the 1950s inside. It's most decidedly not authentic, but still fun.

From here, it's a 240-mile drive to Tucson through the White Mountain Apache Reservation via Hwy 77/Hwy 60. Enjoy the descent; the scenery changes from pines to the short trees and tall bushes of the high desert to the crazy pantomimes of saguaro outside of Tucson.

Grab some sustenance in Tucson at **17** **La Indita**, a vegetarian place that serves Michoacan Tarascan Indian food from Mexico. If you want to try some native cooking at home, pay a visit to the nearby **18** **Native Seeds** retail store. Retire to **19** **Lodge on the Desert**, a 1930s pet-positive resort that focuses on sweet relaxation – whoever's been driving deserves the rest. The next morning, prepare for another time warp at **20** **Arizona State Museum**, the oldest and largest anthropology museum in the state. The museum follows the cultural history of the Southwestern tribes, from Stone Age mammoth hunters to the present.

Even though they disappeared, the engineering and cultural marvels of Arizona's first residents shaped modern Arizona and still wow visitors from around the globe. The people are gone but not forgotten.

Josh Krist

TRIP INFORMATION

GETTING THERE
Phoenix is 150 miles south of Flagstaff and 118 miles north of Tucson.

DO

Arizona State Museum
Follow the history of the Southwestern tribes from Stone Age mammoth hunters to the present. ☎ 520-621-6302; www.state museum.arizona.edu; 1013 E University Blvd, Tucson; suggested donation $3; ✹ 10am-5pm Mon-Sat, noon-5pm Sun

Casa Grande Ruins National Monument
Ranger-led tours November to April. Don't confuse the monument with the modern town of Casa Grande, west of I-10. ☎ 520-723-3172; www.nps.gov/cagr; 1100 W Ruins Dr, Coolidge; adult/child $5/free; ✹ 8am-5pm

Crossing Worlds
Tours on Hopi, Navajo and other Native American cultures last anywhere from 2½ hours to several days. ☎ 928-649-3060; www.crossingworlds.com; Sedona; tours from $80

Heard Museum
A fascinating museum; be sure to check out the busy events schedule. Superb gift shop and café. ☎ 602-252-8848; www .heard.org; 2301 N Central Ave, Phoenix; adult/child/student/senior $10/3/5/9; ✹ 9:30am-5pm

Montezuma Castle National Monument
The 1000-year-old castle-like structure carved into the side of a cliff is a jaw-dropper. ☎ 928-567-3322; www.nps.gov/moca; adult/child $5/free, combination pass with Tuzigoot $8; ✹ 8am-6pm, seasonal variations

Museum of Northern Arizona
Set 3 miles north of downtown Flagstaff, the focus is on the tribes of the top half of Arizona. ☎ 928-774-5213; www.musnaz .org; 3101 N Fort Valley Rd, Flagstaff; adult/teen/student/senior $7/4/5/6; ✹ 9am-5pm

Navajo County Historical Museum
Free Native American dance performances every weekday evening in June and July. ☎ 928-524-6558; www.ci.holbrook .az.us; northeast cnr of East Arizona St and Navajo Blvd, Holbrook; donations appreciated; ✹ 8am-5pm Mon-Fri, 8am-4pm Sat & Sun

Pueblo Grande Museum & Archaeology Park
Excavations here include a ball court and a section of the original canals. ☎ 602-495-0901; www.pueblogrande.com; 4619 E Washington St, Phoenix; adult/child/senior $5/3/4; ✹ 9am-4:45pm Mon-Sat, 1-4:45pm Sun, seasonal variations

Tuzigoot National Monument
Get an up close and personal look at the Sinagua pueblo dwellings. ☎ 928-634-5564; www.nps.gov/tuzi; adult/child $5/free, combination ticket with Montezuma Castle National Monument $8; ✹ 9am-5pm, seasonal variations

Walnut Canyon
Worth calling ahead to make sure the access trail is open (rock falls can close it). If the trail's not open, admission is usually free. ☎ 928-526-3367; www.nps.gov/waca; adult/under 16 $5/free; ✹ 9am-5pm

Wupatki National Monument
Some pueblos stand several stories high. Check the website for details on the Crack-in-Wall overnight trip; it's by lottery only. ☎ 928-679-2365; www.nps.gov/wupa; adult/under 16 $5/free; ✹ 9am-5pm

EAT

Fry Bread House
A small place that gets packed to the gills at lunch. Order a traditional fry bread stuffed with whatever your heart desires. ☎ 602-351-2345; 4140 N 7th Ave, Phoenix; mains $4-7; ✹ 10am-7pm Mon-Sat

TRIP
15

HISTORY &
CULTURE

Kai
Flavorful, authentic Native American cuisine
and great desert views are worth the trip.
☎ 602-385-5726; 5594 W Wild Horse Pass
Blvd, Chandler; mains $35-49, 8-course
tasting menu with wine pairings $200;
🕙 dinner Tue-Sat

La Indita
A fresh spin on Native American cuisine;
vegetarians have lots of choice, but there's
plenty for carnivores. ☎ 520-792-0523; 622
N 4th Ave, Tucson; mains $7-10; 🕙 11am-
9pm Mon-Fri, 6-9pm Sat, 9am-9pm Sun

Native Seeds
Snacks like prickly pear cactus lollipops are
the only things ready to eat, but mixes for
cooking at home are plentiful. ☎ 520-622-
5561; www.nativeseeds.org; 526 N 4th Ave,
Tucson; mixes $6-10; 🕙 10am-5pm Mon-
Sat, noon-4pm Sun

SLEEP

Hyatt Regency Scottsdale Resort & Spa
The hotel has a Native American educational
room and hosts dance and craft demos. It
also has gondoliers who sing – a cultural
smorgasbord. ☎ 480-444-1234; http://scotts
dale.hyatt.com; 7500 E Doubletree Ranch Rd,
Scottsdale; r from $290

Inn at 410
The three-course breakfast is served from
8am to 9am – so wake up, sleepy head. The
Canyon Memories room has a neat Southwest
theme and is worth checking out. ☎ 928-
774-0088; www.inn410.com; 410 N Leroux
St, Flagstaff; r $170-300

Lodge on the Desert
Recover from the road in one of the
hacienda-style casitas; many have patios and
fireplaces. ☎ 520-325-3366; www
.lodgeonthedesert.com; 306 N Alvernon
Way, Tucson; r $200-340; 🐾

Sheraton Wild Horse Pass Resort & Spa
Comfortable rooms, spacious common areas,
and plenty of programs to educate the well-
cared-for guests. ☎ 602-225-0100; www
.wildhorsepassresort.com; 5594 W Wild
Horse Pass Blvd, Chandler; r from $260

Wigwam Motel
Comfy enough on the inside, with plenty of
retro touches, the exterior of the faux wigwams
are fine examples of roadside kitsch. ☎ 928-
524-3048; www.galerie-kokopelli.com
/wigwam; 811 W Hopi Dr, Holbrook; r $48-58

USEFUL WEBSITES
www.arizonaguide.com
http://500nations.com/arizona_tribes.asp

LINK YOUR TRIP
www.lonelyplanet.com/trip-planner

Cowboy Time

WHY GO Sometimes all a city slicker really needs to smile again is get in touch with his or her inner cowperson. Plenty of dude ranches are just an hour or two away from Phoenix, and you'll see why, despite all the hardships, cowboys keep yearning for the wide open spaces.

A first-time visitor would be forgiven for thinking all of the snappy cowgirl outfits worn by women in Scottsdale mean that the spirit of the Wild West is alive and well in the Valley of the Sun, but here's a tip for you, partner: boots and a hat do...not a cowboy make. Would-be cowpokes need to get the heck out of Dodge.

Begin the cowboy adventure with a good meal on the way out of town. Started as a rest stop and general store for weekending Phoenicians on their way to cooler climes, ❶ Pinnacle Peak Patio & Microbrewery is just off the Pima/Princess Rds exit on Loop 101. The steaks are all USDA top-choice beef. The "cowgirl" steak weighs in at a pound. The "cowboy" steak weighs in at a whopping 2lb. Do not even think of wearing a tie (or, wear an old one you don't care about) – it's tradition here to cut them right off and pin them on the wall.

When dinner's done, sip into the cowboy spirit at ❷ Greasewood Flat, just 1.3 miles north on Alma School Rd. Once a stage-coach stop between Phoenix and Fort McDowell, these days the lively, relaxed place is where free spirits – many of them ride steel horses, aka Harleys – share picnic tables under the stars. Bunk down at the ❸ Carefree Resort & Villas, 10 miles northwest of Greasewood Flat in the aptly named desert outpost of Carefree. Cowboy sing-alongs are common, and the luxurious accommodations and desert locale help get you into the slower pace of country life. If you've got the time, try your hand at horseback riding, cattle drives and the other fun on offer.

TIME
3 – 4 days

DISTANCE
175 miles

BEST TIME TO GO
Sep – May

START
Phoenix, AZ

END
Prescott, AZ

ALSO GOOD FOR

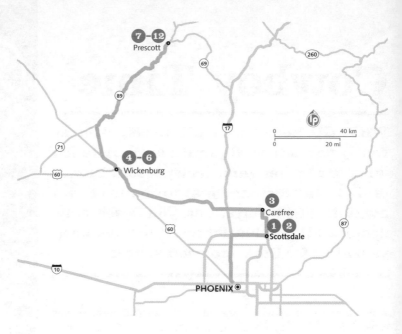

The next morning, head to Wickenburg, the heart of Arizona's cowboy country where old ranch houses sit alone in big patches of ocotillo bushes and mesquite trees. Like so many of the towns in these parts, Wickenburg's history is a tale of prospectors, gold mines and ranchers. Nowadays, guest ranches keep the romance of the Old West alive.

Get the full lowdown on Arizona's cowboy story at the **4** **Desert Caballeros Western Museum,** which in addition to exhibits on history and Native American artifacts, has a world-class collection of American Western artists' work.

Almost any guest ranch gives a pretty good taste of the cowboy lifestyle – albeit prettified to meet modern standards of comfort. The down-home **5** **Flying E Ranch,** a working cattle ranch in the Hassayampa Valley, deserves a look-see. They have "I wanna' be a cowgirl" weekends that will awaken the inner Annie Oakley in even the most genteel womenfolk.

One of Wickenburg's original dude ranches, **6** **Kay El Bar Guest Ranch,** has seen wranglers wrangle and rustlers rustle since 1926. On the National and Arizona Registers of Historic Places, the ranch offers visitors miles of smiles on horse paths through the desert. After a day in the saddle, you'll understand why cowboys walked sort of funny. The heated hot tub and pool don't add up to an authentic cowboy experience, but are much appreciated nonetheless.

Head to Prescott on Hwy 89 to visit the ❼ **Sharlot Hall Museum**, named after the pioneer woman who started it in 1928 to preserve Prescott's legacy as capital of Arizona before it became a state. Sharlot Hall wasn't exactly a wrangler, but she's a good reminder of the important role smart, strong women played in Arizona's early statehood. You go, cowgirl!

"...the burgers are sweet revenge after all that cattle chasing."

Across from the infamous Whiskey Row in downtown Prescott is the columned ❽ **County Courthouse**, which dates from 1916 and is particularly pretty when sporting its lavish Christmas decorations. Often, weekend Western art shows on the plaza around the courthouse come complete with guitar-strumming gents in modern country and western attire. For good eats, try the always-hopping ❾ **Prescott Brewing Company** right across the street. Lots of homemade beer (try the Prescott Porter or Ponderosa IPA), and the burgers are sweet revenge after all that cattle chasing.

People who have spent the last few days doing strenuous activity under the sun probably have throats as dry as prairie grass on a summer's day. The best place to end a cowboy adventure is without a doubt on the centrally located ❿ **Whiskey Row** – the line of bars here is as long as a city block and are busy morning, noon and night.

The first question when arriving at Whiskey Row is what bar's the best. But, the thing to do is take a walk, real slow-like, up and down the row, peeking into each bar until one stands out. If that doesn't work, the ⓫ **Bird Cage Saloon** is a good bet; come for the pours that keep the locals happy and stay for the oddly fascinating collection of stuffed birds. After a few hours in whatever the first bar happens to be, suddenly all of them look pretty inviting.

You'll obviously need a designated driver in these parts, but if that person decides to partake, well-irrigated rustlers can roost at the ⓬ **Hotel St Michael**, right at the beginning (or end, depending on whether you've had one too many or one too few) of Whiskey Row.

TOUGH HOMBRES ONLY

Scottsdale's Cowboy College (www.cowboy college.com) is a wrangler boot camp where for a week you get up with the sun, work a real cattle ranch and unfurl your bedroll at day's end. No hot tubs or room service here, but there are a few days dedicated to horsemanship and lassoing. People back in the city will be mighty impressed, but remember, your cowboy hat won't fit any more if your head swells too much.

And that, compadres, is how the West was won; go on now, git gone.
Josh Krist

TRIP INFORMATION

GETTING THERE
From Phoenix, Cave Creek and Carefree are 35 miles northeast; Wickenburg is 60 miles northwest and Prescott 100 miles northwest.

DO

Desert Caballeros Western Museum
Changing exhibits keep things dynamic and it's a nice place to see depictions of real cowboy life. ☎ 928-684-2272; www.western museum.org; 21 N Frontier St, Wickenburg; adult/under 16/senior $7.50/free/6; ⏱ 10am-5pm Mon-Sat, noon-4pm Sun

Flying E Ranch
Rates include activities and three family-style meals daily; no bar, so BYOB. ☎ 928-684-2690; www.flyingeranch.com; 2801 W Wickenburg Way, Wickenburg; r from $310, seasonal; ⏱ Nov-Apr; ♿

Kay El Bar Guest Ranch
A maximum of 24 guests and access to a huge sprawl of desert; so nice. ☎ 928-684-7593; www.kayelbar.com; Wickenburg; r from $375, seasonal; ⏱ Oct-Apr

Sharlot Hall Museum
More a collection of historic buildings than a traditional museum; see the governor's restored log-cabin "mansion." ☎ 928-445-3122; www.sharlot.org; 415 W Gurley St, Prescott; adult/child $5/free; ⏱ 10am-4pm Mon-Sat, noon-4pm Sun

EAT & DRINK

Bird Cage Saloon
The owners say that some of the birds in the collection are on display at the Smithsonian Institute in Washington, DC ☎ 928-771-1913; www.birdcagesaloon.com; 148 Whiskey Row, Prescott; ⏱ 10am-2am

Greasewood Flat
This outdoor drinking place is a cash-only affair and at night the stars really are big and bright. ☎ 480-585-9430; www.grease woodflat.net; 27375 N Alma School Pkwy, Scottsdale; ⏱ 11am-1am

Pinnacle Peak Patio & Microbrewery
The views of the namesake peak are almost as good as the food. ☎ 480-585-1599; www .pppatio.com; 10426 E Jomax Rd, Scottsdale; mains $15-30; ⏱ 4-10pm Mon-Thurs, 4-11pm Fri & Sat, noon-10pm Sun

Prescott Brewing Company
The food is nearly as good as the microbrews. ☎ 928-771-2795; www.prescottbrewing company.com; 130 W Gurley, Prescott; mains $8-12; ⏱ 11am-10pm, bar until late

SLEEP

Carefree Resort & Villas
A gentle introduction to the pleasures of wide open spaces, the place lives up to the "carefree" in its name. ☎ 480-488-5300; www.carefree-resort.com; 37220 Mule Train Rd, Carefree; r from $169, villas from $209

Hotel St Michael
With a good restaurant downstairs, a free, albeit early, breakfast is included. Two doors down from the beginning of Whiskey Row. ☎ 928-776-1999; www.stmichaelhotel.com; 205 W Gurley, Prescott; r $70-130

USEFUL WEBSITES
www.outwickenburgway.com

LINK YOUR TRIP
www.lonelyplanet.com/trip-planner

Photographing Monument Valley

OUTDOORS

WHY GO The red rocks of Monument Valley and the rounded, wind-carved slots of Antelope Canyon are the trophy shots in any shutterbug's portfolio. Getting close to the rock is the way to avoid the cliché that many a cowboy has wandered across at Monument Valley, and at Antelope Canyon, timing is everything.

After visiting Antelope Canyon and Monument Valley the memories of these places are intense but then one day much later you discover you can't recall exactly what they *really* looked like. The vivid hues, like all things, have faded in memory. Thanks to the magic of photography, though, the colors here can stay alive forever.

With your camera at the ready, head north out of Flagstaff on the US-89. Stop and look back for great shots of the snow-capped San Francisco Peaks looming against the Western sky. Back on the road, the scenery has a limited palette at first – green pine and grey rock – but as the long, straight road loses elevation the desert reclaims the roadside. Unlike the yellow sands presented in many a movie, seen from a speeding car the hues of these dunes undulate from purple to green to black and back again. It's just a preview of the fleeting Technicolor wonders to come but still the best stretch of pavement in the state for finding the snaps that many photographers zoom right past.

After the gas stations and strip malls of outer Flagstaff disappear you're soon on wide open Navajo Nation land, where every 15 miles roadside stalls appear where Native American jewelers sell their silver and turquoise creations. At times, thanks to losing 3000ft of elevation during the course of the journey, you can see the road ahead for what feels like 100 miles but is actually closer to 20 or so.

TIME
2 days

DISTANCE
235 miles

BEST TIME TO GO
Year-round

START
Flagstaff, AZ

END
Kayenta, AZ

ALSO GOOD FOR

HISTORY & CULTURE

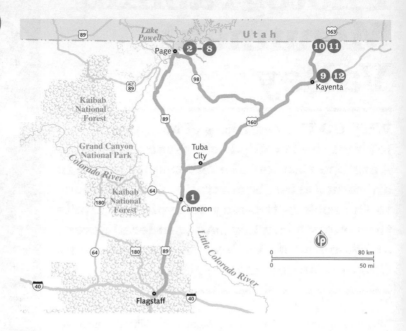

There's only one place for a sit-down meal between Flagstaff and Page, ❶ **Cameron Trading Post** – a historic trading center with its own little post office. It's worth a look, hungry or not.

The town of Page feels like a metropolis after the drive here through sparse landscape straight from a Western movie. Just south of Lake Powell, a massive artificial reservoir set mainly in Utah but whose fingers tickle the northern tip of Arizona, Page is the place for trips to nearby ❷ **Antelope Canyon**.

Freshen up in the spacious suites at ❸ **Debbie's Hideaway**, where the terraced back patio begs for long gab fests under the stars. There's a wheelbarrow full of wood for guests to build a fire in the free-standing fireplace and it's perfectly normal to spin stories around the fire with traveling companions and other guests well into the evening.

Nearby ❹ **Fiesta Mexicana** specializes in huge plates of food for hungry travelers. Its margaritas sneak up on you fast, so beware. Over-indulgers should be consoled by the fact that pretty soon they'll again be on alcohol-free Navajo Nation land. If a visitor wants to sample the nightlife, Page style, check out ❺ **Gunsmoke Saloon**, which boasts Northern Arizona's longest bar and flashy electronic lights to complement the Western-themed decor.

Set up a tour to Upper Antelope Canyon for tomorrow and get ready to snap away. A handful of companies offer tours to Upper Antelope Canyon, but **6** **Antelope Slot Canyon Tours**, owned by Chief Tsotsie, delivers. The company also offers tours to lesser-known Cathedral Canyon. Some of the other tour companies run operations that feel more like cattle calls than guided tours. Ask locals for their recommendations, or, better yet, check out a company in person to see if the general mood is rushed or relaxed.

> "…it's a surprise that, just like in the movies, high noon is the best time to shoot – photos, that is."

Antelope Canyon is divided into two sections. Almost all of the tours go to Upper Antelope Canyon and the flat, sandy bottom makes it navigable for people of all ages and physical conditions. The more strenuous Lower Antelope Canyon sees much smaller crowds. Each section of the canyon is less than a city block long (about a quarter mile), and the shapes and textures bring photographers from around the world.

Since the harsh light of noon usually scrubs away the texture from outdoor shots, it's a surprise that, just like in the movies, high noon is the best time to shoot – photos, that is. Noon is the right time because sunlight can get into the narrow slots of the canyon roofs – as the sun passes overhead the rock changes from grey to pink to red.

Noon is also the time when **7** **Upper Antelope Canyon** gets so packed with people it's hard to walk. Photographers who set up their tripod before the sightseeing tours show up are best off taking a break. Otherwise, expect people walking through the shots and even bumping into the tripod.

The guides here advise to not use a flash – a tripod or at least a monopod holds the camera steady during the long exposure times. The flash gives the rock an odd white spark that looks like a mistake. Metering is a challenge because of the extremes of light and dark. Some snappers like to overexpose their images here to get the detail of the rock and then digitally darken the shot. A "fast" (large aperture) wide-angle lens comes in handy.

"It's important to balance just simply 'being there' versus trying to make good photos. Those really good poster-quality shots require hours of preparation and perfect timing. This is especially important when traveling with a companion, because when I'm trying to get a shot, I'm really in my own world and sometimes it's more important to simply experience a lovely view with my partner than attempt to capture it on a sensor."

Jonathan Steele, Tempe resident and serious shutterbug

In a way it's cheating, but guides often throw dirt into the air to help people capture the beams of light that illuminate the canyon floor like spotlights on a crooked stage.

To get to ⑧ **Lower Antelope Canyon**, follow Hwy 98 east out of Page for 2 miles and look for signs on the left. If you've already gone on the Upper Antelope Canyon tour that day, show your receipt to avoid paying the $6 Navajo Permit Fee again. After parking in a well-signed dirt lot, the cost of a tour is $20 per person, but if you have a tripod (which seems to be the main qualification for being a "real" photographer) you can just pay your $20 and wander the canyon at will for up to four hours.

The tours start whenever the group gets big enough – four seems to be the magic number. The plaque outside the entrance of the canyon has the names of 11 tourists who died in a flash flood here in 1997. Nowadays, the tour guides say, there's a flash-flood detection system located in Upper Antelope Canyon which gives a 20-minute heads up on water danger.

"There are plenty of cactus and juniper trees ready to stand in as extras."

The entrance to Lower Antelope Canyon looks like a small slash in the ground – just a small hole in the desert floor and poof! Once inside it's a narrow world of stairs and ladders and scrambling to find the perfect place to capture the gorgeous rock. If you opt for a guide, most of them are willing to give loads of time to finding the perfect shot.

Spend another night in Page whooping it up at the bar and enjoying the fine art of conversation on the back patio. It's best to let the other worldly colors of Antelope Canyon fade a little in the mind's eye before moving on to take in the subtler hues of Monument Valley.

The next morning, load up on coffee and head 100 miles east to Kayenta, which is really just a small cluster of fast-food places, gas stations and chain hotels at the junction of Hwys 160 and 163. It's the most convenient base for Monument Valley excursions.

Travelers who aren't expecting much after the trip through long stretches of empty road, where even seeing a gas station is an event, will be surprised to stumble on ⑨ **Hampton Inn**. After using the hotel's fast wifi to upload photos, head another 20 miles northeast to ⑩ **Monument Valley Navajo Tribal Park**. If you've seen a Western movie, chances are you've seen Monument Valley – it's visual shorthand in many a film for desolate cowboy country.

It's easy enough to book a jeep or horseback tour on arrival to Monument Valley, but if you want to book ahead, ⑪ **Sacred Monument Tours** gets good marks for its jeep, hiking and horseback outings. Or, in the parking lot of the Monument Valley visitors center, arrange a horseback ride (starting at $140 an hour for two people), or a 2½-hour off-road vehicle tour ($65 per person).

If you want to get back in the saddle but don't want to pony up so much cash, a souvenir stall on the scenic drive loop, near John Ford's Point, can arrange horseback rides for $35 per person, per hour.

The 17-mile dirt road that loops through park is the way to go if you're packing lots of glass or a tripod. There are some off-road sand dunes and arches that are only accessible via guided tour, but there's nothing like having all the time in the world to set up a shot just so. And walking right up to the towers of stone for close-ups gives your photos a whole new feel.

The best time to photograph Monument Valley is at sunrise and sunset. August sometimes brings ominous storm clouds over the valley, while January and February are good months to catch the place with a light dusting of snow. Otherwise, it's a year-round destination as long as you can handle the hot summer days (another good reason to visit at sunrise).

Capturing the sheer scale of it poses the biggest challenge in Monument Valley. The best shots here have something in the background (clouds or the moon usually) or more commonly, in the foreground. There are plenty of cactus and juniper trees ready to stand in as extras. The second biggest challenge is making the colors stand out – there are many shades of deep red here. Avoid the harsh noon sun and use a polarizing filter.

Head back to Kayenta and toast yourself – with the nonalcoholic wine in the Hampton Inn's restaurant – for a full day of shutterbugging. Snuggling into one of the hotel's ultra-comfy beds, don't be surprised if the pictures on the back of your eyelids match the ones you took that day – rest easy knowing that as the memories fade in the months ahead the magic of photography keeps the images bright and clear, forever.

DETOUR

MILE MARKER 13

Head into Utah on Hwy 163 to find mile marker 13. A photo of Monument Valley from here shows the highway heading right into the towering red monoliths. A quick search on any photo-sharing service will turn up a number of the iconic shots – Forrest Gump ended his cross-country run here.

After shaking off the dreams of sleep and powering up on the free breakfast, peek into the **12** **Kayenta Visitor Center** before heading back to Flagstaff. In the summer, the center hosts traditional dances and other cultural events – just ask if it's OK to take a picture.

Josh Krist

TRIP INFORMATION

GETTING THERE
From Flagstaff, head north on US-89 for 140 miles to Page. From Page to Kayenta, take AZ-98 to US-160.

DO
Antelope Canyon
For those who don't want to book a tour in town for the upper canyon, guides can be arranged on-site. ☎ 928-698-2808; Hwy 98; www.navajonationparks.org; adult/child $6/free; 🕒 8am-5pm

Antelope Slot Canyon Tours
Be sure to call ahead at least a few days in advance for the photography tours during summer months. ☎ 928-645-5594; www .antelopeslotcanyon.com; 55 S Lake Powell Blvd, Page; photo tour adult/child $60/35

Kayenta Visitor Center
Between Burger King and the Hampton Inn. The exhibit on the military medals earned by Navajos in WWII is especially interesting. ☎ 928-697-3572; junction Hwys 160 & 163, Kayenta; 🕒 10am-5pm

Monument Valley Navajo Tribal Park
Most of the formations have whimsical names like the Mittens, Eagle Rock, Bear & Rabbit and Elephant Butte. ☎ 435-727-3287; passes not honored, per person $5; 🕒 sunrise-sunset Apr-Sep, 8am-4:30pm Oct-Apr

Sacred Monument Tours
The half-day and full-day photography tours are $250 and $500, respectively, for one to two people; they also do overnight trips on request. ☎ 435-727-3218; www.monument valley.net

EAT & DRINK
Cameron Trading Post
Just north of the Hwy 64 turnoff to the east entrance of the Grand Canyon South Rim. Food, lodging, shopping for Native American goods, and even a post office. ☎ 928-679-2231; www.camerontradingpost.com; 466 Hwy 89, Cameron; mains $10-20; 🕒 7am-10pm

Fiesta Mexicana
The portions are gargantuan and the margaritas are cold and strong. It's also within walking distance from most of the small, independent hotels. ☎ 928-645-4082; 125 S Powell Blvd, Page; mains $8-17; 🕒 11am-9pm

Gunsmoke Saloon
It's the most active nightspot in this part of the state, but everything is relative. ☎ 928-645-1888; www.damplaza.com/gunsmoke .html; 644 N Navajo Dr, Page; 🕒 7pm-2am Tue-Sat

SLEEP
Debbie's Hideaway
The rooms are like small apartments; free laundry facilities and a barbeque stand on the big back porch. ☎ 928-645-1224; www .debbieshideaway.com; 117 8th Ave, Page; ste $40-160; 🗓

Hampton Inn
Kids under 18 stay free and the pool is a perfect place to cool off. ☎ 928-697-3170; www.monumentvalleyonline.com; junction Hwys 160 & 163; r incl breakfast $110-160; 🗓

USEFUL WEBSITES
www.explorenavajo.com
www.pagelakepowelltourism.com

LINK YOUR TRIP
www.lonelyplanet.com/trip-planner

Arizona Architecture

WHY GO Back when green was just a color, Arizona architects were figuring out how to work with the land. From glass domes housing an entire forest to a junk castle to Frank Lloyd Wright's desert complex that's nearly invisible it fits so well into the landscape, this trip takes you to the coolest of Arizona's architecture.

TIME
3 – 4 days

DISTANCE
225 miles

BEST TIME TO GO
Oct – Mar

START
Tuscon, AZ

END
Phoenix, AZ

ALSO GOOD FOR

The journey begins as you leave Tucson and dodge tumbleweeds on Hwy 77 for about 30 miles toward Oracle. Entering ❶ Biosphere 2, you might think you've been transported to the future, or maybe Oz. In a way, you have. This 3-acre enclosed structure was built to be sealed off from the earth (aka Biosphere 1). In 1991, eight biospherians were sealed inside for a two-year tour of duty. A few snafus showed the ecosystems weren't completely self-sustaining, but the participants emerged intact.

After several changes in ownership the site found new life as a university-run earth science research institute. The highlight of the one-hour tour is the huge metal-floored room with a fabric ceiling that acts as an artificial lung – without it, the domes would heat up during the day and burst.

From here, head up to Phoenix via Hwy 79 and I-10 for 115 miles and watch the desert disappear under urban sprawl. To get to Scottsdale's ❷ Taliesin West and see the desert again, overshoot central Phoenix by taking the Loop 101 north to the Cactus Rd exit.

Taliesin West was Frank Lloyd Wright's desert home and studio. Still home to an architecture school and open to the public for guided tours, it's a prime example of his much-imitated organic architecture. The style depends on the environment – desert browns and greens with buildings sunk into the ground to keep them cool, but in a tropical environment a structure would mimic the dense foliage and stands of bamboo.

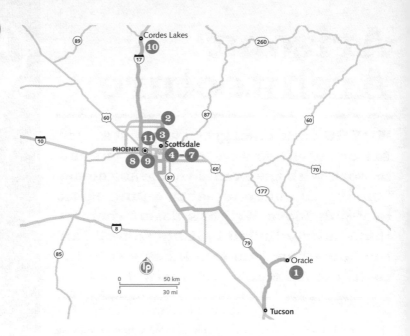

No matter which tour you're on, be sure to notice the effects of Wright's "embrace and release" method. For effect, Wright liked to put small rooms at the entrance of a building (embrace) that then open up to large, airy rooms (release).

About 9 miles southwest of Taliesin West via Cactus Rd and 64th St is another architectural oasis, ❸ Cosanti. The home and studio of Wright student Paolo Soleri, this is where Soleri's signature bronze and ceramic bells are crafted. You're free to walk around – *Star Wars* fans will feel like they're on Luke Skywalker's home planet.

After all this touring, spend the night in Scottsdale's historic ❹ Hotel Valley Ho, a fine example of midcentury modern, with huge windows and lots of uninterrupted space. Gazing over a poolside martini at the sleek, straight lines of the hotel, it's easy to forget that the Rat Pack days are long gone.

While in Scottsdale, be sure to grab a meal at the velvety ❺ Canal at Southbridge. In June 2008, the Scottsdale City Council approved funding for the Soleri Bridge and Plaza, likely the aging architect's last major work. Canal at Southbridge should have great views of the project and dishes like a $30 lobster sandwich seal the deal.

After filling up in foodie heaven, head to the glass-and-steel coolness of ❻ AZ 88, a typical example of upscale Scottsdale style and home of the coldest, tastiest martinis in the area. This is a great staging place for seeing some Scottsdale public art, and the **7** **Scottsdale Museum of Contemporary Art** is next door.

The next morning, head to downtown Phoenix for a visit to the copper-and-glass monolith that houses the **8** **Burton Barr Central Library**. Designer Will Bruder – the unofficial dean of Arizona architects and designer of the Scottsdale Museum of Contemporary Art – says that the strong shape of the library was inspired by Monument Valley. The views of downtown Phoenix from the 5th floor – especially around sunset – are great.

After studying Bruder's masterpiece, call ahead to check the 18-room **9** **Mystery Castle** is open and running tours that day. Equal parts Spanish mission, oversized sand castle and psychedelic mansion, it's eccentric architecture at its best. Fashioned with mostly found material by the late Boyce Gulley, his daughter says he was fulfilling a promise he made to build his princess a castle.

Head to **10** **Arcosanti**, which by design plays by the rules of the desert surrounding it, to spend the night. Located 66 miles north of Phoenix on I-17, it's more of an experiment in urban planning than architecture. A work in progress since the 1970s, it's the embodiment of Soleri's idea to create communities in harmony with their natural surroundings. A mixture of sharply angled concrete buildings and domes that shade the work spaces, everything here except for the bright bronze ingots (soon to be melted and poured) has been faded by the sun to a crisp brown.

Return to Phoenix for a night at the **11** **Arizona Biltmore Resort & Spa.** With architecture inspired by Frank Lloyd Wright, take one of the thrice-weekly walking tours of the 1929 property that looks like the set of a movie about the early 1930s where cigar-chomping captains of industry chase ladies in gowns holding flutes of champagne. Harking back to an age when celebrities had more class than sass, Irving Berlin penned "White Christmas" in his suite and Marilyn Monroe splashed in the pool.

ASK A LOCAL

"It's such a new town that we have an incredible variety of modern architecture – everything from midcentury ranch houses to postmodernism to the latest earth-friendly designs. A lot of it's inaccessible, unfortunately, behind gates and walls. Cruise the nice neighborhoods next to the mountain preserves. Not only will you get great views, but you'll see some amazing private homes."
David Proffitt, architectural journalist

It's true that Arizona's notable buildings might have more going for them in the realm of ideas than aesthetics. But, when the human race is colonizing the galaxy on a Biosphere 2–inspired spaceship and living in Arcosanti-like cities to reduce our use of the ship's resources, we'll have Arizona's architecture to thank.
Josh Krist

HISTORY &
CULTURE

TRIP INFORMATION

GETTING THERE
Tucson is 115 miles south of Phoenix on I-10.

DO
Biosphere 2
The futuristic site is now a University of Arizona–run earth science research institute. ☎ 520-838-6200; www.b2science.org; 32540 S Biosphere Rd, Oracle; adult/child/senior $20/13/18; ☺ 9am-4pm

Burton Barr Central Library
Inspired by Monument Valley, it's the crown jewel in Will Bruder's repertoire. ☎ 602-262-4636; www.phoenixpublic library.org; 1221 N Central Ave, Phoenix; ☺ 9am-9pm Mon-Thu, 9am-6pm Fri-Sat, noon-6pm Sun

Cosanti
Show up in the morning if you want to watch the bells being poured. ☎ 480-948-6145; www.arcosanti.org; 6433 E Doubletree Ranch Rd, Scottsdale; donation appreciated; ☺ 9am-5pm Mon-Sat, 11am-5pm Sun

Mystery Castle
Call ahead to make sure tours are still being offered. ☎ 602-268-1581; 800 E Mineral Rd, Phoenix; adult/child $5/3; ☺ 11am-4pm Thu-Sun Oct-May or by appointment

Scottsdale Museum of Contemporary Art
Another beautiful Bruder creation on the outside, cool contemporary art within. ☎ 480-874-4666; www.smoca.org; 7374 E 2nd St; adult/under 15/student $7/free/5; ☺ 10am-5pm Tue-Wed, Fri & Sat, 10am-8pm Thu, noon-5pm Sun

Taliesin West
Still home to an architecture school and open to the public for guided tours. ☎ 480-860-2700; www.franklloydwright.org; 12621 Frank Lloyd Wright Blvd, Scottsdale; tours $27-60; ☺ 9am-4pm

EAT
AZ 88
A long-time favorite for cool martinis and hot people-watching. ☎ 480-994-5576; www .az88.com; 7353 Scottsdale Mall, Scottsdale; mains from $8; ☺ 11:30am-12:30am Mon-Fri, 5pm-12:30am Sat & Sun

Canal at Southbridge
Substance meets style at this joint accented by velvety booths, a fashion runway and an audiovisual wall. ☎ 480-949-9000; www.canalaz.com; 7144 E Stetson Dr, Ste 250, Scottsdale; mains $11-28; ☺ 11am-midnight

SLEEP
Arcosanti
Rooms here should be booked in advance. There are week- and month-long seminars, a café, concerts and other events. ☎ 928-632-7135; www.arcosanti.org; Cordes Junction; r from $30, Sky Suite $100

Arizona Biltmore Resort & Spa
Sign up for one of the thrice-weekly historic walking tours. ☎ 602-955-6600; www .arizonabiltmore.com; 2400 E Missouri Ave, Phoenix; r from $380

Hotel Valley Ho
Not only a fine example of midcentury modern design, but a centrally located and fun place to stay. ☎ 480-248-2000; www.hotelvalleyho.com; 6850 E Main St, Scottsdale; r $99-600

USEFUL WEBSITES
www.azarchitecture.com

LINK YOUR TRIP
TRIP

www.lonelyplanet.com/trip-planner

Tiny Towns of Rim Country

WHY GO Rim Country – formed by the southern edges of the Colorado Plateau – is the great undiscovered country of Arizona with the most scenic drives, friendly small towns and natural beauty of any one area of the state. Between visits to the towns, there's plenty of Native American sites and outdoor adventure.

TIME
3 – 5 days

DISTANCE
450 miles

BEST TIME TO GO
Sep – Jun

START
Phoenix, AZ

END
Phoenix, AZ

ALSO GOOD FOR

HISTORY &
CULTURE

Rim Country is a gray area on the mental map of most Arizonans. They may or may not have been there – and if so it was either to ski or see the fall colors – and know that it's towards New Mexico. But the exact cities that line the Mogollon (mow-gee-yon) Rim – or even what it is, exactly –aren't so clear. What most people will tell you is that it's beautiful, and rave about drives along sheer white cliffs topped by ponderosa pines and towns with colorful names like Show Low, Strawberry and Snowflake.

Start by heading out of Phoenix on the appropriately named Beeline Hwy (Hwy 87). You know you're about to leave the Valley of the Sun when you see the big fountain of the city of Fountain Hills spouting its jet – once every 15 minutes – a whopping 560ft into the air. The Beeline really starts zigzagging after the tiny town of Sunflower; 32 miles more of snaking roads and you're in ❶ **Payson**, the de facto capital of Rim Country and home to the world's longest-running rodeo.

Get up to speed on Payson and Rim Country at the ❷ **Rim Country Museum**. Walk through the historic buildings of Payson, including a reproduction of the log cabin of Western novelist Zane Grey. Many of his books, including *Under the Tonto Rim*, were written here in the 1920s.

If the exhibits on Grey and rip-roaring Western adventure novels make you want to sleep with an ear to this untamed country, pitch

BEST TRIP

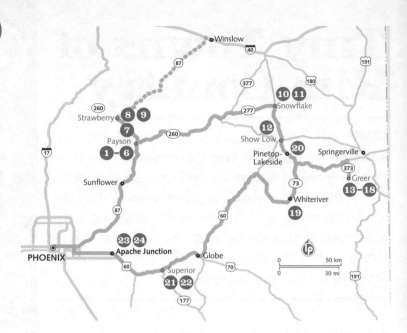

a tent at ❸ **Ponderosa Campground**, 12 miles northeast of Payson on Hwy 260. True to the name, most of the 60 spots here are shaded by tall pine trees. To get the lowdown on other camping and outdoor fun like swimming or fishing in Tonto National Forest – three million acres that spill over most of Rim Country and extend all the way to Phoenix – stop by the ❹ **Tonto National Forest Payson Ranger Station**. Or, if staying in a mock Tudor building is more tempting, check out the ❺ **Best Western Payson Inn**.

The next day, caffeinate with the strong mochas at ❻ **Roadrunner Espresso** before checking out of your room (or tent) and making a day of it at the area's star attraction, ❼ **Tonto Natural Bridge State Park**. Tucked into a lush valley 10 miles northwest of Payson on Hwy 87, you'll feel like you've stumbled onto the set of the TV show *Lost*. The park was discovered by a miner on the run from Apaches, and the cave-filled, thick underbrush is a perfect place to hide out for a few days.

From here continue 10 miles north on Hwy 87 to ❽ **Strawberry**. For a night close to nature that's still comfy, powwow with your traveling mates in a teepee at ❾ **Fossil Creek Llama Ranch**. The ranch offers llama treks that last anywhere from two hours to all day. There are wellness courses and even a goat petting zoo where you can cuddle the critters that supply the milk for the tasty cheese the owners make on the premises.

The next morning, catch Hwy 260 east to ⑩ **Snowflake**, the northernmost city of Rim Country. They get an occasional light dusting of snow but the town is really named after the founders, a Mr Snow and a Mr Flake – seriously. The drive takes you on a gentle roller-coaster ride along the rim and into the edge of the White Mountains. Settled by Mormon pioneers in the late 1800s, there are more than 100 historic homes, many with red brick and white trim. A large number of these old homes have been converted into B&Bs, but ⑪ **Osmer D Heritage Inn** stands out for its food; it's worth trying to book dinner and a room.

> **DETOUR** Take it easy in Winslow, AZ – such a fine sight to see is the small park that faces Route 66 (www .standinonthecorner.com) with a mural that shows one of the key scenes from The Eagles song that put this place on the map. Spend a night in La Posada (www.laposada.org), a luxury hacienda that has hosted many a movie star of yore.

After a scrumptious breakfast at the inn, head south on Hwy 77 until it hits Hwy 260. As you get into the White Mountains you'll pass through ⑫ **Show Low**, where the main drag is named "E Deuce of Clubs." The story goes that long ago two frontier types agreed that the tiny settlement wasn't big enough for the both of them, and whoever could show the low card got to stay. Follow the signs to ⑬ **Sunrise Park Resort**, 65 miles southeast of Snowflake on Hwy 273. From December to April, it has the best skiing in the state – 65 trails crisscross the slopes of three mountains. Between Memorial Day and Labor Day, Sunrise Park is open for mountain biking, hiking, fishing and a scenic sky ride.

Explore Sunrise Park and the nearby Mt Baldy Wilderness Area from ⑭ **Greer**. A bounty of fish swim in the area's waterways and the trout lure anglers from all over. If you're on the hunt for a whopper, ⑮ **Troutback** has half-day fly fishing lessons for beginners and day-long guided trips.

"...the town is really named after the founders, a Mr Snow and a Mr Flake – seriously."

Most people who stay in Greer rent a cabin and do their own cooking; check out www.greerarizona.com for a long menu of choices. Be impressed by the rustic elegance of ⑯ **Amberian Peaks Lodge & Restaurant**, with its big stone fireplace in the main room and food that's dressed up to impress. A river runs through it (the property) and they have cabins on site. Visitors can also hook a cabin at ⑰ **X Diamond Ranch**, and anyone can come by to pay for fishing privileges or a horseback ride.

Energized from nature, float over to the ⑱ **Butterfly Lodge Museum** on the way out of town. It's a restored 1913 home where adventure writer and explorer James Willard Schultz lived with his Blackfoot American Indian wife. Then, buzz towards ⑲ **Fort Apache National Historic Park**, an Army post during the Apache Wars when the muscle of the US military eventually broke Apache resistance. Just 4 miles south of the town of Whiteriver, the park also includes the Apache cultural center. Get the stamp that allows you to visit the Kinishba Ruins, an ancient pueblo dwelling 5 miles west of the fort.

Try your luck at ㉗ Hon-Dah, a gaming resort on tribal land that has it all: ski and snowboard rentals, a restaurant, nightly entertainment, modern hotel rooms and, of course, plenty-o-gaming. Rested and hopefully a few nickels wealthier, take Hwy 73 northwest until it intersects Hwy 60, then make a left to head south. In a land full of mountains that spill into fields of wildflowers, after a few days it's easy to take all of this beauty for granted. But once you start the twisting descent into the Salt River Canyon, the views are so stunning that without stops to gawk open-mouthed at the scenery, drivers will find it difficult to keep their eyes on the not-so-straight and narrow.

FIRE OR HOT AIR IN THE SKY?

The only Rim Country resident who claims interstellar travel is Travis Walton, a logger who says he was abducted near Snowflake by an alien craft in 1975. What makes his story interesting is that there were eyewitnesses and a police manhunt failed to turn up Walton for two days – time on the mother ship, he says. The 1993 movie *Fire in the Sky* is based on his experience.

Snap lots of shots, then continue south on Hwy 60 into ㉑ Superior, where copper country rises toward Rim Country. The standout ㉒ Boyce Thompson Arboretum was built by a mining magnate who had a revelation about the importance of nature; 323 acres support a Noah's Ark of wildlife and plants from deserts around the world.

Finally, to reacclimate to the desert and search for a treasure of biblical proportions, stop in at ㉓ Superstition Mountain Museum in Apache Junction. It has exhibits on the Lost Dutchman Gold Mine, a supposed lode of ore that still draws treasure hunters. Those who think they can sniff out the gold can give it a shot at ㉔ Lost Dutchman State Park, the state's most enduring mining legend, before returning to Phoenix.

Josh Krist

TRIP INFORMATION

GETTING THERE
The town furthest from Phoenix on this trip, Snowflake, is 175 miles northeast.

DO
Boyce Thompson Arboretum
The 1½-mile main trail goes past most of the arboretum's 3200 plant species; taking in dramatic scenery that includes canyon walls and a small lake. ☎ 520-689-2811; http://ag.arizona.edu/bta; 37615 US Hwy 60, Superior; adult/child $7.50/3; ☾ 8am-4pm, seasonal variations

Butterfly Lodge Museum
The home of James Willard Schultz, the adventurer and writer who penned *My Life as an Indian* about his time with the Blackfeet tribe. The art of his son, Lone Wolf, is on display. ☎ 928-735-7514; www.wmonline.com/butterflylodge.htm; adult/youth $2/1; ☾ 10am-5pm, Memorial Day-Labor Day Thu-Sun & holidays

Fort Apache National Historic Park
Cruise through the White Mountain Apache Cultural Center & Museum or take a walking tour of the US military fort. ☎ 928-338-4525; www.wmat.nsn.us; Whiteriver; adult/senior/child $5/3/free; ☾ 8am-5pm Mon-Fri, seasonal variations

Lost Dutchman State Park
Hiking trails abound, but bring lots of water – finding the fabled Lost Dutchman Gold Mine will put you in the history books. ☎ 480-982-4485; 6109 N Apache Trail, Apache Junction; ☾ sunrise-10pm

Rim Country Museum
The region's history in several buildings, including a replica of Zane Grey's cabin. ☎ 928-474-3483; www.rimcountrymuseums.com; 700 Green Valley Pkwy, Payson; adult/teen/senior $3/2/2.50; ☾ noon-4pm Wed-Mon

Sunrise Park Resort
It's worth the trip here just to see the White Mountains at their most scenic. Summer activities abound and the skiing is the best in the state. ☎ 928-735-7669; www.sunriseskipark.com; Greer; day lift tickets adult/child $46/37, r from $69

Superstition Mountain Museum
The Elvis Presley Memorial Chapel is a must-see and it has an interesting exhibit on the Lost Dutchman Gold Mine. ☎ 480-983-4888; www.superstitionmountainmuseum.org; 4087 N Apache Trail, Apache Junction; adult/senior/child $5/2/4; ☾ 9am-4pm

Tonto National Forest Payson Ranger Station
For information on camping and activities in the fifth-largest forest in the United States and to buy a Tonto Pass. ☎ 928-474-7900; www.fs.fed.us/r3/tonto; 1009 E Hwy 260, Tonto; day pass $6; ☾ 8am-5pm Mon-Fri

Tonto Natural Bridge State Park
Tucked into a tiny, forested valley about 10 miles northwest of Payson proper, it protects the largest natural travertine bridge in the world. ☎ 928-476-4202; adult/under 13 $3/free; ☾ 8am-7pm May-Sep, 8am-6pm Apr, Sep & Oct, 9am-5pm Nov-Mar

Troutback
Learn how to catch a whopper – or at least tell one convincingly – with the fly-fishing instructors here. ☎ 520-532-3474; www.troutback.com; Show Low; half-day lessons from $150, trips from $225

EATING
Amberian Peaks Lodge & Restaurant
The great outdoors and classy digs mingle seamlessly – no wonder it's a favorite for weddings. Low season is March to May. ☎ 928-735-9977; www.peaksaz.com; 1 Main St, Greer; r $125-235, 4-person cabin from $200

Osmer D Heritage Inn
A B&B set in a historic house; groups should see if they can get a private dinner. If spending the

night (rooms $105 to $130), three rooms have Jacuzzis. ☎ 928-536-3322; www.heritage-inn .net; 161 N Main St, Snowflake; meals $20

Roadrunner Espresso

This relative newcomer has already become a local favorite for powering up with strong mochas and a mouthwatering assortment of pastries, bagels and sandwiches. ☎ 928-472-7229; 511 S Beeline Hwy, Payson; sandwiches $6; ☷ 6am-5pm Mon-Sat, 8am-3pm Sun

SLEEPING

Best Western Payson Inn

Dependable and good value, this 99-room property in a mock-Tudor building has modern-looking rooms (get a deluxe for extra space). Rates include a modest breakfast. Children under 17 stay free and pets are welcome. ☎ 928-474-3241; www.best westernpaysoninn.com; 801 N Beeline Hwy, Payson; r $70-150; ♿ ♨

Fossil Creek Llama Ranch

Offers two-hour to full-day llama treks as well as wellness courses, spiritual retreats and a goat petting zoo (it makes its own goat cheese). Sleep in a teepee. ☎ 928-476-5178; www.fossilcreekllamas.com; r from $85, hikes from $65

Hon-Dah

If yearning for the flashing lights and clank of coins to balance out all the unspoiled nature, this is a good base with all the mod cons for everything the area has to offer. ☎ 928-369-0299; www.hon-dah.com; 777 Hwy 260, Pinetop-Lakeside; r $100-200

Ponderosa Campground

This USFS site is 12 miles northeast of Payson on Hwy 260 and has 60 tent and RV sites, as well as drinking water and toilets (but no showers). For other area campgrounds, check with the ranger station. ☎ 877-444-6777; www.recreation.gov; near Payson; sites $15; ☷ mid-Apr–Oct

X Diamond Ranch

Cabins with plenty of pretty land between them sleep two to eight people. Horseback riding, fly fishing, an archeological site and a small museum make it a one-stop ranch. ☎ 928-333-2286; www.xdiamondranch .com; btwn Greer & Springerville; rides incl lunch $85, cabins $110-250

USEFUL WEBSITES

www.paysonrimcountry.com
www.wmonline.com

LINK YOUR TRIP

www.lonelyplanet.com/trip-planner

Arizona in Tune

WHY GO Arizona's sun-baked sound, exemplified in the Meat Puppets II album, is a little country, a little rock and roll, with riffs of punk and psychedelia. It wafts from underground clubs, resplendent theaters, even outdoors under the pines on this musical journey from Tucson to Flagstaff.

TIME
4 – 5 days

DISTANCE
450 miles

BEST TIME TO GO
Year-round

START
Tucson, AZ

END
Flagstaff, AZ

ALSO GOOD FOR

CITY

Driving around on a hot day, through the endless strip malls and low, squat houses of Arizona's cityscapes, you wonder how sweet sounds could ever emerge from this place. But at night, on the way to a show, stop a few blocks away on a quiet street and roll down the window. Hear how the far-off music mingles with the sad song of coyotes and the smell of the desert? Now you understand.

Start the music at downtown Flagstaff's ❶ Hotel Monte Vista. The divey downstairs cocktail lounge hosts scrappy rock bands most nights, and there's rarely a cover charge (if so, it's in the $5 range). DJs and karaoke occasionally hijack the airwaves.

The Monte V named many its 50 hotel rooms and suites after celebrities who've slept here. Michael Stipe crashed in room 205; Siouxsie Sioux climbed under the covers in 220. The Freddie Mercury Room (403) may not be your personal rhapsody, but the late Queen front man would have loved its bohemian purple-and-black color scheme and the electric guitar with a theatrical mask hanging off it.

The ❷ Orpheum Theater stands just a few blocks away. Opened in 1911, it screened silent movies and hosted vaudeville acts in its original incarnation. Hundreds of people lined up under the white neon sign to see the shows. They still do, only now the acts are top regional and national bands at this stately spot that's been lovingly restored.

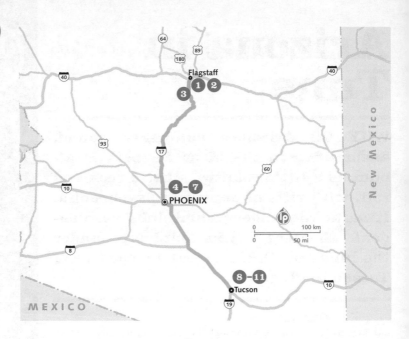

The Orpheum's owners also run ❸ **Pine Mountain Amphitheatre**, an outdoor venue set among hulking evergreens 6 miles south of downtown Flagstaff. Acts from Cracker to BB King play here, where it always feels like a festival. Although, in the middle of a hot Phoenix summer it doesn't matter who's on stage – music lovers make the trip for cool relief.

"Mainstays like Tom Waits test the pristine acoustics when they come through town..."

Speaking of Arizona's capital: Phoenix packs in a huge range of venues, as you'd expect from the country's fifth-largest city. Intriguing new acts grace the small stage at ❹ **modified arts** in a funky brick building downtown. The bands may span genres – alt-country, experimental, roots – but rest assured they're all a few beats outside the mainstream. Be sure to say hi to Kimber, the owner: she's done a huge amount for the local music scene, and the likes of Jimmy Eat World played gigs in her record stores long before they hit it big.

Get up close and personal with bigger draws (think Ani DiFranco, Smashmouth) at ❺ **Celebrity Theatre**. Imagine the intimacy of a small club with the amenities – easy parking, plenty of bartenders and toilets – of a large venue. The revolving stage gives every audience member face time with the stars. And no seat is more than 75ft from the stage, so it's a short span between you and your idol. You might even be able to catch their eye if you yell loud enough.

Phoenix has its own **⑥ Orpheum Theatre** (no relation to Flagstaff's venue), a beautifully restored Spanish Baroque building from 1929. Mainstays like Tom Waits test the pristine acoustics when they come through town, and the Phoenix Symphony plays here on a regular basis. Before the show or during intermission, sink into one of the overstuffed chairs near the bar fireplace.

If all this culture has made you hungry, head over to the **⑦ Rhythm Room**, where there's a little barbecue shack in the parking lot that opens during shows. Bands plug in their amps nearly every night of the week at this rocking little bar, with a heavy emphasis on the blues. If there were an embassy of southern soul in Phoenix, this would be it.

After hopscotching through the musical scene in Phoenix, bunk for a night at one of the cheap national-brand hotels near Tempe's Mill Ave, a lively if somewhat bland-looking strip of themed bars and chain restaurants.

The next day drive down to Tucson for more harmonics. Like the A-minor and E chords on a guitar, the places with the sweetest notes are right next to each other: the **⑧ Rialto Theater** and **⑨ Club Congress**. The Rialto used to have vaudeville acts slapsticking across its stage when it opened in 1920, but now the monsters of rock and hiphop do the honors, along with big names in folk, flamenco and blues.

The dark and moody Club Congress books edgier rock – except when it's club night and a DJ spins the record back and forth. The folks who run this place have a good ear for the best under-the-radar bands strumming their way across the land.

While it's convenient to spend the night at retro, historic **⑩ Hotel Congress**, remember that with two live

ARIZONA MUSICIANS OF NOTE

- Jimmy Eat World (Mesa)
- Meat Puppets (Sunnyslope, Tempe)
- Alice Cooper (Phoenix, Paradise Valley)
- Stevie Nicks (Paradise Valley, Sedona)
- Gin Blossoms (Tempe)
- CeCe Peniston (Phoenix)
- Flotsam and Jetsam (Phoenix)
- DJ Z-Trip (Phoenix)
- Linda Ronstadt (Tucson)

music clubs so close by, it can be a rambunctious scene. Those who prefer quiet should consider the **⑪ Flamingo Hotel**, a classic 1950s motel. Lots of movie stars slept here, including Elvis, who bunked in room 102 in his prejumpsuit days.

Josh Krist

TRIP
20

TRIP INFORMATION

GETTING THERE
Phoenix is about 150 miles south of Flagstaff and 115 miles north of Tucson.

DO
Celebrity Theatre
A 2665-seat theater where no one is more than 75ft from the stage. Amenities galore sweeten the deal. ☎ 602-267-1600; www.celebritytheatre.com; 440 N 32nd St, Phoenix; tickets from $25
Club Congress
Good pours and an eclectic musical line-up of regional buzz bands on the 1st floor of the Hotel Congress. ☎ 520-622-8848; 311 E Congress St, Tucson; covers $3-10
modified arts
This intimate performance and art space downtown feels like you're watching a show at a record store (in a good way). ☎ 602-462-5516; www.modified.org; 407 E Roosevelt, Phoenix; shows $3-5
Orpheum Theater (Flagstaff)
A former vaudeville hall that now hosts top regional and national bands. ☎ 928-556-1580; www.orpheumpresents.com; 15 W Aspen St, Flagstaff; tickets from $15
Orpheum Theatre (Phoenix)
A splendid restored movie house downtown; used by high-brow touring shows and the symphony. ☎ 602-262-7272; 203 W Adams St, Phoenix; tickets from $50
Pine Mountain Amphitheatre
A finger-pickin' treat of outdoor tunes, located south of Flagstaff off exit 337 on I-17. ☎ 928-774-0899; www.pinemountain

amphitheater.com; Fort Tuthill Park, Flagstaff; tickets from $15
Rialto Theatre
A gorgeous 1920 vaudeville and movie theater reborn as a top venue for live touring acts. ☎ 520-740-1000; www.rialtotheatre.com; 318 E Congress St, Tucson; tickets $10-35

EAT & DRINK
Rhythm Room
Cover charges range from a few dollars for local bands (usually early in the week) to about $30 for big-name touring acts on weekends. ☎ 602-265-4842; 1019 E Indian School Rd, Phoenix; ☽ Tue-Sun

SLEEP
Flamingo Hotel
Elvis stayed at this affectionate homage to Tucson's movie history full of posters from old flicks. Relatively quiet. ☎ 520-770-1910; www.flamingohoteltucson.com; 1300 N Stone Ave, Tucson; r incl breakfast $50-70
Hotel Congress
A historic property where old-fashioned radios are the in-room entertainment. Opt for a room at the hotel's far end if you're noise sensitive. ☎ 520-622-8848; www.hotelcongress.com; 311 E Congress St, Tucson; r $70-120; ✿
Hotel Monte Vista
Strong spirits at the bar, friendly spirits in some of the 50 rooms. The onsite lounge hosts live music. ☎ 928-779-6971; www.hotelmontevista.com; 100 N San Francisco St, Flagstaff; r $75-140

USEFUL WEBSITES
www.arizonaguide.com
www.myspace.com/arizonamusicproject

LINK YOUR TRIP
www.lonelyplanet.com/trip-planner
TRIP

Southern Desert Wanderings

WHY GO Imagine walking through the desert, parched, looking for an oasis. In the distance you see a city guarded by prickly saguaros. You stumble into Tucson, and discover that this is the crossroads of Southern Arizona – the perfect base to visit the region's natural, ancient and scientific wonders. Thirst quenched, the adventure begins.

TIME
2 – 4 days

DISTANCE
350 miles

BEST TIME TO GO
Oct – Mar

START
Tucson, AZ

END
Tucson, AZ

ALSO GOOD FOR

HISTORY & CULTURE

Tucson doesn't make a great first impression – there are the strip malls here of many other modern cities, and under the harsh light of the sun it feels like a small maze of concrete and high-speed boulevards. But, look a little deeper and the ugly duckling transforms into a swan. Historic neighborhoods thrive between the freeways, live music joints and gourmet venues have been going strong for decades, and there's a whole street devoted to groovy shopping and good eats. Use it as a base for sorties to the best that Southern Arizona has to offer, and liking Tucson will slowly turn to loving it.

Outside of the city center, the ❶ **Arizona-Sonora Desert Museum** enchants with nearly 2 miles of walking paths between animal and plant habitats. The number of things to see is dizzying so allot plenty of time. The hummingbird aviary is a buzzy blur of wings and watching road runners dart between prairie dogs makes you want to yell "beep-beep!" The museum sits off Hwy 86, about 12 miles west of Tucson.

On the way there you'll pass through the western section of ❷ **Saguaro National Park**, which is actually divided in half by Tucson. True lovers of those wacky cacti in their crazy poses should pay the entrance fee for the park, but just driving along the outskirts you'll see more saguaro than you can shake a spiny stick at.

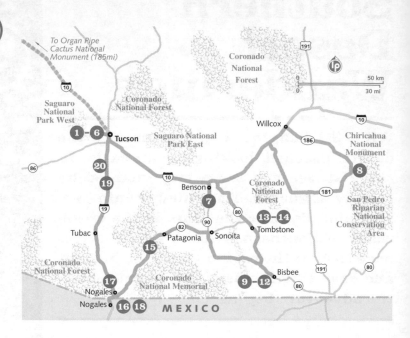

After a day of desert appreciation, enjoy a homemade microbrew and some good Southwestern-style food at ③ **Barrio Brewery**. Set across from the railroad tracks, when a freight train rolls by the beers are only $3. Keep on rollin', freight train. For something more upscale, make reservations at ④ **Café Poca Cosa**, an award-winning Nuevo-Mexican bistro. Take the plunge and order the Poca Cosa plate to let the chef do the deciding. *Muy buenas* margaritas, too.

To get the full Tucson experience (and more trains) spend at least one night at ⑤ **Hotel Congress**. It's especially loud on weekends thanks to the bar and live music downstairs, and you'll hear train horns all night long. With nicely restored but simple rooms that sport rotary phones and only old-timey radios for in-room entertainment, the friendly front-desk staff makes a good thing great.

The next morning, have breakfast at ⑥ **B Line**, a hip café set in the heart of the 4th Ave row of cool restaurants and funky shops. It has strong coffee and tasty breakfast burritos to eat there or to go. Burrito in hand, say *"vaya con dios"* to Tucson for now and head 53 miles towards Benson, gateway to ⑦ **Kartchner Caverns State Park**, a wonderland of spires, stalagmites, soda straws and other ethereal formations five million years in the making.

About 72 miles east of Benson, ⑧ **Chiricahua National Monument** is a gathering of impossibly balanced rocks on top of stone spires sculpted by eons of rain and wind. The remoteness made Chiricahua a favorite hiding place of Apache warrior Cochise and his men. Today it's a hiker's paradise and a redoubt for birds and wildlife. The closest place to spend the night under a roof is at one of the motel chains in Willcox. Or pitch a tent at the Bonita Campground (sites $12), near the visitors center.

"...a wonderland of spires, stalagmites, soda straws and other ethereal formations five million years in the making."

A cool town populated by aging hippies, Bisbee is perched on a hill 70 miles to the southwest. It looks like San Francisco or parts of Vancouver. Get oriented at the **9** Bisbee Mining & Historical Museum to see old photos of Bisbee in its heyday and learn about the copper boom that turned it from a backwater to a full-fledged city. Armed with mining-smarts from the museum, an afternoon with **10** Queen Mine Tours is much more fun. You'll put on a miner's outfit and a lantern before taking a small train straight into the chilly hillside.

Check into the **11** Copper Queen Hotel for a side of luxury with your copper vittles. A comfy place that has all the modern amenities – and a 2nd-floor pool, of all things – the Copper Queen opened in 1902 to accommodate the newly minted (by copper) class and the already wealthy high rollers in town to check on their business interests. The restaurant has great food – the ribs and steaks are divine – and both indoor and outdoor seating. The downstairs bar is a good place to grab a drink, as is the nearby **12** Stock Exchange Saloon, where the chart that tracked changing stock prices during the copper boom days still stands.

The man who first searched for mining riches in what's now Tombstone was told that the only thing he'd find in this dusty corner of the world was his grave:

ASK A LOCAL

"Every time I'm in Tucson I try to visit the **Center for Creative Photography** (www.creativephoto graphy.org), home of the archives of Richard Avedon and Ansel Adams, and a lot of other famous photographers. They have the single best archive of photography in the world. It's a Tucson gem and people rarely know about it because it's on the University of Arizona campus; but they have changing exhibits and anyone can visit."

Jeff Ficker, former Tucson resident

so he named his first silver mine as an insult to nay-sayers. Tombstone's historic downtown, 25 miles north of Bisbee on Hwy 80, has a main thoroughfare that looks just like the dusty, boarded-sidewalk town center in many a Western film. Be sure not to miss the **13** OK Corral, where the most famous gunfight in American history went down – it would be hard to overlook once the shooting starts. A fun place to grab a beverage or a signature "overstuffed Reuben" sandwich in a relatively authentic Wild West place is **14** Big Nose Kate's. Started by Doc Holliday's girlfriend – yes, she had a prominent proboscis – the place sports neat historical photographs and live tunes in the afternoon.

After a half-day of Tombstone, head 50 miles west, mainly on Hwy 82, to Patagonia. This is the home of Arizona's young and growing wine industry. Weekends are the best time to stop by because that's when the majority of the wineries are open for tastings, but ⑮ **Arizona Vineyards**, about 5 miles south of Patagonia, is open daily. The tasting room is as dark and dank as Dracula's den and filled with wacky flea-market furnishings and burning incense.

Only 20 miles southwest of Patagonia, it's easy enough to stroll across the border of ⑯ **Mexico** for a few hours, and some of the area dining and hotel options are fit for silver-screen royalty. Set on 36 acres alongside the Santa Cruz River, ⑰ **Hacienda Corona de Guevavi** is the place to take a vacation from your vacation: dreamy mountain views and vintage courtyard murals abound. At ⑱ **La Roca Restaurant**, mole, margaritas, and a cliffside setting add up to romance south of the border. If you meet a friendly local who's getting on in years, ask about the long-defunct La Caverna restaurant, where stars and gangsters used to mingle in a well-appointed Nogales cave.

> **DETOUR**
>
> A soul-nourishing place under serenely blank skies by day, **Organ Pipe Cactus National Monument** (www.nps.gov/orpi) is known for drug and people smuggling at night. It really is a place of otherworldly beauty – the bulk of the country's organ pipe cacti, which look like big clusters of straight saguaro, are here. It's 81 miles south of Gila Bend and worth a stop, not a stay.

Once Nogales is done with you, head north for 46 miles on I-19 to the ⑲ **Titan Missile Museum**, where the near-death of humanity comes alive. An original Titan II missile site, the actual (deactivated) 103ft-tall missile is still sitting in its launch tube. As part of the nuclear stand-down agreement with the Russians, the glass that covers the missile is angled to avoid glare so that spy satellites can get a clear shot. Ask the tour guide to tell you how one of the USAF higher-ups got a call from his Russian counterpart when a Star Trek movie was filmed here and the Russians weren't notified.

Finally, keep heading north on I-19 for churchin' up at ⑳ **Mission San Xavier del Bac**, 9 miles south of Tucson. A mission was first established here in 1700, but the building that stands today was erected in the late 1700s and has been undergoing a remodel with the help of Vatican experts since the 1990s. The moody candle-lit interior makes it one of the most beautiful buildings in Arizona.

Back in Tucson, you can go your own way, or, take the time to poke around this town full of diamonds in the rough.

Josh Krist

TRIP INFORMATION

GETTING THERE

Tucson is 115 miles south of Phoenix and 64 miles north of Nogales.

VISITING MEXICO

Walking across into Mexico is easiest because crossing with a car invalidates most rental and insurance policies, and you'll need to arrange supplemental coverage. To return to the USA, US citizens need a passport, or a valid picture ID (eg driver's license) and proof of citizenship (eg birth certificate). A passport is the easiest way to go. For more info on crossing, check www.dhs.gov.

DO

Arizona-Sonora Desert Museum

A zoo, a botanical garden and a museum that really deserve a full day of exploration. ☎ 520-883-2702; www.desertmuseum .org; 2021 N Kinney Rd, Tucson; adult/child $10/2; ⏲ 8:30am-5pm Oct-Feb, 7:30am-5pm Mar-Sep

Arizona Vineyards

Come for the atmosphere; with wines called Desert Dust and Rattler Red, the names are interesting, at least. ☎ 520-287-7972; www.nogaleswine.com; 1830 E Patagonia Hwy, Nogales; ⏲ 10am-6pm

Bisbee Mining & Historical Museum

Brings Bisbee's riotous heyday back to life with historical exhibits on the 1st floor and interactive modern mining on the 2nd. ☎ 520-432-7071; www.bisbeemuseum .com; 5 Copper Queen Plaza, Bisbee; adult/child/senior $7.50/3/6.50; ⏲ 10am-4pm

Chiricahua National Monument

This wonderland of impossibly balanced rocks is more than worth the trip. The amenities are scarce so bring food and water. ☎ 520-824-3560; www.nps.gov/chir; Hwy 181; adult/child $5/free

Queen Mine Tours

Definitely one of the best ways to spend 1½ hours in the state. Dress warm, it's cold in them there hills. ☎ 520-432-2071; www .queenminetour.com; 119 Arizona St, Bisbee; adult/child $12/5; ⏲ 9am-3:30pm

Kartchner Caverns State Park

Tours often sell out far in advance, so make reservations – online or by phone – early. ☎ reservations 520-586-2283, information 520-586-24100; www.explorethecaverns.com; Hwy 90, Benson; tours adult/child from $17/9; ⏲ tours 8:20am-4:20pm

OK Corral

This site of the famous gunfight is deliciously kitschy for most adults and the "funniest thing ever" for kids. ☎ 520-457-3456; www.ok-corral.com; Allen St btwn 3rd & 4th Sts, Tombstone; admission $7.50, without gunfight $5.50; ⏲ 9am-5pm

Mission San Xavier del Bac

The moody splendor inside is quite the surprise. Be sure to watch the free video on the restoration. ☎ 520-294-2624; www.sanxaviermission.org; 1950 W San Xavier Rd, Tucson; donations appreciated; ⏲ 7am-5pm

Saguaro National Park

Pronounced sa-Wah-ro, there are 165 miles of hiking trails that thread between these jolly green giants. ☎ 520-733-5153; www .nps.gov/sagu; Tucson; per vehicle $10, valid for 7 days; ⏲ 7am-sunset

Titan Missile Museum

This is the place where the final countdown would have ended life as we know it. ☎ 520-574-9658; www.titanmissilemuseum.org; 1580 W Duval Mine Rd, Sahuarita; adult/child/senior $8.50/5/7.50; ⏲ 9am-4:30pm (last tour), seasonal variations

EAT & DRINK

B Line

Great coffee in the morning and a small wine menu for later in the day. ☎ 520-882-7575; www.blinerestaurant.com; 621 N 4th Ave,

Tucson; mains $7-10; ⊙ 7:30am-9pm Mon-Thu, to 10pm Fri & Sat, to 8pm Sun

Barrio Brewery
Too many trains and tasting all 12 types of beers equals talking in tongue twisters by night's end. ☎ 520-791-2739; www.barrio brewing.com; 800 E 16th St, Tucson; snacks $3-7; ⊙ 11am-1am

Big Nose Kate's
Doc Holliday's girlfriend used to run this joint; live music in the afternoons and the famous longhorn ribs merit a visit. ☎ 520-457-3107; www.bignosekate.com; 417 E Allen St, Tombstone; ⊙ 11am-8pm

Café Poca Cosa
It's all freshly prepared, innovative and beautifully presented. It has the best margaritas in town. ☎ 520-622-6400; 110 E Pennington St, Tucson; mains $16-25; ⊙ lunch & dinner Tue-Sat

La Roca Restaurant
The food will rock you – worth crossing the border to indulge in an exquisite candlelight dinner at this place carved into a stony cliff. ☎ 520-313-6313; 91 Calle Elias, Nogales, Mexico; mains $12-24; ⊙ 11am-midnight

Stock Exchange Saloon
Where miners and those who wanted to relieve them of their fortune used to mingle. Nowadays, it's the place to hang with the locals and hear live music. ☎ 520-432-9924; www.stockexchange saloon.com; 15 Brewery Ave, Bisbee; ⊙ 11am-1:30am

SLEEP

Copper Queen Hotel
A casual late-19th-century elegance with modern amenities; Paul Newman, Boris Karloff and Gore Vidal have all been bedded by this grand old dame. ☎ 520-432-2216; www.copperqueen.com; 11 Howell Ave, Bisbee; r $90-180

Hacienda Corona de Guevavi
This hidden gem was frequented by 'the Duke,' aka John Wayne. ☎ 520-287-6502; www.haciendacorona.com; 348 S River Rd, Nogales, AZ; r $175-225

Hotel Congress
Ask for a room at the far end of the hotel if you're noise sensitive. There's a music club and a tasty restaurant downstairs. ☎ 520-622-8848; www.hotelcongress .com; 311 E Congress St, Tucson; r $70-120; ⊛

USEFUL WEBSITES
www.visittucson.org

LINK YOUR TRIP
www.lonelyplanet.com/trip-planner

Grapes & Hops in the Desert

WHY GO Even local oenophiles often don't know that award-winning wines are produced right here in Arizona. But, as winemaker Fran Lightly will tell you, local varietals are now getting their due. Vineyards cluster in the southern part of the state and around Sedona. Add in esteemed microbreweries, and you're in for a truly spirited vacation.

"In vino veritas," as the ancient Romans were fond of slurring, "In wine, there is truth." To the toga-ed ones, it meant that a loosened tongue tells it like it is. To modern winemakers, it means that every patch of land tells a story through its grapes, and the tale has no lies. Fran Lightly, winemaker at Arizona's pioneering grape producer ❶ Sonoita Vineyards, says the land where he works tells a tale of hot days and cold nights that ends in complex, full-bodied reds.

"We just had a monsoon pass through an hour ago, and it was a full 15 degrees cooler than it is now," Lightly says. "The temperature swings here are amazing. The hot days help the grapes grow, and the cool nights give them their flavor." The state is famous for its variety of landscapes, but here, with vines on the hillside and roller-coaster strips of greenery unfurling beside a river, it feels more like California's lush wine country than sun-baked Arizona.

See for yourself as you motor through the rolling land to Sonoita's hilltop tasting room in Elgin, 9 miles from the town of Sonoita. On weekends, hop on a tractor-drawn vineyard tour and imagine all those grapes filling your glass as a fat cabernet or merlot.

Grab a few bottles and continue with a private tasting in your room at ❷ Duquesne House, an 1898 former boarding house for miners set on

TIME
4 days

DISTANCE
400 miles

BEST TIME TO GO
Year-round

START
Sonoita, AZ

END
Flagstaff, AZ

ALSO GOOD FOR

HISTORY &
CULTURE

Patagonia's original main street. Or appreciate the countryside, the *terroir*, if you will, at ❸ **Spirit Tree Inn**. The peaceful old ranch rests under a copse of towering cottonwood trees, proving yet again that this is fertile land.

After a good night's rest, you'll be ready to drink in the deep, complex flavors at Elgin's ❹ **Callaghan Vineyards**. Robert Parker, the most influential wine critic on earth, recommends a number of Callaghan wines – like the 2002 Petite Sirah – and says that the Arizona vineyard is one of the best-kept secrets in the wine world. Tastings here, like at most Arizona wineries, are weekend-only affairs.

In Sonoita, 16 miles northeast of Patagonia on Hwy 82, ❺ **Dos Cabezas WineWorks** has weekend tastings and is known for its flavor-monster cabernet sauvignon. Still thirsty? Make the 7-mile drive back to Elgin to ❻ **Rancho Rossa Vineyards**. With 17 acres of grapes, it's one of the area's larger vineyards. You'll see the expanse as you drive through to the tasting room, heeding the siren call of the syrah. Critics crowned the 2004 vintage the best red in the state.

Before leaving town, stop in at Sonoita's ❼ **Canela Southwestern Bistro**. The menu specializes in locally grown foods, and the wine list never ceases to amaze – Lebanese and German wines appear alongside bottles from lesser-known winemaking regions in the USA.

Take Hwy 83 north until it hits I-10 to make a quick stop in funky-cool Tucson. Beer lovers will be hopped up for ⑧ **Nimbus Brewing Company**, the largest microbrewery in the state, which sells all ales, all the time. The brewers explain that Tucson's mineral-rich water is perfect for brewing ale – so why make anything else? They flow in shades of gold, red, brown – a veritable Crayola pack of colors. The monkey-themed tap room is the place to learn about them and fill up on tasty bar food before making the 200-mile trek north to Prescott.

Sipping a standout beer or two at ⑨ **Prescott Brewing Company** is much deserved after negotiating the concrete maze where I-10 meets I-17 in Phoenix. Set just a stone's throw from Prescott's Whiskey Row – where 40 wild saloons once crammed into a single block – the brewery's Petrified Porter is heavy enough to count as a meal.

A more delicate drinking experience awaits a block away at ⑩ **Library of Wine & Tea**. The owners focus on Californian and French wines, but toss in Old and New World surprises to keep the palate lively.

Next, it's on to Jerome, a former mining town 36 miles north on Hwy 89. The journey starts innocently enough with miles of strip malls. Then it becomes a twisting, turning uphill drive that eventually lands you smack in the little town's center. After so much hard work, you've earned the right to check in at the ⑪ **Jerome Grand Hotel**. Originally built as a miner's hospital in 1926, Jerome's most luxurious property provides eye-popping views of the Prescott Valley. The on-site restaurant and bar, ⑫ **Asylum**, has a decent wine list, but the cocktails – like the smoky Bloody Mary – are what really make the mature crowd here go crazy.

"Robert Parker says that the Arizona vineyard is one of the best-kept secrets in the wine world."

Take in more valley views at ⑬ **Jerome Winery** – a wine shop set on a large patio with tables, where you can take your pick of 30 local sips. A five-minute twisting downhill walk from Jerome Winery, ⑭ **Grapes** has the tastiest wine list in town. Almost everything on the menu, from gourmet pizza to juicy burgers, comes with a suggested wine pairing.

It's onward to Sedona, 30 miles north on Hwy 89 via a short, winding road. Famous for its red rocks and vortexes of positive energy, Sedona is an undeniable Arizona highlight. Propped up from a 500ft mesa, ⑮ **Sky Ranch Lodge** gives visitors a terrific vantage point to view the town – and its sunsets.

When you come down to earth, ready for a drink, a unique winery excursion awaits. Sure you can drive to ⑯ **Alcantara Vineyards**, but ⑰ **Sedona Wine Tours** lets you float down the Verde River in an inflatable kayak to reach the grounds. Alcantara was the first winery along the river, and it's quickly turning the Verde Valley into a winemaking hot spot. The 2005 chardonnay is a must try and buy. The tasting room is open daily, and on weekends the vineyard hosts tours; August and September are good times to come watch the harvest. And if paddling isn't your thing, you can always stop at Alcantara on the road up from Jerome.

In Cornville ⑱ Oak Creek Vineyards & Winery is also roughly halfway between Jerome and Sedona. A 4-acre (and growing) winery, the tasting room is open every day, and on weekends it's possible to get some face time with owner Deb Wahl. Beer fans unite at Sedona's ⑲ Oak Creek Brewing Company. The microbrewery has been racking up medals at beer festivals for ages. The nutty brown ale packs a punch. Or go for the "Seven Dwarfs" tasting sampler of beers served in 5oz steins.

> **DETOUR**
>
> About 80 miles northeast of Sonoita off I-10, **Willcox** is rising fast as another buzzworthy winemaking region. Sip bubbly at **Coronado Vineyards** (www.coronadovineyards.com) – their dolce veritas tells the story of the area's specialty, white wines, oh-so-sweetly. The **Willcox Chamber of Commerce & Agriculture** (www.willcoxchamber.com) provides further details on the area.

Flagstaff, a 30-mile drive from Sedona through pine trees and air that gets crisper by the minute as the altitude rises, is the perfect place to end our tour of Arizona wine and beer. After settling in at star-studded ⑳ Hotel Monte Vista in the heart of the small, pedestrian-friendly downtown, traipse over to ㉑ Flagstaff Brewing Company. Facing the famous Route 66, the brewery makes a dozen beers on site and has about 100 different types of whiskey. The Sasquatch Stout delivers; so named, one thinks, not for any hairy beasts in nearby woods but for the appearance of a stout lover as he or she makes their way home.

Scholarly imbibers know that ㉒ Brix is oenophile heaven just by the name. A Brix meter is what vintners use to read the sugar content of as-yet-unharvested grapes. The wine menu here is superb, and Brix delivers on fine dining with seasonal, farm-fresh meals prepared with flair.

For a big selection of wines by the glass, head to ㉓ Mountain Oasis in the center of downtown. During lunch, sit at one of the sidewalk tables and watch college students, vacationing families and locals on their muddy mountain bikes pass by.

No matter how you decide to spend your last night of the trip, make a toast: you've now tasted Arizona at its best. Robert Parker's quip about Callaghan Vineyards applies to the whole of Arizona wine. "It's definitely a secret even within Arizona, but we're changing that as fast as we can," says Sonoita's Lightly.

Josh Krist

TRIP INFORMATION

GETTING THERE

Patagonia is off Hwy 82. Prescott, Jerome and Sedona are off Hwy 89. Flagstaff is 310 miles north of Sonoita.

DO

Alcantara Vineyards

The Verde Valley's winemaking trendsetter. Tasting room is open daily and tours are run on weekends. ☎ 928-649-8463; www .alcantaravineyard.com; 7500 Alcantara Way, Verde Valley; tastings $8, tours $5; ⊙ tastings 11am-5pm, tours 11:30am

Callaghan Vineyards

Located about 20 miles east of Patagonia: the critics that matter like their wine. Try the 2002 Petite Sirah or 2005 Callaghan Claire's. ☎ 520-455-5322; www.callaghanvineyards .com; 336 Elgin Rd, Elgin; ⊙ 11am-3pm Fri-Sun

Dos Cabezas WineWorks

Robust, well-priced cabernet sauvignons win raves at Dos Cabezas. The viognier and El Norte, both from 2006, are must-tastes. ☎ 520-455-5141; www.doscabezaswinery .com; 3248 Hwy 82, Sonoita; ⊙ 10:30am-4:30pm Fri-Sun

Jerome Winery

It has 30 wines from Southern Arizona and fantastic views. ☎ 928-639-9067; 403 Clark St, Jerome; tastings $5; ⊙ noon-5pm Mon-Thu, noon-6pm Fri, 11am-6pm Sat, noon-5pm Sun

Oak Creek Vineyards & Winery

Pull up a glass next to winemaker and owner Deb Wahl, who is often here on weekends, to chat. ☎ 928-649-0290; www.oakcreekvine yards.net; 1555 Page Springs Rd, Cornville; tastings from $5; ⊙ 11am-5pm

Rancho Rossa Vineyards

One of southern Arizona's larger wineries, visitors drive through rows of grapes en route to the tasting room. ☎ 520-455-0700; www.ranchorossa.com; 201 Cattle Ranch Lane, Elgin; ⊙ 10:30am-4:30pm Fri-Sun

Sedona Wine Tours

Merrily row your boat to Alcantara Vineyards for a sip of the dreamy wines. The same outfit runs Sedona hiking, biking and vortex tours. ☎ 928-204-6440; www.sedona winetours.com; 2020 Contractors Rd, Sedona; tours $125

Sonoita Vineyards

Started by Gordon Dutt, the man who planted Arizona's first commercial vineyard, the wine here has been served to presidents. ☎ 520-455-5893; www.sonoitavineyards.com; 290 Elgin Canelo Rd, Elgin; ⊙ 10am-4pm

EAT & DRINK

Asylum Restaurant

Great views and a fantastic wine list make this the most upscale place around. ☎ 928-639-3197; 200 Hill St, Jerome; dinner mains $18-29; ⊙ lunch & dinner

Brix

A good selection of wines by the glass and a huge selection by the bottle. ☎ 928-213-1021; 413 N San Francisco St, Flagstaff; mains $23-31; ⊙ dinner Mon-Sat year-round, lunch May-Oct

Canela Southwestern Bistro

A wide-ranging wine list includes some local favorites. ☎ 520-455-5873; www .canelabistro.com; 3252 Hwy 82, Sonoita; mains from $12; ⊙ 5-10pm Thu, 4-10pm Fri-Sun

Flagstaff Brewing Company

Handcrafted brews, live music and lots of whiskey just a stumble away from downtown. ☎ 928-773-1442; www.flagbrew. com; 16 E Rte 66, Flagstaff; ⊙ 11am-2am Mon-Sat, 11am-midnight Sun

Grapes

Everything on the menu has a wine-pairing suggestion. The small gourmet pizzas go great with a red. ☎ 928-634-8477; 111 Main St, Jerome; mains from $10; ⊙ breakfast, lunch & dinner

FOOD & DRINK

Library of Wine & Tea

Run by a Scottish-German couple, you can bet that good beer is on the menu too. ☎ 928-541-9900; www.thelibraryofwine.com; 212 W Gurley St, Prescott; ⏱ 11am-late

Mountain Oasis

Good wines, good food and great people-watching at this casual downtown eatery. ☎ 928-214-9270; 11 Aspen Ave, Flagstaff; mains from $10; ⏱ 11am-9pm

Nimbus Brewing Company

The largest microbrewery in the state capitalizes on the local water profile to make a wide variety of ales. ☎ 520-745-9175; www.nimbusbeer.com; 3850 E 44th St, Tucson; ⏱ 11am-11pm Mon-Thu, 11am-1am Fri & Sat, noon-9pm Sun

Oak Creek Brewing Company

This microbrewery has been racking up the medals at beer festivals for a long quaffing time. ☎ 928-204-1300; www.oakcreekbrew.com; 2050 Yavapai Dr, Sedona; dishes $9-15; ⏱ lunch & dinner

Prescott Brewing Company

The IPA is a great brew to start with, but anything here is good. ☎ 928-771-2795; www.prescottbrewingcompany.com; 130 W Gurley, Prescott; mains $8-12; ⏱ 11am-10pm, bar until late

SLEEP

Duquesne House

Six old-fashioned units each with its own entrance, sitting room and porch. The place for you, a sweetie and a good bottle of red. ☎ 520-394-2732; 357 Duquesne St, Patagonia; r $75

Hotel Monte Vista

In downtown Flagstaff near copious wining and dining options. ☎ 928-779-6971; www.hotelmontevista.com; 100 N San Francisco St, Flagstaff; r Nov-Apr $70-140, May-Oct $75-170

Jerome Grand Hotel

Built as a hospital in 1926, the haunted mansion – like a 1982 Bordeaux – is aging gracefully. ☎ 928-634-8200; www.jeromegrandhotel.com; 200 Hill St, Jerome; r $120-460

Sky Ranch Lodge

Set on 6 acres soaring 500ft above Sedona; drink in the views while sipping on local wines. ☎ 928-282-6400, www.skyranchlodge.com; Airport Rd, Sedona; r $75-190

Spirit Tree Inn

Each room of this historic ranch has desert views and the bunk house is good for small groups. ☎ 520-394-0121; www.spirittreeinn.com; 3 Harshaw Creed Rd, Patagonia; r from $95

USEFUL WEBSITES

www.arizonavinesandwines.com
www.patagoniaaz.com

LINK YOUR TRIP
www.lonelyplanet.com/trip-planner

TRIP

Into the Vortex

WHY GO These towers of red rock in Sedona don't just glow with an otherworldly light at sunset, they concentrate Mother Earth's mojo, or so say the many spiritual pilgrims here, such as tour guide Blair Carl. With a cleaned out body and mind, use the energy of Sedona to tune in to the cosmic radio.

With a rapid-fire intensity, spiritual tour guide Blair Carl draws on references ranging from the Aztec calendar to the New Testament to the study of UFOs. "I tell people to think of themselves like a radio receiver where the tuner has been stuck on one station for a long time," he says. "There are other frequencies out there but we need to quiet ourselves long enough to find them."

It all starts with breathing, and reconnecting with the land, Carl explains. A guide for ❶ **Earth Wisdom Jeep Tours**, he likes to gauge the openness of his passengers to New Age ideals by asking them questions about paranormal experiences they've already had.

Earth Wisdom Jeep Tours visit a few of Sedona's most powerful vortexes, and participants get quiet time at each one to think, meditate or just bask in the view. Vortexes usually dwell in a specific rock formation or a canyon, and there's no one official explanation on what a vortex really is. But, most believers agree that they give off spiritually empowering energy.

"Any vortex tour is a good way to learn about some of the power centers in Sedona and get some ideas on how to get grounded here. After that, I encourage people to strike out on their own," says Carl. The most powerful vortexes are Boynton Canyon, Airport Rock, Bell Rock, and Cathedral Rock. But, as Carl says, feel it out for yourself.

TIME
2 days

DISTANCE
30 miles

BEST TIME TO GO
Year-round

START
Sedona, AZ

END
Sedona, AZ

ALSO GOOD FOR

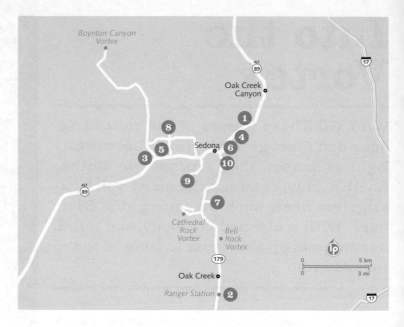

To visit the vortexes solo, you'll need a Red Rock Pass from the ② **Red Rock Ranger District** to park for more than a few minutes in the forest around Sedona; it takes longer than that to get settled for a deep-breathing session. While there, pick up a free map of area hiking and picnic spots. Or get the pass at visitor centers, the ranger station or vending machines at some trailheads and picnic areas.

> "Test the notion that you can never dip your toes in the same river twice."

Carl tells people to eat differently when they come to Sedona seeking clarity, saying that a cleansed body and a cleansed mind go hand in hand. "If in your big-city life you'd normally drink martinis and eat steaks on vacation, try something different here or else you're bringing the same energy to a new place," he counsels.

Even taste buds accustomed to creamy, meaty fare will relish the vegan dishes at ③ **D'lish Very Vegetarian**. It dishes out a good selection of raw foods, which in some circles act as a shock treatment on the intestines to cleanse polluted bodies. Before giving a tour, Carl often stops at ④ **Wildflower Bread Company** on Sedona's main strip. Lines can be long around lunchtime, but the to-go sandwiches provide the perfect sustenance for the body while the mind tries to tune in and turn on.

A well-rested person has a mind more open to whatever truth is out there, or so the thinking goes. Try resting that buzzing brain at one of the basic rooms at the ❺ White House Inn, just a stone's throw from D'lish Very Vegetarian and a short drive to spiritually super-charged Boynton Canyon.

Set on the banks of Oak Creek, ❻ L'Auberge de Sedona recharges guests with pampering fit for a guru. The spa technicians knead the stress away, and testing the notion that you can never dip your toes in the same river twice is a great way to while away the day beside Oak Creek. No matter where visitors stay, Carl advises them to keep a pen and paper beside their bed to record their dreams, saying that some people have more intense dreams after a vortex visit.

Sedona's man-made sacred spaces should not be missed. The spectacular ❼ Chapel of the Holy Cross, a concrete church built into red-rock spires, offers great views of nearby Bell Rock. A consecrated Buddhist shrine, ❽ Amitabha Stupa is set amid piñon and juniper pine and the ubiquitous rocks. According to Buddhist doctrine, anyone who reflects on a stupa is changed by its inherent holiness and grace. There's a smaller stupa further down, and a path between the two is in the works to make it easier for walking meditation and to improve wheelchair accessibility.

The next morning, grab breakfast at ❾ Bliss Café for the ultimate in body-cleansing food. It's all raw and all organic. "For your final day, just keep doing more of the same. Get out and experience the land and feed your body healthy food," Carl says. "Some people might want to visit a psychic or a healer, but just follow your gut. If you get the same feeling from a psychic as you get from those charlatans on TV, just thank them and walk away."

If you've still got that feeling for some spiritual healing, stop in at the friendly ❿ Center for the New Age for a cure for whatever ails you. It has a huge selection of books, crystals and healing stones and a long menu of services, including vortex tours.

What's the sound of one hand clapping? Cynics would answer "slapping," but the truth is, most people do leave Sedona feeling energized. Whether that's from the natural beauty, taking the time to ponder life's riddles, or the vortex radiation that thaws a frozen soul, it doesn't matter so much. Sedona is special, and special things happen here.

Josh Krist

PLAYLIST ♫♫

It's easy to score soundtracks of whale cries and other nature sound, but that doesn't make for good driving music. Usher in enlightenment with:

- "New Age," The Velvet Underground
- "Children of the Sun," Billy Thorpe
- "Woodstock," Crosby, Stills, Nash & Young
- "You May Know Him," Cat Power
- "I'm Beginning to See the Light," The Velvet Underground
- "Atlantis," Donovan
- "In the Light," Led Zeppelin
- "Landslide," Fleetwood Mac

TRIP INFORMATION

GETTING THERE
Sedona is 120 miles north of Phoenix via I-17 and Hwy 179.

DO
Amitabha Stupa
From Hwy 89A, turn right on Andante, left on Pueblo, then head up the gated trail on the right to the Buddhist shrines. Soon to be wheelchair accessible. ☎ 928-300-4435; www.stupas.org; Sedona; ⊙ year-round
Center for the New Age
Find out the color of your aura, regress into past lives or have a psychic tell you the challenges your future holds. ☎ 928-282-2085; www.sedonanewagecenter.com; 341 Hwy 179, Sedona; ⊙ 8:30am-8:30pm
Chapel of the Holy Cross
Three miles south of town on Hwy 179. Drink in the stellar views of vortex heavyweight Bell Rock. ☎ 928-282-4069; 780 Chapel Rd, Sedona; ⊙ 9am-5pm Mon-Sat, 10am-5pm Sun
Earth Wisdom Jeep Tours
With morning, noonish and sunset tours, it also offers outings with a Native American focus. ☎ 928-282-4714; www.earthwisdomtours.com; 293 N Hwy 89A, Sedona; tours $68-98
Red Rock Ranger District
Drop by for a Red Rock Pass (can be purchased online or by phone too) or area maps and information. ☎ 928-203-2900; www.redrockcountry.org; 8375 Hwy 179, Sedona; day/week pass $5/15; ⊙ 8am-5pm

EAT
Bliss Café
The place to go for the ultimate in body-cleansing raw food. It also has plenty of chocolate creations that are pure bliss. ☎ 928-282-2997; 1595 W Hwy 89A, Sedona; mains $6.50-12.50; ⊙ 11am-8pm Mon-Sat, 11am-6pm Sun
D'Lish Very Vegetarian
Try the tamari-glazed walnut burgers or raw zucchini pasta. Earth Wisdom tours often stop here for a bathroom break after Boynton Canyon. ☎ 928-203-9393; 3190 W Hwy 89A, Sedona; dishes $6-12; ⊙ 11am-8pm
Wildflower Bread Company
Both vegetarian- and carnivore-friendly sandwiches are sure to please here, and budget-conscious travelers can stock up on basics. ☎ 928-204-2223; 101 N Hwy 89A, Sedona; dishes $5-10; ⊙ breakfast, lunch & dinner

SLEEP
L'Auberge de Sedona
One of the most opulent properties around keeps winning awards from travel magazines. A riverside cottage is nirvana on earth. ☎ 928-282-1661; www.lauberge.com; 301 Auberge Ln, Sedona; r/cottages from $175/275
White House Inn
Not quite fit for a president, the friendly management makes this good-value, basic motel that much better. ☎ 928-282-6680; www.sedonawhitehouseinn.com; 2986 W Hwy 89A, Sedona; r $65-100

USEFUL WEBSITES
www.lovesedona.com
www.visitsedona.com

LINK YOUR TRIP
www.lonelyplanet.com/trip-planner

Sedona Red Rock Adventure

WHY GO Want an active vacation with a healthy dash of comfort? Take the rolling hills and gentle trails of Sedona, stir in a little woo-woo New Age vortex energy, add a splash of watery fun from nearby Oak Creek and you've got the winning recipe for a red rock adventure.

TIME
3 – 4 days

DISTANCE
90 miles

BEST TIME TO GO
Year-round

START
Sedona, AZ

END
Sedona, AZ

Mountain biking draws the most outdoor adventurers to Sedona, but those who prefer their own rubber soles to a knobby tire can get a move on, too. Almost all biking paths double as hiking paths, plus there are several stunning riverside hikes in nearby Oak Creek Canyon.

Sedona is not all about hiking and biking, though. All sorts of crazy outdoor escapades, from climbs up mighty Cathedral Rock to tubing Oak Creek or kayaking Lynx Lake, are offered by ❶ Sedona Adventure Outfitters & Guides. The group gets bonus points for the "Water to Wine" tour, which mixes floating down a river with wine tasting in a way that's just so, well, Sedona.

If you're a DIY type, swing by ❷ Red Rock Ranger District, the place to pick up a free Red Rock Country Recreation Guide. It's worth checking out the website for a printable map that shows camping spots, picnic areas and trails throughout greater Sedona and Oak Creek.

Travelers coming here to enjoy the great outdoors will appreciate everything ❸ Southwest Inn at Sedona is doing to protect it: the high-ceilinged rooms are filled with energy-saving fixtures (low-water toilets, ceiling fans, fluorescent lights), gas fireplaces and the full range of amenities. The 23-room ❹ Matterhorn Inn has private balconies, perfect for stargazing and resting one's weary body after a hard day on the trails.

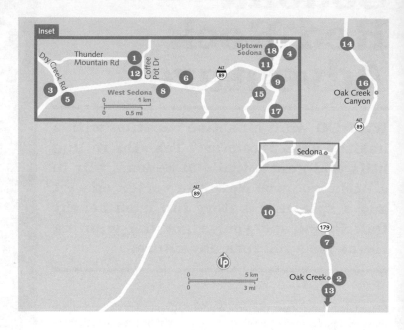

Groups of four will have a grand ole time in a unit at the **5** **Lantern Light Inn.** Lovely gardens + quaint Euro-flavored courtyard rooms + proprietors who help you get the most out of your vacation = an excellent deal.

Make a picnic pit stop at **6** **New Frontiers Natural Market & Deli.** Any trail is doable with creamy French cheese rounds, a bottle of red wine and fresh-baked bread stashed in your bag. If nothing else, the market is a good place to stock up on water. Even though Sedona is where locals come to escape the scorching summer in other parts of the state, that old devil sun is still strong here.

"The Hefeweizen beer has particularly restorative post-trail powers."

Mountain bikers will go ga-ga over Sedona's sheer variety of trails, which include lots of single-track routes carving through the red rocks and dipping down into canyons. Bikes aren't permitted in some wilderness areas, but there are plenty of signs posted so don't worry too much about stumbling into forbidden territory.

A great ride for first-timers is the easy but beautiful Bell Rock Pathway. You can hop on across the street from **7** **Bike & Bean**, a blissful combo of coffee bar, bike-rental place, and information/encouragement provider. The 7-mile round-trip crosses lots of other hiking and biking paths, and it's easy to spend a day exploring.

For experienced riders, there's plenty of poking around on the tracks behind **8** **Mountain Bike Heaven** near Airport Mesa. Yes, the airport here really does sit atop a flattened hill (making it America's most scenic airport, according to locals). It's near a New Age vortex of higher-powered energy, and airport officials in charge of the restaurant occasionally airlift fresh crab to the airport's restaurant.

Because hikers don't have to worry about the sharp descents and technical skills (or lack thereof) that can send mountain bikers helmet-over-heels into rockpiles, finding a sweet walking trail here is easy. Try **9** **Sedona Sports** for recommendations; it also rents GPS units, walking sticks, outdoor-ready baby carriers and mountain bikes, and sells fishing licenses and gear for would-be Oak Creek anglers.

> **ASK A LOCAL**
>
> "[Uptown Sedona] seems to be a bit of a New Age tourist trap. I think it's good to just get out into the rocks and feel what the earth has to offer, which by itself is pretty impressive. The first weeks I was here I did what I can only describe as an emotional detox, and that was just from being present, not from any healing work."
>
> *Paul Dunn, a New Zealander drawn to Sedona*

Just driving around the outskirts of Sedona is a good way to find lightly trodden hiking spots, but if serendipity isn't your bag, any time is a good time to drive the winding 7-mile Red Rock Loop Rd, which is exactly what it sounds like. The drive is paved except for one short section and provides access into **10** **Red Rock State Park,** which has a picnic area next to Oak Creek and six easy hiking trails.

Phew. You've earned the right to get that newly bronzed and toned body to **11** **Mago** for a massage – choices include a mud hand massage, deep neck kneading and intestinal healing, all at decent prices. The massage space is hidden behind the 1st-floor café. This being Sedona, there are spiritual consultations on offer, too. Perhaps the most refreshing way to unwind is at **12** **Oak Creek Brewing Company.** The microbrewery has been racking up medals at beer festivals for ages. The Hefeweizen beer has particularly restorative post-trail powers.

SKY-HIGH

As you might have guessed, it's easy to get high in Sedona – just ring up **Northern Light Balloon Expeditions** (☎ 928-282-2274; www.northern lightballoon.com). They'll pick you up at your hotel and take you up and away at sunrise, when Sedona's reds and golds are at their most vivid. After an hour aloft, they'll return you to solid ground for a champagne breakfast.

Continue with hiking and biking the next day. Or, if the muscles protest too much, saddle up for a different flavor of sore at **13** **M Diamond Ranch** and let a horse do the heavy lifting. The Diamond is a working cattle ranch 14 miles south of town, and it takes small groups on trail rides through the rolling tan and red-rocked land.

For another magical experience, follow Hwy 89A into Oak Creek Canyon and check out ⑭ **Slide Rock State Park**. Short trails ramble past an apple orchard and old farm equipment, but the park's biggest draw are the natural rock slides that swoosh you down into the Oak Creek. This park is jam-packed in summer and traffic in the area can get brutal, so come early or late in the day to avoid the worst congestion.

RED ROCK PASSES

To park in the forest, you'll need to buy a Red Rock Pass (www.redrockcountry.org) from visitors centers, the ranger station or vending machines at some trailheads and picnic areas. Passes go on your dashboard and cost $5 per day or $15 per week. Applicable areas are plastered with signs, which you can ignore if stopping briefly for a photograph.

Under ideal conditions Oak Creek is an enchantress, and will inspire those taken with her to sleep in her green embrace. The ⑮ USFS oversees the camping spots along Oak Creek Canyon. Some are first-come, first-serve, and others accept reservations. Just be sure to arrive on Thursday night or very early on Friday morning to grab an unreserved spot, especially in the summer months.

If you want to sleep near the water of Oak Creek but don't feel like camping, ⑯ **Garland's Oak Creek Lodge**, set 8 miles into the canyon, combines rustic elegance with the casual comfort of your best friend's pad. Rates include a full hot breakfast, cocktails and a gourmet dinner made from organic produce grown on the premises. Adults craving a quiet, authentic getaway flock to the place, and it's often booked solid.

For a good lunch before leaving these scenic environs, try ⑰ **Shugrue's Hillside Grill**. With panoramic views and an outdoor deck to enjoy them, the restaurant serves top-drawer food without a lot of pomp. Fresh fish prepared umpteen ways is just one reason this place is perennially packed to the gills.

If horseback riding at M Diamond Ranch awakened your frontier spirit, have dinner at the ⑱ **Cowboy Club**. It rustles up a fine buffalo burger (or filet mignon, if you're feeling fancy) and you can chow down while perusing the Western-themed wall decor.

Josh Krist

TRIP INFORMATION

GETTING THERE
Sedona is 30 miles south of Flagstaff on Hwy 89A.

DO
Bike & Bean
Easy hiking, biking and vortex-gazing lie just across the street from this cool shop; it's about 5 miles south of town. ☎ 928-284-0210; www.bike-bean.com; 6020 Hwy 179, Sedona; bike hire 2hr/day from $25/$40

M Diamond Ranch
Offering horseback trips that remind you Sedona was once the Wild West. The ranch also hosts cowboy cookouts. ☎ 928-300-6466; www.mdiamondranch.com; 3055 N Forest Rd 618, Rimrock; 1-/2-hr rides $69/90; ☺ Mon-Sat

Mago
The massage and consultation space hides behind the 1st-floor café; follow the unicorn and rainbow paintings. Sedona Story; ☎ 928-282-3875; www.sedonastory.com; 207 N Hwy 89A, Sedona; massages from $15

Mountain Bike Heaven
It's just like the name says, and there's lots of riding just behind the store. ☎ 928-282-1312; www.mountainbikeheaven.com; 1695 W Hwy 89A, Sedona; per day/week $40/140

Red Rock Ranger District
Stop in for a Red Rock Pass (also available online or by phone) or area maps and information; just south of the village of Oak Creek. ☎ 928-203-2900; www.redrockcountry.org; 8375 Hwy 179, Sedona; per day/week $5/15; ☺ 8am-5pm

Red Rock State Park
Take ranger-led nature walks year-round, or moonlight hikes from April to October. ☎ 928-282-6907; www.azstateparks.com; Lower Red Rock Loop Rd; per vehicle $6; ☺ 8am-7pm May-Aug, 8am-6pm Apr & Sep, 8am-5pm Oct-Mar; ♿

Sedona Adventure Outfitters & Guides
The one-stop shop for outdoor adventure tours ranging from bird-watching to vineyard floating to hiking. ☎ 928-204-6440; www.sedonahiking.com; 2020 Contractors Rd, Sedona; tours from $48

Sedona Sports
It rents 'most everything a family of hikers or bikers could need. ☎ 928-282-1317; www.sedonasports.com; 251 Hwy 179, Sedona; bike rentals per half-/full-day $25/35; ♿

Slide Rock State Park
Swoosh down big rocks into the cool creek water or walk the hiking trails. Call for water-quality reports. ☎ 928-282-3034; www.azstateparks.com; Sedona; per vehicle Sep-May $8, Jun-Aug $10; ☺ 8am-7pm Jun-Aug, 8am-6pm Mar, Apr, Sep & Oct, 8am-5pm Nov-Feb

EAT
Cowboy Club
Home of the prickly-pear margarita and lots of beef. There's both a kid-friendly and adult-only section. ☎ 928-282-4200; www.cowboyclub.com; 241 N Hwy 89A, Sedona; mains lunch $9-16, dinner $15-25; ☺ 11am-10pm; ♿

New Frontiers Natural Market & Deli
Healthy groceries and nourishment to pack into a picnic basket. ☎ 928-282-6311; 1420 W Hwy 89A, Sedona; sandwiches $5; ☺ 8am-8pm

Oak Creek Brewing Company
Biking and brews fit together here perfectly. There's a more upscale (and touristed) outpost at Tlaquepaque village. ☎ 928-204-1300; 2050 Yavapai Dr, Sedona; dishes $9-15; ☺ lunch & dinner

Shugrue's Hillside Grill
Great food without having to dress up too fancy-pants; lots of seafood. ☎ 928-282-5300; www.shugrues.com; 671 Hwy 179, Sedona; mains lunch $9-18, dinner $25-30; ☺ lunch & dinner

SLEEP

Garland's Oak Creek Lodge

Often booked solid months in advance. Call ahead for cancellations, especially on weekdays. ☎ 928-282-3343; www.garlandslodge.com; 8067 N Hwy 89A, Sedona; cabins $235-290; ☺ Apr–mid-Nov

Lantern Light Inn

Check-in is Thursday to Saturday night only, but you can stay through the week. ☎ 928-282-3419; www.lanternlightinn.com; 3085 W Hwy 89A, Sedona; r $130-195, guesthouses 2-/4-people $225/310

Matterhorn Inn

The outdoor pool and Jacuzzi are nice for post-hike unwinding; floating on your back you can see the towering red rocks. Pets are $10.

☎ 928-282-7176; www.matterhorninn.com; 230 Apple Ave, Sedona; r $120-180; ☺

Southwest Inn at Sedona

Upper units have the best views. Low water usage for plants and lots of recycling are just a few of the green touches. ☎ 928-282-3344; www.swinn.com; 3250 W Hwy 89A, Sedona; r incl breakfast $130-240

USFS

Operates five campgrounds along N Hwy 89A: Bootlegger, Cave Springs, Manzanita, Pine Flat East, and Pine Flat West. Search the website for rates and availability. ☎ 877-444-6777; www.recreation.gov; Sedona

USEFUL WEBSITES

www.visitsedona.com

LINK YOUR TRIP

www.lonelyplanet.com/trip-planner

Tracing Arizona's Cultures

WHY GO From the Native Americans who first called this place home to the successive waves of adventurers who came to Arizona in search of fame, fortune or just a better life, the history of Arizona is the sum of its pioneering people. Strike it rich – in stories, at least – by retracing their steps.

On a journey from the north of the state to one of the southernmost cities, get ready to trek across more than 1000 years of history. Start at the beginning – or as close to it as possible – in the mountain town of Flagstaff, where the cool climes, plentiful water and food-giving forest must have seemed a godsend to the area's first inhabitants. The ❶ Museum of Northern Arizona is an essential introduction to Native American culture, especially in the northern half of the state.

Move forward in time to an Arizona that wasn't yet a state as you head south on I-17 for 63 miles and look for the signs to Prescott. There, the ❷ Sharlot Hall Museum is a fun place even for the museum-adverse. Instead of the typical museum experience of looking at exhibits, here you wander into log cabins to see them decked out in period furnishings.

Just down the street from the museum, check into the good old days at the ❸ Hassayampa Inn. Opened in 1927, just 15 years after Arizona became a state, it's a good place to get a feel for the days when everybody really did know your name. Prescott feels like a Midwestern town with its antique shops and people who say hi to strangers.

Say "so long, friend" to the Midwestern vibe and head south to thoroughly modern Phoenix. Catching the I-17 is the quickest way to traverse the 100-or-so miles. Have lunch at the all-organic ❹ Arcadia Farms Café and visit the ❺ Heard Museum, where the café is located.

TIME
3 days

DISTANCE
450 miles

BEST TIME TO GO
Year-round

START
Flagstaff, AZ

END
Bisbee, AZ

ALSO GOOD FOR

CITY

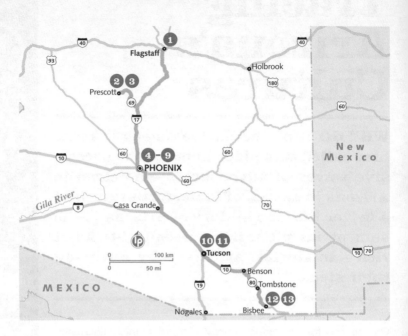

In the museum, peruse the photographs of the late US senator Barry Goldwater, who traveled the state far and wide with his camera and picked up Native American art along the way – much of it on display here.

History and fresh minty flavors collide with a bang at ❻ Pho Bang. It's US senator and former POW John McCain's favorite Vietnamese place in Phoenix – at least according a signed photograph of him that used to adorn the place. At 17th Ave and Camelback Rd, it's just 4 miles from the Heard Museum.

To experience a little slice of Japan transplanted to the desert, head 6 miles south to 3rd Ave and Culver St and wander the ❼ Japanese Friendship Garden. This 3.5-acre park has a koi pond, stone bridges over small ponds, a 12ft waterfall and a tea house. Planners from Phoenix's sister city of Himeji helped design this oasis of calm.

Nearby, at 3rd and Jefferson Streets, pay homage at the ❽ Sun Mercantile Building to the Chinese who came west to build the railways. It's the last building left from Phoenix's Chinatown and activists are fighting to keep it standing. Notice how many of the historic homes in this area have huge front porches; before air conditioning, that's where locals slept on summer nights.

Continue east another 6 miles to see the center of Chinese food and shopping in Phoenix today, the ❾ COFCO Chinese Cultural Center. Imagine a strip mall where all the buildings look like pagodas. There are more than a dozen places to eat and shop here, and the Super L Ranch Market is worth a peek inside for the live fish tanks. Stroll through the on-site gardens – laid out according to the principles of feng shui – to check out replicated landmarks from five ancient Chinese cities. On Chinese holidays the center hosts dances and celebrations.

Let that good Chinese food settle on the 120-mile drive to Tucson through long stretches of suburb that finally give way to citrus fields and patches of tan sand. Spend a night at the ⑩ **Arizona Inn**, another bit of respite from modern times. Sip coffee on the porch, take high tea in the library, lounge by the small pool or join in a game of croquet.

The next morning, take another time warp at the ⑪ **Arizona State Museum**, the oldest and largest anthropology museum in the state. The museum follows the cultural history of the Southwestern tribes, from Stone Age mammoth hunters to the present. With signs in Spanish all over the city, you can bet Mexican culture is alive and well in Tucson. Be sure to cruise through the *barrio historico,* a neighborhood bounded by I-10, Stone Ave, and Cushing and 17th Sts. You'll be treated to great examples of typical Sonoran architecture; houses have colorful, thick adobe walls and those sleeping porches make another appearance.

For a taste of the wild and woolly history of mining, and copper's huge impact on early Arizona (really), take I-10 east to Hwy 80 south to get to Bisbee, once the biggest city between St Louis and San Francisco thanks to the Queen Mine: a major source of copper for cities installing electric lights in the early 1900s. This town on a hill with crazy up-and-down streets was revived by flower-power types in the 1970s who snatched up the Victorian-style houses for a song once the mine shut and the town emptied.

The ⑫ **Bisbee Mining & Historical Museum** does a fantastic job of explaining the decisive role that copper

DETOUR To experience more of the Spanish influence in the region, head 10 miles south of Tucson on I-19 to **Mission San Xavier del Bac**. Blindingly white on the outside, candles and the murmured prayers of the faithful fill the dark interior. Franciscan friars have been conducting services here for two centuries, primarily for the Tohono O'odham. The Spanish, by the way, are the ones who called the Tohono O'odham people Papagos – a slightly insulting term that means "bean-eater."

mining played in Arizona's history and traces Bisbee's journey from small copper camp to rip-roaring boom town to ghost town. End the trip with a few days at the ⑬ **Bisbee Grand Hotel** to relive history – or make some of your own – in one of the themed suites: the Victorian, the Oriental, the Hacienda, and the Western, where you sleep on a bed set inside a covered wagon. Yee-haw!

Josh Krist

TRIP INFORMATION

GETTING THERE
Prescott is 95 miles southwest of Flagstaff via I-17.

DO

Arizona State Museum
Billed as the oldest and largest anthropology museum in the state. ☎ 520-621-6302; www.statemuseum.arizona.edu; 1013 E University Blvd, Tucson; suggested donation $3; ⊙ 10am-5pm Mon-Sat, noon-5pm Sun

Bisbee Mining & Historical Museum
A two-level museum that brings Bisbee's riotous heyday back to life. ☎ 520-432-7071; www.bisbeemuseum.org; 5 Copper Queen Plaza, Bisbee; adult/child/senior $7.50/3/6.50; ⊙ 10am-4pm

COFCO Chinese Cultural Center
After wandering the gardens for free, check out one of the four restaurants here that serve the spectrum of Asian food. ☎ 602-273-7268; www.phxchinatown.com; 668 N 44th St, Phoenix; ⊙ garden 8am-8pm

Heard Museum
Guided tours run at noon, 1:30pm or 3pm (no extra charge) and audio guides are available for $3. ☎ 602-252-8848; www.heard.org; 2301 N Central Ave, Phoenix; adult/child/student/senior $10/3/5/9; ⊙ 9:30am-5pm

Japanese Friendship Garden
Check the schedule for tea ceremony dates or to book a private ceremony for groups. ☎ 602-256-3204; www.japanesefriendshipgarden.org; 1125 N 3rd Ave, Phoenix; adult/child $5/free; ⊙ 10am-3pm Tue-Sun Sep-May

Museum of Northern Arizona
The premier museum in the northern half of the state is set 3 miles north of downtown Flagstaff. ☎ 928-774-5213; www.musnaz.org; 3101 N Fort Valley Rd, Flagstaff; adult/teen/student/senior $7/4/5/6; ⊙ 9am-5pm

Sharlot Hall Museum
Restored buildings include an old schoolhouse and a governor's residence. ☎ 928-445-3122; www.sharlot.org; 415 W Gurley St, Prescott; adult/child $5/free; ⊙ 10am-4pm Mon-Sat, noon-4pm Sun

EAT

Arcadia Farms Café
Uses only organic ingredients for its menu of salads, soups and sandwiches – all with Southwestern zing. ☎ 602-251-0204; www.arcadiafarmscafe.com; 2301 N Central Ave, Phoenix; mains $11-15; ⊙ 9:30am-3pm

Pho Bang
A slice of Vietnam in a not-so-pretty part of Phoenix; service and decor are only OK, but the food is as authentic as it gets. ☎ 602-433-9440; 1702 W Camelback Rd, Phoenix; mains $5-8; ⊙ 10am-9pm

SLEEP

Arizona Inn
Built by Isabella Greenway, Arizona's first congresswoman and a close friend of Eleanor Roosevelt's. The grand old lady still impresses. ☎ 520-325-1541; www.arizonainn.com; 2200 E Elm St, Tucson; r $205-550

Bisbee Grand Hotel
Choose your own thematic adventure in one of the six suites in this restored 1906 building. ☎ 520-432-5900; www.bisbeegrandhotel.com; 61 Main St, Bisbee; r $79-175

Hassayampa Inn
It lives up to its mission of melding yesteryear's charm with modern amenities. Breakfast included. ☎ 928-778-9434; www.hassayampainn.com; 122 E Gurley St, Prescott; r $150-250

USEFUL WEBSITES
www.arizonaguide.com
www.discoverbisbee.com
www.lonelyplanet.com/trip-planner

LINK YOUR TRIP

Flagstaff's Northern Playground

WHY GO Skiing in winter? Yep. Rock climbing, hiking and killer mountain biking in summer? Check, check and check. Flagstaff has you covered season by season. The San Francisco Peaks just north of town are action central – strap in for a downhill ride where the pine trees whoosh by in a green blur.

TIME
3 – 5 days

DISTANCE
60 miles

BEST TIME TO GO
Apr – Sep

START
Flagstaff, AZ

END
Flagstaff, AZ

ALSO GOOD FOR

CITY

The 20-mile radius around Flagstaff is Arizona's playground. Come summer, locals in the hot southern half of the state escape to the cooler altitudes here. In winter, many a Phoenix-area resident has lived the dream of swimming in the morning and schussing down snowy slopes in the afternoon.

No matter what the season, you'll need to set up base camp first. Loads of chain hotels and motels spread out along Route 66, but there's enough low-cost quirk within walking distance of downtown that it's a shame to depend on a car during such a sporty vacation. Flagstaff's two hostels are just south of the train tracks, a maximum 10-minute walk from downtown eating and drinking. Global adventurers of all ages are welcome at ❶ **Grand Canyon International Hostel**. There's a laundry and kitchen on site, and staff can set up the carless (or people who want a break from driving) on well-priced Grand Canyon and Sedona tours. The hostel's sister property, ❷ **Dubeau Hostel**, adds a jukebox, pool tables and foosball to the mix, and attracts a lively crowd. Book in advance to get one of the spartan but comfy-enough private rooms.

Both of the hostels sit mercifully close to ❸ **Hip**, an inexpensive, super-friendly vegetarian restaurant. How they make the vegan enchilada (no meat, no cheese) so flavorsome boggles the mind, but it's so good you might just order seconds.

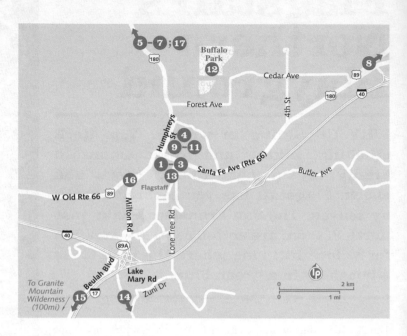

The ④ **Weatherford Hotel** is another central place to rest those barking dogs after a hard day hiking. Built in 1898 in Flagstaff's historic city center, the small property has a faded charm and pretty good prices – as well as a few friendly ghosts. Three of the 10 rooms share a bathroom.

> **ASK A LOCAL**
>
> "The hike to the top of Humphries is supercool – and there's a back way into the mountain: the volcano basin. It's the only place in Arizona with an alpine climate. I've been there a couple times and it's the greenest place in Arizona I've seen."
>
> *James LaPointe, long-time Arizona hiker*

If it's winter, ascend the slopes of the San Francisco Peaks at ⑤ **Arizona Snowbowl**. The resort's 32 ski runs are just the beginning – there's also a terrain park that sees sick shredding by snowboarders, lessons, rentals, meals at the two day lodges and cabins for overnight stays. The powder situation can be wildly unpredictable, so call ahead for conditions. The resort is located 7 miles northwest of Flagstaff on Hwy 180, then another 7 miles on Snowbowl Rd.

If telemarking is more your style, there's nice cross-country skiing at ⑥ **Flagstaff Nordic Center**, 15 miles northwest of Flagstaff. Marked snowshoe trails and a sledding hill round out the winter fun. Actually, sledding is one of Flagstaff's most beloved sports, and almost every hardware and grocery store sells cheap sleds in season.

When it's not winter, this northern area – designated the Kachina Peaks Wilderness Area in 1984 – has a slew of hiking trails worth a day or two of exploration. The trail to the summit of  **Mt Humphries**, the state's highest peak (12,633 ft), begins at Arizona Snowbowl. The first third of the 4.5-mile journey consists of long, looping switchbacks up the side of the mountain.

Even if you have no intention of summiting, the fields of wild flowers and stands of cool pines make the trip worthwhile.

Hardy hikers will love the last third of the trek to the peak – crossing barren fields of volcanic stone above the tree line, it feels like another world. A small rock shelter on the mountain top protects hikers from the cold wind that screams across the bare landscape. Be sure to bring a wind-

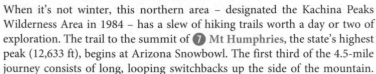

DETOUR About 100 miles southwest of Flagstaff is **Granite Mountain Wilderness**, a center for rock climbing, hiking, fishing and camping. Just 20 minutes away from Prescott via paved roads, the popular 9799-acre area is anchored by the dark, massive slab of – that's right – Granite Mountain. The huge boulders that line many of the hiking paths make the place feel otherworldly. Fido is welcome as long as he's on a leash.

breaker and warm hat. No other trail rivals the view from up here – under perfect conditions you can make out the Grand Canyon, 50 miles north.

Several other hikes in the area afford more leisurely strolling, and most have easy-to-find trailheads and well-marked routes. Not easy, but close to Flagstaff, the steep, 3-mile trek up 9299ft **8** **Mt Elden** rewards with impressive vistas. The trailhead is just past the ranger station on Hwy 89.

No matter what a trail's level of difficulty, realize that you're starting from at least 6900ft of elevation in Flagstaff, and most hikes start even higher than that. This means there's less oxygen in the air, and you'll likely be huffing and puffing more than usual. Altitude sickness is a real concern, so take it easy. Note, too, that some trails have snow on them into late spring.

If you didn't bring your own gear, **9** **Peace Surplus** has hiking, climbing, backpacking and fishing equipment, and a good-sized library of guidebooks for sale. Just a few blocks away, **10** **Aspen Sports** rents backpacks, sleeping bags and tents, as well as skis in winter.

Given that Flagstaff is a college town set in the mountains, it should come as no surprise that half the population spends their weekend astride a mountain bike. But, whereas Sedona has plenty of riding trails for all levels of mountainbikers, the rides in Flagstaff range from challenging to insane. Many trails are close to downtown, but as Bryce Wright (aka "Brycicle") of **11** **AZ Bikes** explains, "The trails are pretty much straight up or straight down, and not for absolute beginners." AZ Bikes rents basic hard-tail and full-suspension mountain bikes, and Bryce and crew can provide details on nearby trails.

No matter what bike shop you use, buy a map or book by Cosmic Ray. His information on Flagstaff rides is invaluable, and the *Arizona Mountain Bike Trail Guide: Fat Tire Tales & Trails* is worth its weight in energy bars if you're planning on visiting other biking spots in the state. Ray's *Fave Hikes: Flagstaff & Sedona* has the footprint profiles of area animals inside the front cover – it's nice to see what critters you're crossing paths with.

The easiest biking trails in the area are accessible from ⑫ **Buffalo Park**, 2 miles northeast of downtown off E Cedar Ave (starts as E Forest Ave). Head to the back of the park – really a big urban walking and biking loop – to get on the gently rolling, wide multiuse paths.

For those looking to ratchet up the adrenaline, you can rock climb all around northern Arizona. And unlike the state's southern region, the stone rarely gets too hot to handle. The best place to dial in to the local scene is ⑬ **Vertical Relief** climbing center: it's "chalk" full of information, gear and, of course, indoor climbing walls. For beginners, the center has a course ($69) with two hours of personal instruction. It can also arrange climbing guides with advance notice.

For bouldering – the art of solving climbing "problems" low enough to the ground that a rope isn't needed – visit ⑭ **Priest Draw**. Imagine lots of steep overhangs and roof problems with big pocket holds. None of the problems are too high – just remember to peel off feet first and all will be fine. Priest Draw is 12 miles southeast of Flagstaff, on National Forest Rd 235. Take Lake Mary Rd to Lake Crimson Rd.

"…even though the climbs are no more than 100ft in length, the ground looks a dizzying distance away…"

If you prefer the sharp end of a rope, the ⑮ **Overlook**, 10 miles south of Flagstaff on Hwy 89A, is a canyon wall full of crack-filled basalt and stellar views of Oak Creek below. Climbers still getting comfortable with heights should know that even though the climbs are no more than 100ft in length, the ground looks a dizzying distance away because of the topography. It's 100% traditional climbing – no bolts allowed.

All this outdoor adventure is bound to make you hungry. Downtown has loads of places to choose from, but ⑯ **Bun Huggers** has been the favorite post-hike/ride/climb spot among locals for decades. After a hard day outside, its juicy burgers taste like…victory.

Before leaving town, make time for a trip to **17** Lava River Cave. Dress warmly and bring a flashlight for this 0.75-mile pitch-black lava tube, where the temperature is about 40°F year-round. Formed 700,000 years ago by molten rock, you can still see evidence of the lava flow in the frozen ripples of the floor. It takes at least an hour round-trip to walk through. The walls of the tubular cave are bare – no groovy stalactites here – but it's a cool way to spend an afternoon.

"After a hard day outside, its juicy burgers taste like… victory."

Admission is free and access is year-round, but roads are closed in winter, so in the colder months you have to cross-country ski or snowshoe in. Travel north on Hwy 180 for 9 miles, turn left 3 miles on Forest Rd 245 (at milepost 230), left again on Forest Rd 171 for 1 mile and one more left on Forest Rd 171B.

At this point there's only one thing left to say about Flagstaff, and we mean it in the nicest possible way: get out of town, now.

Josh Krist

TRIP INFORMATION

GETTING THERE
Flagstaff is located where I-40, I-17 and Hwy 89A meet.

DO

Arizona Snowbowl
Four chair lifts service 32 runs (beginner through expert). In summer, the resort operates a scenic sky ride. ☎ 928-779-1951, snow report ☎ 928-779-4577; www.arizona snowbowl.com; Snowbowl Rd, Flagstaff; half-/full day $40/48

Aspen Sports
Don't want to bother with hauling your gear to Flagstaff? Aspen rents backpacks, sleeping bags, tents, skis and related equipment. ☎ 928-779-1935; 15 N San Francisco St, Flagstaff; ⏰ 10am-6pm Mon-Sat

AZ Bikes
The place for all your mountain-biking needs – Bryce Wright, aka "Brycycle," is happy to suggest trail rides. ☎ 928-773-9881; 5 E Aspen St, Flagstaff; full-day mountain bike rental $30; ⏰ 10am-6pm Mon-Fri, 10am-5pm Sat & Sun

Flagstaff Nordic Center
Ground zero for cross-country skiing. The season is short so call ahead to make sure it's open. Snow-showing trails nearby. ☎ 928-220-0550; www.flagstaffnordiccenter.com; Hwy 180, Coconino County; trail passes $10-15

Peace Surplus
The friendly, helpful staff are more than willing to share their knowledge of northern Arizona's outdoor-action spots. ☎ 928-779-4521; www.peacesurplus.com; 14 W Rte 66, Flagstaff; ⏰ 8am-9pm Mon-Fri, 8am-8pm Sat, 8am-6pm Sun

Vertical Relief
Rock climbers should make this their first stop for gear and info. ☎ 928-556-9909; www.verticalrelief.com; 205 S San Francisco St, Flagstaff; day pass $15; ⏰ 10am-11pm Mon-Fri, noon-8pm Sat & Sun

EAT

Bun Huggers
Meat-lovers adore the mesquite-grilled burgers. Ice-cold beer is on tap, as well. ☎ 928-779-3743; 901 S Milton Rd, Flagstaff; meals under $8; ⏰ 10:30am-1am

Hip
Hip people serve good food that's both meat- and attitude-free. ☎ 928-226-8636; www .hipvegetarianjoint.com; 117 S San Francisco St, Flagstaff; mains from $8; ⏰ 11am-8pm Sun-Thu, 11am-9pm Fri & Sat

SLEEP

Dubeau Hostel
The private rooms are like very basic hotel rooms, but at half the price. Rates include breakfast. ☎ 928-774-6731, 800-398-7112; www.grandcanyonhostel.com; 19 W Phoenix Ave, Flagstaff; dm $18-20, r $41-48

Grand Canyon International Hostel
One of the best independent hostels in the state; it's super clean, run by friendly people. More perks: big free breakfasts and a video lending library. ☎ 928-779-9421; www .grandcanyonhostel.com; 19 S San Francisco St, Flagstaff; dm $18-20, r $38-45

Weatherford Hotel
Eight snug, low-frills rooms (three share one bathroom) and two larger, spiffy ones. ☎ 928-779-1919; www.weatherfordhotel .com; 23 N Leroux St, Flagstaff; r $50-130

USEFUL WEBSITES
www.flagstaffarizona.org

LINK YOUR TRIP

www.lonelyplanet.com/trip-planner

Day Trips from Phoenix

DAY TRIPS

From rows of antique shops to the heart of cowboy country to the city of the future that looks straight out of Star Wars, the Valley of the Sun has many little worlds of adventure circling around it.

PAYSON

Pack a Western novel by Zane Grey and drive up to the cooler climes of Payson. Home to the longes-running rodeo in the United States, buckaroos descend on the town in the middle of August every year to whoop it up. The capital of Rim Country, this is where the desert ends and the ponderosa pines and sheer cliffs of the Mogollon Rim begin. Check out the Rim Country Museum for a glimpse of Payson's Wild West past and take a gander at Zane Grey's reconstructed log cabin. Grab some chow at the Beeline Cafe – as small town and apple pie as you can imagine. Head north to the Tonto Natural Bridge – discovered by a miner on the run from Apaches – and hide out in the lush vegetation with your book. Read a few passages and you'll soon see this beautiful country with the same poetic eye as Grey himself. **Take Hwy 87, aka the Beeline, north for 90 miles. From Payson, Tonto Natural Bridge State Park is an additional 12 miles north on Hwy 87. This last stretch is full of hairpin curves; they don't call it the Beeline for nothing.**

See also **TRIP 19**

WICKENBURG

A lot of places in Arizona will give you a taste of its pioneering past, but Wickenburg wins the award for most authentic. You won't look at the cowboys in Wickenburg, you'll get to play one, if even for just a day. Mosey along on the back of a horse for a few hours, take a jeep tour through the gorgeous desert – after rain the smell of the desert is inspiring, something you'll never forget – or take a historic walking tour. For more of the Old West, take a self-guided tour of Vulture Mine, the hole in the ground that spat out "... tons of gold from the late 1800s until it was closed in 1942, and finish up with a stop at the Desert Caballeros Western Museum. Birders can say hi to their web-footed friends at the Hassayampa River Preserve; 240 species of birds flock together here and it's a rare chance to see the underground Hassayampa River sparkle in the sun. **Take Hwy 60 (Grand Ave) northwest for 60 miles. Vulture Mine is 2 miles west of Wickenburg on Hwy 60, then follow Vulture Mine Rd south for 12 miles. Hassayampa River Preserve is 3 miles southeast of Wickenburg.**

See also **TRIPS 6, 16 & 29**

DOWNTOWN GLENDALE

As close as a person can get to Small Town, USA, and still stay in the Valley of the Sun. Full of festivals, chocoholics are sweet on the Chocolate Affaire – in the three days before Valentine's the owner of Cerreta Candy Company displays a 300-pound chocolate heart. Umm, chocolate. The candy company is open for self-guided tours throughout the year, and it's always a good time to go antique shopping in Glendale. Historic downtown Glendale is 10 city blocks full of charming white picket fence houses and jam-packed with antique stores. If someone in your party isn't excited by antiques and chocolate, and if that person, male or female (no stereotyping here) happens to like football, drop them off for a few hours in Max's Sports Bar – it has the largest collection of football helmets in the country. The fashion-forward love Glendale's many mega-thrift stores. Sure, it takes some time, but since everything old is new again you score the fashions of tomorrow, today. **Glendale is only 9 miles west of central Phoenix via Grand Ave, or take the Glendale Ave exit of either Loop 101 or I-17 (exit name is the same, but different locations).**

See also **TRIPS 11 & 19**

WHITE TANK MOUNTAIN REGIONAL PARK

The 46-sq-mile park drapes across dramatic canyon landscape and is zigzagged by 26 miles of trails, including a grueling one to the top of the 4018ft summit. Come out here after a rainy spell to hike the Waterfall Trail – where after scrambling over some boulders you're rewarded with the sight of luscious waterfalls. At the western edge of the valley, check to see what kind of special events are on that day. Park rangers sometimes do an easy Desert 101 hike that will teach even Arizona natives a thing or two and the two-hour stargazing sessions are a great way to spend the night after a day of hiking. **The park entrance is about 20 miles west of I-17 via Dunlap/Olive Ave, and about 34 miles west of downtown Phoenix.**

See also **TRIPS 24 & 26**

APACHE JUNCTION

Once a year Apache Junction is invaded by damsels in distress and people who talk with funny, supposedly medieval accents. When it's not time for the Renaissance Festival (weekends February through March), this is the place to go for beautiful hiking in the Superstition Mountain Wilderness Area. First, though, stop at Goldfield Ghost Town outside of Apache Junction proper. High noon on weekends sees a mock gun fight at this Old West attraction, which really was a mining outpost back in its day. On Sunday, they even offer real church services to balance out all that outlawin' you've been doing. Stop at the Superstition Mountain Museum to get the lowdown on these rugged, rocky crags; the stone spires here attract rock climbers from all over and there's plenty of hiking at Lost Dutchman State Park, named after the mine just dripping with riches that is supposedly tucked away somewhere here. You'll learn all about it at the museum. Happy treasure hunting. **Apache Junction is 37 miles east of Phoenix on Hwy 60. To get to Goldfield Ghost Town, take Hwy 60 to Idaho Rd/Hwy 88 east and continue for 6.3 miles.**

See also **TRIPS 6 & 19**

CAMP VERDE

Camp Verde was founded in 1865 as a farming settlement and was soon taken over by the US Army. They built a fort here – now Fort Verde State Historic Park – to prevent Indian raids on Anglo settlers. Walking around the well-preserved fort, you'll see the officers' and doctors' quarters, sprint down the parade grounds and study displays about military life and the Indian Wars. Staff occasionally dress up in period costumes and conduct living-history tours; three houses have been completely decked out with period furnishings. It's the best example of what a military outpost really looked like during this turbulent time in Arizona history. **Camp Verde is 90 miles north of Phoenix. To get there, take exit 287 off I-17, go south on Hwy 260, turn left at Finnie Flat Rd and left again at Hollamon St.**

See also **TRIPS 18, 23 & 26**

ARCOSANTI

When you pull off the freeway to get to this place all you'll see at first is a ramshackle few houses anchored by a gas station and a sign pointing the way. Follow the signs and a few miles of dirt road – your car will kick up a lot of dust, but the road is smooth and well traveled – and soon enough you'll be in the parking lot, still wondering what all the fuss is about. Take the steps to the visitors center and sign up for a tour, *then* you'll see a city that looks like what someone imagined the future to look like in 1970. After you understand the ideas behind all that faded concrete, you'll realize the trip was more than worthwhile. The brainchild of ground-breaking architect and urban planner Paolo Soleri, this desert outpost of a new kind of urban planning is based on "acrology;" architecture meets ecology. Radical when conceived in the 1960s, Soleri's ideas now seem on the cutting edge in this age of urban sprawl and global warming. If and when it is finished, Arcosanti will be a self-sufficient village for 5000 people with futuristic living spaces, large-scale greenhouses and solar energy. Spend some time in the gift shop – it sells the famous bronze bells – or grab a meal in the café. **Cordes Junction, the little settlement near Arcosanti, is 65 miles north of Phoenix via I-17. Arcosanti is another 1½ miles from where the paved road ends.**

See also **TRIPS 18, 24, 26 & 29**

SCOTTSDALE/CAVE CREEK

Yep, Scottsdale. Downtown Scottsdale, with all of its bars, restaurants and art, is worth a day, but what we're talking about is North Scottsdale where the lucky few have desert homes. But for the most part it's nothing but cactus in every imaginable shape and lots of mesquite trees to make those steaks you're having later that much tastier. This is where Frank Lloyd Wright saw fit to base his home and architecture school, Taliesin West. The steak houses and woolly bars in this neck of the cacti satisfy: Reata Pass Steakhouse and the next-door Greasewood Flat are good for a lazy, well-irrigated Sunday. Wear a tie to Pinnacle Peak Patio Steakhouse and see what happens. Venture further west into Cave Creek and belly up to the bar at the Horny Toad, a bar-restaurant that locals use as a tasty excuse to see the beautiful landscape. Poke around on Cave Creek Rd; there are plenty of roadside stands selling Western-themed knickknacks and you gotta love the green-neon saguaro-shaped clock. Cave Creek Regional Park has 11 miles of hiking trails that dip up and down into arroyos (desert washes) and are open for mountain biking, hiking and horses. **Cave Creek is 34 miles north of Phoenix via Loop 101 and Scottsdale Rd. It's adjacent to North Scottsdale.**

See also **TRIPS 6, 11, 14 & 16**

GRAND CANYON REGION TRIPS

Living in the Southwest, we know you've seen the Grand Canyon. It is the region's trademark attraction, luring five million visitors a year. But even though you've seen this American icon a million times (admit it), you're secretly impressed by its wedding-cake layers and crazy depth every time you snap a visiting friend's picture from that famous viewpoint on the South Rim. Should you crave more than just another magical sunset photo, we've written 10 trips introducing you to this familiar attraction – and the surrounding region – from a different, more intimate angle. If you like solitude, try our Hiking the North Rim trip; those in search of spirits or art will explore the points of interest on Spirits of the South Rim and South Rim for Artists.

There's a heck of a lot more to the Grand Canyon region than a big hole in the ground. And from the pleasures of Sin City to the truth behind Utah's polygamist culture, we take you road tripping around the western tri-state area. The chapter opens with 48 hours of neon-drenched, outrageous, lose-your-inhibitions fun in America's zany adult funhouse, Las Vegas. Other regional explorations cover lazing on house boats, drinking beer and swimming in Lake Powell's clear turquoise water and getting impressed by red-rock arches and canyon country in Utah's national parks.

PLAYLIST ♫ Set the mood driving to America's most iconic hole with this playlist. Not only does it include music about the Grand Canyon, it also gets you ready to party in Las Vegas and provides a soundtrack for driving through Utah's trippy crimson canyonlands and narrow arches.

- "Grand Canyon," Tracey Thorn
- "Paper Roses," Marie Osmond
- "Utah Carol," Marty Robbins
- "Luck Be a Lady Tonight," Frank Sinatra
- "Leaving Las Vegas," Sheryl Crow
- "Mr Brightside," The Killers
- "Heaven or Las Vegas," The Cocteau Twins
- "The Gambler," Kenny Rogers

BEST GRAND CANYON REGION TRIPS

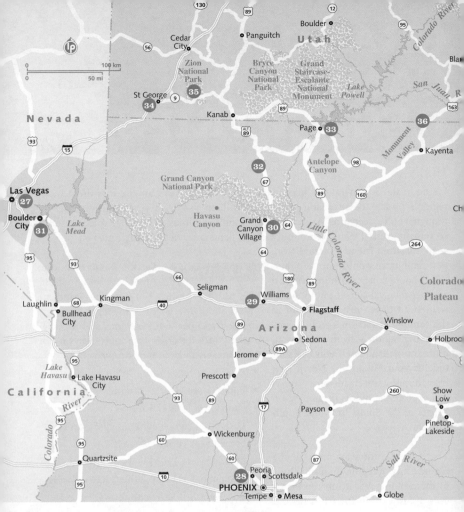

GRAND CANYON REGION TRIPS

48 Hours in Las Vegas

WHY GO Las Vegas is a wild ride. It doesn't matter if you play the penny slots, lay down a bankroll on the poker tables or never gamble at all – you'll leave this town feeling like you've just had the time of your life. Guaranteed.

According to Hollywood legend, the day mobster Bugsy Siegel drove from LA into the Mojave Desert and decided to finish raising a glamorous, tropical-themed casino under the searing sun, all there was here were some ramshackle gambling houses, tumbleweeds and cacti. Nobody thought anyone would ever come here. But everybody couldn't have been more wrong, baby.

Today, Las Vegas welcomes more visitors each year than the holy city of Mecca. In fact, it's the fastest-growing metropolitan area in the USA. Admittedly, its tourist traps, especially on the infamous Strip, are nonstop party zones. But scratch beneath the surface, and you'll find Sin City has much more on tap than just gambling, booze and cheap thrills. There are as many different faces to Nevada's biggest metropolis as there are Elvis impersonators or wedding chapels here.

Sprawled immodestly along Las Vegas Blvd, the Strip is a never-ending spectacle, especially at night with all of its neon lights blazing. Ever since Bugsy's Flamingo casino hotel upped the ante back in 1946, casino hotels have competed to dream up the next big thing, no matter how gimmicky. You can be mesmerized by the dancing fountain show outside of the ① **Bellagio**, an exploding faux-Polynesian volcano in a lagoon fronting the ② **Mirage**, singing gondoliers plying the artificial canals of the ③ **Venetian** or sexy pirates in a mock battle of the scxcs with pyrotechnics galore at ④ **TI (Treasure Island)**. Rise above the Strip's madness inside glass elevators shooting up the half-scale replica of the Eiffel Tower at ⑤ **Paris Las Vegas**, or ascend the 110-story ⑥ **Stratosphere Tower**, where the world's highest thrill rides await.

TIME
2 days

BEST TIME TO GO
Apr– Jun

START
Las Vegas, NV

END
Las Vegas, NV

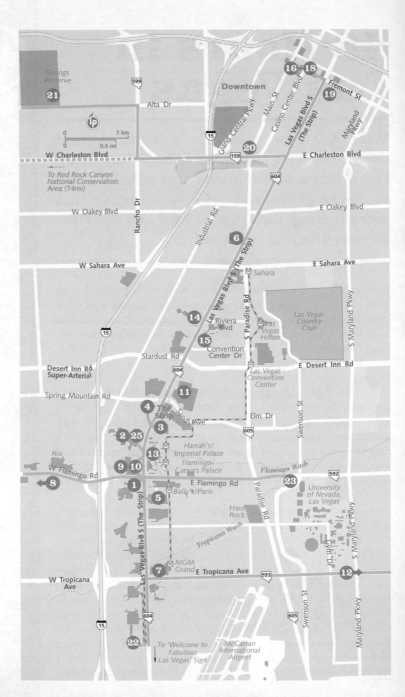

Springs
Preserve
21

Downtown

16 18
19
Fremont St

Main St

Casino Center Blvd

Grand Central Pkwy

Alta Dr

Maryland Pkwy

Las Vegas Blvd S
(The Strip)

0   1 km
0   0.5 mi

W Charleston Blvd
20
159
E Charleston Blvd

15
604

To Red Rock Canyon
National Conservation
Area (14mi)

W Oakey Blvd
E Oakey Blvd

Rancho Dr

Industrial Rd

Las Vegas Blvd S (The Strip)

6

W Sahara Ave
E Sahara Ave

Sahara
15

S Paradise Rd

S Maryland Pkwy

Las Vegas
Country
Club

14
Riviera
Blvd
Las
Vegas
Hilton

15
Convention
Center Dr

Stardust Rd
E Desert Inn Rd

Desert Inn Rd
Super-Arterial
604
Las Vegas
Convention
Center

Spring Mountain Rd

11

4 The
Strip
Sands Ave

Elm Dr
605

3

2 25

13 Harrah's/
Imperial Palace

Rio
Flamingo/
Caesars Palace

9 10
Flamingo Wash

592

W Flamingo Rd
23

8
E Flamingo Rd
University
of Nevada,
Las Vegas

1
Bally's/Paris

5
Hard
Rock

Paradise Rd

Swenson St

Tropicana Wash
Gym Dr

S Maryland Pkwy

7 MGM
Grand E Tropicana Ave
593
12

W Tropicana
Ave

Las Vegas Blvd S (The Strip)

Swenson St

605

Maryland Pkwy

15
604

22

To 'Welcome to
Fabulous
Las Vegas' Sign

McCarran
International
Airport

All of this showy stuff is old hat for Las Vegas. This century-old city is quickly metamorphizing into a sophisticated but still sexy and sybaritic destination. Boutique hotels-within-hotels – for example, the Signature Suites at ❼ MGM Grand or the high-rise ❽ Palms Place – star chefs' restaurants (including a recent invasion of high-flying Frenchmen led by ❾ Restaurant Guy Savoy), and indulgent spas like Caesars Palace's ❿ Qua Baths & Spa, where artificial snowflakes fall in the unusual Arctic Room, are what hip, younger crowds demand. Ironically, this polish and sophistication hearken back to Old Vegas' heyday in the "Fabulous '50s," when mobsters mixed with Rat Pack movie stars and even showgirls dressed in diamonds and silk to just step inside a casino. The most decadent high-roller casino resorts like ⓫ Wynn Las Vegas each have their own galaxy of catwalk couture shops, epicurean restaurants and entertaining diversions, from Broadway shows to nightclubs on par with LA or NYC. To gawk at the VIPs, stroll through the front doors anytime – they're free, and they never close.

You can still find the kitschier and oh-so-cheesy side of Las Vegas. After all, this is the city that brought fame and fortune to flamboyant Liberace, and staged a 1968 comeback show for Elvis outfitted in a rhinestone-studded jumpsuit. Pay your respects at the outrageous ⓬ Liberace Museum, stuffed with hand-painted antique pianos, luxury cars including a mirror-tiled Rolls Royce, and a collection of feathered capes and million-dollar furs. Elvis has indeed left the building, but you can still play blackjack with the King at the ⓭ Imperial Palace, where "dealertainers" do double duty as casino card dealers and celebrity impersonators. Speaking of casinos, there's none tackier than the 1960s ⓮ Circus Circus, where trapeze artists, high-wire workers and jugglers steal center stage. Grab a seat at the revolving Horse-A-Round Bar, made famous by Hunter S Thompson's *Fear and Loathing in Las Vegas*. At the Slots-A-Fun casino next door, grab a coupon book, give the giant slot machine a free spin and scarf down a few 75¢ beers and $1 half-pound hot dogs; then relax and enjoy the laughable lounge acts. At the retro ⓯ Fireside Lounge, a swingin' '70s hideaway, cooing couples nestle into blue-velvet couches and make out like there's no tomorrow.

When you've exhausted the hurly-burly Strip, take yourself downtown to the ⓰ Fremont Street Experience, a five-block-long pedestrian mall with a canopy steroid-enhanced by a super-big Viva Vision screen and 550,000 watts of concert-hall sound. When the 12.5-million synchronized LEDs come on, its silly sound-and-light shows hypnotize passersby (especially anyone who's already drunk on those 99¢ fluorescent-pink margaritas sold in gigantic souvenir glasses). Fremont St is the city's historic quarter, preferred by serious gamblers who find faux volcanoes beneath them; the smoky, low-ceilinged casinos have changed little over the years. Check out the nerve-wracking, no-limit Texas-hold-'em action in the back room at ⓱ Binion's, where the World Series of Poker was born. Then stumble across the street to the ⓲ Golden Nugget, downtown's most posh address, to gawk at the Hand of Faith, the largest chunk of gold ever found, weighing 6lb 11oz. Oh, they've got an outdoor swimming pool with a three-story waterslide that shoots through a live-shark tank, too.

Fremont St is undergoing a renaissance of cool, with indie watering holes and nightclubs popping up, like the ⑲ **Beauty Bar**. On the tattered fringes of downtown, hidden among the vintage-clothing and antiques shops, is the emerging ⑳ **18b Arts District**. On the first Friday night of each month, these streets take on a carnival atmosphere as 10,000 art lovers, hipsters and indie musicians turn it into a big block party, with gallery openings, performance art, live music, fortune tellers and tattoo artists. You'll find more alt-cultural types at the Vegoose music and arts festival, with costumed partying over Halloween weekend, and auteurs at the CineVegas independent film festival in June.

> **DETOUR**
>
> When the ding-ding-ding of the slot machines drives you bonkers, **Red Rock Canyon** (☎702-515-5350; www.redrockcanyonlv.org) is the antidote. The startling contrast between the Strip's artificial neon glow and the awesome natural forces at work in the canyon can't be exaggerated. A 13-mile, one-way loop drive passes striking natural features, panoramic viewpoints and hiking trailheads. To get here from Las Vegas, take I-15 south to Hwy 160 or Charleston Blvd west to Hwy 159, either about a 20-mile drive.

Did you know that this artificial desert oasis also has a greener, more eco-friendly side? The immense ㉑ **Springs Preserve** is planted on the site of the once-bubbling springs that gave Las Vegas its Spanish name, "the meadows." It weaves together cultural and natural history in the OriGen Experience, then imagines a more sustainable future for Nevada at the Desert Living Center, with xeriscaped gardens and interpretive walking trails outside. Back on the Strip, Mandalay Bay's ㉒ **Shark Reef** has some of the world's last remaining golden crocodiles. Go on a behind-the-scenes tour of this walk-through aquarium to find out more about species-conservation efforts. Or if history rocks your world, delve into the Cold War era at the Smithsonian-affiliated ㉓ **Atomic Testing Museum**, when monthly aboveground atomic blasts shattered casino windows as mushroom clouds rose on the horizon, and the city even crowned a "Miss Atomic Bomb" beauty queen.

No matter how many of Las Vegas' multiple personalities you flirt with – kitschy, extravagant, modern, racy, retro, arty or indie – don't leave town without trying the classic stuff. Plug a few bucks into a slot machine. Catch a stage show, whether it's a chintzy showgirl revue or an all-star production in the ever-expanding ㉔ **Cirque du Soleil** galaxy. Stuff yourself at an all-you-can-eat buffet at a luxury casino hotel, or feast at a steakhouse with all the trimmings, of which there are dozens on the Strip (though honestly, we're just as happy with an Angus burger, sweet-potato fries and a liqueur-spiked milkshake from ㉕ **BLT Burger**). Just don't take this city too seriously – or you'll miss out on all the fun.

Sara Benson

TRIP INFORMATION

GETTING THERE

From Albuquerque, take I-40 west to King-man, then US Hwy 93 north; from Phoenix, take US Hwy 60 northwest to I-40.

DO

Atomic Testing Museum

Buy your tickets for this engaging multimedia museum at the replica Nevada Test Site guard station. ☎ 702-794-5161; www.atomic testingmuseum.org; 755 E Flamingo Rd, Las Vegas; adult/child $12/9; ⏱ 9am-5pm Mon-Sat, 1-5pm Sun; ♿

Bellagio

The Italianate resort's faux Lake Como and choreographed fountains are an absurdist antithesis of desert life. ☎ 702-693-7111; www.bellagio.com; 3600 Las Vegas Blvd S; admission free; ⏱ fountain shows 3pm-midnight Mon-Fri, noon-midnight Sat & Sun

Binion's

When the ex-Horseshoe opened in 1951, Texas gambler Benny Binion transformed Fremont St from a row of sawdust gambling halls into classy carpet joints. ☎ 702-382-1600; www.binions.com; 128 E Fremont St; admission free; ⏱ 24hr

Circus Circus

On the Midway you'll find carnival games and circus acts galore. ☎ 702-734-0410; www.circuscircus.com; 2880 Las Vegas Blvd S; admission free; ⏱ shows every 30min 11am-midnight; ♿

Cirque du Soleil

Catch the troupe's signature aerial acrobats at various casino hotels around town. www .cirquedusoleil.com; admission $60-150; various locations; hschedules vary

Fremont Street Experience

Streaking right down the middle of down-town's historic "Glitter Gulch." ☎ 702-678-5600; www.vegasexperience.com; Fremont St, btwn Main St & Las Vegas Blvd; admission free; ⏱ shows hourly dusk-midnight

Imperial Palace

Celebrity impersonators jump up from the blackjack tables to show off their song-and-dance skills. ☎ 702-731-3311; www .imperialpalace.com; admission free; 3535 Las Vegas Blvd S; ⏱ shows every 30 min noon-4am

Liberace Museum

Connoisseurs of kitschy celebrity shrines, don't miss this memorial to 'Mr Showman-ship.' ☐ 702-798-5595; www.liberace.org; 1775 E Tropicana Ave; adult/child $15/10; ⏱ 10am-5pm Tue-Sat, noon-4pm Sun, guided tours 11am Tue-Sat & 2pm Tue-Sun

Mirage

When the volcano erupts, it inevitably brings traffic to a screeching halt. ☎ 702-791-7111; www.mirage.com; 3400 Las Vegas Blvd S; admission free; ⏱ shows hourly 8pm-midnight, from 6pm/7pm in winter/spring

Paris Las Vegas

Gustave Eiffel's original drawings were consulted before building this 50-story replica tower. ☎ 702-946-7000; www .parislasvegas.com; 3645 Las Vegas Blvd S; admission free, tower elevator adult/child $10/7; ⏱ 9:30am-12:30am, weather permitting; ♿

Qua Baths & Spa

A homage to ancient Roman bathing rituals, with social spa-going encouraged in the tea lounge. ☎ 731-7776, 866-782-0655; www .harrahs.com/qua; Caesars Palace, 3570 Las Vegas Blvd S; ⏱ 6am-8pm

Shark Reef

Two thousand submarine beasties call M-Bay's walk-through aquarium home. ☎ 702-632-4555; www.mandalaybay.com; Mandalay Bay, 3950 Las Vegas Blvd S; adult/child $16/11; ⏱ 10am-11pm, last entry 10pm; ♿

Springs Preserve

Forward-thinking eco-museum takes visitors on an incredible trip through historical, cul-tural and biological time. ☎ 702-822-7700;

www.springspreserve.org; 333 S Valley View Blvd; adult/child $19/11; ⏱ 10am-6pm, trails close at dusk; ♿

Stratosphere Tower
High-altitude thrill rides cost extra, but they're pretty much worth it. ☎ 702-380-7777; www.stratospherehotel.com; 2000 Las Vegas Blvd S; adult/child $14/10; ⏱ 10am-1am Sun-Thu, 10am-2am Fri & Sat, weather permitting; ♿

TI (Treasure Island)
Laugh at the hilarious "Sirens of TI" show, in which feisty, bad-girl buccaneers clad in lingerie do battle. ☎ 702-894-7111; www.treasureisland.com; 3300 Las Vegas Blvd S; admission free; ⏱ shows usually 7pm, 8:30pm, 10pm & 11pm

Venetian
Graceful bridges and flowing canals almost capture the romantic spirit of Venice. ☎ 702-414-4300; www.venetian.com; 3355 Las Vegas Blvd S; admission free, gondola rides $12.50-60; ⏱ 10am-10:45pm Sun-Thu, 10am-11:45pm Fri & Sat

EAT & DRINK

Beauty Bar
Swill a cocktail and listen to live bands and DJs inside the salvaged innards of a 1950s beauty salon. ☎ 702-598-1965; www.beautybar.com; 517 E Fremont St; admission free-$10; ⏱ usually 9:30pm-late Sat-Thu, 5pm-late Fri

BLT Burger
French-trained chef Laurent Tourondel dishes up *haute* reinterpretations of classic Americana. ☎ 702-792-7888; www.bltburger.com; Mirage, 3400 Las Vegas Blvd S; mains $12-18; ⏱ 11am-2am Sun & Tue-Wed, 10am-4am Mon & Thu-Sat; ♿

Fireside Lounge
Strangely spellbinding hideaway inside a old-school round-the-clock coffee shop. ☎ 702-735-4177; www.peppermilllasvegas.com; Peppermill, 2985 Las Vegas Blvd S; admission free, mains $8-23; ⏱ 24hr

Restaurant Guy Savoy
Intimate, mod French dining room is the sole US outpost of three-star Michelin chef Guy Savoy. ☎ 702-731-7286; www.guysavoy.com; Caesars Palace, 3570 Las Vegas Blvd S; tasting menu $190-290; ⏱ 5:30-10:30pm Wed-Sun

SLEEP

Golden Nugget
Generously cut, almost gorgeous rooms for anyone hip to the downtown scene. ☎ 702-385-7111, 800-846-5336; www.goldennugget.com; 129 E Fremont St; r $69-250

MGM Grand
There are plenty of rooms and suites to choose from at the world's largest hotel. ☎ 702-891-7777, 800-929-1111; www.mgmgrand.com; 3799 Las Vegas Blvd S; r $80-500; ♿

Palms Place
All-suites condo hotel and co-ed spa lets you flaunt your VIP status in style. ☎ 702-932-7777, 866-942-7773; www.palmsplace.com; 4321 W Flamingo Rd; ste $159-749

Wynn Las Vegas
Five-diamond resort rooms are bigger than your apartment, and come with all the little luxuries. ☎ 702-770-7100, 877-321-9966; www.wynnlasvegas.com; 3131 Las Vegas Blvd S; r $199-515

USEFUL WEBSITES
www.vegas.com
www.visitlasvegas.com

LINK YOUR TRIP
www.lonelyplanet.com/trip-planner

Fantastic Canyon Voyage

WHY GO Take the slow road to Arizona's biggest attraction and weave your way through the heart of cowboy country. Along the way, discover where hippies and New Age followers have claimed whole towns, and get ready to spill your drink when you finally lay eyes on the greatest hole on earth.

TIME
4 – 5 days

DISTANCE
400 miles

BEST TIME TO GO
May – Nov

START
Phoenix, AZ

END
Grand Canyon

ALSO GOOD FOR

Head out of Phoenix on Grand Ave (Hwy 60) and notice how the industrial boulevard that used to be a haven of strip clubs is seeing more cute cafés and hip places to nosh. Sometimes when traffic is light here – rarely – you can beat the train on the tracks that parallels the street – at least for a short time.

On the way, you'll go through ❶ Peoria, a small suburb where wholesomeness and family values still reign supreme – the school-board and city-planning meetings here are often jam-packed because the people here really are that community-minded. Soon you'll pass through ❷ Sun City – it's the original retirement community, and at least one resident of every home has to be over 55. If you're tempted to poke around on the smaller streets, two warnings: many of the streets are circular, so it's pretty easy to get lost; and a golf cart is the preferred mode of transportation for many of the seniors that live here. Pack patience.

About 60 miles northwest of Phoenix, lush desert is crisscrossed by small creeks in ❸ Wickenburg, the dude-ranch capital of Arizona (preferred terminology is "guest ranch," but we'll abide by dude, thank you). It gives a good flavor of what the West was really like. If the kids are fighting in the back seat – or your traveling companion is naughty – take them to the 19th-century Jail Tree, where outlaws were chained in the late-1800s.

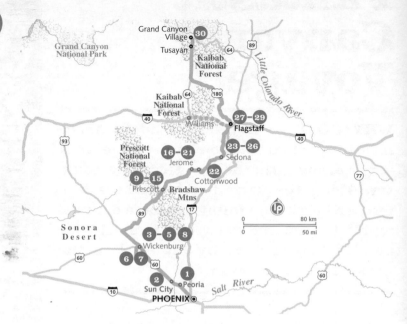

Continue the old-fashioned good times in the lap of modern luxury at ❹ **Rancho de los Caballeros**. The main lodge gives way to cozy rooms decked out stylishly with Indian rugs and handcrafted furniture. Dinner is a dress-up affair, but afterwards you can go all footloose in the saloon.

The next morning, get giddy up at ❺ **Pony Espresso**. Sit a spell on one of the overstuffed sofas of this funky coffee shop with red walls and lots of books and chess tables. Once you've been sustained by the selection of scones and brownies on offer, stock up on sandwich supplies and head out of town, circling down to the ❻ **Vulture Mine**, where Austrian immigrant Henry Wickenburg staked his claim and made his fortune. Take yourself on a guided tour which runs past the main shaft – where $30 million worth of gold was mined – the blacksmith shop and other dusty old buildings. Dogs are welcome here; just ensure they are leashed.

On the way back to Wickenburg, stop to eat your sandwiches at Hassayampa River. Located just southeast of town, this is one of the few riparian habitats remaining in Arizona and a great place for birders to spot everything from hawks to cuckoos. There's a helpful visitor center where you can pick up information and maps.

Now it's time to pump you up – with hearty Teutonic schnitzel, in honor of Herr Wickenburg. Return to Wickenburg, where the ❽ **House of Berlin** will have you saying *"Ich bin ein Berliner"* after chomping your way through the stuffed cabbage rolls, pork chops and other continental classics.

The next morning, head west on Hwy 60 and turn northeast onto Hwy 89/89A – the road with the best scenery and neatest towns in the state. As you drive, first you'll see the western edge of the Bradshaw Mountains, then soon enough you'll see the brown "Now Entering Prescott National Forest" sign, with the yellow cursive letters looking straight from the 1950s. The Sonora desert rises to meet pine trees; juniper (the most twisted and scrubbiest-looking) at the lower elevations and then finally, at the highest elevations, ponderosa.

Drag your eyes away from the forest views: you're nearly in **9** Prescott. The drive through the town is straight-forward enough, but if you do need to stop for directions, wow the locals by pronouncing the last syllable of Prescott as "kit" not "scott." No matter how you say it, this place is like a slice of small-town Ohio in the middle of rugged Arizona. It's two towns, in a way. There's the block-long Whiskey Row, a string of bars that's been quenching the parched gullets of miners, gunfighters and adventurers since the 1800s. Then there's the rest: quiet streets, historic hotels, street fairs outside the old courthouse, antique shopping and three worthy museums, each dedicated to a different side of the Western experience.

Check in to the aptly named **10** Pleasant Street Inn, a four-unit Victorian with forest-green shingle siding set just three blocks from the downtown action. Start the museum tour at **11** Sharlot Hall Museum, a general historical museum and collection of restored log cabins that trace the history of Prescott's territorial capital days. Keep an eye open for the governor's restored log cabin "mansion." After that, duck into the **12** Smoki Museum, which is built like a Native American pueblo. This place showcases Southwestern Native American history from the prehistoric through to the present. Now make your way to the **13** Phippen Museum cowboy and Western art museum, 7 miles north of town. Named after the late George Phippen – a local self-taught artist who helped put Western art on the map – it's worth a visit to see that the range of Western art is broader than oil paintings of weather-beaten faces under broad hat brims.

"...wow the locals by pronouncing the last syllable of Prescott as "kit" not "scott."

Brain full and belly empty, dress up a bit and strut like a brightly plumed bird into the **14** Peacock Room & Bar. Dinner is a touch fancy, but the classic American fare – like slow-roasted prime rib and crab-stuffed salmon – is great. Now you can visit Whiskey Row on a full stomach. In a perfect world, after you pushed open the swinging doors at **15** Palace Saloon and sauntered in, the whole place would get quiet and the music would stop. In reality, someone will politely ask if you want a table or to sit at the bar. Don't let that take away from the old West pedigree of the place; the Earp brothers used to knock 'em back with Doc Holliday at the huge Brunswick bar.

After your night in the saloon, prepare yourself for a completely different world in the short space of 35 more miles on Hwy 89A. ⑯ Jerome, a city with twisting streets that are confusing but make for a fun drive, is an old mining town built into the side of Cleopatra Hill. If Prescott felt small, this place will feel minuscule, but there's a decidedly Bohemian vibe and there seem to be more art spaces than people. Aging hippies run many of the hotels and restaurants – they saved Jerome from decrepitude when Altamont ended an era and they dispersed in search of affordable charm.

> **DETOUR**
>
> **Williams**, 60 miles south of Grand Canyon Village and 35 miles west of Flagstaff on I-40, is a splendid place to base a Grand Canyon South Rim adventure. Plenty of classic Route 66 motels are here, and the old-school homes and train station charm the socks off of visitors. Best of all, visitors can ride the vintage train of the **Grand Canyon Railway** (www.thetrain.com) to the South Rim in comfort and style.

Jerome was a den of sin back when the United Verde Mine was booming in the late 1880s. Drunken miners with pockets full of money stumbled into town, and there were plenty of working girls hoping to make a quick buck of their own. The ⑰ Mile High Inn was the main stage in this drama back when it was a bordello, but now it's a charming seven-room B&B with a downstairs restaurant.

Chat up some burly but friendly-enough bikers (of both sexes) at the nearby ⑱ Spirit Room Bar. It's the main attraction in town; groups of Europeans fresh off their BMW motorcycles politely debate the merits of American beer with weekend hog (Harley) riders inside. Sup at ⑲ Grapes, which feels like an upscale diner with good steaks and lots of yummy wine, and call it a night. Or return to the Spirit Room for a nightcap or two, and maybe make some new friends – an open, friendly attitude goes real far.

The next morning, be sure to visit the ⑳ Jerome Artists Cooperative Gallery before leaving town. Around 30 local artists sell their wares here, and it's a pleasure to wander the place and talk with these creative locals about their adopted home.

Continue northeast on Hwy 89A – trust the signs, not your sense of direction or you'll be going the wrong way down the short stretch of one-way road in the center of Jerome. Two miles outside the town stop at ㉑ Jerome State Historic Park. Recently updated exhibits inside the 1916 mansion of mining mogul Jimmy 'Rawhide' Douglas give a glimpse into just how rootin'-tootin' Jerome was during its mining heyday.

You're now heading to Sedona. On the way, you'll have to slow down through the town center of **22** Cottonwood, where there are a few places to eat and some shops selling curios – underneath the neglected exteriors a lot of these places would charm with enough elbow grease; travelers who are looking to find the next big thing might want to stop and poke around here.

Spend some time in **23** Sedona, but know that the charms reveal themselves slowly. The pull of the place is in the land, and it can take a while to slow down and realize this isn't a huge movie backdrop. New Age types believe that these glowing red rocks hold vortices of high-octane spiritual energy. Outdoors types love the super-scenic hiking and biking trails. Kids just want to slide down the big, slick rocks into Oak Creek at Slide Rock State Park.

Be sure to dedicate some unstructured time to take in the natural beauty here – even if that means just staring at the red rocks. Set on six acres 500ft above the town, **24** Sky Ranch Lodge delivers on its name. The views from the rooms are nothing but blue sky and red rock. After settling in, head over to **25** Red Rock State Park and, if it's between April and October, sign up for a moonlight ranger-led hike. During the day the views impress, but under the pale light of the moon the towers of rock make hikers feel like they're walking through a dream.

Wake up with the sun and watch it rise over the glorious red rocks. After some much-recommended wandering through this special slice of nature, mosey over to **26** D'Lish Very Vegetarian. The vegetarian food is damn good, and even if you're not a vegan you'll find the meal satisfying.

Those who decided to skip Sedona for now can get a big dose of (small) city life in Flagstaff before heading up to one of the seven wonders of the natural world. **27** Hotel Monte Vista is the classic place to stay in Flagstaff – it banks on reputation and location more than on the quality of the rooms, but they are clean and comfy enough

HARMONIC CONVERGENCE

Native tribes have long considered the Sedona area – where the red rocks glow so brightly they look like they're about to explode – a sacred place. It wasn't until 1987 that Sedona's contemporary spirituality arrived in full force. That year, a worldwide meditation event called the Harmonic Convergence gave some people the idea that the Bell Rock formation would open to reveal an alien ship. The UFO never came (or came later, according to believers), but the New Age pilgrims stayed.

and many of them are decorated after the famous celebs who've stayed here: John Wayne, Freddie Mercury, Marilyn Monroe and…Air Supply. The hotel is also right in the heart of historic downtown Flagstaff, bounded on one side by busy Route 66 (and the loud-at-night train that parallels the route) and on the other by the sports paradise of the San Francisco Peaks. Americana meets outdoor adventure here – you're just as likely to see a car with a ski rack on top as a restored Studebaker making the iconic Route 66 trip.

Downtown Flagstaff is full of eating and drinking places. If you're here on a Friday or Saturday evening stop at ㉘ **Mountain Oasis Cafe** – it has flavors from around the world but its weekend prime rib is something to write home about. If it's not a weekend night, the reward is that the nightly stargazing at ㉙ **Lowell Observatory** will be a lot less crowded. Even people who aren't that into astronomy will still dig the old brass-and-wood scientific instruments that give the place a Lemony Snicket vibe. There are plenty of fascinating exhibits and a state-of-the-art space theater, but most people come to see the 1896 24in Clark Telescope where Clyde Tombaugh first spotted Pluto in 1930.

The next morning – and mornings really are best for the 90-mile trip through two national parks to the Grand Canyon Village – take 'er easy on Hwy 180 and Hwy 64. Most people speed to the canyon and miss the transitions on this drive, where there is nary a trace of civilization in sight. At first there are so many trees on the side of the road you're always in the shade and it's easy to feel chilly. You'll see the San Francisco Peaks through the tops of trees moving and jerking like in an old-fashioned movie because of the tricks of perspective at 60mph. Then, there's the big flat of the Coconino Plateau, where if you're lucky you'll see huge fields of little yellow wildflowers. Finally, more trees, but they're taller and straighter here, as if proud of the privileged location near the canyon.

Stop at the ㉚ **National Geographic Visitor Center** in Tusayan to pony up the $25 per-vehicle entrance fee and save yourself what could be a 30-minute wait at the entrance of the park. There's a neat IMAX film about the Grand Canyon here with all the stomach-dropping aerial shots you'd expect from the large-format film company. The real thing is just 7 miles north of here.

The strangest thing about a first-time visit to the Grand Canyon is that a person often expects a slow-build up of beauty with the canyon as the finale. In reality, things just look like they did ever since Flagstaff until you finally make it to the edge. Then, it takes a few minutes to let it sink in that this is live, not a painted scene. Then, well, there aren't the words to do it justice. You'll just have to see for yourself, and try not to spill your drink.

Josh Krist

TRIP INFORMATION

GETTING THERE
Wickenburg, Prescott, Jerome and Sedona are all northwest of Phoenix on Hwy 60 and Hwy 89A.

DO
Hassayampa River Preserve
A place for birders to go loony over 240 feathered residents, on the west side of Hwy 60, 3 miles southeast of town near Mile 114. ☎ 928-684-2772; admission $5; ☺ 7am-11am Fri-Sun mid-May–mid-Sep, 8am-5pm Wed-Sun mid-Sep–mid-May

Jerome Artists Cooperative Gallery
About 30 local artists working in pottery, painting, jewelry and other media sell their creations at fair prices here. ☎ 928-639-4276; www.jeromeartistscoop.com; 502 Main St, Jerome; ☺ 10am-6pm

Jerome State Historic Park
Two miles beyond Jerome en route to Cottonwood, look at the historical displays and the weathered mining equipment outside. ☎ 928-634-5381; www.pr.state.az.us; Hwy 89A, Jerome; adult/child $3/free; ☺ 8am-5pm

Lowell Observatory
Nightly stargazing. During the day 30-minute tours offered hourly between 1:15pm and 4:15pm. ☎ 928-233-3211; www.lowell.edu; 1400 W Mars Hill Rd, Flagstaff; adult/child/student/senior $6/3/4/4; ☺ 9am-5pm Mar-Oct, noon-5pm Nov-Feb

National Geographic Visitor Center
Stop here to pay your entrance fee and cruise through a special lane at the park entrance. ☎ 928-638-2468; www.explorethecanyon.com; Hwy 64, Tusayan; canyon admission per vehicle $25; ☺ 8am-8pm

Phippen Museum
Hosts changing exhibits of celebrated Western artists, including Prescott resident John Coleman. ☎ 928-778-1385; www.phippenartmuseum.com; 4701 Hwy 89, Prescott; adult/under 12 yr/concession $5/free/4; ☺ 10am-4pm Tue-Sat, 1pm-4pm Sun

Red Rock State Park
Ranger-led nature walks year-round, moonlight hikes from April to October. ☎ 928-282-6907; www.azstateparks.com; Lower Red Rock Loop Rd, Sedona; per vehicle $6; ☺ 8am-7pm May-Aug, 8am-6pm Apr & Sep, 8am-5pm Oct-Mar; ♿

Sharlot Hall Museum
More a collection of historic buildings than a tradition museum; see the governor's restored log cabin "mansion." ☎ 928-445-3122; www.sharlot.org; 415 W Gurley St, Prescott; adult/child $5/free; ☺ 10am-4pm Mon-Sat, noon-4pm Sun

Smoki Museum
The lowdown on Southwestern Native American history through artefacts dating from prehistory to the present. ☎ 928-445-1230; www.smokimuseum.org; 147 N Arizona St, Prescott; adult/student/senior/under 12 yr $5/3/4/free; ☺ 10am-4pm Tue-Sat, 1pm-4pm Sun

Vulture Mine
A high-producing gold mine from 1863 to 1942. Head west on Hwy 60, turn left onto Vulture Mine Rd and follow it for 12 miles. ☎ 602-859-2743; Vulture Mine Rd, Wickenburg; admission by donation $7; ☺ 8am-4pm; ♿

EAT & DRINK
D'Lish Very Vegetarian
Try the tamarind-glazed walnut burgers or raw zucchini pasta. The food will impress even die-hard meat eaters. ☎ 928-203-9393; 3190 W Hwy 89A, Sedona; dishes $6-12; ☺ 11am-8pm

Grapes
Everything on the menu has a wine pairing suggestion. Top-drawer pizza, pasta and steak in a classy but lively environment. ☎ 928-634-8477; 111 Main St, Jerome; mains from $10; ☺ breakfast, lunch & dinner

House of Berlin
Schnitzels with noodles and warm apple strudels and other Austro-German classics from Henry Wickenburg's corner of the world. ☎ 928-684-5004; 169 E Wickenburg Way, Wickenburg; dishes $10-16; ☯ lunch Wed-Sun, dinner Tue-Sun

Mountain Oasis Café
Food that ranges from Mediterranean to Japanese to Thai, and cuts of prime rib cooked just right on the weekends. ☎ 928-214-9270; 11 Aspen Ave, Flagstaff; mains from $10; ☯ 11am-9pm

Palace Saloon
There are plenty of framed photos and Old West memorabilia to distract from your pint of Palace Red. ☎ 928-541-1996; 120 S Montezuma St, Prescott; mains $8-20; ☯ lunch & dinner

Peacock Room & Bar
The fancy-pants dining room at the Hassayampa Inn is famous for its classic American dinners. ☎ 928-778-9434; Hassayampa Inn, 122 E Gurley St, Prescott; mains breakfast $6.50-11, lunch $10-14, dinner $18-32; ☯ breakfast, lunch & dinner

Pony Espresso
Scones, brownies and sandwiches provide sustenance. ☎ 928-684-0208; 223 E Wickenburg Way, Wickenburg; mains $4-7; ☯ 7am-8pm Mon-Fri, 8am-6pm Sat & Sun

Spirit Room Bar
A dark, old-timey place with a pool table and a bordello-scene mural on the wall. Live music on weekends and some weeknights. ☎ 928-634-8809; 166 Main St, Jerome; ☯ 10am-2am

SLEEP

Hotel Monte Vista
In downtown Flagstaff, ask for a quiet room if you're afraid the live music at the downstairs bar will irritate. ☎ 928-779-6971; www.hotelmontevista.com; 100 N San Francisco St, Flagstaff; r $70-140 Nov-Apr, $75-170 May-Oct

Mile High Inn
Home of the original mile-high club, apparently. Seven spiffy rooms have funky furnishings. ☎ 928-634-5094; www.jerome milehighinn.com; 309 Main St, Jerome; r with shared/private bathroom $85/125

Pleasant Street Inn
There are just four units; two suites (one with fireplace, the other with private deck), all decorated differently. ☎ 928-445-4774, 877-226-7128; www.pleasantbandb.com; 142 S Pleasant St, Prescott; r $125-175

Rancho de los Caballeros
With a golf course, a spa and fine dining, this 20,000-acre ranch is decidedly upscale. ☎ 928-684-5484; www.sunc.com; 1551 S Vulture Mine Rd, Wickenburg; r $400-620; ☯ mid-Oct–mid-May

Sky Ranch Lodge
Rooms, though fine, make less of an impression than the views. Spend the extra money and get a Rim View room. ☎ 928-282-6400, 888-708-6400; www.skyranchlodge.com; Airport Rd, Sedona; r $80-160

USEFUL WEBSITES
www.outwickenburgway.com
www.nps.gov/grca

LINK YOUR TRIP
www.lonelyplanet.com/trip-planner

Ghosts of the South Rim

WHY GO The South Rim's human side is a crazy quilt of colorful personalities – adventurous entrepreneurs carved out livings as prospectors, tourist guides and rustic hoteliers. Artists and architects, environmentalists and explorers counterbalanced the commercial scene, all the while creating the canyon's history and legends. All these spirited folk have left ghostly remnants of their presence here.

TIME
4 days

DISTANCE
185 miles

BEST TIME TO GO
Jul – Sep

START
Williams, AZ

END
Williams, AZ

Though local Native Americans have lived in the canyon since ancient times, the thrall of the South Rim drew a small stampede of intrepid folk in the late 1800s. Miners found the going too tough to live off mineral claims and turned to the tourist trade. While you're taking in the obvious grandeur of the canyon, get to know it more intimately by seeking out some lingering spirits of the South Rim.

The journey to the South Rim starts in Williams, where Route 66 spirit lives on in old-fashioned soda fountains and refurbished Victorian buildings like the ❶ Red Garter B&B. It's rumored that the apparition of a young woman occasionally makes herself known to guests at this former bordello. Spooked? Check into the friendly ❷ Grand Canyon Hotel instead, as it's haunted only by the charm of its themed rooms and comfortable hostel-style dorms.

Once you're settled in to your digs, head out on the town and have a Williams Wheat beer at the ❸ Grand Canyon Brewery before dinner at Williams' polished but casual ❹ Red Raven Restaurant, where the pork tenderloin with cranberry salsa is complemented by a respectable wine list.

HISTORY & CULTURE

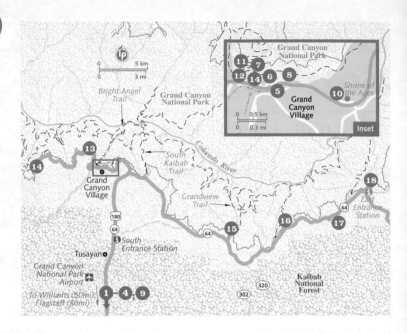

While Williams is admittedly a cute town, it doesn't coast on its looks. It's actually the hub of the ⑤ **Grand Canyon Railway**, which runs restored locomotives to the South Rim. When the railway debuted in 1901, it was *the* preferred mode of transport to the canyon. Despite fading into obsolescence for two decades as car culture burgeoned, the railway's back in business and is now a fun, convenient way to get to the canyon.

> "...the apparition of a young woman occasionally makes herself known to guests at this former bordello."

After your spiritual nocturnes, in the morning lace up your running shoes before you board the train, because you'll want to sprint to ⑥ **El Tovar** for lunch before the crowd catches up. After a bite in the elegant dining room, check in at ⑦ **Bright Angel Lodge & Cabins** and check out its History Room, just off the lobby. The displays explain some history of the Fred Harvey Company, which, along with the Santa Fe Railway, built out much of the South Rim infrastructure and accommodated the tourist boom to the canyon.

Walk eastward along the Rim Trail to enjoy huge canyon views in midday light, which appears to flatten the scenery into a sound-stage backdrop. Browse Zuni fetishes and geode magnets at ⑧ **Verkamp's Curios**, a family store that's been around since 1898, when John George Verkamp started selling souvenirs out of a tent on the rim. Finish with dinner before dark at the ⑨ **Arizona Room** to enjoy a rim-side view over smoky, roasted-vegetable enchiladas.

In the morning, take the Village shuttle to the Shrine of Ages, walking out back to quietly wander the ⑩ Grand Canyon Cemetery, where famous canyon figures have been laid to rest. The first to be buried here was the colorful prospector-turned-guide-turned-postmaster, John Hance.

By 1902 the South Rim had attracted photographer brothers Emery and Ellsworth Kolb, who established a home and studio perched on the rim next to the ⑪ Bright Angel Trail. Shuttle back to ⑫ Kolb Studio, where the brothers used to screen footage of their own wild adventures running the Green and Colorado Rivers in 1911. Have a relaxed lunch before hopping the Hermit Rd shuttle – first stop, ⑬ Powell Point, with a memorial to war veteran and geologist John Wesley Powell, the first to run the length of the Colorado. Pay tribute to the man's bravery, as he not only navigated and mapped the unknown river, but did it with only one arm.

At Hermit Rd's end is an arch leading to ⑭ Hermits Rest. Said hermit, a Canadian prospector and guide named Louis Boucher, lived 3 miles below the rim at Dripping Springs from 1889 to 1912. His namesake stone resthouse, now sheltering a snack bar and gift shop, was designed by South Rim superstar architect Mary Colter. On your way back to the village, take in a canyon sunset at any overlook that catches your fancy.

On your last day, tour Desert View Drive. ⑮ Grandview Point marks the trailhead where miner Peter Berry opened his Grand View Hotel in 1897. Remains of the mine can be seen from the trail, but the hotel is long gone; views from here are as spectacular as they sound. Another stunning view awaits at ⑯ Moran Point, named for Thomas Moran, a landscape painter

DETOUR

We may never know what happened to the Sinagua people, a name given because we have no knowledge of what they called themselves. Around 1425, entire populations suddenly abandoned their pueblos around the central Arizona area for reasons not fully understood. One such abandoned pueblo is beautiful **Walnut Canyon** (www.nps.gov/waca), a dramatic landscape of sheer limestone cliffs and buttes amid ponderosa forest, where you can hike alongside cliff dwellings. Walnut Canyon is 11 miles southeast of Flagstaff off I-40.

whose work aided in designating the Grand Canyon as a national monument in 1908. Further along the road is ⑰ Tusayan Ruins & Museum, where you can walk around the remains of an excavated Puebloan village dating to 1185. Finally, at the end of the road lies the ⑱ Watchtower, another Mary Colter masterpiece, inspired by ancient Puebloan watchtowers. The terrace provides panoramic views of canyon and river, and climbing the circular staircase inside takes you past Hopi murals and leads to the 360-degree views on the top floor. High-tail it back to the village and wave goodbye to the South Rim characters on the late-afternoon train back to Williams.

Wendy Yanagihara

TRIP INFORMATION

GETTING THERE
The South Rim lies 70 miles north of Williams, which in turn is located 35 miles west of Flagstaff.

DO

Grand Canyon Railway
Ride the rails and forgo the hassle of traffic and parking on the South Rim. ☎ 800-843-8724; www.grandcanyonrailway.com; 233 N Grand Canyon Blvd, Williams; adult/child from $75/40; departures from Williams vary seasonally ☽ 8:30-10am; ♿

Kolb Studio
The Kolb brothers' former home and studio now houses a small museum and bookstore. ☎ 928-638-2771; Grand Canyon Village; admission free; ☽ 8am-7pm; ♿

Tusayan Ruins & Museum
The tiny museum features ancient Puebloan split-twig animals found intriguingly in canyon crevices. ☎ 928-638-7888; 22 miles west of Grand Canyon Village, Desert View Dr; admission free; ☽ 9am-5pm; ♿

Verkamp's Curios
Designed by architect Charles Whittlesey, this souvenir shop has been around as long as the Grand Canyon has been a destination. ☎ 928-638-2242, 888-817-0806; www.verkamps.com; Grand Canyon Village; ☽ 9am-6:30pm

EAT & DRINK

Arizona Room
Since it doesn't take reservations, chat up your fellow waitlisters over a cocktail just outside. ☎ 928-638-2631; Grand Canyon Village; lunch $8-13, dinner $16-27; ☽ 11am-3pm Mar-Oct, 4:30-10pm Nov-Dec; ♿

Grand Canyon Brewery
Typical pub fare accompanies the Williams brews. ☎ 928-635-2168; www.grandcanyonbrewingco.com; 233 W Rte 66, Williams; pints $4.50, pitchers $15; ☽ 3pm-midnight Mon-Thu, 11am-midnight Fri-Sun; ♿

Red Raven Restaurant
Fresh, creative and sophisticated cuisine in a casual and unpretentious atmosphere. ☎ 928-635-4980; www.redravenrestaurant.com; 135 W Rte 66, Williams; lunch $6-10, dinner $10-22; ☽ 11am-2pm & 5-9pm Tue-Sun; ♿

SLEEP

Bright Angel Lodge & Cabins
The cabins are most coveted, but lodge rooms (with shared shower) are cozy and immaculate. ☎ 928-638-2631; www.grandcanyonlodges.com; Grand Canyon Village; r $79-90, cabins $111-159, ste $138-333; ♿

El Tovar
By far, the most upscale hotel on the South Rim, with loads of character. ☎ 928-638-2631; www.grandcanyonlodges.com; Grand Canyon Village; r $174-268, ste $321-426; ♿

Grand Canyon Hotel
Reasonably priced and centrally located on Route 66, this historic building has unique rooms and friendly vibes. ☎ 928-635-1419; www.thegrandcanyonhotel.com; 145 W Rte 66, Williams; dm $20, r $60-110; ♿

The Red Garter B&B
With only four rooms and the most delectable pastries in town, it's best to book ahead. ☎ 928-635-1484; www.redgarter.com; 137 Railroad Ave, Williams; r $120-145

USEFUL WEBSITES
www.grandcanyon.org
www.grandcanyonhistory.org

LINK YOUR TRIP
www.lonelyplanet.com/trip-planner

South Rim Art

WHY GO Artists have long been seduced by the natural majesty of the Grand Canyon, and they've left their mark. Now it's your turn to photograph or paint the South Rim, explore the rim's history and shop for Native American art and jewelry along the way.

Two of the most visible artists on the South Rim were – and are – the Kolb brothers, Emery (1881–1976) and Ellsworth (1876–1960), who built their photography studio teetering just above the Bright Angel Trail in 1903. Among their many enterprises was snapping shots of mule-riding tourists heading down the trail. Because there was no running water on the South Rim, they had to run 4.6 miles down to Indian Garden to develop the prints, and then hike back up to ❶ **Kolb Studio** to sell the prints to the tourists.

Go around the studio to find the ❷ **Bright Angel Trailhead**; hike about 2 miles down and you can spot ancient petroglyphs on a boulder above the trail, the marks of anonymous Native American hands from thousands of years before the Kolbs showed up.

See what contemporary Native Americans are creating at ❸ **Hopi House**, one of many buildings on the South Rim designed by architect Mary Colter (1869–1958). Inside, find authentic Native American handicrafts for sale, as well as high-quality pawn jewelry if you're a collector of vintage squash-blossom necklaces or inlaid belt buckles. The building itself was based on traditional Hopi architecture and built from local materials, largely by Hopi workers.

Cross over to ❹ **El Tovar Lounge**, order yourself a prickly-pear margarita to take out to the porch swing and consult *The Guide* (which you'll receive upon entering the park) for current sunrise and sunset

TIME
1 – 3 days

DISTANCE
90 miles

BEST TIME TO GO
Year-round

START
Canyon Village, AZ

END
Tuba City, AZ

ALSO GOOD FOR

OUTDOORS

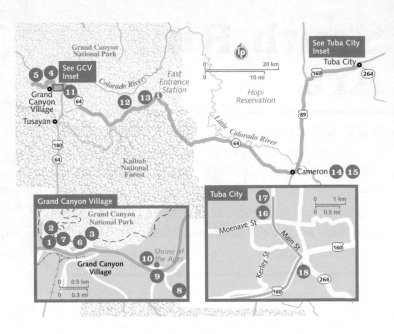

times. This will help you plan your pre-dawn strategy to snap a gallery-worthy sunrise photo tomorrow morning. Noting your ideal wake-up hour, mosey over to your rim-view cabin at the rustic, Colter-designed **5 Bright Angel Lodge & Cabins** and turn in early. Starving artists might find the lodges a bit pricey, in which case **6 Mather Campground** is a good, central place to stay. And if you've totally blown your budget on a tube of alizarin crimson, there's free dispersed camping in Kaibab National Forest, just outside the park.

"...you can't really go wrong – the light transfiguring the spires and buttes is mystical..."

Next morning, stumble bleary-eyed to catch an early Hermits Rest shuttle – or drive yourself if Hermit Rd is open to private vehicles. You've got your camera and tripod, as do a hundred other people with the same idea, but carefully hike beyond any parking lot and you'll find plenty of fine viewpoints. Favorite overlooks for sunrises are **7 Hopi Point** and **8 Pima Point**, but on Hermit Rd you can't really go wrong – the light transfiguring the spires and buttes is mystical from any overlook.

Once you've caught your shot, ride the Village shuttle over to **9 Canyon Village Marketplace** for coffee. It's a pleasant walk from here to the Shrine of Ages, behind which lies the **10 Grand Canyon Cemetery**. You're here to pay your respects to Gunnar Widforss (1879–1934), the Swedish painter whose meticulously layered watercolors depicted the canyon's light and details with stunning sensitivity. You'll also come across the Kolb brothers, who are interred here along with many other of the region's pioneers. Inspired, head over to the bookstore at ⑪ **Canyon View Information Plaza** and peruse the shelves for Widforss prints or discover your new favorite Grand Canyon artist among the posters and books.

Time your departure from the park before sunset, following Desert View Dr to find an overlook to your liking. ⑫ **Moran Point** and ⑬ **Lipan Point** are perennial knockouts, though the former might be a more fitting tribute to Thomas Moran (1837–1926), the British-born painter whose atmospheric landscapes of the American West helped inspire Congress to create the national park system.

RIVER RETREATS

Most Colorado River outfitters (www.gcroa.org) run specialized trips for painters; contact an outfitter directly to see what they offer. One- or two-day painting trips are sometimes offered through **Colorado River Discovery** (www.coloradoriverdiscovery.com) in Page

Head east out of the park and aim for Cameron. It'll be dark by now, so you'll miss the signs saying "Friendly Indians," then "Turn Around Now" followed by "It's Not Too Late" in front of the Navajo stands selling juniperberry-and-bead jewelry during the day. Check in at ⑭ **Cameron Trading Post**, complete with hand-carved furniture and views of the Little Colorado River Gorge, and wake in the morning to the sight of its lush garden, then browse the vast selection of Native American jewelry and handicrafts. If nothing catches your eye, head down the highway to the smaller, sedate ⑮ **Navajo Arts & Crafts Enterprise**, selling jewelry, findings, loose stones and other raw materials.

"There's a deepness and a depth to the Grand Canyon that doesn't exist anywhere else, and so many colors and different textures of rock. And there's the river, of course. I express what's in front of me when it's right in front of me, but I usually try to sit with the place I'm painting and really feel it, and see what catches my eye the most, and get all the colors in my head before I even start."

Serena Supplee, Moab, UT

Traveling deeper into the Navajo Reservation, head up Hwy 89, hang a right at Rte 160, and turn left at the big intersection with Main St. On the corner of Main and Moenave Rds is the funky, octagonal ⑯ **Tuba City Trading Post**, which carries quality Navajo rugs, ranging from Klagetoh patterns to Santa Claus. Just behind the trading post on Main, tuck into a Navajo taco (essentially a taco wrapped in Navajo fry bread instead of a tortilla) at ⑰ **Hogan Restaurant** before heading back out of town. Back at Rte 160 and Main, pore over beads at ⑱ **Mary's Bead Store** at the Tuuvi Travel Center complex, get a cold drink, and hit the road.

Wendy Yanagihara

HISTORY &
CULTURE

TRIP INFORMATION

GETTING THERE
The South Rim of the Grand Canyon lies 92 miles northwest of Flagstaff and 240 miles north of Phoenix.

DO

Cameron View Information Plaza
The Books & More store carries a wide, canyon-centric selection of books, videos, artwork and gifts. ☎ 928-638-0199; Grand Canyon Village; ⌚ 8am-8pm

Hopi House
Worth a look both for its architecture and its wares – a good place for high-quality Native American handicrafts. ☎ 928-638-2631; Grand Canyon Village; ⌚ 8am-8pm May-Aug, 9am-5pm Sep-Apr

Kolb Studio
The Kolb brothers' former home and studio now houses a small museum and bookstore. ☎ 928-638-2771; Grand Canyon Village; admission free; ⌚ 8am-7pm; ♿

Mary's Bead Store
Beads, fetishes and jewelry, conveniently located in the Hopi-run Tuuvi Travel Center. ☎ 928-283-6300; Tuuvi Travel Center, Rte 160 & Hwy 264, Tuba City; ⌚ 8am-7pm Mon-Fri, 10am-6pm Sat-Sun

Navajo Arts & Crafts Enterprise
Navajo cooperative selling jewelry, supplies, and some rugs and pottery. ☎ 928-679-2244; www.gonavajo.com; Hwy 89 & Rte 64, Cameron; ⌚ 8am-7pm Mon-Sat, noon-6pm Sun

Tuba City Trading Post
Established in 1870 in this original building, it carries the usual tourist dreck but also fine handicrafts. ☎ 928-283-5441; Main St & Moenave Rd, Tuba City; ⌚ 8am-6pm Mon-Fri, 8am-5pm Sat & Sun

EAT & DRINK

Canyon Village Marketplace
The deli serves pizza and other simple fare, and the grocery has all the muesli and buffalo jerky you desire. ☎ 928-631-2262; Market Plaza, Grand Canyon Village; mains $5-10; ⌚ 7am-9pm; ♿

El Tovar Lounge
The best place on the South Rim for an evening drink, especially if you can swing a seat outside. ☎ 928-638-2631; www.grand canyonlodges.com; Grand Canyon Village; cocktails $5-7; ⌚ 11am-10pm

Hogan Restaurant
Been wanting to try a Navajo taco? Here's your chance. ☎ 928-283-5260; Main St & Moenave Rd, Tuba City; mains $8-21; ⌚ 6am-10pm Mon-Fri, 7am-10pm Sat & Sun; ♿

SLEEP

Bright Angel Lodge & Cabins
Lodge rooms with private toilets and shared showers have just enough character, though the cabins are the most coveted digs. ☎ 928-638-2631; www.grandcanyonlodges.com; Grand Canyon Village; r $79-90, cabins $111-159, ste $138-333; ♿

Cameron Trading Post
Tour buses and indie tourists alike stop here to shop or to decompress in the famous garden. ☎ 928-679-2231; www.cameron tradingpost.com; 466 Hwy 89, Cameron; ⌚ 6am-10pm May-Aug, 7am-9pm Sep-Apr

Mather Campground
Big, social, with coin-operated laundry, showers and well-dispersed campsites underneath the ponderosa pines. ☎ 800-388-2733; www.recreation.gov; Grand Canyon Village; sites $18; ♿ 🚐

USEFUL WEBSITES
www.nps.gov/grca/supportyourpark/air.htm
www.grandcanyon.org/kolb

www.lonelyplanet.com/trip-planner

LINK YOUR TRIP

Hualapai & Havasupai Journey

WHY GO Where else but here can you walk on a slab of glass suspended above the Grand Canyon's inner gorge? And where else can you find such otherwordly blue-green pools and waterfalls? These singular experiences in sacred places take you from rim to river on reservation lands.

The Grand Canyon's human history goes much further back than to just intrepid river runners and miner-cum-entrepreneurs on the bustling South Rim. But apart from sparse ruins and petroglyphs, the whispers of its earlier Native American culture are not so readily discerned in the national park. But contemporary Native American culture lives on at the Hualapai and Havasupai Reservations, both of which occupy lands along the southern rim of the canyon.

Well-known for their beadwork and basketry, the Havasupai (whose name translates as 'people of the blue-green waters') share the Yuman language with the Hualapai. Both tribes arrived at the Grand Canyon around AD 1150. Today both tribes' economic survival is tied to the tourist trade, although neither participates in the gaming industry. The traditional structure of Havasupai society, based on respect for tribal elders and the tribal council, remains in place despite outside pressures. Meanwhile, the Hualapai ('people of the pine trees') – known for their basketry and dolls but also the newer Grand Canyon West – continue to balance survival with their traditional values of stewardship of land they consider sacred. Each tribe administers its own section of the Grand Canyon independently of the National Park Service, and these vast lands have their own unique attractions.

The trip begins by eschewing the Vegas madness in favor of homey Boulder City: check into the historic ❶ **Boulder Dam Hotel**. Rooms

TIME
5 – 8 days

DISTANCE
420 miles

BEST TIME TO GO
**Apr – May,
Sep – Nov**

START
**Boulder City,
NV**

END
Williams, AZ

ALSO GOOD FOR

OUTDOORS

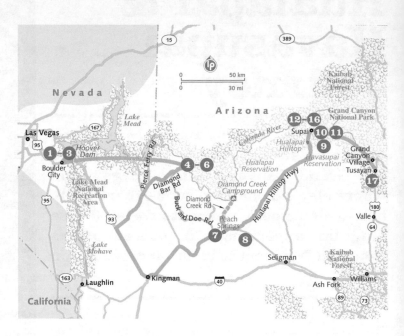

are on the smaller side, but are quaintly classy and within close walking distance of Boulder's small-town commercial district. With the afternoon to spare, drive out to Hoover Dam (Boulder Dam, if you prefer) and tour the cool, cavernous interior of this engineering marvel. When you resurface, beat the desert heat by cranking up the AC and blowing back into Boulder City for a cold drink and a bite to eat at ② **Boulder Dam Brewing Company**. Brewing a 'bolder damn beer,' naturally, the brewpub has a heavenly misted patio, the perfect spot to sip a Hell's Hole Hefeweizen. On the menu is typical pub fare like the classic ploughman's lunch of hearty bread, cheese, pickles and fresh apple slices.

> "...hike down to the 75ft-high Navajo Falls, cascading into a gorgeous swimming hole..."

In the morning, top up the gas tank for the three-hour, tooth-rattling drive to the Hualapai Reservation. Or fly in style with ③ **Scenic Airlines**, whose small planes ferry day-trippers from Boulder City airport to ④ **Grand Canyon West**. Run by the Hualapai tribe, this section of the West Rim offers windswept, unfettered views into the western canyon. And since 2007, novelty reigns with the addition of the much-vaunted ⑤ **Skywalk**. This U-shaped glass bridge cantilevered 4000ft over the canyon lets you look past your feet into the gaping maw below.

Another overlook not to overlook is ⑥ **Guano Point**, a superb picnic spot not so much for its shaded tables but for the post-lunch walk out to the point itself. There, the skeleton of a mine shaft remains, where bat guano (droppings) was once harvested for explosives, fertilizer and cosmetics. After a look at the river from above, descend via helicopter for a short trip on a pontoon boat, or book a full-day rafting trip for the next day with ❼ Hualapai River Runners, based out of Peach Springs. Rafts put in at Diamond Creek and run several fun rapids with a stop for a short waterfall hike, then a helicopter flies you back to the rim.

After a day at Grand Canyon West, the dusty road back through Joshua tree forest puts you onto Route 66. Settle in for the night at ❽ Grand Canyon Caverns & Inn, a quiet roadside motel with all the low-key kitsch and simple comforts you could ask of a Route 66 roadhouse, complete with a faux-ferocious T-rex out front.

Load up on eggs and pancakes at the inn's restaurant on your third morning, before a journey into one of the most magical spots in the Grand Canyon, on the ❾ Havasupai Reservation. Park in the Hualapai Hilltop lot and hoist your pack for the hot but beautiful 8-mile hike down to Supai village at the bottom of Havasu Canyon. Check into ❿ Havasupai Lodge, refuel with a simple burrito at the ⓫ Village Café and go to bed dreaming of blue-green waters.

In the morning, manifest those dreams with a hike down to the 75ft-high ⓬ Navajo Falls, cascading into a gorgeous swimming hole, and ⓭ Havasu Falls, pouring a hundred feet high into another jewel-toned pool. A quarter-mile from Havasu Falls, set up camp at cottonwood-shaded ⓮ Havasu Campground to while away a few days in the canyon. Just beyond lies 200ft ⓯ Mooney Falls, named after the miner who fell to his death here in 1882 – take his misfortune to heart and take the climb down carefully. Chains and ladders aiding the climb can be extremely slippery from the water's spray. ⓰ Beaver Falls, a series of smaller cascades, is another two miles downstream; getting there requires some scrambling, and crossing the creek several times, but in the end you'll be rewarded with several secluded pools near the river.

DETOUR On the Hualapai Reservation, where Diamond Creek flows into the Colorado River, **Diamond Creek Campground** bears the distinction of being the only spot in the Grand Canyon where you can drive directly down to the river. Rafters regularly use Diamond Creek as a put-in and take-out point; campers wishing to sleep by the river can get a first-come, first-served camping permit ($25 per person per night) at the Hualapai Lodge in Peach Springs, an hour's drive from the campground.

If you're short on time but thirsting for a dip in the Havasu pools, flit in for a day or overnight trip with ⓱ Papillon Grand Canyon Helicopters, based out of Tusayan and Las Vegas.

Wendy Yanagihara

TRIP INFORMATION

GETTING THERE
Boulder City is 23 miles from Las Vegas. Take Hwy 93 south from Las Vegas toward Phoenix.

DO

Havasupai Reservation
No lodgings? No love – without a booking, you'll be forced to leave Havasu Canyon. ☎ 928-448-2121; www.havasupaitribe.com; PO Box 160, Supai, AZ; adult/child $35/17.50, plus environmental care fee per person $5; ☽ 9am-5pm

Hualapai Reservation (Grand Canyon West)
The effort to get here and price of admission may be significant, but there's only one Skywalk. ☎ 877-716-9378; www.destination grandcanyon.com; Grand Canyon West, AZ; admission $30, parking $20; ☽ 7am-7pm Mar-Oct, 8am-4:30pm Nov-Feb

Hualapai River Runners
The only company to do one-day river trips in the Grand Canyon. ☎ 928-769-2219, 888-255-9550; www.destinationgrandcanyon.com/runners.html; Hualapai Lodge, 900 Rte 66, Peach Springs, AZ; one-day motorized trips $328; ☽ 8am-5pm; ♿

Papillon Grand Canyon Helicopters
Departures from Boulder City, Las Vegas and Tusayan. ☎ 702-736-7243, 888-635-7272; www.papillon.com; Grand Canyon National Park Airport, Hwy 64, Tusayan, AZ; admission adult/child from $120/100; ☽ 5am-11pm; ♿

Scenic Airlines
Helicopter and fixed-wing aircraft tours to Grand Canyon West. ☎ 702-638-3300, 800-634-6801; www.scenic.com; 3900 Paradise Rd, Suite #185, Las Vegas, NV; 1-day motorized trips $328; ☽ 5am-11pm; ♿

EAT & DRINK

Boulder Dam Brewing Company
Fresh, unadorned pub grub complements the tasty house beers. ☎ 702-243-2739; www.boulderdambrewing.com; 453 Nevada Way, Boulder City, NV; mains $5-9; ☽ 11am-9pm Sun-Thu, 11am-midnight Fri & Sat

Village Café
This Havasupai cafe has a limited and relatively pricey menu, but it's the only game in town. ☎ 928-448-2111; Supai, AZ; mains $10; ☽ 7:30am-7:30pm

SLEEP

Boulder Dam Hotel
Rates at this elegant Boulder Dam landmark include continental breakfast and free wireless internet. ☎ 702-293-3510; www.boulderdamhotel.com; 1305 Arizona St, Boulder City, NV; r $59-109

Grand Canyon Caverns & Inn
A non-cutesy Route 66 motel with amenities like wi-fi, pool, ATM and convenience store. ☎ 928-422-3223, 877-422-4459; www.gccaverns.com; Mile 115, Rte 66, AZ; r $75-85; ♿ ⊗

Havasu Campground
Surprisingly spacious and shaded by cottonwoods, with spring water and pit toilets. ☎ 928-448-2121, 928-448-2141; Havasupai Camping Office, PO Box 160, Supai, AZ; adult/child $17/8.50; ☽ check in 9am-5pm

Havasupai Lodge
Rooms at the lodge sleep up to four people; they have air-conditioning but no TVs or phones. ☎ 928-448-2111, 928-448-2201; www.havasupaitribe.com; PO Box 159, Supai, AZ; r $145; ☽ check-in 8am-5pm

USEFUL WEBSITES
www.destinationgrandcanyon.com
www.havasupaitribe.com

www.lonelyplanet.com/trip-planner

LINK YOUR TRIP

Hiking the North Rim

OUTDOORS

WHY GO Having lived and worked at the Grand Canyon for over 10 years – with a quarter of his job involving actual time roaming the backcountry – Ranger William Reese lets us in on the best of the North Rim, from spectacular sunset overlooks to multiday backcountry treks.

TIME
5 – 15 days

DISTANCE
300 miles

BEST TIME TO GO
May – Oct

START
Jacob Lake, AZ

END
Tuweep, AZ

ALSO GOOD FOR

ROUTE

"I don't wanna say it's like a cult, but people who make the effort to come here typically do their research beforehand; they read up and are more savvy about the Grand Canyon," says Reese. "They're mostly hikers, though not necessarily hardcore hikers, and birders. Some stay for up to two months at a time. But they really run the whole gamut."

Situated about 44 miles from the rim, ❶ Jacob Lake Inn is a welcome place to lay your head at the end of a long drive to the canyon. The inn is equipped with spacious rooms and appealing, heated cabins at the junction of Hwys 67 and 89A. In the morning, get the homemade toast with your eggs at ❷ Jacob Lake Inn Restaurant, and don't forget to pick up a couple of the big, home-baked peanut-butter cookies for later.

Driving through the hills of ponderosa forest that open out on rolling meadows in Kaibab National Forest, look out for mule deer as you approach the entrance to the park. Stop by the ❸ North Rim Backcountry Information Center to pick up a backcountry permit if you plan to do any multiday hikes or camp out on the North Rim. It's also a good idea to drop by just to find out about current weather and road conditions in and around the park.

Then get your first eyeful of the grand North Rim view as you enter the stone portico of Grand Canyon Lodge, pass through the sunroom and out along the narrow, quarter-mile path to ❹ Bright Angel Point; though paved, the path follows the spine of this promontory and has steep dropoffs on either side in some places. But the outcrop gives huge, unobstructed views into the canyon and across to the South Rim. On clear days, you can see all the way to the San Francisco Peaks, over 80 miles south.

Head back in to the rim, pick up sandwiches, salads and drinks at ❺ Deli in the Pines, and then drive out to the ❻ Widforss Point trailhead. This 5-mile trail follows the edge of a forested plateau, a pleasant walk in the shade with great rim-side views most of the way. The trail ends with the expansive views at Widforss Point, where you can enjoy a quiet picnic. Hike back the way you came, or stay the night somewhere in the woods; there's at-large camping here, with a backcountry permit.

> DETOUR
>
> "In the spring, the Thunder River/Deer Creek hike is a great backcountry hike if you have at least three days. At Surprise Valley, if you head east, you'll get to the cave where Thunder River Waterfall flows out. If you head west, there's another river and waterfall. The flowers will be blooming – mariposa lilies, prickly-pear cactus, columbine – it's really pretty."
>
> *Ranger William Reese*

"The North Rim has great hikes through rolling hills and forests of ponderosa pines, firs and spruce. Sometimes you'll even see a few Rocky Mountain maples, which turn a bright fuschia color in the fall, and the aspens turning golden. That's my favorite time here – mid- to late-September, when you have long sunny days, and there's a hard-to-describe sort of magical feeling here," says Reese.

When you arrive back at the lodge, make a reservation at the mule desk for a ride into the canyon the next day with ❼ Canyon Trail Rides, then cross the room and line up a dinner reservation at the ❽ Grand Canyon Lodge Dining Room. Pair your buttery wild salmon with one of the organic wines on the list, or just let the killer views from the high-ceilinged room enhance the flavors of your meal. After dinner, walk back out along the rim and look across the dark canyon at the twinkling lights of Grand Canyon Village on the South Rim. Then fall into sweet sleep in a cabin at ❾ Grand Canyon Lodge or your site at the ❿ North Rim Campground.

On your second day, saddle up for a mule ride down the ⓫ North Kaibab Trail; the full-day trek goes all the way to Roaring Springs, 5 miles down and the main source of water for both the North and South Rims. But if you're here to hike, hoof down on your own feet to see this wealth of water in the desert. With a backcountry permit, you can camp at Cottonwood Campground, 2.2 miles further down from the Roaring Springs trail junction, and hike back out the next day. The trail begins with steep switchbacks through aspen and fir, and on your ascent, you'll want to avoid this last, 3-mile

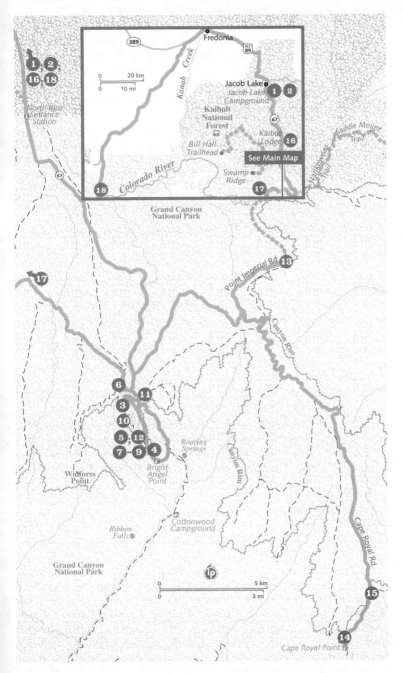

section of the hike during the heat of the day. Passing through Supai Tunnel and crossing the Redwall Bridge, the canyon walls rise steeply as you descend. Though the trail has some steep dropoffs, it's wide and well-maintained, and you'll marvel at how the trail passes from conifer forest to limestone cliff to scrubby desert as you hike.

> **DETOUR**
>
> "There's lots of human history at **Swamp Ridge**: Teddy's Cabin, the North Bass Trail. And it offers easy access to Powell Plateau, a living lab – a few different schools actually study there. It's never been mined, never logged, so there's never been a road there. The huge eco-question is: what would a natural ecological ponderosa forest look like? And this is the answer. You could do a day hike to the rim, or spend several days exploring.
>
> *Ranger William Reese*

Either way you do it, treat yourself on your return with a cocktail from the ⑫ **Roughrider Saloon** – take your glass out to the lodge terrace and put your feet up to drink in the view. Now that you've been below the North Rim, you'll have a deeper appreciation of this massive, complex gorge.

You'll need to wake early the next morning for the full-day hike out to ⑬ **Point Imperial**, along the Ken Patrick Trail. Point Imperial is one of the highest places on the North Rim, at 8800ft, with a terrific view of what explorer John Wesley Powell considered the start of the Grand Canyon. From here you can see Nankoweap, the Vermilion Cliffs, Marble Canyon and the Painted Desert. It's a superb locale for viewing the sunrise, and you can camp here without a backcountry permit as it's in Kaibab National Forest.

If you don't have two days to hike out and back (one day if you can park a vehicle at each end), you can just drive out for a look – the road goes right out to the point. Continue along the road to ⑭ **Cape Royal**, and enjoy an easy ramble to stupendous views of the canyon. There's even a designated wedding site here on a jutting precipice for romantics seeking an appropriately dramatic backdrop to their big day.

"...contemplate the views of the canyon's buttes and spires as the light and shadow slither over them."

With similarly stunning 270-degree views of the Painted Desert, San Francisco Peaks, and good views of where the river has cut into the Kaibab Plateau, ⑮ **Cape Final** is "one of the best places imaginable to watch the sunset," Reese says. "If you're interested in geology, you'll see some really amazing stuff here." You'll often find that the rocky outcrop at the end of the trail is completely deserted, apart from a raven or three. You'll need a backcountry permit if you want to stay at the one primitive campsite perched right next to the edge on the rim, with the bazillion-dollar view all to yourself. Otherwise, try to time your hike for sunset, and bring a headlamp for the 1½-mile walk out.

On the next day, take a high-clearance, four-wheel-drive vehicle to ⑰ **Point Sublime**, a place that lives up to its name. It's hard to get there and totally worth it – this is classic, breathtaking Grand Canyon scenery. Don't even think about taking a low-clearance vehicle down the dirt road, which is deeply rutted in some sections, and be well versed in the art of changing a tire. The 18-mile road to Point Sublime begins at the Widforss Point parking lot and passes through ponderosa forest before reaching a clearing. It then enters the forest again and eventually tapers into piñon and juniper scrub. The point is an excellent place to camp and contemplate the views of the canyon's buttes and spires as the light and shadow slither over them.

Returning from Point Sublime the next day, you'll have to leave the park, drive through the town of Fredonia and take a 61-mile BLM washboard road to get to your next, most remote port of call, so consider spending the night outside the park. Set yourself up in one of the older cabins at the ⑯ **Kaibab Lodge**, 18 miles from the rim, to get a jump on the next day's drive to Tuweep.

With one of the most outstanding overlooks in the park, ⑱ **Tuweep** is not typical of the North Rim. On the western end of the canyon and at a low elevation of 4552ft, it's extremely hot, and has more open views within the canyon, with fewer spires and buttes. The 3000ft vertical drop to the Colorado is nothing if not stunning, and at this point in the canyon, it's only about a mile across to the South Rim. Because of its remoteness, it has more of a wilderness feel to it. There are 10 primitive, first-come, first-served campsites, and as with Point Sublime, you'll need a four-wheel-drive to bump out there on the rough road. Be prepared for the unexpected – bring more water than you think you'll need, a spare tire or two, and your sense of adventure.

DETOUR Allow at least four days to hike the challenging but rewarding rim-to-river **Nankoweap Trail**. Or camp at the trailhead, which itself is located in the Kaibab National Forest. According to Reese, "The geology out there is so fascinating, if you know where the fault lines are going; they are so complex but so distinct. The trailhead is a great viewpoint for that."

Wendy Yanagihara

TRIP INFORMATION

GETTING THERE
Take I-15 north from Las Vegas through St George, then head eastward to Hwy 89 and south on Hwy 67.

DO
Canyon Trail Rides
Book half-day or full-day mule rides upon arrival at the Grand Canyon Lodge on the North Rim. ☎ 435-679-8665; www.canyonrides .com; North Rim; rides $30-125; ⌚ 7am-5pm, mid-May–mid-Oct

North Rim Backcountry Information Office
You'll need a backcountry permit for Cottonwood Campground or one of the campsites on the North Rim. ☎ 928-638-7868; www .nps.gov/grca/planyourvisit/backcountry permit.htm; North Rim; ⌚ 8am-noon & 1-5pm mid-May–mid-Oct

EAT & DRINK
Deli in the Pines
Get packaged but fresh takeout, or eat in at this one budget spot on the North Rim. ☎ 928-638-2611, 928-645-6865; www .grandcanyonforever.com; North Rim; mains $5-10; ⌚ 7am-9pm mid-May–mid-Oct; ♿

Grand Canyon Lodge Dining Room
Although the window tables are the most coveted for the views, you can't really go wrong at any table. ☎ 877-386-4383; www .grandcanyonforever.com; North Rim; mains $5-27; ⌚ 6:30-10am, 11:30am-2:30pm, 4:45-9:45pm mid-May–mid-Oct; ♿

Jacob Lake Inn Restaurant
During the winter, dining is only available at the counter and the kitchen closes a half-

hour earlier. Located 44 miles north of North Rim. ☎ 928-643-7232; www.jacoblake.com; mains $5-15; ⌚ 6:30am-9pm; ♿

Roughrider Saloon
Get espresso and pastries here in the morning, and post-hike cocktails to sip on the terrace in the evening. ☎ 928-638-2611, 928-645-6865; www.grandcanyonforever .com; North Rim; ⌚ 11:30am-11pm mid-May–mid-Oct

SLEEP
Grand Canyon Lodge
Comfortable, quiet cabins with private baths and heaters. ☎ 877-386-4383; www .grandcanyonforever.com; North Rim; r $107, cabins $111-156; ⌚ mid-May–mid-Oct; ♿ ⚘

Jacob Lake Inn
The peaceful, sweet cabins are a better deal than the perfectly comfortable motel rooms. Located 44 miles north of North Rim. ☎ 928-643-7232; www.jacoblake.com; r $108-147, cabins $84-136; ♿ ⚘

Kaibab Lodge
Acceptable alternative if you can't get a booking at Grand Canyon Lodge and don't want to stay as far as Jacob Lake. Located 18 miles north of North Rim. ☎ 928-638-2389; www.kaibablodge.com; cabins $85-155; ⌚ mid-May–mid-Oct; ♿ ⚘

North Rim Campground
Has a general store, a gas station, a coin-operated laundry and ponderosa-shaded campsites. ☎ 928-638-7814; http://reservations.nps .gov; North Rim; campsites $25; ♿ ⚘

USEFUL WEBSITES
www.grandcanyon.org/fieldinstitute
www.kaibab.org

LINK YOUR TRIP
www.lonelyplanet.com/trip-planner

OUTDOORS

Lazing on Lake Powell

WHY GO Controversy be damned, Lake Powell provides a cool respite from the desert heat. Paddling the lake in a kayak is ideal for exploring its small coves and side canyons – or let a guide do the paddling on a smooth-water float on the deep green waters below Glen Canyon Dam.

Even as you approach the lake, a glimpse of its sapphire-blue water through the undulating heat waves is almost enough to cool you down a smidge. Sliding a foot over the side of your kayak feels magnitudes better, and a quick, brave dip in the Colorado will take the edge off any heat-singed soul, as the water temperature hovers around a deliciously shivery 47°F year-round.

Ease onto the water with someone else at the oars with **1** Colorado River Discovery in Page. Running smoothwater floats on motorized or rowed rafts, these trips leaving from Lees Ferry are a relaxed introduction to the steep canyon walls and swirling eddies of the Colorado. Expert guides relate the rich history and geology of the canyon as you drift. Get your land legs back with a midday hike to **2** Horseshoe Bend, about 4 miles south of Page. The payoff is huge, with the trail only three-quarters of a mile and leading to a sudden dropoff at the crazy bend in the river that gives this lookout its moniker.

Backtracking to the dam, browse the interpretive displays at **3** Carl Hayden Visitor Center for some fascinating background on Lake Powell – completion of the enormous Glen Canyon Dam in 1963 culminated in the controversial flooding (and thus demise) of its eponymous canyon, creating Lake Powell in its place. Hour-long tours of the dam depart throughout the day, but if engineering isn't your thing, just wander out back for a look at the dam, and ponder how

TIME
3 days

DISTANCE
190 miles

BEST TIME TO GO
Apr – Oct

START
Page, AZ

END
Marble Canyon, AZ

ALSO GOOD FOR

HISTORY & CULTURE

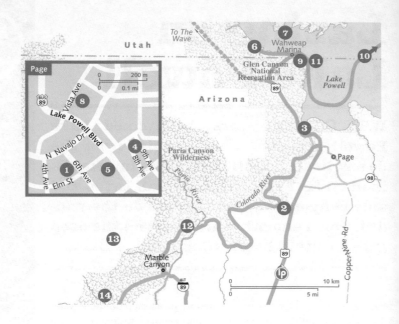

one ecosystem was created as another was destroyed, and how the controlled release of its water impacts communities and ecosystems from the dam to the ocean hundreds of miles away.

As the day's heat dissipates by degrees, check into one of the mom-and-pops on Page's "Old Motel Row". **4 Debbie's Hide A Way** is one favorite, with homey, fully-equipped suites and a slightly loopy garden peppered with tikis out back, an inviting spot for evening beers. For dinner, stroll over to Lake Powell Blvd and snag a terrace table at **5 Fiesta Mexicana** for Mexican comfort food and margaritas. Though both branches on the boulevard serve good *chile rellenos,* be careful which branch you choose, as the terrace-less one doesn't serve booze.

> "…you'll also see catfish jumping and wild ducks and grebes feeding along the shoreline."

But don't overdo it with the powerful margaritas, because next morning you'll be perfecting your power-paddle on Lake Powell. The easiest way to get on the water is to rent a kayak at **6 Lake Powell Boat Rentals** at Wahweap, in Glen Canyon National Recreation Area. You'll be sharing the water with houseboats, wakeboarders and Jet Skiers, but you'll also see catfish jumping and wild ducks and grebes feeding along the shoreline. You could meander the lake's coves and side canyons all day, but even given an hour you can paddle northwest around **7 Lone Rock**, a curious sandstone monolith rising out of the water.

If you're a more ambitious kayaker, consider going DIY. Hit up the friendly boating experts at **8 Bill and Toni's Marine** in Page. The no-nonsense but twinkly-eyed Bill and Toni will set you up with a kayak and everything else you'll need, such as bare-bones roof racks and paddles. They will also offer tips on the best places to launch and explore around the region. If a Jet Ski is more your speed, they rent personal watercraft, too.

After your time on the boat, and shrugging off your PFD (personal flotation device), give the arms a rest and limit yourself to simply lifting a G&T to your lips at the **9 Rainbow Room.** Floor-to-ceiling windows bring the lake right to your table at Page's swankest eatery, where sustainably caught fish and hormone-free beef get their Southwestern flair from flavors like green chile and roasted corn.

> **DETOUR**
>
> It's motionless and rock-solid, but the sinuous sandstone swirl known as **The Wave** in the Paria Canyon–Vermilion Cliffs Wilderness will move you anyhow. Only 10 walk-in permits are issued daily at the **Bureau of Land Management office** (http://paria.az.blm.gov) on Hwy 89 north of Page, just after mile marker 21. Show up before 9am (Utah time!) to enter your name in the daily lottery; if you win a spot, your permit is good for the *following* day. Plan for a six-hour hike.

Save the serious geological mind-boggle for your third day, with a visit to **10 Rainbow Bridge National Monument**, the largest natural arch in the world at 290ft tall and spanning 275ft. Hidden uplake on the Navajo Reservation, one look at the massive red arch against blue sky will explain why it's held sacred significance for local Native Americans throughout the ages. If you're not up for the multiday backcountry hike to Rainbow Bridge, **11 Lake Powell Scenic Cruises** runs full-day trips, departing from Wahweap Marina.

Leaving Lake Powell, have one last splash in the Colorado at **12 Lees Ferry** before spending the night in quiet Marble Canyon. Nestled at the foot of the burnt-orange **13 Vermilion Cliffs**, the roadside **14 Lees Ferry Lodge** is an appealingly unfussy motel, with porch chairs in front of the cobble-stone building providing front-row seats for stargazing before bed.

Wendy Yanagihara

FAR FROM THE MADDING CROWD

Take your sweet time paddling side canyons and sleeping under the stars on a multiday kayak-camping trip. Camping on Lake Powell doesn't require a permit (for stays shorter than 14 days) but does necessitate self-sufficiency and the packing out of all waste. For more information, visit the website for **Glen Canyon National Recreation Area** (www.nps.gov/glca). Be sure to get current information on conditions, as some cuts and canyons may be inaccessible due to varying lake levels.

TRIP INFORMATION

GETTING THERE
Page lies about 135 miles north of Flagstaff, a straightforward drive along Hwy 89 through the Navajo Reservation.

DO
Bill & Toni's Marine
Rent everything from kayaks to personal watercraft to boats here, and get insider information on the best places to explore. ☎ 928-645-2599; pwm@canyon country.net; 803 Vista Ave, Page, AZ; full-day kayak rental $25-45; ☾ 7am-7pm

Carl Hayden Visitor Center
Offers information on local activities and has excellent interpretive displays. ☎ 928-608-6404; Glen Canyon Dam, Hwy 89, AZ; admission free; ☾ 8am-6pm Memorial Day-Labor Day, to 4pm Dec-Feb, to 5pm rest of yr

Colorado River Discovery
Along with smooth-water trips, it also offers kayak backhaul services to Lees Ferry. ☎ 888-522-6644; www.raftthecanyon .com; 130 6th Ave, Page, AZ; half-day river trip adult/child $70/60; ☾ 6am-6:30pm; ♿

Lake Powell Boat Rentals
The easiest way to get on the water: rent, launch, paddle and drop off a kayak at Wahweap. ☎ 928-645-1111; www.lakepowell .com; Wahweap Marina, UT; full-day kayak rental $28; ☾ 7am-7pm

Lake Powell Scenic Cruises
Enjoy a full-day cruise on Lake Powell, the highlight of which is Rainbow Bridge. ☎ 800-528-6154; www.lakepowell.com; Lake Powell Resort, 100 Lakeshore Dr, Page, AZ; adult/child $148/92; ☾ 7am-7pm; ♿

EAT
Fiesta Mexicana
As festive as the name suggests, with down-home Mexican fare. ☎ 928-645-4082; 125 South Lake Powell Blvd, Page, AZ; mains $7-12; ☾ 11am-10pm

Rainbow Room
Lake views take the cake at Lake Powell Resort's restaurant. ☎ 928-645-1162; www.lakepowell.com; Lake Powell Resort, 100 Lakeshore Dr, Page, AZ; mains $12-28; ☾ 6am-10pm

SLEEP
Debbie's Hide A Way
Suites at Debbie's come complete with full kitchens, bathrooms and spacious living areas. ☎ 928-645-1224; www.debbies hideaway.com; 117 8th Ave, Page, AZ; r $39-159; ♿

Lees Ferry Lodge
The 10 rooms at this small motel are uniquely and comfortably furnished, and the porches are perfect for watching sunsets. ☎ 928-355-2231; vclodge@yahoo.com; Hwy 89A, Marble Canyon, AZ; r $70-112; 🐾

USEFUL WEBSITES
www.nps.gov/glca
www.nps.gov/rabr

LINK YOUR TRIP
www.lonelyplanet.com/trip-planner

Polygamy Country

WHY GO Upswept hairdos and pastel prairie dresses, averted eyes and gaggles of children. No, you haven't stepped into a Laura Ingalls Wilder time warp, this is modern-day southeastern Utah, where the Mormon religion holds strong, and a polygamous splinter group has taken the faith to some pretty serious extremes.

Polygamy has been causing controversy ever since Mormon prophet Joseph Smith revealed the principle in 1843. Within a few years the church leader had been murdered and the Saints driven from Illinois to the Utah Territory. But for all the effect polygamy had in populating western states (second church president Brigham Young was purported to have had as many as 35 wives, 65 children and countless great-great-great grandchildren – this author included), the practice lasted a surprisingly short time. The official Mormon church, known as the Church of Jesus Christ of Latter Day Saints (LDS) today, espoused plural marriage for only 50 years. In fact, the LDS excommunicates multiple marriers.

That doesn't mean the practice faded away. Start talking to residents in the staunchly Mormon ① St George, and you may be regaled with stories of polygamous friends or suspiciously large broods of similar-age kids tumbling out of minivans. St George is, after all, the closest urban center to Hildale-Colorado City, the town where an estimated 7000 polygamy-practicing members of a cult-like splinter sect, the Fundamentalist Church of Jesus Christ of Latter-day Saints (FLDS), live.

Start your day in St George as the Mormon pioneers would have. OK, so settlers wouldn't have sipped espresso, but they would have recognized the baked cinnamon-apple smell wafting from the ② Bear Paw Café.

TIME
2 days

DISTANCE
90 miles

BEST TIME TO GO
Sep – Oct

START
St George, UT

END
Hildale, UT

ALSO GOOD FOR

HISTORY & CULTURE

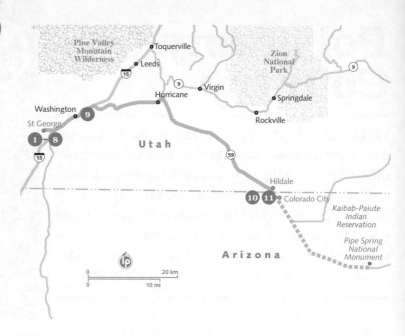

Fruit and nuts were some of the first local crops planted. Look for the mulberry trees (planted to feed silk worms) that shade the old town streets as you stroll past mercantile buildings on N Main and Tabernacle Sts. The dry goods are gone, but you can still lap up ice cream under pressed-tin ceilings at ❸ **Thomas Judd's Store** (c 1911), part of the Green Gate Village Inn historical B&B community.

"Don't worry, no one will try to convert you – unless you ask."

To get a feel for high-end pioneer polygamist life, mosey over to the ❹ **Brigham Young Winter Home** (1873), where in October apples drip from some of the original orchard trees. Young, and presumably several of his wives, were among the first "snowbirds" to flock to St George for the mild winters. Though not as lavish as today's clifftop getaways, the intricately carved woodwork does belie a richer-than-thou lifestyle.

During Brigham Young's 30-year tenure, the 1877 ❺ **St George Temple** was the only temple completed and in service. Unless you're a member, entry's barred, but you can admire the huge slabs of hand-chiseled rock, plastered and painted a glowing white. At night, uplighting makes the scene all the more ethereal. Exceptionally polite visitors center volunteers will happily answer questions. (Don't worry, no one will try to convert you – unless you ask.) But note that members aren't big on talking about polygamy these days. It's no wonder, considering the crimes that have been associated with polygamous offshoot sects. If you want to get the real story, you'll have to descend the back stairway and search through the stack at the ⑥ **Book Cellar**. Margi and Karin stock frank Mormon and FLDS memoirs, and have some tales to tell themselves.

After dining on artisanal entrées at the ⑦ **Painted Pony**, take your bedtime reading back to your room in the ⑧ **Seven Wives Inn**, where the original owner of the 1873 Victorian sequestered polygamists fleeing persecution in a secret attic room. Stay in the "Jane" room and you'll be sleeping under the same eaves where the current innkeeper's ancestor once hid (yes, he did have seven wives).

If day one was dedicated to mainstream Mormonism, day two represents the radical fringe. First stop is any superstore near St George, like the ⑨ **Walmart** in Washington. Be respectful, but you'll be hard pressed not to notice FLDS women cruising the aisles in ankle-to-wrist dresses, their long hair teased skyward and wrapped in a bun. What looks like several generations (mother, daughter, granddaughter) are likely to be "sister wives," all married to one man.

Other than a proliferation of 17,000-sq-ft houses (for multiple wives and even more multiple children), the twin towns of ⑩ **Hildale-Colorado City** on the Utah–Arizona state line appear pretty normal. But this is where FLDS leader Warren Jeffs imposed increasingly strict edicts in this polygamous community before his conviction in 2007 – including the widely reported actions of closing the schools, banning private books (TV had long been taboo), banishing teenage boys out onto the streets of St George and forcing girls as young as 13 to marry men 40 years their senior.

We don't recommend driving around town too much; nonresidents have been followed and police are FLDS members. But do pop into the ⑪ **Merry Wives Café**; it's run by those in a less insular polygamist sect from Arizona. As you admire the large family portraits and the pastoral mural of women romping through a field hand-in-hand, it starts to sink in. Not much has changed in 150 years. Polygamy is still practiced, and it's still stirring things up.

Lisa Dunford

RELIVING HISTORY

Meet the big man, Brigham Young himself, with **Historic St George Live!** (www.stgeorge live.org). Costumed docents lead bus tours to historic sights where noted 1870s residents tell their stories and answer questions. In addition to the church president, look for local missionary and farmer Joseph Hamblin.

> **DETOUR** Twenty miles from Colorado City, **Pipe Spring National Monument** (www.nps.gov/pisp) is quite literally an oasis in the desert. The constant supply of water attracted both Paiute Native Americans and Mormon settlers. During the late 1800s, the ranch here was a stop on the "Honeymoon Trail" – a route Arizona Mormons followed traveling to be married at the St George Temple.

TRIP INFORMATION

GETTING THERE
From Las Vegas follow I-15 northeast 120 miles then take Utah exit 6 west into St George.

DO
Book Cellar
A fiercely independent bookstore in conservative country, Book Cellar carries roughly 20,000 new and used titles. ☎ 435-652-0227; www.sgbookcellar.com; 130 N Main St, St George; ☻ 10am-5pm

Brigham Young Winter Home
The furnishings aren't all original, but this house museum well illustrates the second Mormon president's life. ☎ 435-673-2517; www.lds.org; 67 W 200 North, St George; admission free; ☻ 9am-5pm

St George Temple
Brigham Young dedicated the town's temple in 1871. Find out more at the public visitors center. ☎ 435-673-5181; www.lds.org; 440 S 300 East, St George; ☻ visitors center 9am-9pm

Thomas Judd's Store
Admire the original 1911 store building while satiating your sweet tooth with the candy and ice cream sold here. ☎ 435-628-6999; 76 W Tabernacle St, St George; ☻ 10am-5pm; ⚐

Wal-Mart
Extremist FLDS church members often shop at this supercenter between St George and Hildale-Colorado City. ☎ 435-628-2802; 625 W Telegraph St, Washington; ☻ 24 hr

EAT
Bear Paw Café
Ooohhh those fluffy Belgian waffles and juicy blueberry pancakes…and there's

a coffee barista on-site. ☎ 435-634-0126; 75 N Main St, St George; mains $5-9; ☻ 7am-2pm

Merry Wives Café
Come to see the polygamist family portraits, stay for the good daily specials like the fried shrimp. ☎ 435-874-9425; Hwy 59, Hildale; dishes $5-10; ☻ 11am-7:30pm Mon-Sat

Painted Pony
Layers of flavor (think green leeks enlivening sweet potato hash), make this St George's top restaurant. ☎ 435-634-1700; 2 W St George Blvd, St George; mains $20-25; ☻ 11am-10pm Mon-Sat

SLEEP
Green Gate Village
Grassy lawns separate the nine historic buildings, filled with antiques, that comprise this B&B community. ☎ 435-628-6999, 800-350-6999; www.greengatevillageinn.com; 76 W Tabernacle St, St George; r incl breakfast $99-139

Seven Wives Inn
Character oozes from each of 13 individually decorated rooms (one has a hot tub inside a Model T Ford). ☎ 435-628-3737, 800-600-3737; www.sevenwivesinn.com; 217 N 100 West, St George; r incl breakfast $80-180

SUGGESTED READS
For more on life inside the FLDS, pick up Carolyn Jessop's book *Escape* or the DVD documentary *Under the Banner of Heaven*.

USEFUL WEBSITES
www.lds.org
www.sgcity.org

LINK YOUR TRIP
www.lonelyplanet.com/trip-planner

Written in Stone: Utah's National Parks

WHY GO Stare at the swirling pattern long enough and you'll swear you can see the red rock move. Hiking through Utah's five national parks, you get to test your limits and bear witness to the earth's power at its most elemental. Here the story of wind and water is written in stone.

TIME
8 days

DISTANCE
400 miles

BEST TIME TO GO
May – June, Sep – Oct

START
Zion National Park

END
Canyonlands National Park - Needles District

ALSO GOOD FOR

227

Though the whole alphabet soup of Southern Utah's national parks – Zion to Arches, west to east – lies within the Colorado plateau, each region has its own distinctive features. Start at the lowest elevation (just 3800ft on the canyon floor) in **1** Zion National Park and you can feel the desert heat. Temperatures in July consistently top 100°F, and late October still has warm, sunny fall days. The park's red canyon cliffs are so strikingly dramatic that it's hard to imagine that the little Virgin River carved them.

The carved red rock views from the winding and main canyon drive (on a shuttle system in summer) are great. But to get a real feel for the place, hike **2** The Narrows, the slender canyons along the river's north fork. In an easy-does-it day, you can trek a few miles north from Riverside Walk to experience the sheer fluted walls closing in and then slosh back. Adrenaline junkies will shuttle out early to the Narrows trailhead near Chamberlain's Ranch so they can complete the full 16-mile, 13-hour journey in a day. Plan to get wet: at least 50% of either hike is in the river.

Prefer dry land? More than one hiker has challenged their fear of heights on **3** Angel's Landing. Here the 5-mile one-way trail is so steep (1450ft ascent) and narrow (5ft at some points) that there's a wide spot known as "chicken-out point." To conquer one cleft formed by wind and water, 22 stonework switchbacks were carved into the rock.

Thankfully, an exertion-filled day doesn't necessarily need to end in a night on the hard ground. The motel rooms at the ❹ **Zion Lodge** may not be much to look at, but the lodge provides a front-row seat for the kaleidoscope of colors reflected off red rock at sunset. Your best bet for dinner is in nearby Springdale, where you can savor ancho chile–seared lamb paired with one of hundreds of wines at ❺ **Spotted Dog Café**. The town is so laid-back, you won't even have to change out of your hiking togs.

WHAT'S A VIRGIN TO DO?

Fourteen miles west of Springdale, it's hard to miss the town of Virgin. Have your picture taken inside the 'Virgin Jail' or 'Wild Ass Saloon' before you feed the deer, donkey and llama in the petting zoo, or buy ice cream in the Trading Post. What pure kitschy fun! The tiny outpost town has another claim to fame – in 2000 the council passed a law requiring residents own a gun. It's a $500 fine if you don't.

A more isolated and even-terrained hiking experience is to be had if you drive out to ❻ **Kolob Terrace Rd**, 14 miles west of Springdale. Stunning views of carved red rock pop up at every turn as you weave in and out of park lands. Thirty-eight miles north, turn off toward ❼ **Lava Point** for an excellent overlook, a six-site first-come, first-serve campground, and higher-elevation hikes that lead to cool, flower-filled meadows.

Stay over a second night because you also want to explore the one-10th-as-visited Kolob Canyons arm of Zion NP, 40 miles (70 minutes) northwest. In some ways the 5-mile scenic route starting from ❽ **Kolob Canyons Visitor**

Center is even more stunning than the main drive. Here the cliff walls are closer and the roads are paved with red rock asphalt (yes, it's really red), making the experience all the more colorfully intense. At the end of the road, follow ❾ Timber Creek Overlook Trail (0.5 miles) up a 100ft ascent to a small peak with expansive finger canyon views.

The next day, broad leaves and deciduous trees give way to evergreen needles and soaring pines as you make your way from Zion to ❿ Bryce Canyon National Park. Though only 77 miles northwest, a 4000ft elevation change sets Bryce a world apart. Here the freeze-and-thaw of winter snows has gotten under the earth's skin. Expanding fissures created the spindly spires and sherbet-colored fins (thin walls of rock) that stand like sentinels in ⓫ Bryce Amphitheater. Best viewed from Sunset and Sunrise Points, you can also hike below the lookouts and experience the awe of these sandcastle shapes from below. Zig-zag 521ft down from Sunset Point along Navajo Trail through Wall Street slot canyon, under arches and past hoodoos – all glowing an eerie orange. Follow the Queen's Trail along the canyon floor up to Sunrise Point and back along the overlooking rim for a fairly strenuous 3-mile loop (you climbed down, you have to climb up).

ASK A LOCAL

"For end of the day photography it's the tremendous views off Kolob Terrace Rd. Here you stand at the extreme western edge of the Colorado Plateau and can see the land fall away beneath your feet. To the north are beautiful vistas into the Kolob finger canyons and Hop Valley. If you're fortunate, you may glimpse the sizable elk herd that frequents the large meadow to the southeast of the Hop Valley trailhead."
Michael Plyler, Director, Zion Canyon Field Institute, Springdale

Bryce does have a lodge, but you can't visit the park without noticing the sleep-shop-eat-and-outfit-for-all-adventures complex ⓬ Ruby's Inn, sprawling just north of the entrance. What was originally just a motel gained town status in 2007 and has been a family-owned part of the landscape since 1919. Everybody passing through to Bryce stops here at one time or another – to sleep, get gas, have a meal, or book a helicopter or horseback ride; it's an experience.

Driving west from Bryce on Hwy 12, almost all you see south of the road – expansive plateaus, candy cane–striped sedimentary hills, uplifted ridges – belongs to the nation's largest park. ⓭ Grand Staircase-Escalante National Monument (GSENM) is bigger than Rhode Island (1.9 million acres) and about a zillion times more desolate. Entry is free and infrastructure is limited to the towns along the park's edge; dirt roads traverse the expanse. ⓮ Upper Calf Creek Falls is the GSENM's most accessible and popular day-hike trail (2 mile round-trip). Start on the spur road between mile markers 81 and 82 off Hwy 12. Cairns lead the way down a fairly steep trail with far-ranging views. When the trail splits, veer toward the lovely pools and swimming hole on the upper trail.

Your most comfortable bet is to base yourself in the microscopic town of Boulder at ⑮ **Boulder Mountain Lodge** (66 miles northeast of Bryce), a rustic eco-lodge with high-thread-count sheets. Then you can dine on soulful, earthy preparations of locally raised meats and site-grown organic vegetables at the associated ⑯ **Hell's Backbone Grill**. If you can tear yourself away after waking up to birdsong on the 15-acre wildlife sanctuary you should at least go for one backroad drive through the GSENM.

RABBITS & RATTLESNAKES

No, it's not the name of a new band; rabbit and rattlesnake are the kinds of sausages you can try at **Buffalo Bistro** (www.visiteastzion.info/ buffalobistro.html) in Glendale. Hang out on the rustic back porch while your buffalo ribs sizzle on the grill and the boisterous owner-chef holds court. Stop for dinner en route from Zion to Bryce (April through October, reservations advised); who knows, the Testicle Festival (Rocky Mountain oysters served) may even be on.

Just west of town, the rough gravel-and-dirt ⑰ **Hell's Backbone Rd** climbs steadily uphill for 14 miles before reaching a one-lane bridge teetering above a plunging canyon sure to give you vertigo. Cut the engine, get out and listen to the wind funneling up the canyon while giant crows float silently on the thermals above. Look to the east, where Boulder Mountain is carpeted with deep-green forests and stands of quaking aspens that turn a gorgeous gold in September.

Do pay a visit to ⑱ **Anasazi State Park** before you continue on. Thousands upon thousands of pottery shards, on display in the museum, were excavated here in the 1950s. Outside are the scant remains of the Ancestral Puebloan archaeological site, inhabited from AD 1130 to 1175.

Ever wondered what happens when the earth's crust buckles? See for yourself at ⑲ **Capitol Reef National Park**, 48 miles northeast of Boulder. The rocky valleys, petrified yellow sand dunes and steep switchbacks along Hwy 12 hint of the geography to come. Over the course of millions of years, a 100-mile-long monocline fractured and uplifted, creating Waterpocket Fold, the centerpiece to Capitol Reef NP. (The formation once blocked settlers' westward migration like a 'reef' blocks a ship's passage.) An interpretive drive leads south along the fold, past abandoned homesteads and orchards where the sweet smell of free-for-your-picking pears, apricots, peaches and apples hangs in the air June through October. Pitch your tent next to the fragrant fields at ⑳ **Fruita Campground** and listen as the Fremont River babbles along.

If you're camping there's little reason to go into the closest town, Torrey, 11 miles west. Well, except to eat at one of southern Utah's best restaurants,

㉑ **Café Diablo.** Its stylized Southwestern cooking – including succulent vegetarian dishes – bursts with flavor. Even if you order just appetizers ($9 to $11) and dessert, you won't leave hungry.

You have to venture north into the park to get an up-close view of the monocline's Capitol Dome. Arrange a shuttle and bike rental from ㉒ **Backcountry Outfitters** and you can pedal the 58-mile loop through ㉓ **Cathedral Valley.** An otherworldly landscape of stark desert (bring water!) studded with rounded hills of volcanic ash and towering sandstone monoliths rewards the effort. The sedimentary layers you see – chocolate browns, ashen grays, sandy yellows and oxidized reds – together reveal 200 million years of history.

"...reaching a one-lane bridge teetering above a plunging canyon sure to give you vertigo."

If Capitol Reef reveals the passage of time, ㉔ **Arches National Park,** 142 miles northeast, captures a snapshot. Almost all of the rock you see here is entrada sandstone, a muddy-to-orangish-red stone laid down during the Jurassic period. The namesake arches formed when salt pockets raised up the earth and water erosion tore it down. Freeze-and-thaw continues to slough off rock, creating arches (which will all eventually collapse). Book ahead for a ㉕ **Fiery Furnace** guided hike, so you can explore the maze of spectacularly narrow fissures and giant fins that are the first step in arch formation.

The king of all named park features is ㉖ **Delicate Arch.** You've seen this one: it's the unofficial state symbol and is pictured on just about every piece of Utah tourist literature ever printed. The 3-mile round-trip trail to it ascends slickrock, culminating in a wall-hugging ledge. If you've filled up on the homemade scones and jam for breakfast at the lovely ㉗ **Sunflower Hill B&B** where you're staying, you may not need it. But you could bring a picnic lunch, ditch the crowds by passing beneath the arch and drop down to enjoy it on the other side several yards away.

Your sizable base town, Moab, 5 miles south of the park, is a good place for stocking up on everything. It's also ideally located to reach several other parks as day trips. In the morning you're off to see one of the

> **DETOUR**
>
> A Salvador Dali–like rock fantasy, a field of giant stone mushrooms or an acid trip the creator went on? You decide what the stadium-like valley of stunted hoodoos resembles. We think the 3654-acre **Goblin Valley State Park** (www.stateparks.utah.gov), 58 miles northeast of Capitol Reef, looks like a big playground. Follow the trail down from the overlooks, then you're allowed to climb down, around, even over, the evocative 'goblins' (2ft- to 20ft-tall rock formations). Detour west off Hwy 24 along a signed, paved road 12 miles to the entrance.

Canyonlands National Park sections, but first stop on the way in to ㉘ **Dead Horse Point State Park,** where the views pack a wallop. Peer down 2000ft to the Colorado River and 100 miles across a mesmerizing stair-step red-rock landscape. (You might remember this epic vista from the final scene in *Thelma & Louise*.) Legend has it that cowboys blockaded the mesa to corral wild horses, and that they forgot to release them upon leaving. The stranded equines died within view of the unreachable water below, hence the name.

JUMP OFF A CLIFF

Hiking into a slot canyon so slender you have to turn sideways and rappelling down a cliff face (or climbing up one) are just a few of the adventures available in southern Utah. Unless you're an expert, you'll need a guide. Outfitters are found in pretty much every town adjacent to a park. In Springdale, contact **Zion Adventure Company** (www.zionadventures.com), in Escalante, **Excursions of Escalante** (www.excursions-escalante .com), and in Moab, the **Moab Adventure Center** (www.moabadventurecenter.com).

Ten miles further on (30 northwest of Moab) lies ㉙ **Canyonlands National Park – Islands in the Sky District**. Think of this as the overview section of Canyonlands, a RVer's special, with paved drives and easy-access lookouts. Here vast serpentine canyons tipped with white cliffs loom high over the Colorado and Green Rivers, their waters 1000ft below the rim at Islands in the Sky.

For the more adventurous, ㉚ **Canyonlands National Park – Needles District**, 75 miles south of Moab, is where you can hike down in and among the skyward-jutting spindles and spires, blue-hued mesas and majestic buttes. Trek the awesome 11-mile ㉛ **Chesler Park Loop** through desert grasslands, past towering red-and-white-striped pinnacles and between deep and narrow fractures (some only 2ft across). Elevation changes are mild, but the distance makes it a moderate-to-difficult day hike. Don't forget to stop on the way back to Moab to see the hundreds of petroglyphs at the ㉜ **Newspaper Rock Recreation Site**. Note that the impressive panel of horse and human etchings photographs better in the late-afternoon sidelight.

And leave plenty of time to get back to Moab for your reservation at casually elegant ㉝ **Center Café**, which supports the local farmers market and youth garden. Lingering over sautéed shrimp with cheddar-and-garlic grits served in the back garden, you have ample opportunity to reflect on not only the earth's bounty but the tumultuous forces that created it. Now if your calves would just stop throbbing from so many days of hiking.

Lisa Dunford

TRIP INFORMATION

GETTING THERE
From Las Vegas, Zion National Park is a 160-mile, 70-plus-mph drive northwest up I-15 and off onto smaller Hwy 9.

DO
Anasazi State Park
The ruins aren't as evocative as some in southeastern Utah, but Ancestral Puebloan museum exhibits are well worth seeing. ☎ 435-335-7308; www.stateparks.utah.gov; Main St/Hwy 12, Boulder; admission $4; ☺ 9am-5pm

Arches National Park
Stop at the visitors center to see a park-overview video, check ranger-led activity schedules, reserve your tickets for a Fiery Furnace hike and buy maps. ☎ 435-719-2299; www.nps.gov/arch; Hwy 191; admission per vehicle/week $10; ☺ visitors center 8:30am-6:30pm

Backcountry Outfitters
In addition to 4WD and hiking packages, Backcountry Outfitters also rents bicycles ($38 per day) and ATVs ($150 per day) and provides shuttles. ☎ 435-425-2010; www.ridethereef.com; 677 E Hwy 24 at Hwy 12, Torrey; ☺ 9am-6pm

Bryce Canyon National Park
The visitors center sells loads of maps and books and gives out info about weather, road conditions and campsite availability. ☎ 435-834-5322; www.nps.gov/brca; Hwy 63; admission per vehicle/week $25; ☺ visitors center 8am-6pm

Canyonlands National Park – Island in the Sky District
Pick up your overlook driving tour CD for $10 (or rent it for $5) before you drive out to the fabulous vistas. ☎ 435-259-4712; www.nps.gov/cany/island; Hwy 313; admission per vehicle $10, includes Needles District; ☺ visitors center 8am-6pm

Canyonlands National Park – Needles District
Ask rangers about the 4WD roads the park is known for. Even if you're hiking, watching can be quite a show. ☎ 435-259-4711; www.nps.gov/cany/needles; Hwy 211; admission per vehicle $10, includes Island District; ☺ visitors center 8am-6pm

Capitol Reef National Park
Watch the short film, then ooh and aah over the 64-sq-ft park relief map, carved with dental instruments. Ranger-led hikes available. ☎ 435-425-3791; www.nps.gov/care; cnr Hwy 24 & Scenic Dr; scenic drive $5; ☺ visitors center 8am-6pm

Dead Horse Point State Park
To escape the small (but sometimes chatty) crowds at the main overlook points, take a walk around the mesa rim. ☎ 435-259-2614; www.stateparks.utah.gov; admission $10; ☺ visitors center 8am-5pm, trails dawn-dusk

Kolob Canyons Visitor Center
Admission to Zion National Park's main section includes admission to Kolob Canyons, and vice versa. Hold onto your receipt. ☎ 435-586-0895; Kolob Canyons Rd, off I-15; admission per vehicle/week $25; ☺ visitors center 8am-4:30pm

Newspaper Rock Recreation Area
This tiny, free turn-out showcases a single large sandstone rock panel packed with more than 300 petroglyphs attributed to Ute and Ancestral Puebloan groups. www.blm.gov; Hwy 211

Zion National Park
Rangers are on hand to answer questions and lead interpretive hikes from the main visitors center. Mandatory shuttle rides (April through October) start there. ☎ 435-772-3256; www.nps.gov/zion; Hwy 9; admission per vehicle/week $25; ☺ visitors center 8am-6pm

EAT

Café Diablo
Don't miss the creative Southwestern cuisine here. For something you won't find back home, try the rattlesnake cakes. ☎ 435-425-3070; 599 W Main St, Torrey; mains $20-24; ⏲ 5-10pm Apr-Oct

Center Café
Center Café's chef-owner draws from regional American and Mediterranean influences. Budgeteers: come for the small plates served from 3pm to 6pm. ☎ 435-259-4295; 60 N 100 West, Moab; small plates $6-11, mains $18-30; ⏲ 3-10pm

Hell's Backbone Grill
This is foodie destination dining. Save room for desserts such as chimayo-chile ginger cake with butterscotch sauce. ☎ 435-335-7464; Boulder Mountain Lodge, cnr Hwy 12 & Burr Trail Rd, Boulder; mains $12-22; ⏲ 5-9:30pm Apr-Nov

Spotted Dog Café
Don't be put off by the white tablecloths and black-shirted waiters; snobbery is not on the menu at this upscale hiker's fave. ☎ 435-772-3244; Flanigan's Inn, 428 Zion Park Blvd, Springdale; mains $19-28; ⏲ 5-10pm

SLEEP

Boulder Mountain Lodge
Watch the birds flit by at the wildlife sanctuary and stroll through the organic garden. Don't forget to recycle – Boulder Mountain Lodge has a strong eco-aesthetic. ☎ 435-335-7460; www.boulder-utah.com; cnr Hwy 12 & Burr Trail Rd, Boulder; r $97-175; ♿

Fruita Campground
June through August, the 71 first-come, first-served riverside sites fill up by noon. Drinking water, pit toilets available. ☎ 435-425-3791; www.nps.gov/care; Scenic Dr, Capitol Reef National Park; campsites $10; ♿

Ruby's Inn
Motel rooms, hotel suites, post office, grocery store, ATV rental and outfitter tours are just some of the facilities at Ruby's. ☎ 435-834-5341; www.rubysinn.com; 1000 S Hwy 63, Bryce Canyon; r $81-145; ♿

Sunflower Hill B&B
Kick back in an Adirondack chair amid the manicured gardens of two inviting buildings – an early-20th-century home and a 100-year-old farmhouse. ☎ 435-259-2974; www.sunflowerhill.com; 185 N 300 East, Moab; r incl breakfast $155-225

Zion Lodge
Despite a late-'90s American motel style, this park lodge is admirably green: 85% of its power comes from solar and wind, and lodge vehicles are all hybrids. ☎ 435-259-4295; 60 N 100 West; r $150-180

USEFUL WEBSITES
www.nps.gov
www.utah.com

LINK YOUR TRIP   www.lonelyplanet.com/trip-planner

Trail of the Ancients

WHY GO Dusty and desolate, hot and hardscrabble: parts of southeastern Utah were so forbidding that they were the last to be mapped in the continental US. Yet it's precisely this isolation that has preserved the rocky natural wonders and numerous Ancestral Puebloan ruins and petroglyph sites for us to ponder.

Dramatic chocolate-red buttes and layered mesas grow smaller in your rear-view mirror as you head north from ❶ Monument Valley. Not to worry, there are plenty more sights – both ancient-man and nature made – on this route around Utah's nearly uninhabited southeastern corner. Turn north up Hwy 261 and branch off to ❷ Goosenecks State Park Overlook to see how the San Juan River's path carved tight turns through 1000ft of sediment, leaving gooseneck-shaped spits of land untouched.

Back on Hwy 261, get ready for a ride. You'll ascend ❸ Moki Dugway, a roughly paved, hairpin-turn-filled road section that rises 1100ft in just 3 miles. Miners 'dug out' the extreme switchbacks in the 1950s to transport uranium ore. It's far from wide by today's standards: you can't see what's up around narrow corners, but you can see down the sheer dropoffs. Those afraid of heights (or in trailers over 24ftlong), steer clear.

From about AD 900 to 1300 Ancestral Puebloans (or Anasazi) inhabited this region; theories abound as to why they left (drought, deforestation?) but none have been proven. You'll need one of the limited day-use permits to get your first glimpse of their inhabitation in the wild and twisty canyons of ❹ Grand Gulch Primitive Area. Call the Monticello Bureau of Land Management (BLM) office to reserve ahead and pick it up near the trailhead at ❺ Kane Gulch Ranger Station. Then you can scrabble 4 miles down Kane Gulch to a view of Junction Ruin cliff dwelling. Hundreds of sites have been identified in the backcountry.

TIME
3 days

DISTANCE
180 miles

BEST TIME TO GO
May – Jun & Sep

START
Monument Valley, AZ

END
Mexican Hat, UT

ALSO GOOD FOR

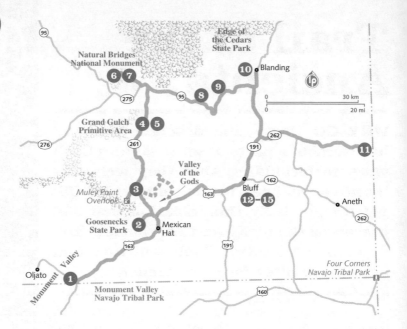

You've reached your day's destination when you get to ⑥ **Natural Bridges National Monument,** a dark-stained, white-sandstone canyon with three stone bridges formed by under-flowing water. The oldest, the beautifully delicate Owachomo Bridge, spans 180ft but is only 9ft thick. All are visible from a 9-mile winding loop road with easy-access overlooks and downhill trails.

> **ASK A LOCAL**
>
> "It is very difficult for me to designate a favorite archaeological site. If I had to pick it would be the next place I find that I've never seen before. After 15 years of trekking in Grand Gulch, for example, I still find new sites."
>
> *Larry Sanford, llama trekking guide, Bluff*

After a star-filled night at the ⑦ **Natural Bridges Campground,** pack your gear, fill your water jugs and get going. The overgrown (and not terribly evocative) roadside ⑧ **Mule Canyon Ruins** are 27 miles along. Pottery here links the population (c AD 1000 to 1150) to the Mesa Verde group in southern Colorado. A few miles further are the even more intriguing ⑨ **Butler Wash Ruins,** associated with the Kayenta group (c 1300 AD) of northern Arizona. Scramble a half-mile over slickrock boulders, following the cairns, and be rewarded with an overlook of a cliff dwelling with sacred kivas, habitation and storage rooms.

To learn more about the area's ancients, your next stop should be ⑩ **Edge of the Cedars State Park** (really a museum) in Blanding. The trove of archaeological evidence here has been gathered from across southeastern Utah. Outside, climb down the rickety ladder into a dark, earthy-smelling ceremonial kiva c AD 1100. Can you feel a power to the place? The encroaching sub-division makes you wonder what other amazing sites remain hidden under neighboring houses.

Unlike the state park, ⑪ Hovenweep National Monument exists in splendid isolation. Most of the eight towers and unit houses you'll see in the Square Towers Group were built from AD 1230 to 1275. Imagine stacking clay-formed blocks to create such tall structures on little ledges. The masonry skills are impressive indeed, but what caused the need for defensible settlements? You could easily spend a half day hiking around the gorge's ruins, thinking about how much we don't know about the people who lived here.

You can afford to take your time on the route; your base camp for the night is just 40 miles west and south in the tiny-tot town of Bluff, which has fewer people than places to stay. The best is ⑫ Recapture Lodge, an old-fashioned, multistory wooden motel where long-time resident owners and staffers know and care deeply about the region.

GO WITH A GUIDE

Sadly enough, many invaluable area archaeological sites have been vandalized by pot-hunters. The old maxim "take only pictures" bears repeating. Do not move or remove any artifacts; it's against the law. The best way to explore afield is with well-informed, responsible guide outfits like **Far Out Expeditions** (www.faroutexpeditions.com) and **Buckhorn Llama Company** (www.llamapack.com).

Then again, if you really want to rough it, you can. Three miles east of "town," scrubby vegetation and the trickling San Juan River help cool things off at ⑬ Sand Island Campground & Petroglyphs. You oughta stop here to see the freely accessible alien and equine-esque figures carved high into the rock wall (from 900 to 2500 years ago) anyway.

Wherever you stay, make sure to eat at ⑭ Cow Canyon, a rambling house-restaurant where local ingredients star on a daily-changing world-food menu. And in the morning try Native American fry bread (saucer-shaped fried dough) in a bacon-and-egg sandwich at ⑮ Twin Rocks Trading Post. The attached shop and gallery vends crafts by Navajo and Ute artisans.

DETOUR ➤ Think of the gravel road through **Valley of the Gods** (aka "mini Monument Valley") as a do-it-yourself roller coaster, with sharp, steep hill-ocks and quick turns around the sandstone monoliths. Allow an hour-plus for the 17 miles between Hwys 163 and 261. And be careful; this author's little Volkswagen made it – barely. You'll need a 4WD if it's rained.

Another desolate 47 miles through undulating rockland and you are back where you started. But, we're warning you, after your time in the stark splendor of these ancient sites, you may just hate to get back to civilization.

Lisa Dunford

TRIP INFORMATION

GETTING THERE
Monument Valley, straddling the Utah–Arizona state line, is 430 miles east and north of Las Vegas in the middle of nowhere.

DO

Edge of the Cedars State Park
See how museum curators are piecing together the past in the pottery reconstruction lab. ☎ 435-678-2238; www.stateparks.utah.gov; 660 W 400 North, Blanding; admission $5; ⊙ 9am-5pm

Grand Gulch Primitive Area
Call the Monticello BLM office permit line to reserve ahead your limited-capacity pass for hiking or overnighting in Grand Gulch. ☎ 435-587-1532; www.blm.gov; Hwy 261; day-use $2, overnight $8

Hovenweep National Monument
Six sets of Ancestral Puebloan sites were home to a sizable Ancestral Puebloan population before abandonment c AD 1300. ☎ 970-562-4282; www.nps.gov/hove; park entrance per week $3; ⊙ trails dawn-dusk

Kane Gulch Ranger Station
Pick up advance-reserve Grand Gulch permits opposite Kane Gulch trailhead (some walk-ins available). Located 4 miles south of Hwy 95. Hwy 261; ⊙ 8am-noon

Natural Bridges National Monument
See the bridges from disabled-accessible overlooks or hike down into the valley to the spans themselves. ☎ 435-692-1234; www.nps.gov/nabr; Hwy 275; admission $6; ⊙ 7am-sunset, visitors center 8am-5pm

EAT

Cow Canyon
Only a handful of fresh-made entrées are on offer any given evening at this eclectic eatery. ☎ 435-672-2208; cnr Hwys 191 & 163, Bluff; mains $11-18; ⊙ 5-9:30pm Thu-Mon Apr-Oct

Twin Rocks Trading Post
Diner-like meals include hearty stews and sandwiches. Owner Craig Simpson is a font of local lore. ☎ 435-672-2341; 913 E Navajo Twins Dr, Bluff; mains $5-12; ⊙ 7am-9pm

SLEEP

Natural Bridges Campground
Fairly sheltered sites cluster in red sand among scraggly trees. Pit toilets and grills; water at the visitors center. ☎ 435-692-1234; www.nps.gov/nabr; Hwy 275; campsites $10

Recapture Lodge
Rooms are comfy (if basic) and super knowledgeable staffers put on slide shows May to September. ☎ 435-672-2281; www.recapturelodge.com; Hwy 191, Bluff; r incl breakfast $46-76

Sand Island Campground
Pitch your tent beside the San Juan River at some of the 27 first-come, first-served sites. Pit toilets, drinking water. ☎ 435-587-1500; www.blm.gov; Sand Island Rd, Bluff; campsites $10; ⊙ May-Oct

SUGGESTED READS
- *Ancient Ruins of the Southwest,* David Noble
- *House of Rain: Tracking a Vanished Civilization,* Craig Childs

USEFUL WEBSITES
www.blandingutah.org
www.bluff-utah.org

LINK YOUR TRIP
www.lonelyplanet.com/trip-planner

NEW MEXICO TRIPS

Strewn with boughs of blood red ristras and earth-tone adobes, and smelling of sage, piñon and roasting green chile, the "Land of Enchantment" is like nowhere else in the country. Home of Billy the Kid, the world's most famous UFO crash site and America's only Hispanic governor, New Mexico is also the country's *it* destination du jour. Who's coming? Hollywood production companies (seems everyone is shooting a movie here), Richard Branson (he's planning to launch tourists into outer space from his Virgin Galactic Spaceport in 2010) and more than 15 million visitors a year (not all from this planet).

DH Lawrence, Georgia O'Keeffe and the Cohen brothers all found inspiration in the state's ethereal backdrop of mesas, mountains and unique light, and so did we. These 22 New Mexico trips take you to the most famous, obscure, artsy, offbeat and sometimes on-the-path attractions in the state. From hand-loomed blankets on the Fiber Arts Trail, an extraordinary meal in Santa Fe or cheesy alien schlock at the shop in Roswell, art is everywhere in New Mexico and plays an integral role in many of our trips. But gallery hopping is far from New Mexico's only sport. The state doubles as a giant outdoor playground. And we take you to the sickest mesa-top single track outside Gallup, and have you shredding powder, skiing around the Enchanted Circle. Whether you are exploring hidden hot springs, stargazing a black-velvet desert sky or sampling the best barley-wines in the state, these trips aim to introduce New Mexico from a fresh perspective.

 **PLAYLIST** New Mexico has inspired more than one artist to pen a song about here. Below is a mixture of our favorite music from, about or perfect for rocking out to while road tripping here. We call it the Land of Enchantment Mix.

- "Santa Fe," Bellamy Brothers
- "The Ballad of Billy the Kid," Billy Joel
- "About an Hour Ago," OAR
- "Rio," Duran Duran
- "Scenic World," Beirut
- "New Mexico Rain," Michael Hearne
- "Texas, New Mexico Line," Jed & Kelley
- "New Mexico Sky," Tony Schueller

BEST NEW MEXICO TRIPS

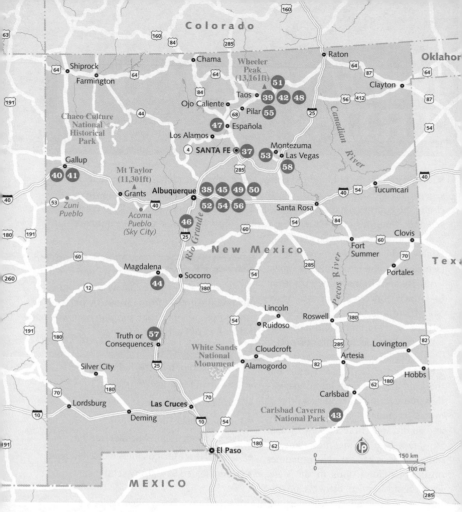

NEW MEXICO TRIPS

48 Hours in Santa Fe

WHY GO Bewitching Santa Fe dates back to 1610, and is one classy old gal. Home to world-class galleries, museums, restaurants, and even opera, Santa Fe wins most people over on the first go. But just in case, we've created a 48-hour insider itinerary sure to grab even the hardest hearts.

Welcome to Santa Fe, a city that makes its own rules, yet never forgets its long and storied past. The country's oldest state capital (she's turning 400 this decade) is a bewitching place where adobes are set against a Sangre de Cristo mountains backdrop. From art to opera, hot green chile to fiery red ristras, ornate churches and world-class resorts, every part of this oasis in the high desert is saturated with creative flair. The city is home to a motley crew of characters, including yuppie gringo artists, New Age hippie transplants, Spanish families that have called the city home for centuries, illegal Mexican immigrants, reclusive ex-Hollywood producers and ageless movie stars. All have come for the privacy and space.

Begin at the historic Plaza. Santa Fe's heartbeat, it dates back to the city's beginning. Native Americans sell their jewelry and pottery along the wall outside the ❶ Palace of the Governors. Arrive early for the best selection. Each piece is unique, so have a long stroll. We'd suggest browsing the length of the portale (awning) before making a purchase – there is so much variety. Look out for silver pendants and bracelets that integrate red coral into traditional turquoise and silver designs. We love the chunky silver pendants, made with blocks of different colorful stones, that many artists are beginning to create. Whatever your choice, the jewelry sold here is guaranteed to be innovative, and hand-crafted by Native Americans in New Mexico. Head inside the Palace of the Governors to check out the museum. Built in 1610 by Spanish officials, it is one of the oldest public buildings in the USA. Today it's a museum, with more than 17,000 objects reflecting Santa Fe's Native American, Spanish, Mexican and American heritage. Next door, the ❷ Museum of Fine Arts features

TIME
2 days

BEST TIME TO GO
Aug – Oct

START
Palace of the Governors, Santa Fe

END
Dragon Room Bar, Santa Fe

TRIP
37
CITY

a collection on par with heavy-hitters like New York City's Met. There are more than 20,000 pieces in the collection, including a section by regional artists.

Hungry after museum-hopping? Visit the ❸ French Pastry Shop. Order the divine crepes, filled with everything from ham and cheese to strawberries and cream, or a cup of the best French onion soup in town. After lunch, grab the M Line bus from the Plaza or hop in your car and drive 3 miles southwest to Santa Fe's other main museum district, renowned Museum Hill. Our favorite museum in Santa Fe is located here. The ❹ Museum of International Folk Art houses more than 100,000 objects from more than 100 countries. The exhibits aren't simply arranged behind glass cases; the historical and cultural information is concise and thorough; and a festive feel permeates the rooms. The Hispanic wing displays religious art, tin work, jewelry and textiles from northern New Mexico and the Spanish colonial empire, dating from the 1600s to the present.

After lunch head to Santa Fe's Rodeo Dr, ❺ Canyon Road, for a little million-dollar painting browsing. Once a footpath used by Pueblo Indians, then the main street through a Spanish farming community, Santa Fe's most famous art avenue began its current incarnation in the 1920s, when artists led by Los Cincos Pintores moved in to take advantage of the cheap rent. Today more than 90 of Santa Fe's 300 galleries are found here. From rare Native American antiquities to Santa Fe School masterpieces to wild contemporary work, it's all for sale. It can seem a bit overwhelming, so we'd suggest just wandering. Stop in at the ❻ Pushkin Gallery. Owned by the family of poet Alexander Pushkin, this gallery shows Russian masters including Nikolai Timkov and Vasily Golubev as well as more modern work. After you've gallery hopped your heart out, it's time for a different kind of Canyon Rd shopping experience. At ❼ El Milagro Herbs, the resident herbalist mixes invigorating body sprays, healing tinctures and re-laxing bath salts. Try the Desert Dweller Deep Moisturizing Lotion; it cures even the driest skin. In the heart of the Canyon Rd chaos is one of the city's best dinner joints, ❽ El Farol. The ambience is rustic adobe, the steaks are plump and chef James Campbell Caruso's tapas are delectable. If you're in town on a Wednesday night, there is a flamenco dinner show ($60). After eating, it's time for dancing at the ❾ Cowgirl Hall of Fame. The famous watering hole boasts Western-style feminist flair, an outside patio and live music after 9pm. Try the unique smoky-tasting Mescal margarita on the rocks.

Check into one of Santa Fe's classiest hotels for two nights. Steps from the plaza, the ❿ Inn & Spa at Loretto offers superspacious rooms done up in modern Southwestern style. Have a good-night cocktail at the lobby bar and look up at the ceiling. Each panel is hand-painted. Don't sleep in; you'll want to get to ⓫ Tia Sophia's for breakfast before the line gets too out of control. This is the city's favorite morning eating option, and you'll find celebs and locals alike stuffing their mouths with delicious green chile–soaked egg, cheese and meat burritos.

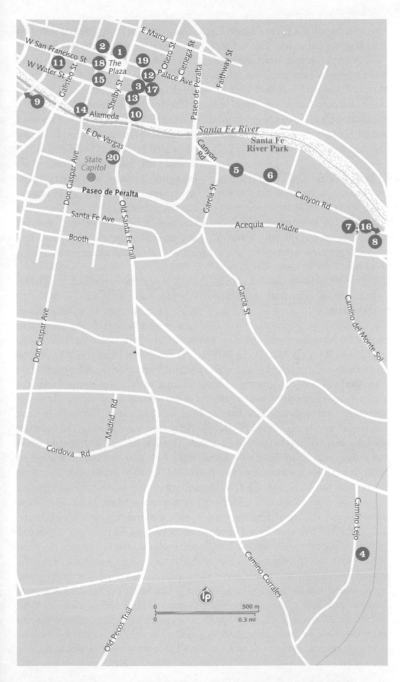

Construction on the ⑫ **St Francis Cathedral** began in 1869, when Archbishop Jean Baptiste Lamy was sent to Santa Fe by the pope with orders to tame the wild Western outpost town through culture and religion. Convinced that the town needed a focal point for religious life, he initiated work on what is now the city's landmark building. Visit the small chapel inside, where the oldest Madonna statue in North America is housed. Constructed between 1873 and 1878, the nearby ⑬ **Loretto Chapel** is modeled on St Chapelle in Paris and home of the city's most photographed site – the Miraculous Staircase. Legend has it the staircase came to be after the chapel's nuns prayed for help in building a circular stairwell. Shortly after sending off their godly message, a traveling carpenter, believed afterward to be St Joseph, arrived, constructed a wooden spiral staircase with two 360-degree turns and no central or visible support and left without charging for his labors.

OPERA IN THE GREAT OUTDOORS

If you are lucky enough to be in Santa Fe in July or August, don't miss an al fresco opera (www. santafeopera.org) performance. The site alone is an architectural marvel, with views of wind-carved sandstone wilderness. Arrive for a tail-gate two hours before the show begins. You'll see everything from pizza on the roof of someone's car to crystal, linen and candles in the bed of a pickup truck.

Have a fast fuel-up lunch at ⑭ **Del Churro Saloon**, which serves pub grub so good even Gov. Richardson eats it. Then spend the afternoon mountain biking some of the state's best intermediate single track. You can rent a bike from ⑮ **Melo Velo Bicycles**. Follow Upper Canyon Rd north to the well-signed parking lot at Cerro Gordo Rd and ride the ⑯ **South Dale Ball Trails**. It's a challenging course, starting with a superlong, hard and rocky uphill climb, followed by a series of harrowing switchbacks. But you'll be reward with supreme isolation and outstanding views. Get back in time for sunset and a margarita at the ⑰ **Belltower Bar**. During the summer months, this rooftop bar at the La Fonda Hotel is the premier spot to catch the setting sun. Santa Fe serves some of the best margaritas in the state, so go ahead and get a little tipsy (you don't have to drive anywhere). This time drink your tequila at the ⑱ **Ore House**, which has more than 40 types of margaritas. Splash out and order a sipping tequila. Made from 100% blue agave tequila, the Herradura Suprema is as smooth as this cactus liquor gets, and costs $50 per shot. For a more realistically priced beverage order our favorite margarita, the Santana Rita, made with smooth El Milagro Respado tequila and Grand Marnier; it has a delicious smoky-sweet tang. Plus the heated 2nd-story patio offers great Plaza people-watching. The family-run, James Beard Award–winning restaurant ⑲ **The Shed**, has been serving New Mexican fare in a atmospheric 1692 adobe since 1953 and is where to head for dinner. Afterwards, cap off your 48 hours in Santa Fe with a Black Dragon margarita inside a 300-year-old adobe building at the ⑳ **Dragon Room Bar**. It is a consistent top favorite of locals and Hollywood visitors alike.

Becca Blond

TRIP INFORMATION

GETTING THERE
Santa Fe is about 60 miles north of Albuquerque on I-25. Take exit 282, St Francis Dr, and follow the signs to the downtown plaza.

DO

El Milagro Herbs
Mixed by a resident herbalist, this little shop is stocked with goodies for your skin and body. ☎ 505-820-6321; www.milagroherbs.com; 1020 Canyon Rd, Santa Fe

Loretto Chapel
The chapel is now a museum; stop in to see the Miraculous Staircase or to light a candle for a loved one by the impressive altar. ☎ 505-982-0092; www.lorettochapel.com; 207 Old Santa Fe Trail; admission $3; 🕐 9am-6pm summer, 9am-5pm winter

Melo Velo Bicycles
Has info about area trails and offers half-day to 10-day bike tours. ☎ 505-982-8986; www.sunmountainbikeco.com; 102 E Water St, El Centro gallery; rentals per hr $9, day $45; 🕐 9:30am-5pm Mon-Sat, 10am-4pm Sun

Museum of Fine Arts
Features works by regional artists and sponsors regular gallery talks and slide lectures. ☎ 505-476-5072; www.museumofnewmexico.org; 107 Palace Ave; admission $8, 5-8pm Fri free; 🕐 10am-5pm Tue-Sat, to 8pm Fri

Museum of International Folk Art
Arguably the best museum in Santa Fe, with straightforward, fun, almost pop-like exhibits. ☎ 505-476-1200; www.moifa.org; 706 Camino Lejo; admission $8; 🕐 10am-5pm Tue-Sat

Palace of the Governors
One of the oldest public buildings in the country. Don't miss the Native American jewelry for sale out front. ☎ 505-476-5100; www.museumofnewmexico.org; 100 Palace Ave; admission $8, 5-8pm Fri free; 🕐 8am-5pm Tue-Sat, to 8pm Fri

Pushkin Gallery
Russian masters and contemporaries are featured at this landmark gallery. It also sells museum-quality Orthodox icons and lacquer boxes. ☎ 505-982-1990; www.pushkingallery.com; 550 Canyon Rd; telephone for opening hours

St Francis Cathedral
Look for a Hebrew inscription on the front of this Catholic Church. Legend has it Lamy had the words carved as a thank you to Jewish friends that contributed money to church construction. ☎ 505-982-5619; 131 Cathedral Pl; 🕐 8am-5pm; mass 7am & 5pm Mon-Sat, 8am, 10am, noon & 5pm Sun

EAT & DRINK

Belltower Bar
Watch the sun sink into a fiery pink ball while sipping on a smooth and limey margarita at Santa Fe's ultimate roof-top bar. ☎ 505-982-5511; 100 E San Francisco St; 🕐 5pm-sunset Mon-Thu, 2pm-sunset Fri-Sun May-Oct

Cowgirl Hall of Fame
Margaritas are what to drink, BBQ brisket is what to eat. There's also a billiards room. ☎ 982-2565; 319 S Guadalupe St; mains $8-13; 🕐 11am-midnight Mon-Fri, 8:30am-midnight Sat, 8:30am-11pm Sun, bar to 2am Mon-Sat, to midnight Sun

Del Churro Saloon
Serves inexpensive pub grub and huge margaritas in atmospheric environs. There's a blazing fire in winter; in summer tables spill out onto the sidewalk patio. ☎ 505-982-4333; Inn of the Governors, 101 W Alameda; mains under $6; 🕐 6.30am-late

Dragon Room Bar
Visit after 9pm on Tuesday, Thursday or Saturday to hear live music. The Black Dragon margarita is what to drink. ☎ 505-983-7712; 406 Old Santa Fe Trail

El Farol
This popular restaurant and bar, set in a rustically authentic adobe, features live music nightly. Tapas are what to order. ☎ 505-983-9912; 808 Canyon Rd; lunch $8-18, dinner $25-50; ⏲ 11:30am-late; ♿

Ore House
With more than 40 different margaritas you can't go wrong drinking at the Ore House. There's a cozy Old West bar inside, a heated roof-top patio outside. ☎ 505-983-8687; 50 Lincoln Ave

French Pastry Shop
Along with a host of quiches, sandwiches, cappuccino and of course pastries, it does delicious stuffed crepes and French onion soup. ☎ 505-983-6697; La Fonda Hotel, 100 San Francisco St; mains $3-7; ⏲ 7am-2pm

Tia Sophia's
Santa Fe's favorite breakfast spot, it is always packed. Order a breakfast burrito. There's a shelf of books for the kids. ☎ 505-983-9880; 210 W San Francisco St; mains $3-9; ⏲ 7am-2pm Mon-Sat; ♿

The Shed
We can't get enough of the red and green chile smothered chicken enchiladas topped off with a big scoop of homemade guacamole. ☎ 505-982-9030; 113½ E Palace Ave; lunch $8-10, dinner $9-20; ⏲ 11am-2:30pm & 5:30-9pm Mon-Sat; ♿

SLEEP

Inn & Spa at Loretto
Warm woven rugs cover Frette linens on beds and local art hangs on dark red walls. Wi-fi is available. ☎ 505-988-5531; www.hotelloretto.com; 211 Old Santa Fe Trail; r from $250

USEFUL WEBSITES
www.santafe.org
www.santafegalleries.net

LINK YOUR TRIP
www.lonelyplanet.com/trip-planner

Albuquirky

WHY GO Most Albuquerque locals agree that their city is a bit off-kilter. But ask why, and no one can say exactly. Walk its neighborhoods, meet the folks who live here and visit its under-the-radar museums on this tour through the quirky side of Albuquerque.

Just about everybody in Albuquerque, from turquoise-studded ol' timers to sleepy-eyed students, eventually finds their way to the ❶ Frontier Restaurant. Join the line, take your number and people-watch over a green chile–drenched breakfast burrito. After breakfast, wander east on Central Ave, perusing the eclectic mix of tattoo parlors, clothing boutiques and New Age shops around the ❷ University of New Mexico and in ❸ Nob Hill. Detour up Monte Vista St a few blocks to the ❹ Spaceship House, a private residence designed by legendary architect Bart Prince, an Albuquerque native, and guarded by copper dinosaurs. Just past Carlisle Blvd is the Route 66 classic ❺ Cowboys & Indians Antiques, stuffed with high-end jewelry, pottery and basketry, as well as flea-market finds like cowboy dishes from the 1920s. Walking into this tiny shop (as much a museum as a store) is like discovering your grandparents' attic. It's dusty, dark and strangely removed from the buses and traffic just outside the door.

While the city has the standard art and history museums, it's the little museums that best represent the city's funky spirit. Even if you have no interest in their subjects, they're worth a visit. Bob Meyers, director of the ❻ American International Rattlesnake Museum, clearly loves his snakes. You'll find him in his two-room homage to rattlers most days, joking around with customers and fielding questions on the museum's less hospitable residents. In addition to what is allegedly the world's largest collection of live rattlesnakes, don't miss the snake-themed beer-and-wine-bottle collection or the freaky 1976 movie poster for *Rattler*.

TIME
3 days

BEST TIME TO GO
Year-round

START
Frontier Restaurant, Albuquerque, NM

END
Casa de Sueno, Albuquerque, NM

ALSO GOOD FOR

CITY

247

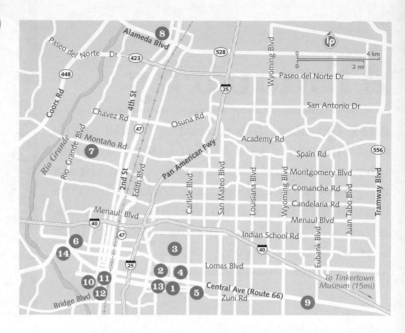

For those who prefer high-speed thrills to scaly chills, head to the ❼ **Unser Racing Museum**, honoring Albuquerque's famous NASCAR family. The museum, designed in the shape of a racing wheel with Al Unser Sr's 1971 Indy 500–winning car rotating in the center, features more than 30 shiny cars from Indy 500 and Pikes Peak races. The nondescript white-washed wall in the parking lot ended Al Unser Sr's bid for the 1989 Indy 500 title. Alan lost to Emerson Fittipaldi when he hit the wall, so he bought it and had it moved lock, stock and barrel to the museum.

ASK A LOCAL

"Albuquerque is a great city to live because everything goes. People gravitate here. They're transitioning in their lives, and they feel the spirit of the city. This is the place for mind, body and spirit conditioning. It's eclectic and welcoming."
Adrian Cramer

Thanks to the wind patterns called the Albuquerque Box, Albuquerque is a popular destination for hot-air balloon enthusiasts year-round and the International Balloon Fiesta (www.balloonfiesta.com) is held annually over the first week of October. Get a sense of balloon life at the modern ❽ **Albuquerque International Balloon Museum** with life-size balloons filling its high ceilings and several interactive exhibits exploring everything from the sport's earliest experiments to hot-air balloons in Native American art.

New Mexico, famous as the birthplace of the atomic bomb, embraces its atomic identity. At the ❾ **National Atomic Museum**, press a button to hear an oddly comical Einstein doll explain, with a jolting German accent, his theory of relativity, and examine America's uneasy embrace of atomic energy at the funny and slightly disturbing exhibit on atomic popular culture. One of the oddest pieces in the display is the bottle of La Bomba wine, from a Los Alamos winery, with a mushroom cloud on its label.

The Hispanic neighborhood of ⑩ **Barelas**, established in the late 1600s, is Albuquerque's oldest district. In the early 1990s, historic preservationists teamed with local activists to clean up and revitalize the downtrodden Barelas, opening a Hispanic cultural center and protecting historic buildings. At its north end sits ⑪ **Ruppe B Drug**, a nondescript room featured in the Smithsonian's traveling exhibit on folk life. While you'll find a few drugstore basics, like Tylenol and Maalox, the heart of Ruppe's business lies in its traditional Hispanic and Native American cures. The aged Maclovia Zamora, a *yerbera* (healer) who learned traditional healing from her grandmother, who herself was a *curandera* (traditional Hispanic folk healer), listens patiently to customers' ailments and selects herbs from the plastic baskets and hooks against the wall. "Steep this, mixed with this, and a little bit of this," she recommends, in a voice that in itself is healing. "But don't use boiling water. Drink a few cups of the tea, and that headache will go away." And you listen because she knows. Before leaving, check out the glass case of unusual soaps and lotions,

 **DETOUR** Duck and wind your way through the 22-room **Tinkertown Museum**, stuffed floor to ceiling with Ross J Ward's 20-year collection, including a 60ft miniature replica of an Old West town, Ward's wood carvings and a Buddha in a glass-bottle shrine. It's in the foothills of the Sandias (I-40 east, exit 175).

including rattlesnake and turtle cream, and take a moment at the strangely moving altar at the store's center. Down the street, the always-crowded ⑫ **Barelas Coffeehouse**, with its oddly short counter and simple decor, serves what many claim is the best New Mexican homecooking in the city.

When you're ready to call it a day, head for dinner at ⑬ **Annapurna's World Vegetarian Café**, where you can take a dry-erase board quiz to determine your ayurvedic body type before ordering and the owner offers personalized menu selections. After a dessert of fresh coconut served whole with a straw and zucchini cake, retreat to ⑭ **Casa de Sueno** for the night. Designed as an artists' colony in the 1930s, this adobe compound with 21 casitas hosted slews of artists and writers through the years, many attracted to the city's quirky vibe and distinct personality.

Yes, Albuquerque is a funny place. It's the kind of place folks stumble into on their way to somewhere else. We'll just stay for a couple years, they say. And 30, 40 years later, they're still here, watching the Sandias turn red at sunset.
Jennifer Denniston

TRIP INFORMATION

GETTING THERE
Albuquerque sits at the intersection of two major interstates, I-40 and I-25, 63 miles south of Santa Fe.

DO
Albuquerque International Balloon Museum
More than anyone thought they'd want to know on the history, culture, sport and science of hot-air balloons. ☎ 505-768-6020; www.balloonmuseum.com; 9201 Balloon Museum Dr, Albuquerque; adult/child $4/3; ☽ 9am-5pm Tue-Sun; ♿

American International Rattlesnake Museum
Like walking into the home of a good friend who just happens to be a snake fanatic with the world's largest collection of live rattlesnakes. ☎ 505-242-6569; www.rattlesnake .com; 202 San Felipe St NW, Albuquerque; adult/child $2.50/3.50; ☽ 11:30am-5:30pm Mon-Fri, 10am-6pm Sat, 1-5pm Sun, seasonal variations; ♿

Cowboys & Indians Antiques
As much a museum as a store, this small Route 66 gallery sells quality antique Western, Native American and Hispanic art and memorabilia. ☎ 505-255-4054; www .cowboysandindiansnm.com; 4000 Central Ave SE, Albuquerque; ☽ 10am-6pm

National Atomic Museum
Check out B-21 bombers, the history of Madame Curie, displays on atomic culture and more. ☎ 505-245-2137; www.atomic museum.com; 601 Eubank Blvd SE, Albuquerque; adult/child 6-17 $6/4; ☽ 9am-5pm daily; ♿

Ruppe B Drug
Maclovia Zamora dispenses traditional Native American and Hispanic healing remedies at this 100-year-old business. ☎ 505-243-6719; 807 4th St SW, Albuquerque; ☽ 10am-6pm daily

Unser Racing Museum
You gotta love a museum with this much passion, even if you've never watched a NASCAR race in your entire life. ☎ 505-341-1776; www.unserracingmuseum.com; 1776 Montano Rd NW, Albuquerque; adult/child 7-12 yr $7/3; ☽ 10am-4pm daily; ♿

EAT
Annapurna's World Vegetarian Café
Even dedicated carnivores will enjoy tasty grains, veggies and fruit dishes. Vegan and gluten-free options. ☎ 505-262-2424; 2201 Silver Ave SE, Albuquerque; mains $4-10; ☽ 7am-8pm Mon-Wed, 7am-9pm Thu-Sat, 10am-2pm Sun

Barelas Coffeehouse
Classic neighborhood restaurant with a city-wide following. ☎ 505-843-7577; 1502 4th St SW, Albuquerque; mains $4-12; ☽ 7:30am-3pm Mon-Fri, to 2:30pm Sat

Frontier Restaurant
Albuquerque institution since 1971 for cheap and delicious green-chile stew and fresh-squeezed OJ in a no-frills space on old Route 66. ☎ 505-266-0550; 2400 Central Ave SE, Albuquerque; mains $4-8; ☽ 5am-1am daily

SLEEP
Casa de Suenos
Historic casitas (small houses) close to shops and museums in Old Town. Many suites have a kiva fireplace or hot tub, and a full breakfast is included. ☎ 800-665-7002; www .casadesuenos.com; 310 Rio Grande Blvd SW, Albuquerque; ste $150-189

USEFUL WEBSITES
www.itsatrip.org
www.publiclands.org

www.lonelyplanet.com/trip-planner

LINK YOUR TRIP
TRIP

Brewpub Crawl

WHY GO Whether you're craving a cold Green Chile Beer on the banks of the Rio Grande, or a strong barley wine with a side of bluegrass in a cozy Santa Fe bar, beer aficionados on a mission for the perfect microbrew can plan an entire holiday around New Mexico's fantastic brewpubs.

TIME
5 days

DISTANCE
415 miles

BEST TIME TO GO
May – Oct

START
Taos, NM

END
Silver City, NM

ALSO GOOD FOR

CITY

Northern New Mexico is the state's brew mecca. Start your microbrew crawl in ❶ Taos. It only takes a heartbeat to fall head over heels in love with this tiny and isolated town. Let your senses absorb sage and piñon in the air, the sweeping mesas cresting at the pointy, often snow-white tip of Taos Mountain and you're in for a delightful experience.

It's definitely an acquired taste and we admit Taos's signature Green Chile Beer – infused with roasted green chiles during the brewing process – isn't for everyone, but try at least one or two of these unique beers at ❷ Eske's Brew Pub, a crowded Taos institution. Although the ❸ Alley Cantina doesn't brew its own beer, it still has a decent selection of bottled beers. The coolest thing about the Cantina isn't the beverage selection, however; it's the location in the oldest building in Taos. Built in the 1500s by forward-thinking Native capitalists as the Taos Pueblo Trading Post, nowadays you can catch live music ranging from Zydeco to rock and jazz seven days a week. Bed down at the ❹ Laughing Horse Inn, which has funky rooms, a hot tub under the stars and a hippie-commune atmosphere. Prepare your body for another day of beer tasting with breakfast at ❺ Sustaining Cultures. It's a New Agey outpost where you order a "wheatgrass hopper" with a side of at-your-table tarot-card reading.

Whether you choose to take the high road or the low road, it's a gorgeous drive to historic ❻ Santa Fe. Founded in 1609, it is Ameri-

BEST TRIP

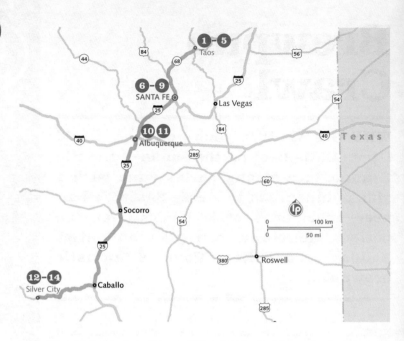

ca's oldest capital and the home of New Mexico's oldest microbrewery: the **7 Santa Fe Brewing Company**. Officially incorporated in 1892 – although it had been experimenting with brewing since miners arrived in the late 1870s – the Santa Fe Brewing Co shut its doors just four years later when the market dried up. It took a hundred years, but the brewing company reopened in 1988 – it didn't really expand until today's co-owner Brian Lock and his two partners took over the brewery in 1997. Beer geeks will love the tasting and touring side of the brewery, where they have eight beers on tap, all made on premises, plus a guest beer or two. The Santa Fe Pale Ale, which is bottled and sold in restaurants and shops around the Southwest, is the most well-known beer served. It has a fulfilling flavor with a crisp-hoppy bite. But also make sure to sample the house favorite, the Nut Brown Ale. Another interesting selection includes the Imperial Porter, which is a virtual Black Forest of dark, malty goodness.

> **ASK A LOCAL**
>
> "I really like the different seasonal brews, each one in the proper time of year, a pilsner in summertime, a porter in winter, a bock in spring. Our Nut Brown is a "sessions" beer – this means you can easily down more than one – but our 20th Anniversary beers are really exciting!"
>
> *Brian Lock, owner, Santa Fe Brewing Company*

The **8 Second Street Brewery**, in the city's revitalized Railyard District, is another popular brewpub in Santa Fe. Second Street serves handcrafted

English-style beers created on site. Try the Cream Stout and grab a bite to eat here, then stay for the live music. Sleep at the Spanish hacienda–style ❾ La Fonda, which has a very unique folk-art character.

Just an hour south of Santa Fe, ❿ Albuquerque is worlds apart. This working-class city has a real grittiness about its sprawling adobe subdivisions and rocky mesa tops. It's the kind of place requiring a bit of digging to appreciate – or maybe just some good beer, which can be found, and even created by you, at ⓫ Kelly's Brewery. Located inside a streamlined Texaco station that was considered one of the most modern facilities on Route 66 in the 1960s, it serves a rotation of homemade beers and prides itself on being a real brew-it-yourself pub. Guests can select a recipe, and be guided through the two-hour process of actually brewing their own beer. You'll have to wait two weeks before you can drink your creation, but if you can swing back through Albuquerque it's worth returning to bottle your product and taste the fruits of your labor.

It's a 238-mile trek southwest from Albuquerque to ⓬ Silver City, but if you're looking to drink locally made brews in New Mexico's coolest Wild West town, then it's worth the drive. The ⓭ Silver City Brewing Co serves a range of homemade ales and lagers. We like the 'Fat' Strong Scotch Ale. At 9.2% alcohol it packs quite a punch. A gold medal winner at the Great American Beer Festival, the 'Fat' Strong is a big, dark, supermalty brew that tastes almost like a fine Scotch whiskey. If you are interested in learning about the craft, ask to chat with the head brewer. End your New Mexican brewpub tour in Silver City's most venerable sleeping establishment, the ⓮ Palace Hotel. In a restored 1882 hostelry, it has 19 affordable rooms all decorated in old-fashioned Territorial style.

Aaron Anderson

BEER MAKING IN NEW MEXICO

Although several breweries were already making the pale European-style beers introduced to Americans when the Santa Fe Brewing Company opened in 1892, beer historians consider it the state's first microbrewery because it took beer making to a whole new level. Regional flavors were added during fermentation and alcohol levels were tweaked – leading to the creation of darker, richer and sometimes almost tangy-tasting beers. Plus the brews were made in small batches – so each barrel tasted slightly different.

TRIP 39

TRIP INFORMATION

GETTING THERE
Taos is 135 miles northwest of Albuquerque. Take I-25 north to Hwy 285 north and follow it to Hwy 68 north into town.

DO

Alley Cantina
Live music almost nightly. ☎ 505-758-2121; 121 Terracina Lane, Taos; pub grub $6-14; ☽ from 11:30am

Eske's Brew Pub & Eatery
A crowded local hangout with 25 microbrews and good food; try a hearty bowl of Wanda's green-chile stew. ☎ 505-758-1517; 106 Des Georges Lane, Taos; pub grub $6-10; ☽ 4-10pm Mon-Thu, 11am-10pm Fri-Sun

Kelly's Brewery
Call ahead to reserve a spot for brewing your own beer. It costs $150 for a 72-gallon batch. If you just want to sample, go to the onsite pub. ☎ 505-262-2739; 3226 Central Ave SE, Albuquerque; ☽ 8am-midnight

Santa Fe Brewing Company
Go on a tour, stop by the tasting room or grab a burger and a pint at this popular brewery. ☎ 505-424 3333; www.santafe brewing.com; 35 Fire Place, Santa Fe; mains from $7; ☽ 7am-9pm Sun-Thu, to 10pm Fri & Sat, tours noon Sat, by appointment.

Second Street Brewery
Excellent homemade beer and New Mexican and American dishes; sit outside on the big patio, or inside the brewery. ☎ 505-982-3030; www.secondstreetbrewery.com; 2nd St, Santa Fe; ☽ 11am-10pm, to 11pm Fri & Sat

Silver City Brewing Co
Grab delicious pizza, calzones and wings with your beer at this popular brewery. ☎ 575-534-2739; 101 E College Ave, Silver City; mains from $6; ☽ 11am-10pm

SLEEP & EAT

La Fonda
Vibrant and historic; the rooftop bar is perfect for sunset cocktails. ☎ 800-523-5002; www.lafondasantafe.com; 100 E San Francisco St, Santa Fe; r from $225

Laughing Horse Inn
This unique inn offers one-of-a-kind rooms inside a meandering 120-year-old Spanish adobe hacienda. ☎ 800-776-0161; www.laughinghorseinn.com; 729 Paseo del Pueblo Norte, Taos; r $75-160

Palace Hotel
Rooms at this historic hotel vary in size, but all are comfortable. ☎ 575-388-1811; www.zianet.com/palacehotel; 106 W Broadway, Silver City; r from $45

Sustaining Cultures
A New Age joint serving sandwiches, the best salad bar in Taos and hearty breakfasts. ☎ 505-751-0959; 114 Doña Luz St, Taos; mains $5-10; ☽ 9:30am-5:30pm Mon-Sat

USEFUL WEBSITES
www.beer100.com/brewpubs_l_to_n/newmexico.htm

LINK YOUR TRIP
www.lonelyplanet.com/trip-planner

Ice Caves & Wolf Dens on Highway 53

WHY GO Forget Route 66, get your kicks on Hwy 53 between Gallup and Grants. The alternative route features a trippy line-up of weird and wonderful distractions – lava badlands, ice caves, wolves and historical graffiti – set against a surreal landscape of crimson arches, crumbling pueblos and volcanic craters.

TIME
2 days

DISTANCE
85 miles

BEST TIME TO GO
Aug – Oct

START
Gallup, NM

END
Grants, NM

ALSO GOOD FOR

Used for centuries as a Zuni, Hopi and other Pueblo Indian trade route, Hwy 53 runs parallel to Route 66 and serves up a Pandora's box of one-of-a-kind attractions. Reach the byway via Hwy 602 south from ❶ Gallup pausing at the ❷ Ellis Tanner Trading Company on the way. The shop doubles as a sort of social gathering place for the Navajo community and still operates a functional trade counter. If you don't have anything to swap, your dollar is good in the huge pawn room. Dig around for one of the unique pieces of turquoise jewelry tucked away behind a collection of vintage sheep-wool rugs in the massive pawn room.

It doesn't matter how small a New Mexican town is, if it's on the map, it likely has a restaurant where the community gathers for gossip, fresh guacamole and green-chile stew. In the Navajo sheep-farming village of ❸ Ramah, just east of the entrance to Hwy 53, this restaurant is the ❹ Stage Coach Café. Whether you order a T-bone or enchiladas, make sure to sweeten your experience with a slice of creamy, crusty pie for dessert.

Animal lovers will want to make a short 20-minute detour to the ❺ Wild Spirit Wolf Sanctuary after lunch. A non-profit organization, it provides food, shelter, love and even a multivitamin to abused and abandoned wolves and wolf-dogs that are unable to survive in the wild. Take a right on BLM Rd 125, about 10 miles east of Ramah,

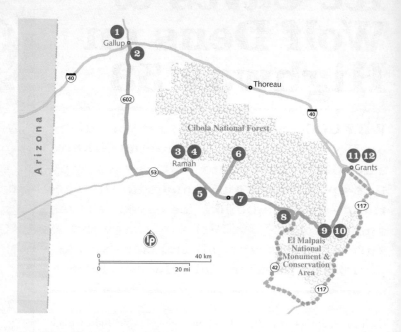

and follow it 8 miles to BLM Rd 120. Turn right onto this gravel road and continue for 4 miles to the sanctuary. You can take a tour (offered six days a week). Besides learning all about wolf-conservation efforts, behavior and eating habits, tours take visitors on walks through the natural-looking habitats and allow you to get quite close to these big, shaggy, long-nosed, dog-like creatures.

DETOUR For a real backcountry adventure, take a detour to El Malpais' Wild Western side. County Rd 42 leaves Hwy 117 about 34 miles south of I-40 and meanders through 40 miles of Bureau of Land Management (BLM) country. It passes several craters, caves and lava tubes (reached by signed trails) and emerges at Hwy 53 near Bandera Crater. Since the road is unpaved, it's best to have a high-clearance 4WD. Go with a companion – this is an isolated area.

Having got your wolf fix, get back on Hwy 53 and head for some ancient graffiti. 6 **El Morro National Monument**, also called "Inscription Rock," has been autographed by passers-by since 1250, when the first pueblo petroglyphs were etched near the top of this 200ft hunk of sandstone rising above a permanent pool of water. Spanish conquistadors, Anglo pioneers and railway surveyors all paused to fill their canteens at the 200,000-gallon waterhole, and when they stopped many couldn't help leaving a record of their visit behind. It's quite a sight – more than 2000 messages were carved into the soft rock before President Teddy Roosevelt turned El Morro into America's second national monument.

By this point you'll be ready to relax, and luckily the region's best B&B is in El Morro's backyard. The ❼ **Cimarron Rose** sits in a peaceful locale in the Zuni Mountains just east of the national monument, and the innkeepers take pride in being eco-friendly. Rainwater is collected and used as utility water, and grey water is reused to water trees. Two goats and a horse organically fertilize Cimarron's perennial gardens, which provide food and shelter for more than 80 species of birds.

After devouring a big and delicious Cimarron Rose breakfast, it's time to explore the volcanic badlands. Privately owned ❽ **Bandera Ice Cave**, known to Pueblo Indians as Winter Lake, is a chunk of green-tinted ice (the color comes from Arctic algae) frozen inside part of a collapsed lava tube. The subterranean cave stays frozen year round – the ice on the cave floor is 20ft thick and temps never rise above 31°F! Reach the volcanic crater where the cave sits on one of several easy walking trails from the concession visitors center.

Haven't had enough lava? Good. ❾ **El Malpais National Monument** is your next destination. Pronounced el mahl-pie-*ees*, which means "bad land" in Spanish, the monument consists of almost 200 sq miles of lava flows abutting adjacent sandstone with a number of hiking trails departing from access points along Hwy 117. Keep an eye out for the impressive ❿ **La Ventana Natural Arch**, visible from Hwy 117 about 17 miles south of I-40. Stop by the national monument's information center in Grants, or ask at the ranger station at the park entrance for backcountry camping permits and park maps.

ALL ABOUT LAVA

All told, five major flows have been identified in **El Malpais National Monument**, with the most recent one pegged at just 2000 to 3000 years old. Prehistoric Native Americans may have witnessed the final eruptions since local Indian legends refer to "rivers of fire." Scenic Hwy 117 leads modern-day explorers past cinder cones and spatter cones, smooth *pahoehoe* lava and jagged lava lava, ice caves and a 17-mile-long lava-tube system.

Your trip ends in ⓫ **Grants**. Once a booming railway town, and then a booming mining town, today it is simply a trucker's stop on Route 66 with one interesting museum. Located at the town's now defunct uranium mine, kids love the hands-on exhibits at the ⓬ **New Mexico Mining Museum**. Although a lack of demand has ceased mine operations, this remains America's largest uranium reserve.

Becca Blond

TRIP INFORMATION

GETTING THERE
From Gallup, 140 miles west of Albuquerque on I-40 (Route 66), take Hwy 602 south to Hwy 53 east.

DO

Bandera Ice Cave
Look for this private tourist concession 25 miles southwest of Grants. ☎ 505-783-4303; www.icecaves.com; adult/child 5-12 yr $8/4; ☼ 8am-4:30pm; ♿

Ellis Tanner Trading Company
One of the Southwest's largest functional, traditional Indian trading posts, it's been run by the same family for four generations. ☎ 505-863-4434; www.etanner.com; cnr Nizhoni & Hwy 602; ☼ call for hr

El Malpais Information Center
Stop by the Grants Visitors Center for free backcountry camping permits. ☎ 505-285-4641; www.nps.gov/elma; 123 E Roosevelt Ave, Grants; ☼ 8am-4:30pm Mon-Fri

El Malpais National Monument
The ranger station at the entrance to this volcanic badland has maps and info on hiking in the national monument. ☎ 505-783-4774; www.nps.gov/elma; Hwy 53; ☼ 8:30am-4:30pm

El Morro National Monument
A nationally protected 200ft sandstone outcrop covered with thousands of years of graffiti; located about 52 miles southeast of Gallup. ☎ 505-783-4226; www.nps .gov/elmo; adult/child $3/free; ☼ 9am-5pm, to 7pm in Jun-Aug

New Mexico Mining Museum
Kids can't get enough of the "world's only uranium museum." It's a hands-on place with metal-cage descents into the 'Section 26' mine shaft. ☎ 505-287-4802; adult/child 7-18 yr $3/2; ☼ 9am-4pm Mon-Sat; ♿.

Wild Spirit Wolf Sanctuary
Walk with the wolves at this sanctuary that gives abused and injured wolves and wolf-dog mixes a new lease on life; tours of the animals' homes last around one hour. ☎ 505-775-3304; www.wildwolf sanctuary.org; Forest Rd 120; adult/child $5/3; ☼ 11am-3.30pm Tue-Sun

EAT & SLEEP

Cimarron Rose
Two Southwestern-style suites with tiles, pine walls and hardwood floors are offered at this eco-friendly B&B off Hwy 53 between El Morro and El Malpais National Monuments. ☎ 505-783-4770; www.cimarronrose.com; 689 Oso Ridge Rd; ste $110-185

Stage Coach Cafe
Friendly service, Mexican and American dishes and a big selection of pies. ☎ 505-783-4288; 3370 Bond St/Hwy 53, Ramah; mains $6-10; ☼ 10am-6pm Mon-Sat, to 4pm Sun

USEFUL WEBSITES
www.ancientway-route53.com

LINK YOUR TRIP

www.lonelyplanet.com/trip-planner

OUTDOORS

Mountain Biking Gallup

WHY GO Move over Moab, it's Gallup's turn in the saddle. Whether it's racing down psychedelic-orange slickrock, lung-busting up high desert mesas or dropping into narrow aspen glades, the nearly 200 miles of single track around this old Route 66 motoring town is the wickedest mountain biking in New Mexico.

Once just another fading pit stop on old Route 66, Gallup has been reinvented as New Mexico's mountain-biking capital. From aspen forest to high desert, slickrock to mesa, beginner to advanced, the single-track trails here are big on variety, but small on crowds. Unlike Moab, Gallup has yet to become a trend.

Gallup's trail networks are a homegrown community initiative, built by locals, with more trails added every year. Pay a visit to ❶ **High Mesa Bikes** for the latest trail scoop. Owner Albert Ortega helped build Gallup's trail systems and doles out advice with a smile.

After stocking up on maps and power bars, it's (almost) time to hit the trail – you can ride right to the trailhead; it's just 3 miles north of Gallup. From downtown, go north on Hwy 491 to Chino Loop Rd and look for the gravel parking lot on the left side; this is the ❷ **Gamerco Trailhead**, the eastern entrance to the excellent ❸ **High Desert Trail System**. High Desert boasts 23 miles of exposed mesa top and crumbly terrain – read loose rocks and sand – on three loops of varying difficulty that can be ridden in one mammoth circuit or individually. Warm up on ❹ **First Mesa Loop**, the only track suitable for beginners. Fly downhill for half a mile, cross a flat, boggy stretch scented with cedar, then start a long, slow burn to the top of the first mesa and the Six Flag Junction. If you're feeling good – and you're at least an intermediate cyclist – turn right and continue

TIME
3 days

DISTANCE
150 miles

BEST TIME TO GO
May – Oct

START
Gallup, NM

END
Gallup, NM

ALSO GOOD FOR

HISTORY & CULTURE

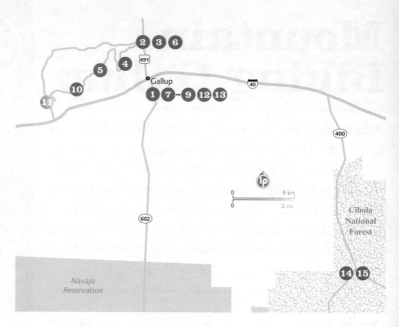

on to the more challenging **5** Second Mesa Loop; combined it's a 13-mile round-trip jaunt. Otherwise turn right and head back around the mesa to the starting gate for an 8-mile round trip. After your ride, refresh yourself with an ice-cold beer from the take-away liquor shop next to the Gamerco trailhead called **6** The Tropics (a local favorite).

> **DETOUR**
>
> To really get off the line, visit the **Twin Springs Trailhead**. Located 35 miles southeast of Gallup off Hwy 400, Twin Springs already has 70 miles of forest trails, with more planned. Don't miss the ride through the mesmerizing 2.5-mile-long aspen corridor. The slickrock is also pretty killer. Ask Albert at High Mesa Bikes for trail recommendations.

After a day of bumpy thrill riding, you'll be ready for an original Route 66 crash pad, the **7** El Rancho Hotel. Popular with the Hollywood crowd from the '30s to the '60s – Humphrey Bogart, Katherine Hepburn, and John Wayne – it's now listed as a National Historic Site. Check out the superb two-story open lobby decorated in Navajo-meets-rustic-lodge style. The hotel's **8** El Rancho Restaurant is in a slightly kitschy spaghetti Western setting. (Nearly all the "leading lady" dishes are of the fruit with sorbet or cottage cheese variety.) After dinner, sip a margarita at the hotel's old-time **9** 49ers Bar.

On day two, mix things up and start with the most challenging trail, the **10** Third Mesa Loop. This trail crosses the highest mesa top and starts from the western end's **11** Mentmore Trailhead. When combined with the Second Mesa Loop it is an awesome, but very technical, 15-mile leg and lung buster – the views alone are worth the effort. The trail starts with a climb up the northern ridgeline, then pops down to the Second Mesa Loop, with its numerous cliffside overlooks. Take a breather at Six Flags Junction before starting a long, gnarly climb up a narrow track that's literally carved into the crumbly rock wall. It's appropriately named the "House of Pain."

Return to El Rancho for some well-earned slumber. Spice up your gastro variety with a visit to the off-the-path **⑫ Genaro's Café** and a green-chile burger – ask for the chile on the side, unless you want a soppy bun. It also serves classic Mexican food like tamales and *chile rellenos*.

> **ASK A LOCAL**
>
> "On the Plush Trail there's this really cool old alligator juniper tree that takes about three people to put their hands around it and the bark looks like real alligator skin. There are carved benches under the tree, and that's where we relax, take a break, drink a beer, and then we drop down into the aspens. It's so beautiful up there."
>
> *Albert Ortega*

Fuel up on your third day with a full breakfast at the **⑬ Coffee House** – local art on the walls, overstuffed couches and newspapers, and of course strong espresso. The Zuni Mountains are your next stop, about 15 miles southeast of Gallup and best reached by car. From Gallup head east on I-40 to exit 33 onto Hwy 400 and follow this road for 7.7 miles to the parking lot on the right for the **⑭ Mile Marker Three Trail System**. Running through the Cibola National Forest, the trailhead is at 7500ft – a thousand-foot gain from High Desert – and has lots of tree cover, which makes biking here much cooler. The 68-mile trail system is true forest single track – the path is 2ft at its widest! Beginners should ride the 8-mile **⑮ Quaking Aspen Trail** past ponderosa pines and gangly white aspens. It's a real mountain-bike trail, with loose rocks and all, but the climbs and descents aren't too technical.

"After a day of bumpy thrill riding, you'll be ready for an original Route 66 crash pad..."

Our favorite ride at Three Mile incorporates a number of trails to form a perfectly balanced – one third flat, one third up and one third down in alternating orders – 16-mile loop. The loop doesn't have a name, but is easy to follow. Take Quaking Aspen to the Plush trail, then jump on Turkey Nest and follow it to the Y2K trail, which eventually leads back to Quaking Aspen and the main parking lot.

Aaron Anderson

TRIP INFORMATION

GETTING THERE
Gallup is 139 miles west of Albuquerque on I-40 (Historic Route 66).

DO
High Desert Trail System
The visitors center has maps; take the Chico/Gamerco exit of I-40 to reach the main trailhead. ☎ 800-242-4282; www.galupnm.org; 701 Montoya Blvd; ⊙ 8am-5pm Mon-Fri

High Mesa Bikes
Rents bikes, has loads of info on the Mile Marker Three and High Desert Trail Systems and sells the latest outdoor gear. ☎ 505-863-3825; www.highmesabikes.com; 123 W Coal Ave; rentals per day $35-65; ⊙ 10am-6pm Tue-Sat

EAT & SLEEP
49ers Bar
Have a cocktail at the congenial Old West bar in the El Rancho. There's music nightly. ☎ 505-863-9311; www.elranchohotel.com; 1000 E Hwy 66; ⊙ 7am-midnight

Coffee House
A mellow atmosphere attracts locals, artists, bikers and musicians. Sandwiches and strong espresso are on the menu, and there's wi-fi. ☎ 505-726-0291; 203 W Coal Ave; mains $4-10; ⊙ 7am-9:30pm Mon-Thu, to 11pm Fri & Sat, to 4pm Sun

El Rancho
Hollywood goes authentic Native American at Gallup's best, and only, full-service lodging option. ☎ 505-863-9311; www.elranchohotel.com; 1000 E Hwy 66; r $65-100

El Rancho Restaurant
New Mexican and American cuisine is served amid old Hollywood photos and frontier surroundings at this restaurant inside the hotel of the same name. ☎ 505-863-9311; www.elranchohotel.com; 1000 E Hwy 66; mains $8-20; ⊙ 7am-midnight

Genaro's Café
Enjoy generous portions of favorites like Stuffed Poblanos and Sopaipillas at this hidden gem. If you like it hotter, the red chile will make you feel right at home. ☎ 505-863-6761; 600 W Hill Ave; mains $6-12; ⊙ 10:30am-8pm Tue-Sat

The Tropics
Stock up on cold microbrews right across from the Gamerco trailhead at this take-away shop. It's where all the locals go for the best microbrew selection after (and sometimes during!) a sick single-track day. ☎ 505-863-9298; 503 Chino Ave; beer from $4

USEFUL WEBSITES
www.gallupnm.org
www.gallupwaypoints.com

LINK YOUR TRIP
www.lonelyplanet.com/trip-planner

Pueblo Life

WHY GO Be it the sweet scent of frying dough or the sparkle of silver and turquoise bracelets displayed in an adobe shop window, Native American customs are part of New Mexico's soul. On this trip the culture and history of four of the state's 19 distinct pueblos are explored.

TIME
3 days

DISTANCE
310 miles

BEST TIME TO GO
Jun – Aug

START
Taos Pueblo, NM

END
Zuni Pueblo, NM

To understand New Mexico, home to the fifth-largest Native American population, you must visit her pueblos. The experience may not be the happy tourist attraction you were expecting: many offer little for visitors outside of festival weekends, serving as home to groups of long-displaced people, complete with schools, shops and gathering places. On this trip we take you to sacred ruins and ceremonial dances but also expose you to the all-too-often harsh reality of life for the average Native American living on reservation land. Poverty, alcoholism and anger are visible here. At the end, you'll have experienced much, and gained an appreciation of the complex Native American cultures and belief systems.

One of New Mexico's best-preserved adobe dwellings is the ultra-famous ❶ Taos Pueblo, the largest multistoried pueblo still existing in the USA. Built around 1450, it's been continuously inhabited by the same tribe ever since and was designated a World Heritage Site in 1992. Shop for fine jewelry, *micaceous* (an aluminum mineral found in local rocks) pottery and other arts and crafts just outside the main pueblo entrance at the well-respected ❷ Tony Reyna Indian Shop. We like the turquoise necklaces, bracelets and rings. The general public has the best chance of seeing traditional dances in July and August, when many festivities are opened to the public. Plan your summer visit to Taos Pueblo to coincide with the huge ❸ Taos Pueblo Powwow, which features Plains and Pueblo Indians gathering for dances and workshops as this centuries-old tradition continues. Of all the pueblos in northern New Mexico, Taos Pueblo has the most events and celebrations open to the public. This age-old

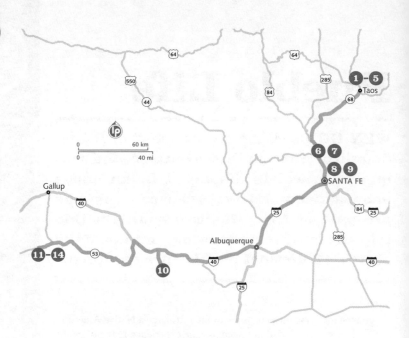

gathering includes workshops and dances and is open to the public. Everyone's favorite spot for grub, ④ **Tewa Kitchen** serves a host of Native treats like *phien-ty* (blue-corn fry-bread stuffed with buffalo meat), *twa chull* (grilled buffalo) or a bowl of heirloom green chile grown on pueblo grounds. Native Americans legalized casinos in an attempt to raise money for their impoverished communities, and Indian reservations are the only place you can gamble in the state. Head to ⑤ **Taos Mountain Casino**. It's a cozy joint, where you can blow your cash in an alcohol- and smoke-free environment – don't expect a whiskey with your hand of cards; booze is banned at New Mexican casinos.

Don't linger too long at the blackjack table; you have much more to see before dark. From Taos Pueblo head southeast to ⑥ **Nambé Pueblo**. At the base of the Sangre de Cristo mountains, just driving here is amazing. The road cuts through dramatically sculpted sandstone and over piñon-scented hills. Perhaps because of the isolated location (or inspirational geology), Nambé has long been a spiritual center for the Tewa-speaking tribes, a distinction that attracted the attentions of Spanish priests intent on conversion by any means necessary. After the Pueblo Revolt and Reconquista wound down, Spanish settlers annexed much of their territory. Although the Native Americans living here lost much of their land, the place still remains inhabited and spiritually important today. And Nambé's remaining lands have a couple of big attractions, including ⑦ **Lake Nambé**. It was created in 1974 after the US federal government dammed the Rio Nambé, flooding historic ruins but creating an important reservoir that attracts non-motorized boaters and trout lovers. There's nowhere to sleep around Nambé Pueblo, so go south to ❽ **Santa Fe** and spend the night at the posh ❾ **Inn at Loretto**, modeled after the Taos Pueblo. Start early on day two as your next two pueblos are a few hours' drive west. You can grab dinner at the hotel's swish but affordable Luminaria. Dine under the romantic canopies on the patio or inside modern, candlelit environs. Either way, chef Brian Cooper is making local waves for his original contemporary American dishes served with a signature Santa Fe twist. There's live music in the evenings.

There are few more dramatic mesa-top locations than ❿ **Acoma Pueblo** (they don't call it "Sky City" for nothing), sitting 7000ft above sea level and 367ft above the surrounding plateau 63 miles southwest of Albuquerque. It's one of the oldest continuously inhabited settlements in North America: people have lived here since the later part of the 11th century. The pueblo is famous for pottery, which is sold by individual artists on the mesa. Traditional Acoma pottery is made from clay dug on the reservation and then painted. Ask before buying if this is how the vase or mug you are looking at was made, as there is a distinction between this traditional method and what locals call "ceramic" pottery (it is made elsewhere with "inferior clay" and simply painted by the artist).

THE ORIGINAL APARTMENTS

Pueblos are the original apartments, unique among the country's Native American dwellings. These adobe structures can have up to five levels, connected by ladders, and are built with varying combinations of mud bricks, stones, logs and plaster. In the central plaza of each pueblo is a kiva, an underground ceremonial chamber that connects to the spirit world.

Return back to I-40 from Acoma Pueblo and head west towards Gallup, turning off onto scenic Hwy 53 and then to the ⓫ **Zuni Pueblo**. Take some time to walk around and soak up the history. Besides ancient stone houses and beehive-shaped mud ovens, you'll pass the massive ⓬ **Our Lady of Guadalupe Mission**, featuring impressive locally painted murals of about 30 life-size kachinas (Hopi spirit dolls). The church dates from 1629, although it has been rebuilt twice since then. It's a good example of the Christian missionary influence on the area. The ⓭ **Ashiwi Awan Museum & Heritage Center** displays early photos and other tribal artifacts and is worth a quick visit. End your Native American odyssey with a good night's sleep at ⓮ **Inn at Halona**. Rooms here are decorated with local Zuni arts and crafts, and this is the only place to stay on the pueblo.

DETOUR For a comprehensive overview on visiting New Mexico's pueblos, stop by Albuquerque's **Indian Pueblo Cultural Center** (www.indianpueblo .org). Operated by the pueblos themselves, you'll get an idea of what to expect from each distinct village. A historical museum here traces the development of Pueblo cultures; exhibits compare cultures through languages, customs and crafts; an art gallery features changing exhibits and a restaurant serves Pueblo fare.

Becca Blond

HISTORY & CULTURE

TRIP INFORMATION

GETTING THERE

Taos Pueblo is 135 miles from Albuquerque. Follow I-25 to Hwy 285 to Hwy 68, all going north to Taos town; turn right on Pueblo Rd and continue 3 miles.

DO

Acoma Pueblo

Visitors can only reach Sky City on guided tours leaving every 45 minutes from the visitors center. ☎ 505-469-1052; I-40 exit 96, 13 miles south; tours adult/child $10/7; ☾ closed Jul 10-13, early Oct

Ashiwi Awan Museum & Heritage Center

Will cook traditional meals for groups of 10 or more ($10 per person) with advance reservations. ☎ 505-782-4403; Ojo Caliente Rd, Zuni Pueblo; admission by donation; ☾ 9am-5pm Mon-Fri

Lake Nambé

The Pueblo's most popular attraction, it's great for trout fishing from oar-boats. ☎ 505-455-2304; Hwy 101, Nambé Pueblo; per car per day $10; ☾ 7am-7pm Apr-Oct

Nambe Pueblo

Set in a dramatic mountain location just 18 miles north of Santa Fe. ☎ 505-455-2036; www.nambefalls.com; Hwy 503, Nambe Pueblo

Taos Mountain Casino

One of the coziest casinos in New Mexico. ☎ 505-737-0777; www.taosmountain casino.com; Taos Pueblo Rd, Taos Pueblo; ☾ 8am-1am Sun-Wed, 8am-2am Thu-Sat

Taos Pueblo

It's been lived in since 1450 and is the biggest and most famous pueblo in the state.

☎ 505-758-1028; www.taospueblo.com; Taos Pueblo Rd, Taos Pueblo; adult/child $10/5, photography or video permit $5; ☾ 8am-4pm, closed for 10 weeks starting in Mar

Taos Pueblo Powwow

Rare public access to dances and workshops. ☎ 505-758-1028; www.taospueblopow wow.com; Taos Pueblo Rd, Taos Pueblo; admission $5; ☾ 2nd week in Jul

Tony Reyna Indian Shop

Big collection of arts and crafts from around New Mexico. ☎ 505-758-3835; Taos Pueblo Rd, Taos Pueblo; ☾ 8am-noon & 1-6pm

Zuni Pueblo

Information and photography permits available from the tourist office. ☎ 505-782-7238; Halona Plaza, Zuni Pueblo; ☾ 8am-5:30pm

SLEEP & EAT

Inn at Halona

Room service is provided by a grocery store in the back. ☎ 505-782-4547, 800-752-3278; www.halona.com; 1 Shalaka Dr, Zuni Pueblo; r from $79

Inn at Loretto

Modeled after the Taos Pueblo, this gorgeous old hotel has wi-fi and a great spa. ☎ 505-988-5531; www.hotelloretto.com; 211 Old Santa Fe Trail, Santa Fe; r from $250

Tewa Kitchen

Excellent Native American cooking. ☎ 505-751-1020; Taos Pueblo Rd, Taos Pueblo; mains $6-13; ☾ 11am-5pm Wed-Mon, to 7pm Jun-Aug

USEFUL WEBSITES

www.indianpueblo.org
www.nativewiki.org

LINK YOUR TRIP

www.lonelyplanet.com/trip-planner

Out of This World

WHY GO Whether you go in a spaceship, the mother ship or atop a mushroom cloud, New Mexico is fully devoted to blasting you off planet earth. The birthplace of the atomic bomb, alien mania and intergalactic space travel lures X-files fanatics and nuclear-fission junkies lusting to uncover occult Americana's soul.

This trip begins with a serenade of bats in New Mexico's wild south. Follow the two-lane highway across a bleached and blinding desert to ❶ Carlsbad Caverns National Park. The only caverns in the state are also some of the world's biggest and the home of a quarter-million-strong population of Mexican-free tail bats. Take the ?-mile subterraneous walk 029ft down to the Big Room. The 1800ft-long, 255ft-high chamber is capable of dropping even the most clenched jaws. Be above ground at sunset, when hundreds of members of Carlsbad's healthy bat population swarm out of the caves and hunt for dinner. It's a wacky way to start your out-of-this-world adventure.

After you've seen the bats, start thinking about visitors from another planet, because you'll be jumping on the "extraterrestrial highway" (Hwy 285) heading north to ❷ Roswell next. In the heady post-WWII baby-making summer of 1947 an unidentified flying object fell out of the sky here and America's fascination with little green men from outer space went mainstream. Believers are convinced the UFO was an alien spaceship, while the government swears it was a top-secret weather balloon. At this point the truth doesn't matter. Roswell has become the mother ship of the USA's alien subculture. Visit the ❸ International UFO Museum & Research Center for the full scoop.

Crash in Roswell for the night. It's not the most interesting city to sleep, filled with a slew of generic chains, but your next destination,

TIME
5 days

DISTANCE
605 miles

BEST TIME TO GO
Apr – Jun

START
Carlsbad Caverns National Park, NM

END
White Sands National Monument, NM

ALSO GOOD FOR

HISTORY & CULTURE

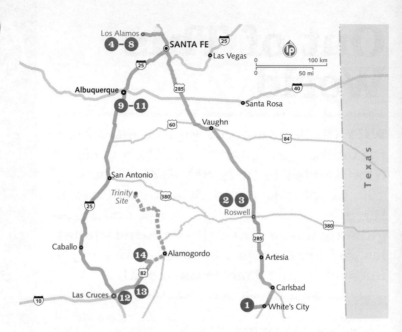

④ Los Alamos, is a 250-mile drive northwest and is best reached in daylight. The birthplace of the atomic bomb, Los Alamos sits in a pretty 7400ft mesa-top location and is a fascinating study in American pop culture. You can't actually visit the Los Alamos National Laboratory, where nuclear science was born, but the well-designed **⑤ Bradbury Science Museum** walks you through atomic history with more than 40 high-tech interactive exhibits. Also stop at the **⑥ Los Alamos Historical Museum,** displaying pop-culture artifacts from the Cold War. Los Alamos' stunning Jemez Mountains locale is worth a night of your life. Spend it in the East Room at the **⑦ Adobe Pines B&B** – it has a balcony with amazing views. Grab dinner at the **⑧ Canyon Bar & Grill,** which does a great green-chile cheeseburger.

DETOUR

On the first Saturday in April and October detour to the **Trinity Site** in the northern corner of the White Sands Missile Range to see where the first atomic bomb was detonated on July 16, 1945. The blast, which created an 8-mile-high mushroom cloud visible for hundreds of miles and a quarter-mile crater, took place in a desolate area ironically known as the Jornada del Muerto (Journey of Death). The **Alamogordo Chamber of Commerce** (www.alamogordo.com) has tour info and dates.

Retrace your tracks to Santa Fe the next morning, then take I-25 south to Albuquerque. The **⑨ National Museum of Atomic Nuclear Science & History** features an impressive collection of nuclear weapons (relax, the warheads aren't attached but everything else is real) and activities for kids. Albuquerque's atomic-alien nightlife theme aligns itself perfectly with this trip's chakras, so hit the blue-collar clubs and sophisticated biker bars around bustling Central Ave *après* dark. The appropriately named ⑩ **Launch Pad** is a retro-meets-modern gathering place for people of all tribes (and planets). Treat your body to an otherworldly nutritional experience on night number three. ⑪ **Los Poblanos** is on an organic farm surrounded by lavender fields. The B&B's six rooms feature kiva fireplaces. Breakfast here means tasting some of the farm's 75 varieties of fruits and vegetables cultivated without the use of any synthetic chemicals. Talk about out of this world.

Continue south on I-25 through a bleached desert of agave and yucca to ⑫ **Las Cruces**. Wedged between the sparkling waters of the Rio Grande and the fluted Organ Mountains, beautiful Las Cruces is sadly one of New Mexico's poorest cities. Locals hope this changes in 2010, when Britain's rebel billionaire Sir Richard Branson starts blasting tourists into outer space from the ⑬ **Southwest Regional Spaceport** 25 miles east of town. A cool $200,000 will buy you a 90-minute, 62-mile straight-up ride on a Virgin Galactic spaceship. With reclining seats, big windows and a pressurized cabin to eliminate the need for wearing unfashionable space suits, Branson hopes it will entice everyone from honeymooners to visitors from outer space. "We might even be able to allow those aliens who landed at Roswell 50 years ago in a UFO a chance to go home," he jokes.

THE TRUTH IS OUT THERE?

The US government has changed its story about the Roswell crash enough times to turn even a flying-saucer skeptic into a conspiracy theory believer. The first press release identified the object as a disk, but a day later the disk had become a weather balloon. The feds then confiscated all the previous press releases, cordoned off the area and posted armed guards to escort curious locals from the crash site. Calls were supposedly placed to a local mortician about the availability of small, hermetically-sealed coffins.

"Albuquerque's atomic-alien nightlife theme aligns itself perfectly with this trip's chakras..."

Your trip started with a quarter million bats. End it at the world's largest pure gypsum dune field, the otherworldly ⑭ **White Sands National Monument**, which resembles a frosted, almost hairspray-stiff version of sand drifts found on coastal beaches. Drive the 16-mile scenic loop into the heart of the cocaine-colored dunes, making sure to get out and climb, romp, slide and roll around. Stay for sunset when watered-down sunlight paints the white canvas a heavenly pink, purple and gold. It's a hell of a visual.

Becca Blond

TRIP 43

TRIP INFORMATION

GETTING THERE
Carlsbad Caverns National Park is 305 miles south of Albuquerque and 23 miles south-west of Carlsbad town on Hwy 180/62.

DO

Bradbury Science Museum
A children's section at this atomic-history museum features hands-on activities including computer programs. ☎ 505-667-4444; www.lanl.gov/museum; Central Ave; admission free; 🕐 10am-5pm Tue-Sat; 🚲

Carlsbad Caverns National Park
The park covers 73 sq miles and has nearly 100 caves. If you want to scramble to lesser-known areas, ask about Wild Cave tours. ☎ 800-967-2283; www.nps.gov/cave; 3225 National Parks Hwy; adult/child $6/3; 🕐 8am-5pm, to 7pm late May–mid-Aug

International UFO Museum & Research Center
The museum library claims to have the most comprehensive UFO-related materials in the world. And we have no reason to be skeptical. ☎ 575-625-9495; www.iufomrc.org; 114 N Main St; admission free; 🕐 9am-5pm

Los Alamos Historical Museum
Pick up a self-guided Los Alamos walking-tour pamphlet at this museum preserving atomic-era pop culture. ☎ 505-662-4493; www.losalamos.com/historicalsociety; 1921 Juniper St; admission free; 🕐 9:30am-4:30pm Mon-Sat, 11am-5pm Sun

National Museum of Atomic Nuclear Science & History
This kid-friendly museum uses interactive activities to introduce young ones to atomic history. ☎ 505-245-2137; www.atomic museum.com; 1905 Mountain Rd NW; adult/child $5/4; 🕐 9am-5pm; 🚲

White Sands National Monument
The dunes, 15 miles southwest of Hwy 82/70, cover 275 sq miles and are composed of gypsum, a chalky mineral used in making plaster of Paris. ☎ 575-679-2599; www.nps.gov/whsa; admission $3; visitors center 🕐 8am-7pm Jun-Aug, to 5pm Sep-May

EAT & SLEEP

Adobe Pines B&B
In an adobe building, there are five appealing rooms with wi-fi. ☎ 505-661-8828; www.losalamoslodging.com; 1601 Loma Linda Dr, Los Alamos; s/d $78/88

Canyon Bar & Grill
The best place for a beer and basic bar grub. Live music and dancing on Friday; karaoke Thursday. ☎ 505-662-3333; 163 Central Park Sq, Los Alamos; mains $5-12; 🕐 11am-2am Mon-Sat, to midnight Sun

Los Poblanos
On an organic farm five minutes' drive from the Old Town and within walking distance of the Rio Grande. ☎ 505-344-9297; www.lospoblanos.com; 4803 Rio Grande Blvd NW, Albuquerque; r $145-250

Launch Pad
The hottest spot for local live music. ☎ 505-764-8887; www.launchpadrocks.com; 618 Central Ave SW, Albuquerque; 🕐 7pm-1am

USEFUL WEBSITES
www.atomicarchive.com
www.weirdload.com/nm-ufo.html

LINK YOUR TRIP
www.lonelyplanet.com/trip-planner

Fiber Arts Trail

WHY GO Dishing up dramatic mountain-meets-adobe scenery and 71 shopping stops, the Fiber Arts Trail is the ultimate girls' green road trip. Go ahead, buy the soft, blue sheep-wool shawl you're already wrapped in and the hand-loomed Navajo blanket. Shopping at these artisan-owned rural galleries is sustainable and 100% guilt free.

TIME
3 days

DISTANCE
230 miles

BEST TIME TO GO
Aug – Oct

START
Magdalena, NM

END
Silver City, NM

You won't find any chain stores on the three Fiber Arts Trail loops, but you will discover numerous artist-owned galleries where the merchandise is original and always made in New Mexico. The concept behind the trail is to put fiber arts galleries in rural communities on the map. Currently, it's not unusual for artists in poor communities to drive hundreds of miles to sell their craft. These daily long hauls aren't just bad for the earth's carbon footprint; they also put strain on families. The Fiber Arts Trail creators hope to eliminate this variable by bringing the market to the artist, establishing permanent sustainable arts-based tourism in the rural towns where these artisans tend to live.

It would take an entire book to cover all 71 stops and three loops on the Fiber Arts Trail (happily, an easy-to-follow tourism booklet has been written) so we've concentrated on our favorite portion of the Southern Loop. Our good-for-humanity shopping trip begins in ❶ Magdalena, 27 miles west of Socorro. It's hard to believe Magdalena, now a sleepy colony of artists and society drop-out types, was the region's commercial hub for 50 years after its 1884 founding. About 30 artists work out of ❷ Pepper's Gallery, each with a unique personality that is expressed in the varied creations on display – you'll find everything from decorative gourds to Navajo rugs. Mosey down the street to ❸ Magdalena Arts Gallery when you are finished. You can grab

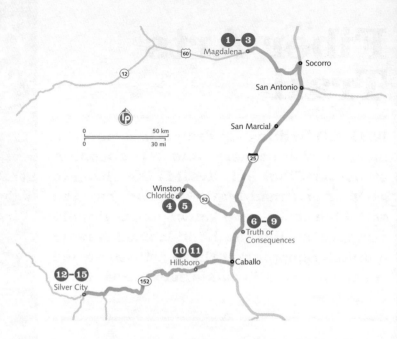

a latte from the attached coffee shop and check out the collection of baskets, drums, wall art and other one-of-a-kind pieces for all budgets.

Located 120 miles southwest, the ghost town of ❹ Chloride is the next stop on this artsy adventure. A random collection of rotting wooden shacks, it went bust just 20 years after booming in 1879. Check out the 200-year-old "hanging tree" on Wall St in the center of town, used to hang criminals in the 19th century. Then visit the ❺ Monte Cristo Gift Shop & Gallery. Today the roomy two-room adobe with a false Western front is an artist's cooperative selling paintings and Southwestern arts and crafts. But back in 1880, it was the most popular saloon and dance hall in town.

"Check out the 200-year-old 'hanging tree' on Wall St in the center of town..."

You will be tired after a full day of shopping and winding mountain roads, so bed down in quirky ❻ Truth or Consequences, 40 miles to the southeast. Have dinner at ❼ Los Arcos, known for its sumptuous steaks, before hitting the healing waters, and then your bed, at the swanky ❽ Sierra Grande Lodge & Spa. On your way out of T or C, pay a visit to ❾ Celestial Creations. Food has always been a form of art in New Mexico, and at Celestial they showcase it as such – check out the salsas and spices made from local green and red chiles. The gallery features art from across the state, including beautiful Native American made–kachina dolls and dreamcatchers.

South of T or C take Hwy 152 west into silver country, pausing in ⑩ Hillsboro, New Mexico's hottest up-and-coming ghost town. The charming little place was revived by local agriculture after mining went bust, and today it's known for a Labor Day Apple Festival. Pause for a sandwich and coffee at the ⑪ Barbershop Café before continuing west. Here the road winds up, up, up to the 8220ft summit of Emory Pass (pull off and check out the stupendous views) before descending into ⑫ Silver City, our favorite New Mexican Wild West town. The streets are dressed with a lovely mish-mash of old brick and cast-iron Victorians and thick-walled blood-red adobes, and the place still emits a frenetic frontier vibe. Billy the Kid spent some of his childhood here, and a few of his old haunts are mixed in with modern coffee shops and quirky galleries. ⑬ The Common Thread is home to the Southwest Women's Fiber Arts Collective, a nonprofit cooperative devoted specifically to connecting, and promoting the work of, female fiber artists. You can buy their imaginative creations at the gallery. Grab a beer and grub at ⑭ Silver City Brewing Company after purchasing the last baskets, blankets, rugs and pottery of the trip. The microbrewery serves a rotating selection of ales and lagers, made on site, and good hot wings. Spend your last night at Silver City's most venerable lodging house, the gracefully aging ⑮ Palace Hotel.

Becca Blond

FINDING YOUR WAY ON THE FIBER ARTS TRAIL

The concept of the New Mexico Fiber Arts Trails is to cultivate interest and awareness of the state's rich and unique fiber arts heritage, as well as bring opportunities for artists to prosper without having to leave their home community. The state has put a lot of money into the initiative, and has created a fabulous glossy *New Mexico Fiber Arts Trails Guide*.

TRIP INFORMATION

GETTING THERE
From Albuquerque take I-25 south to Socorro, then head west on Hwy 60, 27 miles to Magdalena.

DO

The Common Thread
The gallery features the work of the Southwest Women's Fiber Arts Cooperative. ☎ 575-558-5733; www.fiberarts collective.org; 107 W Broadway St, Silver City; 🕑 10am-5pm Mon & Thu-Sat

Celestial Creations
Showcases art from around New Mexico for all budgets. ☎ 575-894-7591; www.celestial-creations-nm.com; 220 Date St, Truth or Consequences; 🕑 11am-5pm Mon, Tue & Thu-Sat, 11am-4pm Sun, closed Wed

Peppers Gallery
A cooperative featuring the work of 30 local artists. It's on the right-hand side of the road at mile marker 113. ☎ 575-854-3696; 100 First St, Magdalena; 🕑 9am-5pm Thu-Sun

Magdalena Arts Gallery
Adjoins the Bear Mountain Coffee Shop in the center of town. ☎ 575-854-3318; www.magdalenaartsgallery.com; 902 First St, Magdalena; 🕑 10am-4pm Wed-Mon

Montecristo Gift Shop & Gallery
There is no numbered address, but Monte Cristo is easy to spot — it's one of the few operational buildings in Chloride. ☎ 575-743-0493; Wall St, Chloride; 🕑 10am-4pm Mon-Sun

EAT

Barbershop Café
The sandwiches are delicious at this café; inquire about rooms ($60) if you need to crash. ☎ 575-895-5283; 200 Main St, Hillsboro; mains $5-12; 🕑 11am-3pm Wed, Thu & Sun, to 8pm Fri & Sat

Los Arcos
The most upscale place to dine, inside or out, in town. ☎ 575-894-6200; 1400 N Date St, Truth or Consequences; mains $15-25; 🕑 5-10pm

Silver City Brewing Company
If interested in the craft of beer making, ask to chat with the head brewer. Pizza and calzones are served with a rotating selection of microbrews. ☎ 575-534-2739; 101 E College Ave, Silver city; mains from $6; 🕑 11am-late

SLEEP

Palace Hotel
A restored 1882 hostelry, it has 19 rooms that vary from small (with a double bed) to two-room suites (with king- or queen-size beds) outfitted with refrigerators and microwaves. ☎ 575-388-1811; www.zianet.com/palace hotel; 106 W Broadway, Silver City; r from $45

Sierra Grand Lodge & Spa
Nonguests are charged $25 for the first person then $5 per additional person to use the pool. Rooms and suites are a mix of luxe and tranquil and have wi-fi access. ☎ 575-894-6976; www.sierragrandelodge.com; 501 McAdoo St, Truth or Consequences; r from $99

USEFUL WEBSITES
www.nmfiberarts.org

LINK YOUR TRIP
www.lonelyplanet.com/trip-planner

Farm to Table: Organic New Mexico

WHY GO Santa Fe local Richard Harris spent a year researching New Mexico's artisan farms for his book "Artisan Farming: Lessons, Lore and Recipes." Over lunch at Harry's Roadhouse, his favorite Santa Fe eatery, he shared some of his favorite spots and scenic drives.

TIME
3 days

DISTANCE
210 miles

BEST TIME TO GO
May – Aug

START
Albuquerque, NM

END
Albiquiu, NM

ALSO GOOD FOR

Driving along these dirt roads and side highways into the river valleys of northern New Mexico, you may see a farmer in his field, darkened by the sun despite his straw hat, leaning on his shovel and watching the water flow from the communal acequia (irrigation ditch) into his field. He stands, ready to divert the water as it meanders gently, adjusting the dirt so the water fills straight furrows along his seedlings. It's the acequias, clear and shallow, beautiful and promising, and the people who rely on them, that give New Mexico farming its distinct culture.

This trip takes you away from the Walmarts and McDonalds, shopping carts and processed foods, to a part of the country where everything runs a little slower and demands a little more patience. Begin with a stay at ❶ **Los Poblanos Historic Inn** in Albuquerque. This 1934 hacienda, with spectacular mountain views, and breakfasts made from ingredients provided by its own organic farm, sits on 25 acres of gardens and fields. Farmer Monty grows everything from lavender to chile, and you can walk along the historic acequia, swim in the tiled pool or simply sit in the gardens, watching the cotton from the cottonwood trees drift in the wind.

From Los Poblanos, drive past the corrals and farms lining Rio Grande Boulevard, turn left at Alameda Ave, cross the Rio Grande and turn right on Corrales Rd to the village of ❷ **Corrales**. Side roads cut east, past vineyards and orchards, to dirt trails through the Rio Grande bosque, and it's not unusual to see folks riding horses along the main

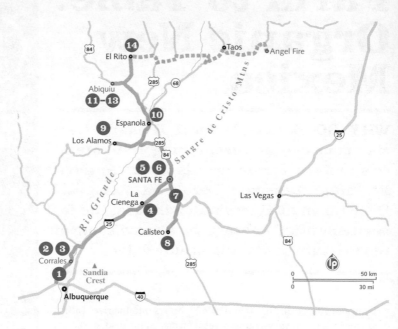

drag. Stop at ③ **Heidi's Organic Raspberries** for a taste of red-chile raspberry jam; in late July and early August, grab a bucket and pick your own berries.

About 45 miles north of Corrales is the 200-acre ④ **El Rancho de las Golondrinas**, originally built around 1710 to accommodate travelers on the Camino Real. During weekend festivals in the summer and fall, period-dressed docents demonstrate wool spinning, hide tanning and other tasks typical of colonial New Mexico. At the Harvest Festival in October, you can stomp on the grapes to make wine, cook your own tortillas, and taste beans, biscochittos (anise cookies), green chile and other traditional New Mexican food.

"Green-chile and piñon meatloaf, goat cheese made on site, fresh berry cobbler served warm with whipped cream..."

In ⑤ **Santa Fe**, stop for lunch at tiny ⑥ **Pasqual's** or ⑦ **Harry's Roadhouse**, both with excellent food focusing on locally grown ingredients. Try the grilled salmon burrito with black beans, goat cheese and cucumber salsa at Pasqual's, followed by thee sinful dessert sampler. Don't let the long lines scare you off. Harry's, an adobe with several rooms and gardened patio, feels more like a roadside diner, New Mexico style. Spend the night at the rambling ⑧ **Galisteo Inn**, a country retreat just south of Santa Fe. The inn serves upscale dinners (be sure to make advance reservations) and organic breakfasts.

Drive Hwy 84 north from Santa Fe up to **9** **Second Bloom Inc**, a small goat farm in Los Alamos that makes goat-milk soaps and lotions. Try the Mesa Herbal, made with New Mexico comfrey root and oats. In the farmlands surrounding Española, 20 miles northeast of Los Alamos, visit **10** **Santa Cruz Farm**. Using nothing but solar energy, this vegan and organic farm grows more than 70 different kinds of produce and welcomes visitors year-round.

Wind along the Chama River Valley to the town of **11** **Abiquiu**. Founded in 1754, Abiquiu today is home to an eclectic population of Hispanic farmers, organic-farm newcomers and

FARMERS MARKETS

Of New Mexico's many farmers markets (www .farmersmarketsnm.org), one of the biggest and best is the **Santa Fe Farmers Market** (www.san tafefarmersmarket.com), held Tuesday and Saturday morning from 7am to 12pm May through September, from 8am October through April at the Farmers Market Pavilion (in the Santa Fe railyard). Here, growers from across northern New Mexico sell organic veggies and fruits, cheeses, jellies and more.

artists and is most famous as the heart of Georgia O'Keeffe country. About five minutes past Bodes General Store is **12** **Purple Adobe Lavender Farm**. Showcasing 15 varieties of organic lavender, it offers private tours and classes, and sells oils, soaps and lotions made on site. Spend the night at **13** **Las Parras de Abiquiu**, a small organic vineyard in the bosque west of Hwy 285. If you're lucky, Stan will include some of his homemade raisins along with your evening tray of cookies or bread, nuts and sugar-snap peas, strawberries or other goodies from his garden.

Finish your trip about 15 miles north of Abiquiu at **Walter's Place**, a tiny adobe restaurant with orchards and a small courtyard that fills your spirit as well as your belly. It feels as if you're eating in someone's home, and they are cooking their favorites for you. Green-chile and piñon meatloaf,

DETOUR ⮞ At the tiny **Ritchie-Slater Winery** (www.ritchie-slat erwinery.com) in mountain country just north of Taos, Lan and Charlot Slater forgo standard grapes in favor of making wine from pears, apples, blackberries and other local fruit. While the distinctive flavor is not for everyone, the spectacular views of the meadow and woods from the winery's informal patio make this a great place for wine tasting.

goat cheese made on site, fresh berry cobbler served warm with whipped cream and a glass of fresh goat milk. Everything homemade, everything fresh, everything delicious. Take *that*, McDonalds!

Jennifer Denniston

TRIP INFORMATION

GETTING THERE
Albuquerque sits at the intersection of I-40 and I-25, 63 miles south of Santa Fe.

DO
El Rancho de las Golondrinas
Living museum and working farm with colonial Spanish buildings. Weekend festivals. ☎ 505-471-1261; www.golondrinas.org; 334 Los Pinos Rd, La Cienega (I-25, Exit 276B); 10am-4pm Wed-Sun Jun-Sep;

Heidi's Rasberry Organic Farm
Bucolic raspberry farm in Rio Grande Valley. ☎ 505-898-1784; www.heidisrasberryfarm .com; PO Box 1329, Corrales; seasonal variations;

Purple Adobe Lavender Farm
Fields of lavender along the Chama River. ☎ 505-685-0082; www.purpleadobelavend erfarm.com; Hwy 84, between Miles 210 & 211, PR 1622, No 31, Abiquiu; 10am-4pm, May-Aug;

Santa Cruz Farm
Pick your own strawberries, blackberries and raspberries, as well as green chile and veggies. ☎ 505-514-1662; House 830, El Llano Rd, Espanola; by appointment;

Second Bloom Inc
A goat farm that makes deliciously smooth goat's-milk soap and lotions. ☎ 505-672-1485; www.secondbloomfarm.com; 248 Rio Bravo, Los Alamos; Jun-Sep;

EAT
Harry's Roadhouse
Casual local hang-out is a favorite for comfort food with a Southwestern twist. ☎ 505-989-4629; 96 Old Las Vegas Hwy, Santa Fe; mains $8-15; 7am-10pm daily;

Pasqual's
Bustling Santa Fe hotspot features organic fare and local produce. ☎ 505-983-9340; 121 Don Gaspar Ave, Santa Fe; mains $8-30; 7am-3pm Mon-Sat, to 2pm Sun, 5:30-10pm daily;

Walter's Place
Tiny home with eclectic homecooking. Bring your own wine or beer. ☎ 505-581-4498; 1179 Main St, El Rito; mains $12-17; 5-10pm Fri & Sat, May-Oct;

SLEEP
Galisteo Inn
Historic ranch with viga ceilings, thick adobe walls and exquisite dinners. ☎ 866-404-8200; www.galisteoinn.com; Hwy 41, Galisteo; r & ste $85-275;

Las Parras de Abiquiu
Organic vineyards and handsome casita in Chama River valley. ☎ 505-685-4200; www .lasparras.com; Hwy 84, Mile 213-41, Abiquiu; r $130;

Los Poblanos Historic Inn
Rambling hacienda surrounded by organic farm. ☎ 505-344-9297; www.lospoblanos .com; 4803 Rio Grande NW, Albuquerque; r $155-255;

USEFUL WEBSITES
www.greenchile.com
www.pickyourown.org/NM.htm

SUGGESTED READS
- *A Garlic Testament: Seasons on a Small New Mexico Farm*, Stanley Crawford
- *Mayordomo: Chronicle of an Acequia in Northern New Mexico*, Stanley Crawford
- *·Pueblo Indian Agriculture*, James Vlasich
- *·Slow Food: The Case for Taste*, Carlo Petrini

LINK YOUR TRIP
www.lonelyplanet.com/trip-planner

On Location in New Mexico

WHY GO With A-list looks, versatile style, Wild West attitude and more than 500 films on her 120-year-long resume, New Mexico was a movie star well before her 2007 Oscar sweep. Filmmaker-turned-sculptor and "Barney Miller" creator Ted Flicker takes us on location to see why Hollywood is so obsessed about making movies here.

TIME
4 days

DISTANCE
125 miles

BEST TIME TO GO
May – Aug

START
Isleta Pueblo, NM

END
Abiquiu, NM

Begin your silver-screen odyssey 16 miles south of Albuquerque at ① Isleta Pueblo, the birthplace of New Mexican filmmaking. The state's first movie, shot here in 1898, was a 50-0second documentary about Native American children. The schoolhouse where *Indian Day School* was shot still stands today. Although New Mexico has been in the movie business for over a century and a fifth now, the industry has really exploded in the last three years, when 150 of the more than 500 movies filmed here were made. Ted Flicker, a Hollywood writer and director turned Santa Fe sculptor, has been watching the state's film industry since relocating here in 1986, and credits Gov. Bill Richardson's administration with the production surge.

"New Mexico now offers a support network for filming and more financial incentives than any other state," he says. "There's no reason not to shoot here. It's even beautiful."

Best known for creating TV's smash hit *Barney Miller,* Flicker also wrote and directed 1967's most controversial movie, *The President's Analyst.* The political satire made enough fun of J Edgar Hoover, Flicker said, to get him blacklisted from the industry until the FBI chief died. Although Flicker has since traded his director's chair for a potter's wheel and clay, he remains in touch with the Hollywood scene as a voting member of the Academy of Motion Pictures. And should he start making movies

BEST TRIP

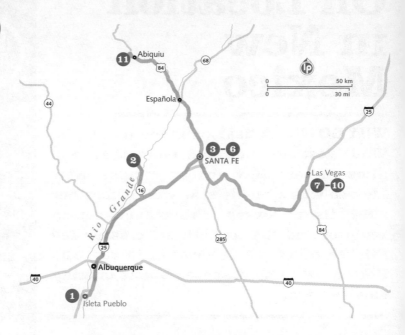

again, Flicker knows exactly where he'll film: ❷ **Kasha-Katuwe Tent Rocks National Monument**. An easy drive north on I-25 from Isleta Pueblo, Flicker describes it as being "like no other place in the world. Giant spires of rock are topped by smooth tent-like domes. It's something to see. The canyon is deep and mysterious. Some places are so narrow you have to squeeze through. Somewhere in the middle is a wide opening ideal for an alfresco lunch scene."

> *"The canyon is deep and mysterious. Some places are so narrow you have to squeeze through."*

Bring a video camera to shoot your own movie among oversized cartoonish boulders and pale yellow slot canyons. The main trail ends on top of a long teepee-like rock overlooking a narrow canyon. Stand at the edge and angle your lens slightly upward, we discovered, and you'll get a great shot that appears to be filmed standing on a cloud hanging in a deep blue sky.

It takes a little over an hour to reach your home for the night, the oldest operating state capital in the USA – ❸ **Santa Fe**. Visit the ❹ **Video Library** first. This DVD-rental shop is paradise for silver screen buffs. Besides a big selection of off-the-grid indie films, the store has an entire wall of movies filmed in New Mexico. Rent a few; we're taking you to a hotel with a DVD player tonight. Grab *No Country for Old Men* if you haven't seen it. You're going to the town where it was filmed tomorrow. By this point you'll be starving, so follow Flicker's instructions and go to ❺ **Ristra** for dinner. His favorite restaurant is an intimate place where the waiters learn your name, and the melt-in-your mouth steaks are cooked to order. Spend the night at **6 La Posada**. Not only is it ultra romantic, it has that promised DVD player and a big flat-screen TV to watch your chosen selection on.

It's OK to stay in bed watching videos until final check-out time as your next destination, **7 Las Vegas**, is just one hour north on I-25. *No Country for Old Men,* which took home four Oscars in 2007, was filmed largely in Las Vegas. Not only did the town double for the plains of west Texas, the I-25 overpass played the US–Mexican border crossing bridge. They've been shooting movies in Billy the Kid and Doc Holiday's old stomping ground for decades now. Other classics include *Wyatt Earp, Easy Rider* and *North Country.* Have a meal at **8 Charlie's Spic & Span Bakery & Café,** where locals come to gossip between mouthfuls of stuffed *sopapillas.* Keep your ears open. If they're shooting a movie in town, you'll hear about it at Charlie's. Plan to arrive in Las Vegas on a Thursday, Friday or Saturday, so you can watch a movie at the old-fashioned **9 Fort Union Drive-In**. It's one of New Mexico's few remaining drive-ins. Spend the night at the **10 Plaza Hotel**. It's charming, historic and good value.

GOING GREEN

Whether you are interested in being an extra in a movie filmed in New Mexico, the latest state industry news or your favorite film's back story, visit www.nmfilm.com for comprehensive info. The website also has loads of info on New Mexico's Green Filmmaking initiative that encourages producers to think sustainable when creating movies and TV shows here. There are even opportunities to win green-filmmaking grants.

Take the backroad over the Sangre de Cristo mountains to **11 Ghost Ranch,** one of the top places to shoot movies in New Mexico and your final destination. Leaving Las Vegas, jump on Hwy 518 north that winds through rugged wilderness and forest land until you reach the junction with Hwy 68, then go south. When you hit Hwy 84 head north again, pass tiny Abiquiu (home of Georgia O'Keeffe) and 25 minutes later you'll reach Ghost Ranch. It's a Presbyterian retreat (open to the public) and a favorite location with Hollywood filmmakers. Eighteen movies have been shot amid the spectacular red-rock and box-canyon scenery here, including *Indiana Jones & the Crystal Skull* (2008) and *The 3:10 to Yuma* (2007). But the place is still best known for its 1991 role

MADE IN NEW MEXICO

Ironically, Disney's *High School Musical,* set in Albuquerque, is one of the few movies not really made in New Mexico. On the flip side, over 500 other films were made here, including the portion of *21 Grams* set in a seedy hotel. The hotel was Leisure Lodge in Grants (filmmakers repainted it to look old and dirty for the movie). Stay in room 117 to sleep where Benicio Del Torro's character anguished.

in the Billy Crystal dude-ranch classic *City Slickers.* Ghost Ranch is a great place to spend your last night. Take time to sit outside after dark and stare at the night sky. Not only is the area supposedly rife with UFO activity (aliens were featured in the last *Indiana Jones*), it also twinkles brightly with constellations.

Becca Blond

HISTORY &
CULTURE

TRIP INFORMATION

GETTING THERE
Isleta Pueblo is 16 miles south of
Albuquerque on I-25; take exit 215.

DO
Fort Union Drive-In
Just north of town, this classic drive-in theater
has great views of the surrounding high desert.
☎ 505-425-9934; 3300 7th St, Las Vegas; per
car $5; ☾ evenings Thu-Sat May-Sep.

Isleta Pueblo
Call to check if it's possible to see the schoolhouse where New Mexico's first movie was
made. The pueblo also has a casino resort.
☎ 505-869-3111; I-25 exit 215; ☾ casino
8am-4am Mon-Thu, 24 hr Fri-Sun

Video Library
This supercool Santa Fe movie-rental shop
stocks an entire wall of made in New
Mexico DVDs. The staff is friendly and
knowledgeable. ☎ 505-983-3321; 120 E
Marcy St No 1, Santa Fe

SLEEP & EAT
Charlie's Spic & Span Bakery Café
Locals choose Charlie's for lattes in the morning and New Mexican diner fare after dark.
It's also the place to catch up on all the latest
gossip. Bring your lap-top, there is wi-fi.

☎ 505-426-1921; 715 Douglas Ave, Las
Vegas; mains $4-9; ☾ 6.30am-9.30pm

Ghost Ranch
Digs are dorm beds, but quality cafeteria-style
meals produced with locally raised meat and
organic veggies are included in the nightly rate.
Call ahead to make sure there's space. ☎ 505-
685-4333; www.ghostranch.org; US Hwy 84;
tent/RV sites $16/23, dm $45-80

La Posada
World-class service puts this hotel in a league
of its own. Your every need is catered to on
this beautiful, shady, 6-acre property a few
blocks from the Plaza. ☎ 866-331-7625;
www.laposada.rockresorts.com; 330 E Palace
Ave, Santa Fe; r from $175

Plaza Hotel
Las Vegas' most celebrated and historic lodging is also excellent value. ☎ 505-425-3591;
www.plazahotel-nm.com; 230 Old Town
Plaza, Las Vegas; r incl breakfast from $69

Ristra
Ristra attracts a devoted group of regular cli-
entele who come for its casual intimacy and
excellent food. The contemporary American
menu is influenced by the flavors of France
and the Southwest, and changes seasonally.
☎ 505-982-8608; 548 Agua Fria St, Santa
Fe; mains $20-40; ☾ 5-9.30pm

USEFUL WEBSITES
www.nmfilm.org

LINK YOUR TRIP
www.lonelyplanet.com/trip-planner

Take the High Road...and the Low Road

WHY GO Whether you take the High Rd or the Low Rd, follow the mountains or the river, the way to Taos is dotted with timeless adobe villages where the green chile is spicy, the church is home to healing dirt and the intricately woven blankets are still loomed by hand.

Spend a little time in the region where the mighty Rio Grande flows past the crimson-hued Sangre de Cristo (Blood of Christ) mountains, healing water bubbles from boiling springs and the high desert air is scented with sage and pine and you'll understand why New Mexico calls itself the "Land of Enchantment". From Santa Fe, follow Hwy 285 north to ❶ Española, the starting point for the High and Low Rds to Taos.

Drive Hwy 76, known as the ❷ High Road, first. The small towns along the more famous route are filled with crumbling adobes, rusting pick-ups, graying snow in winter and sun-baked clay in summer. They often look half-abandoned, but look closely and you'll find they're rich in weaving and other Native American handicraft workshops-cum-offices. The road, which winds through river valleys, skirts high, cartoon-like sandstone cliffs and passes numerous wood-carving and weaving studios-cum-shops.

The first, and our favorite, stop is ❸ Chimayó. Originally established by Spanish families in possession of a land grant, it is home to a fabulous old adobe church and an equally fabulous New Mexican restaurant. Whatever you do, don't miss the famous ❹ Santuario de Chimayó, built in 1816. Legend has it the church's dirt has healing powers. The back room serves as a shrine to its miracles – canes, wheelchairs, crutches and other abandoned medical aids all hang like trophies from the thick adobe walls. Kneel into a hole in the ground

TIME
4 days

DISTANCE
150 miles

BEST TIME TO GO
Jun – Sep

START
Santa Fe, NM

END
Santa Fe, NM

ALSO GOOD FOR

FOOD & DRINK

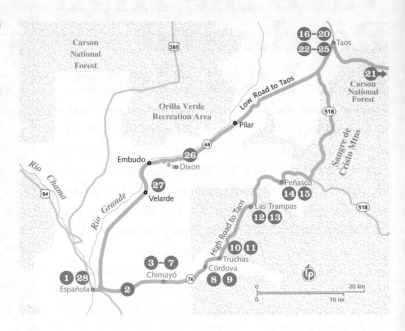

and smear some dirt on your ailing body. Pay a visit to ⑤ Centinela Traditional Arts for naturally dyed hand-loomed blankets, vests and pillows. Irvin Trujillo, a seventh-generation Rio Grande weaver whose carpets are featured in collections across the country, runs and works out of the 20 artist cooperative. ⑥ Rancho de Chimayó serves classic New Mexican cuisine courtesy of the Jaramillo family's famed recipes and is where you should eat dinner. The atmosphere is as fantastic as the fresh lime margaritas. Spend the night at unpretentious ⑦ Casa Escondida, with beautiful rooms and a hot tub made for stargazing.

The next morning follow Hwy 76 to the east as it climbs high into the Sangre de Cristo Mountains. After about 3 miles of sharp ascent look for the sign pointing right and down to Quemado Valley and ⑧ Córdova. The small village is best known for its unpainted, austere *santos* (saint) carvings created by masters such as George López and José Delores López. Stop and check out their work at ⑨ Sabinita López Ortiz shop. The shop also sells intricate wood-carvings made by the proprietor, Sabinita, a member of the same artistic family.

From Cordova, Hwy 76 continues to wind up the mountains, ascending higher and higher until reaching tiny and dramatic ⑩ Truchas (meaning trout in English). The town showcases rural New Mexico at its most sincere. The ramshackle town was originally settled by the Spaniards in the 18th century, and feels as if it never left that era. The setting for Robert Redford's *Milagro Beanfield War* is a mishmash of narrow roads, most unpaved, leading to yards of red dirt and crumbling adobe homes. Despite the obvious poverty, Truchas is a determined little place, with some quality galleries and workshops well worth supporting. The town is best known for its woven textiles, and ⓫ Cordova's Handweaving Workshop is a good place to buy them. Run by a friendly fourth-generation weaver named Harry, here you can watch him at work between browsing his beautiful blankets, place mats and rugs. Continue on to ⓬ Las Trampas next and look for the 1760 ⓭ Church of San José de Gracia. Although raided countless times by Apache warriors, it was never destroyed. Original paintings and carvings remain in excellent condition, and self-flagellation blood stains from the Los Hermanos Penitentes (a 19th-century secretive religious order with a strong following in the northern mountains of New Mexico) are still visible. ⓮ Peñasco is the next community along the route. By now you'll likely be hungry, so stop for lunch at the ⓯ Sugar Nymphs Bistro. The family-run restaurant is the social hang-out for this tiny community, and serves everything from fresh-pressed cider to piñon couscous.

In Peñasco, hop on Hwy 518, which winds north along the western edge of the Sangre de Cristo mountains and national forest land to ⓰ Taos. Attracting suitors for centuries now with her kiss of canyons and art, Taos is a great lover, stunningly beautiful and bursting with outdoor adventures.

"Attracting suitors for centuries now with her kiss of canyons and art, Taos is a great lover."

The residents are an eclectic lot: a mix of neo-hippies, ski-bum drop-outs, environmentally conscious artists and reclusive celebs – Julia Roberts and Donald Rumsfeld both have houses here. More than 30% of Taos' residents call themselves artists, and the mountain town with magical light is home to more than 80 galleries. ⓱ Guadalupe Plaza is the city's historic heart. Just west of the main intersection of Kit Carson Rd and Paseo del Pueblo Sur, it has been a social gathering place since the 1600s. The plaza is completely enclosed by ancient adobe buildings with deep portals. After strolling around the square, walk down the city's art alley, historic ⓲ Ledoux St.

Check into ⓳ La Fonda de Taos for two nights. The landmark hotel was formerly owned by notorious playboy Saki Karavas and is a sexy place to sleep. The hotel houses a small collection of DH Lawrence's erotic paintings ($3 admission) in a private viewing room – be sure to check them out. For great people-watching over the plaza head to the 2nd-floor patio of ⓴ Ogelvie's Taos Grill & Bar. It serves views with its chicken mole, and garlic and black-pepper rib-eye. Kick back with a couple of fresh lime margaritas. Spend your second day in Taos in the great outdoors. Hike, bike, fish, raft – the list of warm weather activities is endless. In winter it's all about the skiing and snowboarding on ㉑ Taos Ski Valley, 20 miles north of downtown. Visit the gigantic

㉒ **Taos Mountain Outfitters** to get started. The shop rents, sells and has info on everything you need to play outside. Or rent a full-suspension mountain bike and grab local trail maps at the ㉓ **Gearing Up Bicycle Shop**. Before hitting the single track, cycle 3 miles northwest of downtown (make a left on Hwy 64) and visit the innovative ㉔ **Greater World Earthship Development**. This collection of environmentally savvy homes is the brainchild of architect Michael Reynolds. His idea was to develop a building method that "eliminates stress from both the planet and its inhabitants." Buried on three sides by earth, the Earthships are designed to heat and cool themselves, make their own electricity and catch their own water. Sewage is decomposed naturally, and dwellers grow their own food. Head downtown to historic ㉕ **Doc Martin's** for dinner. Relax by the kiva fireplace and pop the cork on one of its award-winning wines. Then dive headlong into the most delicious *chiles rellenos*. This is where the city's intellectuals gather.

Return to Santa Fe on the ㉖ **Low Road**. The route winds along the Rio Grande and the air is thick with the scent of cedar. Hwy 68 is faster mileage and speed-limit wise, but go slow. Running beside the Rio Grande River for much of the way, it's also an angler's paradise, with plenty of good fly-fishing spots. Bring a picnic lunch and stop at one of the tables perched above the river to eat. Keep an eye on the river in summer – you'll see dozens of tourist-packed white-water rafts rush by. The road cuts through the Rio Grande Canyon for a while – gorgeous – before popping out amidst the apple orchards around Velarde. Your final stop before returning to Española is the family-run ㉗ **Black Mesa Winery**. Although the first wineries opened in this part of New Mexico more than 400 years ago, production fizzled over the last century, and only now are vineyards making a comeback. Owners Lynda and Jerry Burd know all about the revitalization of the New Mexico wine industry, and a trip to their vineyard is a must for wine hobbyists.

 DETOUR Just before the Black Mesa Winery, take a slight detour east on Hwy 75 to the small farming community of **Dixon**, home to a few galleries and our favorite vineyard in the west, **La Chiripada Winery** (www.lachiripada.com). We can't get enough of its inexpensive white wines (less than $20 a bottle; we like the Riesling best). Don't miss out on the tastings offered from 10am to 5pm Monday through Saturday and from noon to 5pm on Sunday. If you can't make it to the vineyard, check out the **tasting room** on the historic plaza in Taos.

It's just a short sprint back to Española, where you should treat yourself to a final night on the road sleeping at swanky ㉘ **Rancho de San Juan**. This little gem just north of town features first-class rooms, a spa and great service in a spectacular setting. Many consider its restaurant New Mexico's best.
Becca Blond

TRIP INFORMATION

GETTING THERE
From Santa Fe take Hwy 285 north for 15 miles to Hwy 76 north to Taos; return via Hwy 68 south.

DO

Black Mesa Winery
New Mexican wines. ☎ 505-852-2820; www .blackmesawinery.com; 1502 NM 68, Velarde; ☻ 10am-6pm Mon-Sat, noon-6pm Sun

Cordova's Handweaving Workshop
Gorgeous hand-woven blankets, place mats and rugs. ☎ 505-689-2437; www.la-tierra .com/busyles; Main Truchas Rd, Truchas; ☻ call for hr

Centinela Traditional Arts
Naturally dyed blankets, vests and pillows are sold at this cooperative gallery. ☎ 505-351-2180; www.chimayoweavers.com; NM 76, Chimayó; ☻ 9am-6pm Mon-Sat, 10am-5pm Sun

Church of San José De Gracia
One of the finest surviving 18th-century churches in the USA. Hwy 76, Las Trampas; admission free; ☻ 9am-5pm Mon-Sat Jun-Aug

Gearing Up Bicycle Shop
Rents mountain and hybrid bikes (hour/day/ week $10/35/125), full-suspension bikes (per day $50) and road bikes (per day $45). ☎ 575-751-0365; 129 Paseo del Pueblo Sur, Taos; ☻ 9am-6:30pm

Greater World Earthship Development
The tour office is located 1.5 miles past the Rio Grande Gorge Bridge on US Hwy 64 west. ☎ 575-751-0462; http://earthship.org; US Hwy 64; tours $5; ☻ 10am-4pm

Sabinita López Ortiz
Austere *santos* and other intricate local wood carvings are for sale. ☎ 505-351-4572; County Rd 9, Córdova; ☻ variable

Santuario de Chimayo
An impressive old adobe church with a history of working healing miracles. ☎ 505-351-4889; NM 76, Chimayó; admission free; ☻ 9am-5pm, mass 11am Mon-Sat & noon Sun

Taos Mountain Outfitters
A great all-around outdoor shop that sells the latest gear and has loads of info on area activities, especially hiking. ☎ 575-758-9292; www.taosmountainoutfitters.com; 114 S Plaza, Taos; ☻ 10am-5pm

Taos Ski Valley
Check the resort website for ski-and-stay deals, including week-long packages with room, board, lessons and lift tickets. ☎ 866-250-7274; www.skitaos.org; half-/full-day lift ticket $47/63

EAT

Doc Martin's
Bert Philips (the Doc's bro-in-law) and Ernest Blumenschein cooked up the idea of the Taos Society of Artists at this cozy New Mexican restaurant. ☎ 505-758-1977; 125 Paseo del Pueblo Norte; mains $5-35; ☻ 7am-10pm

Ogelvie's Taos Grill & Bar
Great views from the patio; serves New Mexican and American favorites including good steaks. ☎ 505-758-8866; 103 E Plaza, Taos; lunch $8-11, dinner $10-26; ☒

Rancho de Chimayó
Amazing New Mexican homecooking and the perfect margarita in atmospheric Southwestern environs. ☎ 505-351-4444; www .ranchodechimayo.com; 300 County Rd 98; mains $8-16; ☻ 11:30am-9pm Mon-Fri, 8:30am-10:30am Sat & Sun, closed Mon Nov-Apr

Rancho de San Juan
A fabulous, award-winning restaurant (mains $35) and inn just north of downtown Española. ☎ 505-753-6818; www.ranchode sanjuan.com; 34020 Hwy 285, Española; r & ste $275-675; ☻ 6-8pm Tue-Sun

Sugar Nymphs Bistro
Fill up on New Mexican diner fare, including pizza, at this cozy, crowded family restaurant in tiny Peñasco. ☎ 505-587-0311; 15046 State Rd 75, Peñasco; mains $5-15; ☺hr vary, call ahead; ♿

SLEEP
Casa Escondida
Eight beautiful rooms and a hot tub. ☎ 505-351-4805; www.casaescondida.com; 64

County Rd 100; r $99-149

La Fonda de Taos
Gorgeous, all-adobe, upscale hotel with a sexy vibe; no children under 13. ☎ 800-833-2211; www.hotellafonda.com; 108 S Plaza, Taos; r $239

USEFUL WEBSITES
www.newmexico.org/explore/scenic_byways/highroad.php
www.taoschamber.org

LINK YOUR TRIP
www.lonelyplanet.com/trip-planner

In the Footsteps of DH Lawrence

WHY GO A haven for writers and artists, New Mexico holds a prominent place in American literature. Edward Borins, owner of Santa Fe's Garcia Street Books, and Nancy Rutland, owner of Albuquerque's Bookworks, take us on a tour of the state's storytelling tradition.

TIME
3 days

DISTANCE
205 miles

BEST TIME TO GO
Aug – Oct

START
Santa Fe, NM

END
Santa Fe, NM

ALSO GOOD FOR

FOOD &
DRINK

Beginning in the early 20th-century, writers from DH Lawrence to Mary Austin found their way to Santa Fe and Taos, finding freedom, inspiration and transformation in the dusty shadows of sunset mountains and the idealized communal culture of the pueblo people. Pack a notebook and pen, and follow in their footsteps.

One of the most influential characters of New Mexico's literary parlors was Mabel Dodge Luhan, a writer and socialite from Greenwich Village, who arrived here in 1917. In her 1929 memoir, Luhan describes how the New Mexico sun "entered into one's deepest places and melted the thick, slow densities. It made one feel good. That is, alive." She moved to ① Taos, started a writers' colony and married a man from Taos Pueblo. Her sprawling adobe home, in which she entertained Ansel Adams, Georgia O'Keeffe, Alfred Steiglitz and hosts of other artists, became home to Dennis Hopper (he reputedly wrote *Easy Rider* here) and is now the ② Mabel Dodge Luhan House. The inn, with kiva fireplaces and gardens, hosts regular writers' workshops.

Luhan invited British author DH Lawrence and his wife Frieda to her writers' colony, and in September 1922 they arrived in Taos. In 1924 Luhan supposedly gave them the 160-acre Kiowa Ranch in exchange for the manuscript of *Sons and Lovers*. Though the ranch itself is closed to the public, Lawrence fans make a pilgrimage to the ③ DH Lawrence Memorial. As the story goes, when Lawrence died in 1930, Frieda was so determined to keep Luhan from spreading Lawrence's ashes throughout

the property that she mixed them up with the cement that was used to make the memorial's alter.

Notorious in his day for his doctrines of sexual freedom, Lawrence suffered censorship and persecution for not only his writing but also his art. For $3, see his ❹ **Forbidden Paintings**, condemned as obscene and seized from a London gallery in 1929, at La Fonda Hotel on the Taos Plaza. After a peek at Victorian England erotica, walk a few blocks to the ❺ **Moby Dickens Bookstore**, stuffed with great Southwestern reads. Pick out a few to enjoy under the cottonwoods of ❻ **Kit Carson Park & Cemetery**, the final resting place of Mabel Dodge Luhan and Kit Carson.

> **DETOUR** A couple hours east of Albuquerque on I-40 is **Santa Rosa**, birthplace of Rudolfo Anaya and the setting for the town created in his *Bless Me Ultima*. The **Rudolfo Anaya Sculpture Garden**, with a larger-than-life statue of Anaya and pages of Anaya's books cast in bronze embedded in the walkways, is a must-see for Anaya fans.

Taos resident John Nichols captured northern New Mexico in his 1974 novel *The Milagro Beanfield War*. Robert Redford filmed the 1988 movie south of Taos in the farming village of ❼ **Truchas**. From here, continue past the adobe churches, orchards and desert hills, past Española and up to ❽ **Los Alamos**. Author William Burroughs and Gore Vidal attended the Los Alamos Ranch School (1917–43), a boys' boarding school; Burroughs was expelled for taking the hypnotic drug chloral hydrate. Check out the former school, now called **9 Fuller Lodge**, and peruse the nearby **10 Los Alamos Historical Museum**, with displays on the school, the Manhattan Project and the region's natural history.

From Los Alamos it's a 35-mile drive to **11 Santa Fe**. Before the tourists and the T-shirts, the malls and the whole foods, this was a dusty little town of adobe houses and afternoon siestas. Explore the city's literary history on a walking tour with **12 Storytellers and the Southwest**. Santa Fe continues to attract authors, many of whom host gatherings at the Lensic Theater as part of the **13 Lannan Foundation Readings and Conversations** and book-signing events at **14 Garcia Street Books** and **15 Collected Works**. These small, independent bookstores boast an excellent selection of Southwestern literature. For dinner, head to tiny **16 Acqua Santa**, popular with visiting authors, whose photos line the wall, and serving creative American cuisine with a focus on seasonal and local ingredients.

The former home of Witter Byner (1881–1968), a poet and pillar of the Santa Fe Writers' Colony famous for hosting raucous parties, is now the **17 Inn of the Turquoise Bear**, a B&B with gardens and evening wine and cheese.

Finish your jaunt through literary New Mexico with a walk on the 16-mile **18 Paseo del Bosque Trail** in Albuquerque (I-25 south 50 miles to the Alameda exit, west to the parking lot before the bridge). Wind your way along spur trails to the silent shores of the Rio Grande River, the languorous lifeblood of the New Mexican desert, and relax with Jimmy Santiago Baca's *Spring Poems Along the Rio Grande* or Paul Horgan's *Great River: The Rio Grande in American History*. Afterwards, head to **19 Bookworks**, in the city's rural north valley, where Rutland can guide you deeper into literary New Mexico.

NEW MEXICO LITERATURE

In addition to these classics, check out the addictive mysteries by Tony Hillerman and Michael McGarrity.

- Mabel Dodge Luhan, *Edge of Taos Desert: An Escape to Reality*
- John Nichols, *The Milagro Beanfield War*
- Willa Cather, *Death Comes to the Archibishop*
- Rudolfo Anaya, *Bless Me Ultima*
- N Scott Momaday, *House Made of Dawn*
- Leslie Marmon Silko, *Ceremony*
- Frank Waters, *The Man Who Killed Deer*
- Jimmy Santiago Baca, *Black Mesa Poems*
- Oliver LaFarge, *Laughing Boy*

"New Mexico," Lawrence wrote, "… changed me forever. In the magnificent fierce morning of New Mexico, one sprang awake, a new part of the soul woke up suddenly." After a few days in his footsteps, breathing in the piñon fires and the desert sage, perhaps you too will find that there's just something about this place that does, indeed, wake up the soul.

Jennifer Denniston

HISTORY & CULTURE

TRIP INFORMATION

DO

Bookworks
Wonderful bibliophile hang-out, with a great childrens'-book section. ☎ 505-344-8139; 208 W San Francisco St, Santa Fe; ⏱ 9am-9pm Mon-Sat, to 7:30pm Sun; ♿

Collected Works
Independent bookstore only blocks from the Santa Fe Plaza. ☎ 505-988-4226; 108 S Plaza, Santa Fe; ⏱ 9am-9pm Mon-Sat, 10am-6pm Sun; ♿

DH Lawrence Memorial
Shrine to the literary giant on the grounds of his ranch; located 20 miles north of Taos on Hwy 522. ☎ 575-776-2245; Hwy 522, San Cristobol; ⏱ dawn-6pm daily; ♿ 🐾

Garcia Street Books
Voted Santa Fe's best bookstore six years in a row. ☎ 505-820-7258; www.garcia streetbooks.com; 376 Garcia St, Santa Fe; ⏱ 9:30am-6pm daily; ♿ 🐾

Lannan Foundation Readings & Conversations
Nationally acclaimed writers and poets read and discuss their work. ☎ 505-986-8160; www.lannan.org; 313 Read St, Santa Fe; ⏱ Sep-May

Los Alamos Historical Museum
Cool museum housed in the former Los Alamos Ranch School's apartments for visiting parents. ☎ 505-662-6272; 1921 Juniper St, Los Alamos; ⏱ 9:30am-4:30pm Mon-Sat, 1-4pm Sun; ♿

Moby Dickens Bookstore
A curl-up-your-feet kind of bookstore with excellent selection of Southwestern literature. ☎ 575-758-3050; 124 Bent St, Taos; ⏱ 10am-6pm Sun-Thu, to 7:30pm Fri & Sat; ♿ 🐾

Storytellers & the Southwest
Walk through Santa Fe's historic and contemporary literary tradition. ☎ 505-989-4561; barbarah@newmexico.com; Santa Fe Plaza, Santa Fe; 2-hr tours $20; ⏱ by appointment

EAT

Aqua Santa
Bustling one-room adobe with open kitchen and small patio. ☎ 505-982-6297; 451 W Alameda, Santa Fe; mains $14-35; ⏱ noon-2pm Wed-Fri, 5:30-9pm Tue-Sat

SLEEP

Inn of the Turquoise Bear
Throngs of authors and artists once gathered here for what Ansel Adams called "Bymer Bashes." ☎ 505-983-0798; www .turquoisebear.com; 342 E Buena Vista St, Santa Fe; r $99-235; ♿ 🐾

Mabel Dodge Luhan House
Echoes of New Mexico's literary giants linger in the adobe walls and viga ceilings. ☎ 575-751-9686; www.mabeldodgeluhan.com; 240 Morada Lane, Taos; r $99-235; ♿

SUGGESTED READS
- *Utopian Vistas: The Mabel Dodge Luhan House and the American Counterculture*, Lois Palken Rudnick
- *Walks in Literary Sana Fe: A Guide to Landmarks, Legends and Lore*, Barbara Harrelson
- *Turn Left at the Sleeping Dog: Scripting the Santa Fe Legend 1920–1955*, John Pen LaFarge
- *Literary Pilgrims: The Santa Fe & Taos Writers' Colonies 1917-1950*, Lynn Cline

USEFUL WEBSITES
www.santafewritersconference.com
www.unm.edu/~taosconf/

LINK YOUR TRIP
www.lonelyplanet.com/trip-planner

Hiking the Jemez

WHY GO Hike through mountain streams and meadows of thick grass and wildflowers, pink volcanic rock valleys covered with piñon and juniper, chamisa and blooming cactus, ancient dwellings and the butterscotch smell of Ponderosa pine, then soak those dusty bones in the healing waters of the Jemez's natural hot springs.

Speeding along I-25 from Albuquerque, the Jemez Mountains register as little more than a massive protrusion of green to the west, a backdrop to the light shows of the summer monsoons. But to those who take the time to wind through them, these remnants of a rich and violent volcanic history offer the essence of New Mexico, its desert and mountains, its dust and streams, its quirky spirit and expansive landscape.

From I-25, head west at exit 242 towards Bernalillo, just north of Albuquerque. At the Walgreens, turn left and drive about a mile to the **1** Range Café for a hikers' breakfast of heuvos rancheros or organic oats and fruit. Afterwards, continue on Hwy 505 through the desert expanse of Zia Pueblo to San Ysidro, the beginning of the **2** Jemez Mountain Trail National Scenic Byway. Head north on Hwy 4, and within miles the brown desert transforms into brilliant red-sandstone valleys, capped in most places by pink volcanic tuff formed by volcanic ash erupted two million years ago from the Jemez volcanoes. Pass Jemez Pueblo, stopping for beans and Navajo tacos at a roadside stand at **3** Red Rocks, a small expanse of desert shrub surrounded by vertical red-sandstone cliffs, and to pick up hiking maps, check on current conditions and peruse the small museum in the **4** Walatowa Visitor Center across the street.

From here, the road follows the stream-like Jemez River, squeezed between cottonwoods and willows on the left, and the canyon wall on

TIME
2 – 3 days

DISTANCE
80 miles

BEST TIME TO GO
May – Oct

START
Albuquerque, NM

END
Los Alamos, NM

ALSO GOOD FOR

HISTORY & CULTURE

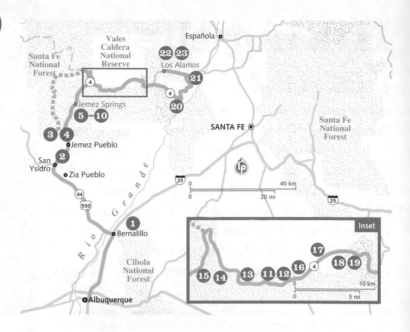

the right, past several fishing pullouts, to **5** **Jemez Springs**. Stretched along Hwy 4 and without a centralized downtown, this tiny mountain town offers several galleries, a coffee shop, a few restaurants and a handful of B&Bs, including the lovely **6** **Canon del Rio**. A family-style breakfast is served in a massive great room, with tiled floors and plenty of sun. Enjoy the view of red cliffs towering over the river from the inn's lovely pool and zen gardens.

An even quieter alternative lies down the road at **7** **Casa Blanca Guest House and Garden Cottage**. Two private casitas hidden in the terraced gardens of roses, grass, willows and wildflowers make a perfect base for area hiking. Relax in the hammock on the riverbank, and help yourself to fruit from the orchard or veggies from the garden. Across the street, **8** **Laughing Lizard Inn Café** offers organic salads, veggie-laden pizza and patio dining. For a cold Fat Tire and a game of pool, head to **9** **Los Ojos Bar and Grill**, a popular watering hole with tree-stump bar stools and a jukebox.

The area's geology offers a different style of watering hole. Molten magma miles below the surface warms the area's waters, creating natural hot springs rich in what some claim are healing and therapeutic minerals. Avoid the bathhouses in the town of Jemez Springs, and head instead to the low-key and friendly **10** **Giggling Springs** nearby. Forget about those deadlines and headlines, and lose yourself for a day soaking in the hot springs and cooling off in the creek. The tiny shop sells bathing suits and bathrobes as well as herbal tea and smoothies.

Just north of town is the 8-mile ⑪ **East Fork Trail No 137**. Divided into three sections with four access points along Hwy 4, this hike winds through the Santa Fe National Forest and is excellent for both families and experienced hikers. The best stretch is the northernmost 4.5-mile section from the tiny parking lot at ⑫ **Las Conchas** to ⑬ **East Fork Trailhead.** Here, the trail follows the Jemez River (which is really more of a mountain stream) for the first couple miles, offering plenty of opportunity to splash in the clear water, fly-fish in the riffles and relax in meadows, before climbing gently into the aspen. Trail 137A and 137B spur off, cutting steeply into the canyon to swimming holes, where the water is actually deep enough to swim. At the East Fork Trailhead, the trail crosses Hwy 4 and continues about a mile past a parking lot to ⑭ **Jemez Falls**. From here, it's 2.5 miles to ⑮ **Battleship Rock**. Though this massive rock formation towering above the pines has little claim to fame besides its vague resemblance to a battleship, it is hugely popular and crowded on summer weekends. If you just want to picnic by the river, the quiet ⑯ **Las Conchas Fishing Access**, a few minutes north past the Los Conchas trailhead, has several tables and grills. You can walk about 10 minutes along the river, and then the trail ends.

Unlike anywhere else in New Mexico, the vast, wild, surreally quiet and sublimely beautiful 89,000-acre ⑰ **Valles Caldera National Preserve** is open to the public on a limited basis by reservation and lottery for hiking, skiing, fishing, elk hunting and other activities. The preserve rests in an ancient volcanic crater with young volcanic peaks separated by expansive valleys of treeless grassland, springs, streams and bogs. As early as 10,000 years ago, Ancestral Puebloans not only hunted and fished the region, but collected obsidian (volcanic glass) for arrowheads. Examples of these black, glassy stones lie along the 3-mile round-trip ⑱ **Coyote Call Trail** or the 2-mile round-trip ⑲ **Valle Grande Trail** that wind gently through woods and fields. Both are accessible from Hwy 4 without fee or reservation.

> **ASK A LOCAL**
>
> "It's difficult to describe the caldera because it's so amazing. If I didn't catch a single fish, it wouldn't matter. The scenery alone sets it apart. We saw some elk, some coyotes. Our 1-mile fishing beat, a 45-minute drive in, was completely secluded. It had a little cabin, and my wife spent the day on the porch reading. I head to Los Ojos every trip, not for the food but for the ambience. It's a complete escape up there."
>
> *Lane McIntyre, Corrales*

A private ranch from 1890 to 2000, when the federal government purchased the caldera for $100 million, this area has remained home to thousands of elk, bear, mountain lions and other wildlife. The collapsed volcanic field, called Valles Grande and visible from Hwy 4, is only 20% of the entire preserve; to really appreciate its silence and beauty you must hike its interior. Trails range from 1-mile guided human and natural-history hikes to the 7-mile Cerro Secco and Cerro del Abrigo trails. Though you must make a reservation for both guided and unguided hikes, as well as wildlife-viewing trips and winter sleigh rides, the preserve has informal and intimate one-hour geology and history van tours for walk-in visitors.

> **DETOUR**
>
> Blasted out from the volcanic tuff by the railroads in the 1920s, **Gilman Tunnels** lie 5 miles north from Hwy 4 on paved State Rd 485. The Guadalupe River cuts through the desert valley, making this a spectacular drive. From the tunnels, the gravel Forest Rd 126 climbs 18 miles through the aspen to Hwy 126. Turn left to **Fenton Lake State Park**, with a 35-acre lake set at 7900ft and surrounded by ponderosa.

From the caldera, Hwy 4 twists and turns like a whip through the dense ponderosa of the Pajarito Plateau, offering panoramic views of the desert below to the east, to ⑳ **Bandelier National Monument**. Ancestral Puebloan cliff dwellings are accessible on the easy 1.2-mile Main Loop Trail, and there are hundreds of acres of backcountry hiking. Climb up ladders into the dwellings and imagine what life must have been like here 10,000 years ago. The 5-mile round-trip Falls Trail follows the creek most of the way on its descent down the red canyon walls to the Rio Grande. Though it's an easy hike, you won't see many people. Lizards scurry across the path, and yellow-bellied birds flutter past while hawks soar above. The first of the trail's two waterfalls is a classic tumult against the dry, rocky backdrop, while the second is a gentle tumble from a shallow pool. Take a book and a picnic to the second, about a mile and a half from the trailhead, and sit on the huge boulder under the cottonwoods. You could easily spend hours here in the sun, splashing in the shallow, rocky-bottomed creek and breathing in the desert air.

BACKCOUNTRY HIKES & HOT SPRINGS

Ask at the Jemez Ranger District (☎575-829-3535) for details on **San Antonio Hot Springs**, one of the nicest of the area's many natural hot springs, and unmaintained trails through the Dome Wilderness. The **St Peter's Dome Trail-Number 118** leads to the Dome, a geologic feature formed when magma pushed up the rock, and connects to wilderness trails in Bandelier National Monument.

Twelve miles north of the monument's main entrance is ㉑ **Tsankawi**, a section of the park that sees very few visitors. Hike along a rocky trail, used by Tewa Pueblo people who lived here in the 1400s, past untouched cliff-dwellings and petroglyphs. You can literally see the soot left from their fires that burned thousands of years ago on the cave ceilings. Sit with the hot, dry wind in your face, in the sublime silence of the desert, and look out over miles upon miles of chalky white and gentle orange mesas, speckled with the low-lying green piñon trees, to the snow-capped Sangre de Cristo Mountains in the distance.

This hike through the Jemez ends at sleepy little ㉒ Los Alamos. Famous as the birthplace of the atomic bomb, Los Alamos is today home to Los Alamos National Laboratories. Stay at any of a handful of chain motels, and head to ㉓ Chile Works for breakfast. Popular with scientists and academics in this company town, this tiny shack squeezed next to Sonic serves famously addictive green chile and the best breakfast burrito in the Jemez.

Jennifer Denniston

TRIP INFORMATION

GETTING THERE
Albuquerque lies at the intersection of I-40 and I-25, 63 miles from Santa Fe.

DO
Walatowa Visitor Center
Small museum on the history and culture of the Jemez Pueblo. Also provides hiking maps and details. ☎ 505-834-7235; 7413 Hwy 4, Jemez Pueblo; ☉ 8am-5pm daily; ♿

Giggling Springs Hot Springs
Sip fresh smoothies and three-berry tea at these privately owned natural hot springs. ☎ 575-829-9175; www.gigglingsprings .com; 40 Abousleman Loop, Jemez Springs; per hr/day $15/35; ☉ 11am-12pm Wed-Sun

Bandelier National Monument
Spectacular 32,000-acre national monument includes 70 miles of trails and some of best and most accessible Ancestral Puebloan cliff dwellings in New Mexico. ☎ 505-672-3861; www.nps.gov/band; 15 Entrance Rd, Los Alamos; per vehicle $12 (7 days); ☉ 8am-6pm Jun-Aug, 9am-4:30pm Aug-May; ♿

Valles Caldera National Preserve
Advance reservations required for hikes in this 89,000-acre preserve. ☎ 866-382-5537; www.vallescaldera.gov; 18161 Hwy 4; hiking adult/child $10/5, van tours $5; ☉ walk-in van tours 10am, 12pm, 2pm & 4pm daily May-Oct; ♿

EAT
Range Café
Fuel up with huge plates of 21st-century diner fare before winding up into the Jemez. ☎ 505-867-1700; 925 Camino del Pueblo, Bernalillo; mains $6-15; ☉ 7:30am-9pm Sun-Thu, to 10pm Fri & Sat; ♿

Laughing Lizard Inn & Café
Patio dining and an eclectic menu in the tiny mountain town of Jemez Springs. ☎ 505-867-1700; 925 Camino del Pueblo, Bernalillo; mains $6-15; ☉ 7:30am-9pm Sun-Thu, to 10pm Fri &Sat; ♿ 🐾

Chili Works
Walk-up window with New Mexican fare drenched in some of the best chile in New Mexico. Cash only. ☎ 505-662-7591; 1743 Trinity Dr, Los Alamos; mains $5; ☉ 6am-2pm Mon-Sat; ♿ 🐾

DRINK
Los Ojos Restaurant & Saloon
Hunting lodge meets biker bar with mountain lions, elk and bear on the walls. ☎ 505-829-3547; 17596 Hwy 4, Jemez Springs; ☉ 11am-when it gets slow daily Mon-Sat

SLEEP
Casa Blanca Guesthouse & Garden Cottage
Fully furnished casitas (small houses) nestled beside a stream among an oasis of orchards. ☎ 575-829-3579; 17521 Hwy 4, Jemez Springs; casitas $110-170; ♿

Canon del Rio
Handsome rooms and riverside lounging beside red-rock cliffs. Strict seven-day cancellation policy during the summer. ☎ 575-829-4377; 16445 Hwy 4, Jemez Springs; d $129-139

USEFUL WEBSITES
www.jemezmountaintrail.org
www.fs.fed.us

LINK YOUR TRIP
www.lonelyplanet.com/trip-planner

Margarita Marathon

WHY GO If New Mexico had a state drink, it would be the margarita. With nearly every restaurant serving some variation of the sweet and tangy concoction, where do you spend your hard-earned cash and saved-up calories? Follow our tour to find smooth tequila, hand-squeezed lime and a Grand Marnier nirvana.

TIME
3 days

DISTANCE
185 miles

BEST TIME TO GO
Sep – Nov

START
Albuquerque, NM

END
Chimayo, NM

Start your margarita marathon in ❶ Albuquerque. Suffering in the sybaritic shadow of Santa Fe, Albuquerque is too often skipped as far as destinations go. But to understand New Mexico, and especially her margaritas, you must visit her biggest and grittiest city. Make sure to snap a photo in front of the giant sign outside ❷ Sadie's telling you "in 1897 in this location nothing happened." The restaurant is more than just an Albuquerque institution, it also serves the best damn margaritas in the city – and you don't even have to splurge on the expensive tequila to enjoy their fresh, limey goodness. Go with a carafe of the Grand Gold margarita, and a side of chicken blue-corn tortilla enchiladas topped with vegetarian green chile and guac.

From Albuquerque it's a quick drive up I-25 to your next stop, America's oldest capital, ❸ Santa Fe. The all-adobe city is filled with fabulous art, culture and architecture. And it serves some of the freshest margaritas around. Upon arrival head to the historic Plaza and the heated roof-top bar of the ❹ Ore House, home of our favorite margaritas in Santa Fe. With 40 different types of margaritas on the menu, it's a really good place to learn your tequila. The cheapest margaritas are made with gold tequila, Triple Sec and pre-mixed Sweet & Sour, all of which you should avoid if possible (the taste is rough and sickly sweet). Instead opt for a translucent silver tequila or a honey-colored Anejo and Reposada. These agave tequilas are aged for at least two months, and taste much smoother and fuller. A good margarita should never be

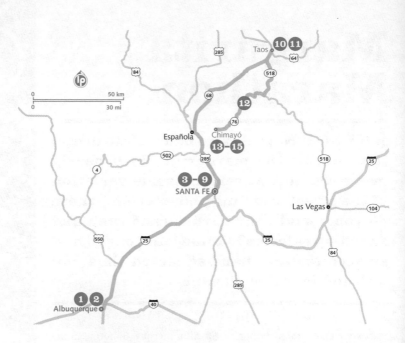

mixed with only Sweet & Sour, but should be made with at least 50% freshly squeezed lime juice. We like our margaritas made with 100% fresh lime. If you find this too tart, ask the bartender to add a splash of orange juice to sweeten it. Much of the sweetness in a margarita comes from its final ingredient: citrus liquor. Triple Sec is the bottom-of-the-barrel sweetener Cointreau and Grand Marnier are much better. Cointreau is more subtle and smoky, while Grand Marnier (our personal favorite) lends more sweetness and body to your fermented-cacti concoction. At the Ore House we love the Santana Rita, made with El Milagro Reposada and Grand Marnier. It has just the right amount of sweetness and tang. For something slightly less sugary, try the SandyRita with Sauza Commemorativo Anejo and Cointreau. It's also less expensive.

ASK A LOCAL "Personally, I think Cointreau is best with silver tequilas; you get a smooth and smoky taste. If you like Grand Marnier, it goes best with Anejo or Reposada tequilas. You get a more full body, sweet taste. The best tequilas are aged and meant to be sipped. A high-quality, 100% agave tequila that's been properly aged tastes like a fine Scotch."

Kate Taylor, Server, Ore House, Santa Fe

Santa Fe is a great town for a margarita roof-top pub crawl. The **5 Belltower Bar** atop La Fonda hotel is the premier spot to catch one of those patented New Mexican sunsets while sipping top-shelf margaritas – frozen or on the rocks, both are delish. When it comes to tequila-fueled nightlife, you can't beat the **6 Cowgirl Hall BBQ & Western Café**. Order the Mescalita margarita.

It's super smoky and different tasting (made from a mescal cacti base). Wash it down with the restaurant's house specialty, BBQ brisket (we like it best in the quesadillas, add green chile of course). At night the bar features some of the rowdiest bands and country dancing in the city. Parents won't feel left out – their kids will dig the onsite playground.

Spend the night at the **7 Inn of the Governors**; not only are rooms elegant with kiva fireplaces, the hotel is within stumbling distance of the Plaza and has a bar that just happens to serve the best-value margaritas in the city. Have a nightcap margarita at the adjacent **8 Del Churro Saloon**. Although the quality isn't the best in the city, you'll be tipsy enough at this point not to care. Plus for less than $7, you get a huge shaker of the house concoction, which fills your massive margarita glass twice! If your stomach is churning from too much booze, then try one of the delicious cheese-stuffed peppers. It feeds two and costs less than the margarita! It's no wonder Gov. Bill Richardson chooses to dine here. Take care of your hangover and wake up with a breakfast burrito smothered in spicy green chile and a cup of strong coffee at **9 Tia Sophia's**, where local artists and visiting celebrities alike take their morning nosh.

THE STRAIGHT-UP TEQUILA TRUTH

Fine tequila is like fine Scotch: meant to be sipped and savored. The most expensive, smoothest sipping tequilas are made from small batches of aged 100% blue agave, a cactus native to the Southwest and Mexico. And just like fine Scotch, the sky is the limit when it comes to price. To sample one of the best tequilas on the market – the 100% blue agave Herradura Suprema – will cost you $50 a shot in a Santa Fe bar!

With your stomach full, follow the Low Rd to **10 Taos** (it's just as pretty and gets you to the next margarita faster than taking the High Rd). Go straight to the **11 Adobe Bar** upon arriving. The packed street-side patio serves the state's finest margaritas from a classic Taos crash pad. And with creaky chairs and the warm kiva fireplaces, this bar screams New Mexican history.

Taos is a beautiful city, but you have more margaritas to taste. So jot down notes for the future, and drive south on the **12 High Road**. The drive is gorgeous, skirting cartoon cliffs and edging past pine forests as it winds through the mountains to charming **13 Chimayó**. Originally established by Spanish families with a land grant, it is home to a fabulous old adobe church and an equally fabulous New Mexican restaurant, where you can have your last margarita (or three as you're sleeping in town). The **14 Rancho de Chimayó** restaurant is also famed for the Jaramillo family's classic New Mexican cooking and wonderful old-school hacienda ambience. Spend your last tequila-soaked night at the unpretentious **15 Casa Escondida** just down the road. It features eight beautiful rooms and a hot tub.

Becca Blond

TRIP INFORMATION

GETTING THERE
Albuquerque is at the crossroads of I-25 and I-40 and is one hour south of Santa Fe.

DO

Adobe Bar
Fabulous margaritas are served at this always-packed bar in a gorgeous old adobe building. ☎ 505-758-2233; 125 Paseo del Pueblo Norte, Taos; ☽ from noon

Belltower Bar
This rooftop bar is the best spot in Santa Fe for a killer margarita-and-sunset-view combo. ☎ 505-982-5511; 100 E San Francisco St, Santa Fe; ☽ 5pm-sunset Mon-Thu, 2pm-sunset Fri-Sun May-Oct

Cowgirl Hall of Fame & Western Café
Wacky Western feminist flair and a huge patio, plus delish margs and melt-in-your-mouth BBQ. ☎ 982-2565; 319 S Guadalupe St, Sante Fe; mains $8-13; ☽ 11am-midnight Mon-Fri, 8:30am-midnight Sat, 8:30am-11pm Sun, bar to 2am Mon-Sat, until midnight Sun; ♿

Del Churro Saloon
An atmospheric old joint with copper-topped tables, lots of vegetation and a blazing fire in the winter. Margs are supersized. ☎ 505-982-4333; Inn of the Governors, 101 W Alameda, Santa Fe; mains under $6; ☽ 7am-late

Ore House
With more than 40 different types to choose from, there's bound to be a margarita for everyone. ☎ 505-983-8687; 50 Lincoln Ave, Santa Fe; ☽ 11am-late

Rancho de Chimayó
In an adobe hacienda, this restaurant features old-school ambience, delicious homecooked New Mexican food and well-mixed margaritas. ☎ 505-351-4444; 300 County Rd 98, Chimayó; mains $8-16; ☽ 11:30am-9pm Mon-Fri, 8:30am-10:30pm Sat & Sun, closed Mon Nov-Apr

Sadie's
A massive place with a barn-like atmosphere, Sadie's is an Albuquerque institution serving the city's best margs. ☎ 505-345-5339; 6230 4th St NW, Albuquerque; mains $5-13; ☽ 10am-10pm Mon-Sat, 10am-9pm Sun; ♿

Santuario de Chimayo
As many as 30,000 people make an annual pilgrimage to this c 1816 church, famous for its miraculous dirt, every year on Good Friday. ☎ 505-351-4889; NM 76, Chimayo; admission free; ☽ 9am-5pm, mass 11am Mon-Sat & noon Sun

SLEEP & EAT

Casa Escondida
A highly recommended Southwestern B&B, this is a low-key place with a hot tub for soaking sore limbs, and eight gorgeous rooms. ☎ 505-351-4805; www.casaescondida.com; 64 County Rd 100, Chimayó; r $99-149

Inn of the Governors
An intimate place to slumber. Rooms have working kiva fireplaces, wi-fi and Southwestern decor. ☎ 505-982-4333; 101 W Alameda, Santa Fe; r from $135

Tia Sophia's
Breakfast is the meal of choice, with fantastic burritos and other Southwestern dishes. The shelf of kids' books helps little ones pass the time. ☎ 505-983-9880; 210 W San Francisco St, Santa Fe; mains $3-9; ☽ 7am-2pm Mon-Sat; ♿

USEFUL WEBSITES
www.tequilasource.com

LINK YOUR TRIP
www.lonelyplanet.com/trip-planner

Skiing the Enchanted Circle

WHY GO Northern New Mexican skiing is all about long runs through icicle-dipped glades of fir, fast slams down steep shoots and awesome expert terrain. And now that snowboarders can ride the slopes at Taos Ski Valley, there's no excuse for powder hounds not to shred their way around the Enchanted Circle's low-key mountain resorts.

TIME
3 days

DISTANCE
80 miles

BEST TIME TO GO
Dec – Mar

START
Taos Ski Valley

END
Red River

Start in New Mexico's top snow destination, the ❶ Taos Ski Valley. It's the kind of place people move to in order to say they've "ski bummed" for a couple years. Those who have done so tell us there is just something special about the snow, challenging terrain and laid-back atmosphere that makes this mountain more addictive than hot cocoa.

Once exclusive to skiers, Taos Ski Valley recently let snowboarders start riding her 70-plus trails. Boasting 300in of all-natural powder and a peak elevation of 11,819ft, Taos is also a technical rider's dream. From zipping down steep tree glades to jumping off cliffs into untouched snow bowls, this resort has a 2612ft vertical drop and more than 50% of its terrain is marked expert. If you just feel like playing on the rails and jumps, head to the terrain park that also features a cross obstacle course for skiers. When your legs are feeling sore, ride down to the ❷ Snakedance Condominiums & Spa at the bottom of the lifts. You can soak your muscles in the hot tub, warm up in the sauna or even call the concierge to arrange an in-room massage! Grab dinner and an *après*-ski drink at ❸ Tim's Stray Dog Cantina, a ski-valley institution famous for its flame-roasted red and green chile.

There's only one road in and out of Taos Ski Valley – Hwy 150 – and it takes you right past ❹ Taos Cow Ice Cream. Stop on your way out

the next morning for a breakfast-time cone of sweet, edible snow (well ice cream, but close enough). It's a good snack to munch on your drive to the next resort. Hwy 150 merges with Hwy 64 near Taos town (20 miles from the resort) and is called the Enchanted Circle byway. Follow the road as it winds through snow-capped pine forests and past the jagged peaks of the Sangre de Cristo range. **5** **Angel Fire Resort**, about 26 miles east of Taos, is your next ski-hopping trip stop. As if the 2077ft vertical drop and 450 acres of trails weren't enough, Angel Fire also offers the opportunity to try off-the-grid winter sports like riding the mountain on a skateboard without wheels or a bike outfitted with skis. Plus the resort boasts a Chris Gunnarson–designed, 400ft-long, competition-quality half-pipe with a wicked 26% grade. The resort is the best place to sleep, offering ski chalet–style rooms and excellent child-care facilities. Visit the **6** **Roasted Clove** for dinner. The town's long-established favorite dining option pairs interesting Southwestern-influenced American cuisine with fine wine.

> *"Stop for a cone of sweet, edible snow to munch on your drive to the next resort."*

Head out early on day three and get ready for a little car time. Kick back, pump the stereo and watch the meadows of snow and thick tracks of forest flash by. Just north of Eagles Nest look west for a great view of Wheeler Peak, New Mexico's highest mountain. Is your dog joining you for this road trip? He'll always be grateful if you take him to the **7** **Enchanted Forest** for cross-country skiing – well, you ski and the dog can run alongside. New Mexico's premier Nordic ski area boasts 34km of groomed trails near the 9820ft Bobcat Pass, including a 5km ski trail designated especially for dogs and their guardians.

It's a short and scenic drive from the Enchanted Forest to the **8** **Red River Ski Resort** in the center of Red River town. Old West meets German ski chalet in this village of cheerfully painted ticky-tacky shops and art galleries, along with six historic buildings and plenty of dilapidated mines, all gleaming in the high desert sun. New Mexicans drive from across the state to ski at Red River, as the prices here are about $20 less than the other resorts. If you're traveling with the kids, or just learning how to ski, it's a good destination as there are numerous kid and newbie packages. The resort is surrounded completely by national forest land, including the Wild Rivers Recreation Area, and there are plenty of tree glades and

A LITTLE BIT OF HISTORY

Home to 13,161ft Wheeler Peak, crystalline lakes, huge tracks of forest and rolling steppes carpeted with windswept meadows, there's a reason they call this 84-mile eye-candy byway the Enchanted Circle. Most towns along the loop were founded in the 1880s gold rush by Anglo settlers looking for the mother lode. It never quite panned out, however, and the abandoned mines and ghost towns are highlights of the trip. Those settlers who remained turned to tourism and opened major ski resorts at Angel Fire and Red River.

chutes for intermediate and expert skiers to dip into. The terrain park is a work of art with lots of boxes and rails for tricks. Bed down at the German style **9** **Alpine Lodge**, which runs a slew of stay-and-ski packages and has two hot tubs on the property. Grab a meal at **10** **Shotgun Willies**, a long-time local favorite. The house specialty is the BBQ, which is served by the pound. Order the brisket combo. Red River is a favorite stop on the country-and-western music circuit, so end your trip with a night of cocktails and line dancing at the popular **11** **Bull o' the Woods Saloon.**

Becca Blond

TRIP INFORMATION

GETTING THERE
To reach the Taos Ski Valley, take Hwy 64 north out of Taos to the blinking light, and veer right on Hwy 150 toward Arroyo Seco. The trip is 20 miles.

DO

Angel Fire Resort
Angel Fire is big on snow-sport variety, and the resort's rooms are the best in town. ☎ 800-633-7463; www.angelfireresort.com; NM 434; half-/full-day lift tickets $44/59; r $150-300; ⛄

Enchanted Forest
This dog-friendly Nordic ski area hosts exotic Moonlight Ski Tours on the Saturday before a full moon. ☎ 800-966-9381; www.enchanted forestxc.com; NM 38; adult/child $12/5; ◷ 9am-4:30pm Nov-Mar; 🐾

Red River Ski Area
Half-price weekends during the beginning of December and deals on multiday stays including accommodations make this resort even more appealing. ☎ 800-331-7669; www.redriverskiarea.com; half-/full-day lift tickets $41/55.

Red River Ski Resort
Kid-friendly ski resort that's also good for newbies. Tree glades and chutes for more advanced riders. ☎ 800-331-7669; www .redriverskiarea.com; half-/full-day lift tickets $41/55; ◷ Dec-Mar; ⛄

Taos Ski Valley
Check the resort website for ski-and-stay deals, including week-long packages with room, board, lessons and lift tickets. ☎ 866-250-7274; www.skitaos.org; half-/full-day lift tickets $47/63

SLEEP & EAT

Alpine Lodge
Go online for specials, from college day room discounts, kids-stay-and-ski-free deals and early-season lift-ticket discounts. Condos sleep six. ☎ 575-754-2952, 800-252-2333; www.thealpinelodge.com; 417 Main St, Red River; d $74-86, condos $185-312

Bull o' the Woods Saloon
This is one of a handful of pubs that bring in live country bands on weekends. ☎ 575-754-2593; Main St, Red River

Roasted Clove
This long-established restaurant is everyone's favorite fine dining. ☎ 575-377-0636; www .roastedclove.com; 48 N Angel Fire Rd, Angel Fire; mains $17-35; ◷ 5pm-10pm Wed-Mon

Shotgun Willie's
BBQ is the house special, but the breakfasts are the perfect hang-over cure. ☎ 575-754-6505; cnr Main St & Pioneer Rd, Red River; mains $6-12; ◷ 7am-7pm

Snakedance Condominiums & Spa
Check online for ski-and-stay specials. This giant place at the bottom of the lifts offers ski-lodge–style accommodation with loads of amenities. ☎ 800-322-9815; www.snaked-ancecondos.com; 110 Sutton Pl; r $65-250; ⛄

Taos Cow Ice Cream
Famous for all-natural ice cream, baked goods and subs. ☎ 505-776-5640; 485 Hwy 150; mains & cones $2-7; ◷ 7am-7pm

Tim's Stray Dog Cantina
Fabulous northern New Mexican cuisine, fresh margaritas and a big selection of bottled brews. ☎ 505-776-2894; 105 Sutton Pl; mains $4-12; ◷ breakfast, lunch and dinner

USEFUL WEBSITES
www.enchantedcircle.org
www.taosvacationguide.com

LINK YOUR TRIP
www.lonelyplanet.com/trip-planner

Rock It: A Geology Expedition

WHY GO University of New Mexico geology professor Yemane Asmerom takes us across lava flows and through canyons of pink volcanic tuff to rocks rich in dinosaur bones, shows us where to collect fossils, and directs us to some great geology museums on this trip into New Mexico's geologic past.

TIME
5 days

DISTANCE
200 miles

BEST TIME TO GO
Dec – Mar

START
Albuquerque, NM

END
Taos, NM

ALSO GOOD FOR

OUTDOORS

Fuel up for rock hunting with a plate of huevos rancheros at ❶ Flying Star, Asmerom's favorite Nob Hill haunt. Then begin your exploration of New Mexico geology with a visit to the University of New Mexico (UNM). Examine the state's rocks, minerals and fossils at the on-site ❷ Geology Museum and take a few minutes to read up on the area's plate-tectonic and paleoclimatic history. Down the hall, explore the solar system at the ❸ Meteorite Museum, which boasts a one-ton meteorite, before heading west on Central Ave to the ❹ Museum of Natural History, where you can walk through the interior of a volcano, complete with not particularly realistic boiling lava below your feet.

For a good night's rest, Asmerom recommends ❺ Nora Dixon Place in his rural hometown of Corrales. Walk a half-mile down the road to the Rio Grande bosque or sit in the courtyard to watch the setting sun turn the Sandia Mountains watermelon. Though it's tempting to spend the morning relaxing with coffee in the sun, you'll want to get an early start. A long day of volcano hopping begins at the "Three Sisters" at ❻ Petroglyph National Monument. These spatter cones (created about 150,000 years ago by lava sputtering up from cracks in the earth) poke up a few hundred feet from the grassy lava flatlands. Climb to the top for spectacular views of the Rio Grande Rift, with the Sandia Mountains bounding the rift to the east, the volcanoes and their lava flows forming the western margin, and the Rio Grande River down its center.

HISTORY & CULTURE

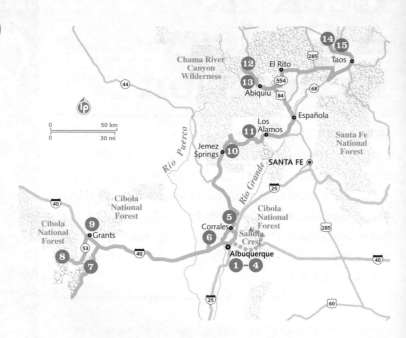

Continue west on I-40, through the endless plains and valleys punctuated by sandstone- or basalt-topped mesas, just over 100 miles to the 26,300-acre **⑦ El Malpais National Monument**, one of many volcanic regions along the Jemez Lineament, a line of volcanic activity that stretches from El Capulin in Raton, NM, to Springerville,

> **DETOUR** The Sandia Mountains are a tale of two slopes. Formed by the Rio Grande Rift, the west slope exposes 1.4-billion-year-old granite roots under parched desert scrub. The east side is capped with 300-million-year-old, water-retaining limestone, and thus thriving alpine forests. The billion-year-long gap in time represented by the contact between granite and limestone is visible 300ft downhill from the **Doc Long Picnic Area** on the road to Cedar Crest (I-40 exit 175).

AZ. Named after the Spanish word for badlands, El Malpais's raw landscape of jagged black lava flows and desert shrubs, searing under the summer sun, offers miles of hiking trails, primitive camping and scenic drives.

Twenty-eight miles south of Grants on Hwy 53, fire and ice intertwine at **⑧ Ice Cave and Bandera Crater**. A short climb reveals a great view into the Bandera Crater, the largest cinder cone in the region. Another trail winds through the lava to an ice cave, an exposed portion of lava tube which maintains a below-freezing temperature year-round.

Back in the '50s, when folks thought we were going to run the world on nuclear energy and the US was building nuclear bombs, uranium mining in the Grants area boomed. Before returning to Albuquerque, stop at the

9 New Mexico Mining Museum in Grants, where a cage takes you down into a recreated uranium mine.

Return for a late dinner and another night in Corrales, before packing up and heading north on Hwy 4 to the Jemez Mountains, a gigantic, low-profile volcano that erupted huge amounts of volcanic ash two million years ago. Drive through the red-rock canyon of the Jemez River, past layers of volcanic tuff, pumice, lava and obsidian, stopping for a scramble over the travertine deposit of the sulphur-smelling **10** Soda Dam.

A turnout on the west side of Hwy 4, 15 miles north of the Wallatowa Visitor Center, offers great fossil picking through ancient sea-floor sediment, and there are several stretches along Hwy 4 where you can pull over and pick up pumice, lava and obsidian. Pause to read the roadside marker on the geology of the ranchlands of **11** Valles Grande, the Jemez's collapsed volcanic crater. On weekdays, the caldera offers walk-in geology van tours that depart from the visitors center, visible from Hwy 4.

From here, drive through Los Alamos and Espanola and follow Hwy 84 up onto the Colorado Plateau to **12** Ghost Ranch. New Mexico's state fossil, the dinosaur Coelophysis, was first discovered in the fossil-rich beds of the ranch in 1947. You can often see Ghost Ranch's own paleontologist, Alex Downs, excavating dinosaur bones at the paleontology museum here. Several hikes lead through exposed large sections of rock from the Mesozoic, the age of dinosaurs (250 million to 66 million years ago).

RIO GRANDE RIFT

The Rio Grande Rift is a linked series of 10-million-year-old north–south trending valleys stretching from southern Colorado through New Mexico and into Texas. Rifting – the stretching and thinning of the earth's crust – resulted in sunken valley floors with outer edges defined by volcanoes resting atop fractures in the crust (which served as magma conduits) or mountains formed by uplift and rotation of huge granite blocks. The Three Sisters cinder cones on the west side of Albuquerque are an example of the former, the Sandia Mountains the latter.

After a swim in **13** Abiquiu Reservoir, head through El Rito and on up to Taos. An unpaved road descends the Rio Grande Gorge through hundreds of feet of lava and crosses the river. The rocks on the east side of the valley are ancient metamorphic rocks, mostly schists, with shiny micas, round garnets and crossed staurolites, while the rocks on the west are lava erupted within the past few million years.

Continue on Hwy 68 through Embudo Canyon to the dramatic stretch of the **14** Taos Plateau, formed by volcanic eruptions and cut by an 800ft canyon formed by the Rio Grande River. The view from **15** Rio Grande Gorge Bridge is enough to inspire just about anyone to a career in geology.
Jennifer Denniston

TRIP INFORMATION

GETTING THERE
Albuquerque sits at the intersection of I-40 and I-25, 63 miles south of Santa Fe

DO

El Malpais National Monument
Black lava oozed from a cluster of volcanoes until as recently as 2000 years ago, and several lava flows here look younger still. ☎ 505-783-4774; www.nps.gov/elma/; 123 E Roosevelt Ave, Grants; 9am-4pm Mon-Fri;

Geology Museum
Small but well-presented museum with a focus on local geology. ☎ 505-277-4204; Northrop Hall, University of New Mexico, Albuquerque; 7:30am-noon, 1-4:30pm Mon-Fri;

Ghost Ranch
Hike through one of the country's most prolific quarries of the Triassic era and visit the tiny but excellent paleontology museum. Various accommodations available. ☎ 505-685-4333; www.ghostranch.org; Hwy 84, btwn Miles 225 & 226, Abiquiu; seasonal variations, closed Dec;

Ice Cave Bandera Volcano
Hike around the side of the most pristine and accessible volcanoes in the country. ☎ 888-423-2283; www.icecaves.com; I-40 exit 81; adult/child 5-12 yr $9/4; 8am-1 hr before sunset;

Meteorite Museum
Excellent selection of meteorites including many exceptionally large specimens. ☎ 505-277-4204; Northrop Hall, University of New Mexico, Alburquerque; 9am-4pm Mon-Fri;

Museum of Natural History
Excellent exhibits on New Mexico geology designed with the layman in mind, as well as lots of fun stuff for kids. ☎ 505-841-2802; www.nmnaturalhistory.org; 1801 Mountain Rd NW, Albuquerque; 9am-4pm Mon-Fri;

New Mexico Mining Museum
Bone up on uranium mining in the heart of uranium country. ☎ 505-287-4802; 100 North Iron Ave, Grants; 9am-4pm Mon-Sat;

Petroglyph National Monument
Trails through the flat, grassy Volcano Day Use Area lead past three volcanic cinder cones. The petroglyphs are in another area. ☎ 8505-899-0205; www.nps.gov/petr/; 6001 Unser Blvd NW, Albuquerque; dawn-dusk;

EAT

Flying Star
Chow on everything from organic oats to Asian stir-fry tofu or burritos smothered in red chile. Corrales has another branch. ☎ 505-255-6633; 3416 Central SE, Albuquerque; mains $5-12; 6am-11:30pm Sun-Thu, to 12pm Sat & Sun;

SLEEP

Abiquiu Inn
Spacious casitas (small houses) with full kitchens and screened-in porches overlooking the bosque. Handsome Southwestern doubles also available. ☎ 505-685-4378; www.abiquiuinn.com; 21120 Hwy 84, Abiquiu; r $140-195;

Nora Dixon Place
Quiet bed and breakfast in an historic village north of Albuquerque. ☎ 505-898-3662; www.noradixon.com; 312 Dixon Rd, Corrales; r $102-124;

USEFUL WEBSITES
www.geoinfo.nmt.edu/tour/
www.publiclands.org

SUGGESTED READS
• *Basin and Range,* John McPhee
• *Roadside Geology of New Mexico,* Halka Chronic

www.lonelyplanet.com/trip-planner

LINK YOUR TRIP

Hot Springs & Swimming Holes

OUTDOORS

WHY GO There's nothing like floating on your back in a mineral-heavy pool, inhaling steam and the scents of sage and desert, staring at a velvet sky twinkling with diamonds. Once you've spent an evening in New Mexico's enchanting hot springs – it doesn't matter if it's commercial or au natural – you'll be hooked for life.

TIME
5 days

DISTANCE
575 miles

BEST TIME TO GO
Dec – Mar

START
Montezuma Hot Spring Pool, NM

END
Gila Hot Springs Vacation Center, NM

Sometimes the best things in life are free, if you know where to look. In the case of steaming water, you can't beat the natural ❶ Montezuma Hot Spring Pool, about 7 miles northwest of ❷ Las Vegas (the original Sin City, popular with Billy the Kid, not the neon-lit metropolis that gangster rappers and pop stars now frequent) on Hwy 65. Besides their reputed curative and therapeutic powers, these admission-free soaking pools are especially alluring under the light of a full moon. Stay in Las Vegas afterwards, at the historic ❸ Plaza Hotel. Sleep in if you like, it's only an hour's drive south on I-25 to ❹ Santa Fe, your next stop. The oldest state capital in the USA doesn't boast its own natural springs, but it is home to the most zen retreat in the state, ❺ Ten Thousand Waves Japanese Resort & Spa, the perfect place for pampering. Follow a long soak in the mountainside hot tubs (some private, others public) with a hot-stone massage or exfoliating body wrap. Spend the night in one of the 13 gorgeous free-standing guesthouses. It's so relaxing here, you'll never want to leave.

Except you should. Otherwise you'll miss ❻ Ojo Caliente Hot Springs, the state's most famous hot-springs resort (for good reason). The shabby chic place, about an hour's drive north of Santa Fe, features five pools against a backdrop of crumbly, orangey sandstone monoliths and baby-blue New Mexico sky. Ojo Caliente's most unique facet is its springs are each fed by an independent water source containing

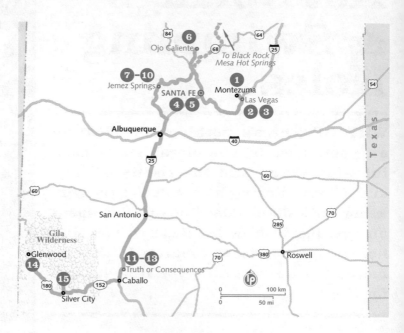

different mineral contents. The enclosed Soda Spring Pool, meant to help relieve digestion problems, is about as relaxing as it gets; it's full of steam and perfect for floating in the mist. The al fresco cliffside Iron Pool has a floor made from natural pebbles that gently exfoliate your feet as you soak up the blood-cleansing and immunity-boosting waters. Don't forget to fill up a water bottle from the fountain at the Lithium spring to swig on a day when your mood could use a little elevation!

> *"When your skin has turned reptilian from mineral-pool soaking, head to the Laughing Lizard Inn…"*

South of Ojo Caliente, the road meanders past sculpted rock formations and ruins of abandoned pueblos into the heart of the Jemez Mountains, the world's largest volcano. The gorgeous village of ⑦ **Jemez Springs** is constructed around a cluster of hot mineral pools – the result of an underground lava flow – on the Jemez River. The rustic ⑧ **Jemez Springs Bath House**, which also does great massages, is one of two places in town to experience the water's healing magic. Nearby ⑨ **Giggling Springs** is the other, and the choice of many locals who praise its superhot and therapeutic pools. The site of the state's oldest bathhouse (c the late 1880s), Giggling Springs' hot pool is right next to the Jemez River, which acts as a great cold plunge, should the heat become too much! The original bathhouse still stands at the end of the driveway, welcoming visitors to the stacked red-rock pool of hot, healing water. When your skin has turned reptilian from mineral-pool soaking, head to the ⑩ **Laughing Lizard**

Inn across the street from Giggling Springs to bed down in one of its funky rooms. The attached café serves a mean green chile and has live music on weekend nights.

It's a 200-mile drive from the Jemez Mountains south to ⑪ **Truth or Consequences**. But it's worth the long slog along I-25 to reach this quirky city's famous hot mineral pools where Native Americans, including Geronimo, have bathed for centuries. The water here ranges in temperature from 98°F to 115°F. Most of T or C's hotels and motels double as spas. The swankiest place to take a hot dip by far is ⑫ **Sierra Grande Lodge & Spa**, which added two new mineral baths and a holistic spa last year. The resort charges non-guests $25 for the first person, then $5 for each additional person, to use its mineral springs. For a more casual experience, ⑬ **Riverbend Hot Springs** has six outdoor tubs by the river and a hippie hostel vibe. It costs between $10 and $15 per person to soak.

From Truth or Consequences head southwest about 200 miles to Silver City, then take Hwy 180 north for another 44 miles to the ⑭ **Gila National Forest Ranger Station**. The country's first designated wilderness area, the Gila Wilderness, is also the largest roadless area in the USA outside Alaska. If you're looking for isolated and undiscovered hot springs amid a brilliant tableau of wild mountains, remote canyons and millions of trees, the Gila is where to go. Our favorite series of hot springs in the forest are just a short hike up Middle Fork River from the forest ranger station. Backtrack towards Silver City when you're finished, and take Rte 15 north for 39 miles to pet-friendly ⑮ **Gila Hot Springs Vacation Center**. Your final swimming hole has been used by Native Americans for centuries. There is primitive camping by the springs, or you can shack up in one of the simple rooms. Either way, you'll have a brilliant (and warm) view of southern New Mexico's star-streaked sky from a mineral pool in the middle of nowhere. Now that's a good ending.

Becca Blond

> **DETOUR** Take Hwy 522 north from Taos for 11 miles to reach the best free soaking in northern New Mexico: **Black Rock Mesa Hot Springs**. The series of pools bubble out of the Rio Grande River and form one large, natural soaking pool that's well-maintained by local volunteers. The temperature is perfect, and so are the narrow canyon views. The hot springs are just outside the village of Arroyo Hondo. From Hwy 522, make a left just north of Herb's Lounge onto County Rd 005. Follow the dirt road for nearly a mile (it turns to the right) to the parking lot at the bottom. Scramble down the canyon on a maintained trail to the river and plunge into the black-rock pool at the bottom – you can't see the springs until you're nearly on top of them!

TRIP 53

TRIP INFORMATION

GETTING THERE
From Albuquerque, head north on I-25. Exit at Las Vegas and drive 5 miles north on Hwy 65 to Montezuma.

DO
Giggling Springs
Loved by locals for its superhot water, these private springs are just across the street from the best hotel in town. ☎ 575-829-9175; 40 Abouslemen Loop; per hr $15; ⏱ 11am-5pm

Gila National Forest Ranger Station
The starting point for the trail to the Middle Fork hot springs pools. ☎ 575-539-2481; Hwy 180; ⏱ 8am-4:30pm

Gila Hot Springs Vacation Center
Used by Native Americans since ancient times, these springs are in a pet-friendly resort. ☎ 575-536-9551; www.gilahot springsranch.com; Hwy 15; pool admission $3, tent/RV sites $12/17, r from $50; 🐾

Jemez Springs Bath House
Have a healing soak in a private tub at this rustic Old Western bath house. ☎ 505-829-3303; www.jemezspringsbathhouse.com; 62 Jemez Springs Plaza; per hr $10-15; ⏱ 10am-8pm

Montezuma Hot Spring Pool
This au-natural, community-maintained hot soaking pool is especially enchanting on a moonlit evening. ☎ 505-454-4200; Hwy 65, Montezuma; admission free; ⏱ 5am-midnight

Ojo Caliente
Our favorite high-desert hot-springs escape. ☎ 800-222-9162; www.ojocalientespa.com; 50 Los Baños Dr; pool admission weekday/ weekend/after 6pm $16/22/12, massages $50-125, wraps $10-90, facials from $50, luxury packages from $125

Ten Thousand Waves Japanese Resort & Spa
Santa Fe's favorite Japanese spa welcomes doggies with custom-sized beds and bones! Humans get soaking tubs, massages and zen bedrooms. ☎ 505-982-9304; www.ten thousandwaves.com; 3451 Hyde Park Rd, Santa Fe; r $99-279; 🐾

EAT & SLEEP
Laughing Lizard Inn
A great guesthouse with cozy rooms and an attached café (mains $5-11). ☎ 505-829-3108; www.thelaughinglizard.com; NM 4; r $49-64, ; ⏱ restaurant 11am-8pm Tue-Sat, 11am-6pm Sun, limited hr in winter

Plaza Hotel
Las Vegas' most celebrated and historic lodging is also excellent value. ☎ 505-425-3591; www.plazahotel-nm.com; 230 Old Town Plaza, Las Vegas; r incl breakfast from $69

Riverbend Hot Springs
Dormitory-style accommodations in cabins, trailers and teepees. The hot spring tubs are spread along the river. ☎ 575-894-7625; www.riverbendhotsprings.com; 100 Austin St; dm/camping $24/20, r $40-100

Sierra Grande Lodge & Spa
Chakras align at this oasis. Guest rooms are luxe and tranquil and there's a holistic spa. ☎ 575-894-6976; www.sierragrandelodge .com; 501 McAdoo St; r from $99

USEFUL WEBSITES
www.discovernewmexico.com/hotsprings /index.htm

www.swimmingholes.org

LINK YOUR TRIP
www.lonelyplanet.com/trip-planner

Following the Turquoise Trail

WHY GO You can zip from Albuquerque to Santa Fe in under an hour on the highway, but taking the old turquoise trading trail is the quintessential quirky rural New Mexican road trip. Here, the hippies ride Harleys around ghost-gone-gallery old mining towns and the three-ring circus is found inside the museum.

A National and Historic Scenic Byway, the Turquoise Trail has been a major trade route since at least 2000 BC. That's when local artisans began trading Cerrillos turquoise with communities in present-day Mexico – the first rocks were dug up by Native Americans around AD 100. Today it's a quixotic rural New Mexican road trip and a journey back in history. First up is the ❶ **Tinkertown Museum**, located about 1 mile down the trail. The museum is the life's work of Ross J Ward, and one of those places you have to see to believe. Ward has created an entire animated Western miniature town and three-ring circus that includes thousands of intricately carved wooden figurines. The artist is also famous for his kooky words of wisdom like "eat more mangos naked."

New Mexico's small towns pride themselves on being off-beat and unique, and the next town en route, Madrid, is no different. Here the hippies ride Harley Davidsons and bikers frequent the modern art galleries. A bustling company coal-mining town in the 1920s and '30s, ❷ **Madrid** (pronounced *Maa*-drid) was all but abandoned after WWII. In the mid-1970s, the company's heirs sold cheap lots to tie-dyed wanderers who have built a thriving arts community with a sprinkling of New Age shops and biker bars. Unlike the uniform adobe brick comprising most New Mexico towns, Madrid's buildings are wood, giving the place an almost northeast coal-town vibe. By the time you arrive, you'll be hungry (especially if you've logged serious miles on Sandia Crest). Stop by the ❸ **Mine Shaft Tavern** for pub

TIME
2 days

DISTANCE
65 miles

BEST TIME TO GO
Sep – Nov

START
Albuquerque, NM

END
Santa Fe, NM

ALSO GOOD FOR

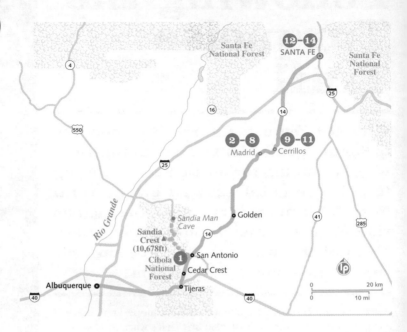

grub and a chance to chat with the locals at the "longest stand-up bar in New Mexico." Built in 1946, the 50ft shotgun bar has been Madrid's favorite attraction for decades. There's live music on weekends.

Spend the night at ❹ **Madrid Lodging**, which has a couple of two-room suites and an outdoor hot tub in a well-tended, colorfully painted 1930s boarding house. Check in for two nights – you have a full day ahead of you. Go gallery hopping the next morning. Madrid may be a one-street town, but it is home to dozens of art shops. Visit ❺ **Fuse Arts** for first-rate abstract designs and ❻ **Seppanen & Daughters Fine Textiles** for amazing rugs. For lunch try ❼ **Mama Lisa's Ghost Town Kitchen**, where everything from the bread to the stew is made from scratch. The menu changes daily, but there's always something spicy and New Mexican featured. Take in the afternoon show at the ❽ **Madrid Melodrama & Engine House Theatre**. Whether you have kids, or are one at heart, this place puts on a Wild West how, staring a steam locomotive, mining desperados, scoundrels, vixens and other storied characters from the Victorian era that leave you with an old-fashioned happy feeling at the end. Admission includes a six-shooter loaded with marshmallows to unload at the villains.

From Madrid it's a quick 3 mile sprint to your next stop. Native Americans have been digging for turquoise in the hills north of tiny ❾ **Cerrillos** since the 1st century. With unpaved streets and a vibe reminiscent of a Spanish village from the late 1800s, the old mining town feels wonderfully lost in time. Explore the history at the ⑩ **Cerrillos Turquoise Mining Museum & Petting Zoo**, a top-drawer roadside attraction. It packs five rooms with Chinese art, pioneer-era tools, mining equipment dating to 3000 BC, bottles and antiques excavated from an abandoned area hotel, and anything else the owners thought was worth displaying. For $2 more you can feed the goats, llamas and unusual chickens. Or head into the mountains and go for a horseback ride. The ⑪ **Broken Saddle Riding Co** has one- to three-hour horseback rides through juniper-dotted hills and abandoned mines. Along the way, you'll learn about local history and geology; don't forget a camera to capture the spectacular views.

After two days of hiking, horseback-riding and gallery hopping you'll be more than ready to soak those tired limbs upon arriving in ⑫ **Santa Fe**. Head straight to ⑬ **Ten Thousand Waves Japanese Resort & Spa** for a massage and a soak in an al fresco private hot tub built for two. Inhale the piñon and savor the silence and steam. Finish your trip down the Turquoise Trail buying a chunk of the blue stone that started it all. The best place to purchase the semiprecious stone, which is usually set in sterling silver jewelry, is from the Native American artists selling their work under the *portales* (overhangs) in front of the ⑭ **Palace of the Governors** on the downtown square. The artists are part of a state initiative that allows Native Americans to sell jewelry and art in front of the palace. It's a tradition that began in the 1880s, when Tesuque artisans began meeting the train with all manner of wares. Today up to 1200 members, representing almost every New Mexican tribe – some drive as far as 200 miles – draw lots for the 76 spaces under the vigas each morning.

Becca Blond

DETOUR

The views from the top of 10,678ft **Sandia Crest** are straight out of a John Denver music video. Sacred to Sandia Pueblo, the pink hued granite mountain's summit is the highest point on the Turquoise Trail. Reach it from Sandia Crest Rd (NM 165), which intersects with NM 14 in Cedar Crest. The steep, winding road is lined with picnic spots and trailheads. Don't miss the easy 1 mile roundtrip hike to **Sandia Man Cave**, where North America's oldest human encampment was discovered in 1936.

GOT ROCK?

Cerrillos has been in the mining business since AD 100, when Native Americans discovered turquoise. Spanish explorers followed, building the first mine in North America. By the late 1800s Cerrillos was a rip-roaring prospector town with 21 saloons. Although best known for its top-quality turquoise, gold, silver and zinc have also been extracted. In fact, Thomas Edison once spent many thousands of dollars on a laboratory meant to refine gold without using water. But unlike the light bulb, this experiment never turned on.

TRIP INFORMATION

GETTING THERE
From Albuquerque take I-40 east for 10 miles to the Tijeras/Cedar Crest exit. Follow the signs for Hwy 14 north.

DO
Broken Saddle Riding Co
This company runs one- to three-hour horseback rides through juniper-dotted hills and abandoned mines. ☎ 505-424-7774; www.brokensaddle.com; off County Rd 57; rides $55-90; ☽ by appointment

Cerillos Turquoise Mining Museum & Petting Zoo
Five rooms with Chinese art, pioneer-era tools, mining equipment dating to 3000 BC, bottles and antiques excavated from an abandoned area hotel among other relics. ☎ 505-438-3008; 17 Waldo St, Cerrillos; admission $2; ☽ 9am-sunset

Fuse Arts
First-rate abstract art is on display at this interesting gallery. ☎ 505-438-4999; 2878 Hwy 14, Madrid; ☽ call for hr

Madrid Melodrama & Engine House Theatre
You get to shoot marshmallows at the bad guys with your very own six-shooter at this summer-time melodrama in the Old Coal Mine Museum. ☎ 505-438-3780; 2814 NM 14; adult/child $10/4; ☽ 3pm Sat & Sun May-Oct

Seppanen & Daughters Fine Textiles
Textiles are the focus at this gallery, specifically Navajo and Tibetan rugs. Brightly colored wooden animals from Oaxaca are also on sale. ☎ 505-424-7470; 2879 NM 14, Madrid; ☽ call for hr

Tinkertown Museum
The life's work of one man, this amazing museum consists of an intricately carved miniature Western town and three-ring circus complete with mechanical people and cars. ☎ 505-281-5233; www.tinkertown.com; 121 Sandia Crest Rd; adult/child $3/1; ☽ 9am-6pm Apr-Nov; ☝

EAT & SLEEP
Madrid Lodging
Colorful two-room suites, wi-fi and an outdoor hot tub make this well-tended place the pick of the town. ☎ 505-471-3450; www.madridlodging.com; 14 Opera House Rd, Madrid; r $110-130

Mama Lisa's Ghost Town Kitchen
Whatever you do, don't miss the red chile chocolate cake, the specialty at this traditional New Mexican café. The menu rotates, but everything is cooked fresh. ☎ 505-471-5769; Rte 14, Madrid; mains from $5; ☽ call for hr

Mine Shaft Tavern
Around for more than 60 years, this bar is the local choice for cold beer, pub grub and good music. ☎ 505-473-0743; 2846 NM Hwy 14, Madrid; mains $5-15; ☽ noon-12pm

Ten Thousand Waves Japanese Resort & Spa
Stay in one of the 13 gorgeous, zen-inspired guesthouses and indulge in massages, facials and soak time in one of the private mountainside hot tubs. ☎ 505-982-9304; www.tenthousandwaves.com; 3451 Hyde Park Rd, Santa Fe; r $99-279

USEFUL WEBSITES
www.byways.org/explore/byways/2094/
www.turqouisetrail.org

LINK YOUR TRIP

www.lonelyplanet.com/trip-planner

Rafting & Fishing the Rio Grande

OUTDOORS

WHY GO Whether it's casting for trout in early fall or rushing rapids in late spring, playing on the Rio Grande near Taos is a heavenly treat. Rife with fly-fishing spots and wild white water, this stretch of river flows through New Mexico's most magical, sage-scented, crimson canyon scenery.

TIME
4 days

DISTANCE
40 miles

BEST TIME TO GO
Apr – Sep

START
Pilar, NM

END
Questa, NM

It takes only a few moments watching the blue ribbon dancing past crimson cliffs and through craggy mocha canyons to fall in love with the Rio Grande around Taos. Rafting and fly-fishing are the two top ways to enjoy the river, so we've combined both into one action-packed trip. Begin in New Mexico's rafting capital, tiny **1** Pilar. Warm up riding the **2** Racecourse, a 5-mile stretch of white water just south of town. You can join one of the half-day trips run by **3** Los Rios River Runners. The biggest of the Racecourse's nine named rapids is "Big Rock." When the river is running fast (early in the season) it's a Class IV. Adrenalin junkies should drive a solo inflatable kayak down the Racecourse.

After drying off, follow Hwy 68 north for 16 miles to beautiful and artsy **4** Taos. You'll be starving, and probably craving a beer, so go straight to **5** Eske's Brew Pub, which serves roasted green chile infused beer. It's definitely an acquired taste, but if you're adventurous enough to be on this trip in the first place you can handle a 12oz glass of this spicy beer. Wash the green chile aftertaste away with more green chile – order a burrito smothered in hearty green-chile stew! Your hotel is 10 miles from Taos, just west of the **6** Rio Grande Gorge Bridge, the USA's third-highest suspension bridge, which is featured in *Easy Rider* and *Natural Born Killers*. The environmentally savvy **7** Greater World Earthship Development, your home for two nights, is just past the 650ft-high bridge. A cross

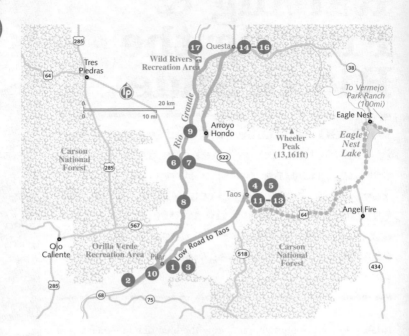

between organic Gaudí architecture and space-age fantasy, the sustainable dwellings are made from recycled tires, aluminum cans and sand, with rain catching and gray-water systems to minimize their carbon footprints. Buried on three sides by sod, and with strange solar paneling sticking off their roofs, the dwellings resemble hastily camouflaged alien spaceships from afar; inside they are chic and up to date, exactly as one would expect an extraterrestrial home to look.

> **DETOUR** Fly-fishing enthusiasts won't want to miss a visit to **Vermejo Park Ranch** (www.vermejo parkranch.com) on Hwy 555 about 40 miles west of Raton. Maintained by Ted Turner as a premier fishing and hunting lodge, this beautifully situated 920-sq-mile enterprise offers fly-fishing clinics from June through August. Rates include all meals and activities and cost around $350 per person.

Your second day is devoted to rafting New Mexico's most celebrated stretch of white water. You can either run the 15-mile-long **8** **Taos Box** with a commercial trip – Los Rios River Runners are just one of a dozen companies who offer rafting trips here – or in your own boat. The most exciting rafting is between May and June, when water levels are at their peak. The rapids to keep an eye out for include "Dead Car" and "Powder Line Falls" (both Class IV) and the "Rock Garden," the biggest rapid of them all, a technical Class IV plus. If you have your own boat, it's free to run the Taos Box, but you need to register at the launch site. To get here, take Hwy 522 east from Taos to Arroyo Hondo and turn left just north of Herb's Lounge (a bar). The

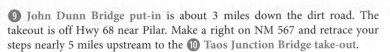

9 John Dunn Bridge put-in is about 3 miles down the dirt road. The takeout is off Hwy 68 near Pilar. Make a right on NM 567 and retrace your steps nearly 5 miles upstream to the **10** Taos Junction Bridge take-out.

Return to Taos for dinner at historic **11** Doc Martin's. Relax by the kiva-style fireplace and pop the cork on one of its award-winning wines, then dive headlong into the most delicious *chiles rellenos*. The **12** Alley Cantina is the oldest building in town, constructed in the 1500s by forward-thinking Native American capitalists. Today it's a good bar to catch live music ranging from Zydeco to rock and jazz. Devote day three to fly-fishing. Visit **13** Los Rios Anglers in Taos for the scoop on good spots and to pick up bait. The company also runs tailored trips to unspoiled private lands threaded with secret sparkling streams. Some of the best public fishing is just south of Pilar on the Rio Grande. The quiet portion of the river north of the Racecourse is where to go for cutthroat trout and northern pike up to 32in in length – the record fish was 54in long, which is just shy of 5ft!

"...inside they are chic and up to date, exactly as one would expect an extraterrestrial home to look."

Historic **14** Questa, 40 miles to the northwest, is your final destination. It's the jumping-off point for your final rafting trip. Have an early dinner at the **15** Questa Café, a Southwestern diner beloved for its Frito pie, chile-cheese fries (go for red) and home-made desserts. And get a good night's sleep at the basic but comfortable **16** Kachina Motel. The 6-mile-long **17** Upper Box is New Mexico's most technical white water and can only be run in spring. Congress designated this portion of the Rio Grande one of the nation's eight original Wild and Scenic Rivers in 1968, and this set of rapids is in a remote, steep-walled volcanic canyon. The three biggest rapids – NCO, Hell Hole and Big – all start with huge drops in a fast-flowing current. The hardest part of the ride, however, is the straight-up, nearly mile-long hike after taking out!

HOT (SPRING) BOXING WITH BUBBLY

If you're lucky enough to be rafting the Taos Box in a private boat, bring some bubbly to sip while soaking in the hot springs along the way. The first homemade set of pools is just south of the put-in on the left bank. The second set is about 2 miles further downstream – and easier to spot. Watch for a gash in both sides of the sheer canyon wall. The remnants of an old stagecoach trail, it signals your next soaking spot on the river's right bank.

Becca Blond & Aaron Anderson

TRIP 55

TRIP INFORMATION

GETTING THERE
Pilar is 116 miles north of Albuquerque. Take I-25 for 57 miles to Hwy 285 north, continue for 28 miles and merge onto Hwy 68 north; Pilar is another 28 miles north.

DO
Los Rios Anglers
This tackle shop sells fishing licenses and runs personalized, guided fly-fishing trips. Staff are friendly; don't be shy about asking where to cast your reel. ☎ 575-758-2798; www.losrios.com; 126 W Plaza; day trips 1/2/3 people $250/275/450

Los Rios River Runners
The best-known company rafting the Taos Box and Racecourse. ☎ 575-776-8854; www.losriosriverrunners.com; Rio Grande Gorge Visitors Center, Hwy 68, Pilar; Taos Box $100, Racecourse $50; ☺ 8am-6pm

EAT & DRINK
Alley Cantina
Live music almost nightly. ☎ 505-758-2121; 121 Terracina Lane; pub grub $6-14; ☺ from 11:30am

Doc Martin's
Bert Philips (the Doc's bro-in-law) and Ernest Blumenschein cooked up the idea of the Taos Society of Artists at this cozy restaurant. ☎ 505-758-1977; 125 Paseo del Pueblo Norte; mains $5-35; ☺ 7am-10pm

Eske's Brew Pub & Eatery
Check out this crowded hang-out with 25 microbrews on and good food. ☎ 505-758-1517; 106 Des Georges Lane; pub grub $6-10; ☺ 4-10pm Mon-Thu, 11am-10pm Fri-Sun

Questa Café
The best place in Questa for hearty New Mexican fare. ☎ 575-586-9631; 2422 NM 522; mains $4-10; ☺ 6am-10pm Mon-Sat, 6am-3pm Sun

SLEEP
Greater World Earthship Development
Rent an Earthship for a boutique-chic, solar-powered experience. Look for the office 1.5 miles west of the Rio Grande Bridge on Hwy 64. ☎ 505-751-0462; www.earthship.org; US Hwy 64, Taos; r $125-175

Kachina Motel
Pretty basic, but cute, clean and right on the water. ☎ 575-586-0640; 2306 NM 522, Questa; r $80

USEFUL WEBSITES
www.nmparks.com
www.sdcmountainworks.com/water/whitewater.php

LINK YOUR TRIP
www.lonelyplanet.com/trip-planner

New Mexico's Wine Countries

FOOD & DRINK

WHY GO Small boutique wineries hidden in the Rio Grande bosque and dotting the piñon-studded hillsides of central and northern New Mexico, boast award-winning wines, many crisp, fruity and the perfect accompaniment to the state's chile-infused cuisine. Pick your designated driver and hit the road!

TIME
3 days

DISTANCE
230 miles

BEST TIME TO GO
May – Nov

START
Albuquerque, NM

END
Santa Fe, NM

ALSO GOOD FOR

OUTDOORS

The oldest winemaking region in the country, the first vineyards in New Mexico were planted by a Franciscan monk and a Capuchin monk in 1629 at the San Antonio de Padua Mission at Senecu, on the east bank of the Rio Grande, just north of present-day San Antonio. Grown from a cutting called vitis vinifera, or "mission grapes," the grapes at Senecu provided sacramental wine to missionaries throughout the state. In 1880, during its peak wine production, more than 3150 acres of grape vines in New Mexico and the territory produced more than a million gallons annually. By the 1920s, Rio Grande flooding, a particularly harsh climate and Prohibition killed the industry in the state, and it wasn't until 1978 that the winemaking returned to New Mexico.

Today, wineries in New Mexico are small mom-and-pop affairs, and though some have national reputations, most sell their wines only to local markets, or from their wineries alone. Begin a wine-tasting trip through New Mexico with wineries hidden in the outskirts of ❶ Albuquerque, a city that despite its western sprawl and choking traffic boasts several well-preserved pockets of farmland along the Rio Grande. Settle into a handsome Southwestern room at ❷ Los Poblanos Historic Inn, a former ranch surrounded by lavender fields in the summer and pumpkin patches in the fall. A big lawn, shaded by cottonwoods, sits next to a tiled pool (the oldest in Albuquerque), perfect for whiling away an afternoon with a bottle of wine and a book. Walking trails meander through the inn's gardens and organic farm, along the centuries-old acequia (irrigation ditch) and past the chickens

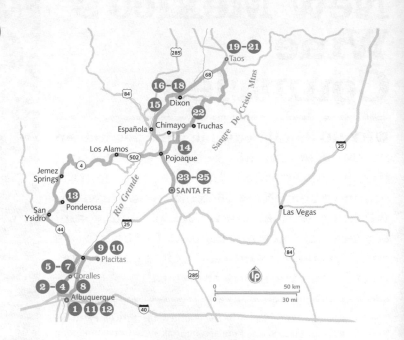

and goats. Breakfast includes fruit and veggies grown on-site, and the inn is 100% committed to an environmentally friendly agenda.

Across the street from Los Poblanos is ③ **Anderson Valley Vineyards**, a tiny winery at the end of a dirt road. Its Red Chile Cabernet, a simple cab infused with red-chile powder, changes subtly but distinctly when eaten with a chocolate kiss. Only in New Mexico! From here, head down the road to the stately ④ **Casa Rondena**, the most elegant of New Mexico's wineries. The high-ceilinged tasting room is housed in one of several Mediterranean-style buildings that cluster together among the arbors, and there are several tables outside by the pond where you can sit with your glass of wine.

Situated north on Rio Grande Blvd and west across the Rio Grande is ⑤ **Corrales**, a small farming community squished amongst cookie-cutter developments and the floodplains of the Rio Grande bosque. Call in advance for a visit to ⑥ **Milagro Vineyards**, family owned and one of the smallest wineries in New Mexico, with a tasty hand-crafted blend of Zinfandel, Merlot and Cabernet called Corrales Red and an odd T-shirt featuring a bow-tied pig enjoying a glass of wine. Don't miss ⑦ **Corrales Winery**, a lovely spot with a kiva-style tasting room with a semicircle of windows that offers spectacular views of the vineyards and the distant Sandia Mountains. Owned by a retired Sandia lab engineer, this winery makes some of the best wine in New Mexico, but it isn't sold in stores so stock up.

Two final wineries in and around Albuquerque couldn't be more different. The vineyards of the **8** **Gruet Winery** are located hours away in the state's agricultural south, but the winemaking facilities and tasting room is located along I-25 in Albuquerque; the winery's excellent offerings more than compensate for this unpleasant location. Indeed, Gruet is the largest and most nationally recognized of New Mexico wines, and its sparkling whites earn rave reviews. Continue north on I-25 and about 6 miles east to **9** **Placitas**, sheltered in the foothills of the Sandia Mountains and boasting a 19th-century mission church and excellent hiking, where you'll find the charmingly low-key **10** **Anasazi Fields Winery**. Vintner Jim Fish focuses on wines handcrafted from his own plums, apricots, peaches and blackberries. Distinct and unique, they're not sweet, as many fruit wines are. It's an acquired taste, but what better place to begin an exploration into a different kind of wine than sitting in this oasis, listening to the desert wind or sitting by the kiva fireplace. Their whimsical cranberry wine, surprisingly tasty, is popular during the Thanksgiving holidays.

After a siesta back at Los Poblanos, head down Rio Grande Blvd to Central Ave for dinner at **11** **Artichoke Café**, a local favorite with a fantastic wine list. Sit at the wine bar or head straight to the decidedly urban dining room or tiny courtyard for organic and locally grown fare cooked with creative flair and a New Mexican twist. For something more casual, **12** **Zinc Wine Bar & Bistro**, a couple miles east on Central Ave, has sandwiches and California-inspired bar food.

The next day, from Albuquerque drive west on Hwy 550 (I-25 exit 242) and north on Hwy 4 about an hour to **13** **Ponderosa Winery**, hidden in the piñon and juniper Ponderosa Valley of the Jemez Mountains. It's worth coming here just to sit in a rocker on the wraparound porch, lazily watching the grapes grow and not doing much of anything. Continue through the mountains, climbing several thousand feet to Los Alamos, and wind down to the Rio Grande Valley on Hwy 502 and south a half-mile on Hwy 285 for a stop at **14** **Kokkoman**, an excellent wine shop with wines from around the state and the world. From here, head north on Hwy 285 and east towards Taos on Hwy 68 to **15** **Black Mesa Winery**, best known for its Coyote Red and Antelope Red, in Velarde.

SOUTHERN WINE TRAIL

The hot days and cool nights of southern New Mexico are perfect for wine growing, and many central and northern wineries source their grapes from vineyards here. While the handful of wineries alone are not worth the drive, stop by if you're in the area visiting **White Sands National Monument** or **Carlsbad Caverns**. Wine shops in and around Albuquerque and Santa Fe carry wines from throughout the state.

After a green-chile burrito at **16** **Embudo Station**, idyllically situated on the quiet banks of the Rio Grande, continue up the river to **17** **Vivac Winery** for a dessert of handmade chocolate (try the red-chile pyramid) and a tasting flight of complex reds. A few miles down Hwy 76, in the farming town of Dixon, is ⑱ **La Chiripada Winery**. Housed in a white adobe surrounded by arbors and cottonwoods, this is one of the most pleasant stops on the trip through New Mexico wine country. Take a glass of Rio Embudo and relax on the steps before returning to Hwy 68 toward ⑲ **Taos**, about 25 miles north.

WINE FESTIVALS

Expect plenty of chile, *biscochitto*, cheese and, of course, wine at these annual celebrations.

- Toast of Taos Wine Festival, Taos (www.toastoftaos.com)
- Albuquerque Wine Festival, Albuquerque (www.abqwinefestival.com)
- Southern New Mexico Wine Festival, Las Cruces (www.snmwinefestival.com)
- Harvest Wine Festival, Las Cruces (www.wineharvestfestival.com)
- Bernalillo Wine Festival, Bernalillo (www.newmexicowinefestival.com)
- Wine Festival at Rancho de las Golondrinas, Santa Fe (www.ranchodelasgolondrinas.com)
- Santa Fe Wine and Chile Fiesta, Santa Fe (www.santafewineandchile.org)

The historic ⑳ **Old Taos Guest house**, set on several grassy acres with fruit trees, grape arbors and panoramic views from its courtyard, offers beautiful Southwestern-style rooms and suites and delicious breakfasts. Uncork that bottle you picked up along the way and relax in the hammock before heading to dinner at the richly tapestried ㉑ **Joseph's Table**. Try the duck-fat fries and an organic buffalo burger at the intimate Butterfly Bar, or indulge in an upscale culinary extravaganza in the formal dining room.

Looping back from Taos, take the ㉒ **High Road**, stopping at historic churches, galleries and hillside villages along the two-hour drive back to ㉓ **Santa Fe**. Here, just down the street from the town plaza, is the ㉔ **Santa Fe Vineyards** tasting room. Perhaps best known for its vaguely erotic O'Keeffe-esque labels, works of art in and of themselves, its wines have won several awards at the New Mexico State Fair and the Bernalillo Wine Festival.

End your trip through New Mexico wine country with piñon-crusted goat cheese and trout baked in adobe at ㉕ **La Casa Sena**. Both the formal dining room and the cantina offer excellent food and an award-winning wine list, but it's the courtyard, with a fountain and set with white tablecloths, that gives this place its charm. And just in case you find yourself wishing you had bought a few more bottles of your favorites on your trip through New Mexico wine country, don't worry. Its boutique wine store next door offers an excellent selection from New Mexico and beyond.

Jennifer Denniston

TRIP INFORMATION

GETTING THERE
Albuquerque sits at the intersection of I-40 and I-25, 63 miles south of Santa Fe.

DO
Anasazi Fields Winery
Bring a picnic to enjoy in the desert wilderness behind the winery. ☎ 505-867-3062; www.anasazifieldswinery.com; 26 Camino de los Pueblitos, Placitas; ☼ noon-5pm Wed-Sun Apr-Dec, weekends & by appointment Jan-Mar; ♿

Anderson Valley Vineyards
Friendly winemakers nestled in the Rio Grande valley north of downtown Albuquerque. ☎ 505-344-7266; 4920 Rio Grande Blvd NW, Albuquerque; ☼ noon-5pm Wed-Sun

Black Mesa Winery
A small winery in the Velarde valley, just off the highway on the way to Taos. ☎ 505-852-2820; 1502 Hwy 68, Velarde; ☼ 10am-6pm Mon-Sat, noon-6pm Sun

Casa Rondena Winery
The most elegant tasting room in the state has grandiose buildings and peaceful gardens. ☎ 505-344-5911; www.casarondena.com; 733 Chavez Rd, Albuquerque; ☼ 10am-6pm Wed-Sat, noon-6pm Sun

Corrales Winery
Lovely little winery, set in a rural village north of Albuquerque, makes some of New Mexico's best reds. ☎ 505-898-5165; 6275 Corrales Rd, Corrales; ☼ noon-5pm Wed-Sun

Gruet Winery
The biggest winery in New Mexico with nationally recognized sparkling wines. ☎ 505-821-0055; www.gruetwinery.com; 8400 Pan American Freeway, Albuquerque; ☼ 10am-5pm Mon-Fri, from noon Sat, tours 2pm daily

Kokkoman
Huge selection of wine, including most New Mexico wines, and knowledgeable staff.

☎ 505-585-2260; 34 Cities of Gold Rd, Pojoaque; ☼ 10am-6pm Mon-Sat, from noon Sun

La Chirlpada Winery
With a little white adobe tasting room, acres of vineyards and cottonwoods lining the acequia, this peaceful winery is one of the prettiest in the state. ☎ 505-579-4437; www.lachiripada.com; Hwy 75, Dixon; ☼ 10am-5pm Mon-Sat, from noon Sun; ♿

Milagro Vineyards
Husband-and-wife team make a Corrales Red and Corrales White at their tiny winery in the Rio Grande bosque. ☎ 505-898-3998; www.milagrowine.com; 985 W Ella, Corrales; ☼ by appointment only

Ponderosa Valley Vineyards
Hidden in the foothills of the Jemez Mountains, several miles from the main highway. ☎ 505-834-7487; www.ponderosawinery.com; 3171 Hwy 290, Ponderosa; ☼ 10am-5pm Tue-Sat, from 12pm Sun; ♿

Santa Fe Vineyards
Beautiful labels and award-winning wine with a downtown Santa Fe tasting room. ☎ 505-982-3474; www.santafevineyards.com; 235 Don Gaspar, Santa Fe; ☼ 11am-5pm Mon-Sat, from noon Sun

Vivac Winery
One of the newest wineries in New Mexico; brothers Jesse and Chris Padberg specialize in complex reds. ☎ 505-579-4441; 2075 Hwy 68, Dixon; ☼ 10am-6pm Mon-Sat, from noon Sun; ♿

EAT
Artichoke Café
Slick wine bar with cozy interior and outstanding menu of eclectic contemporary American fare. ☎ 505-243-0200; 424 Central Ave SE, Albuquerque; mains $12-31; ☼ 11am-3:30 Mon-Fri, 5:30-10pm Tue-Sat, to 9pm Sun & Mon

Casa Sena
Perfect winelist and courtyard dining in downtown Santa Fe. ☎ 505-988-9232;

125 E Palace, Santa Fe; mains $14-39; ☏ dining room 11:30am-3pm Mon-Sat, from 11am Sun, 5:30-10pm, cantina 5:30 and 7:30 seating Jun-Oct, limited seating Nov-May; ⟨⟩

Embudo Station
Perfectly situated for lunch between winery visits, with riverside tables in the shade of the cottonwoods. ☎ 505-852-4707; Hwy 68, Embudo; mains $8-15; ☏ noon-8pm Apr-Oct, seasonal variations; ⟨⟩

Joseph's Table
A luscious interior of dark wood and silk, exquisite food and excellent wine list. ☎ 505-751-4512; Hotel La Fonda, 108A South Taos Plaza, Taos; mains $11-39; ☏ 11:30am-2:30pm Mon-Fri, 5:30-10pm daily

Zinc Wine Bar & Bistro
Live music, wine flights and casual dining down the street from the University of New Mexico. ☎ 505-254-9462; 3009 Central NE, Albu-querque; ☏ 11am-2:30pm and 5-10pm Mon-Fri, to 11pm Sat & Sun, cellar bar 5pm-1am

SLEEP

Los Poblanos Historic Inn
Rambling hacienda surrounded by gardens and an organic farm and set in the heart of New Mexico's central wine district. ☎ 505-344-9297; www.lospoblanos.com; 4803 Rio Grande NW; d $155-255

Old Taos Guesthouse
A 180-year-old former ranch with 7 acres of orchards, grape arbors and grass; boasts handsome Southwestern rooms and delicious breakfasts. ☎ 575-758-5448; www.oldtaos.com; 1028 Witt Rd, Taos; d $85-175; ⟨⟩ ⟨⟩

USEFUL WEBSITES
www.nmwine.com
www.winecountrynm.com

LINK YOUR TRIP
www.lonelyplanet.com/trip-planner

Geronimo Trail Scenic Byway

ROUTE

WHY GO Escape civilization and travel back in time on the Geronimo Trail, where rugged black mountains collide with a sun-bleached desert, the air reeks of sage, and the road stretches on forever. Linger in well-preserved ghost towns and be time-ported to the raucous 1880s, when outlaws and silver prospectors ruled the towns in the Old West.

TIME
4 days

DISTANCE
105 miles

BEST TIME TO GO
Jun – Sep

START
Truth or Consequences, NM

END
Silver City, NM

ALSO GOOD FOR

HISTORY & CULTURE

The newly minted Geronimo Trail Scenic Byway (named for the feared Apache warrior who held out against Mexican and US raiders until his capture in 1886) is the perfect escape route if you need to go off the grid for a few days. Following in the footsteps of Apaches, pioneer prospectors and the US calvary, this series of rural roads is not only rich in history, it's also blessed with a seemingly endless amount of wide open spaces. Commercial traffic is nearly non-existent and billboards are banned, so there is little to distract your eye from the mesmerizing expanses of sage- and mesquite-scented desert or the rugged beauty of New Mexico's longest mountain chain, the Black Range. The route is graced with multiple well-preserved ghost towns, relics of the short-lived late-19th-century silver boom, where if you listen close enough, we swear you can hear the spirits whisper.

Start your trip in quirky little ❶ **Truth or Consequences**, home to a growing number of New Age hippies, off-the-grid artists and sustainable living eco-warriors. Usually referred to as T or C, Truth or Consequences is a kooky little high-desert oasis on the banks of the Rio Grande. It was called Hot Springs until the 1950s, when the town changed its name to that of the era's most popular radio game show, Truth or Consequences, in a tourism gimmick. More than half a century later, the stunt has paid off. The town has gained a reputation as the place for arty-holistic types to move to and drop out – the

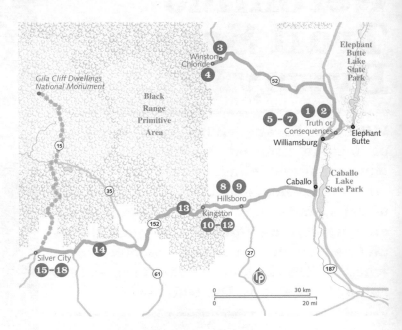

geothermal energy is said to be comparable to that found at Sedona's vortexes. Crystal shops, herbalists' offices, yoga studios, eclectic art galleries and off-the-wall boutiques clutter the shabby-chic main drag. They are the offerings of the spiritual seekers, healers, writers and painters who came here to find their vision, but need to earn their bread and butter at the same time. After paying the well-respected ❷ **Geronimo Springs Museum** a quick visit – get the scoop on the name change and info about the byway – hit the road. Oh, and don't worry that you haven't properly explored T or C, you'll be back.

Head north out of T or C on the I-25 frontage road heading west into the Cuchillo Mountains. Turn left onto Hwy 52 and get ready to explore the ghosts of centuries past. The road winds over the mountain tops and through scrub-oak desert to the eccentric former mining town of ❸ **Winston**, named in honor of a former shopkeeper who gave out generous lines of credit at his store after the silver market crashed in 1893 and prospectors lost everything. Today the town is little more than an array of old wood buildings fronting a wide meadow. It's home to just a few residents. A few miles further up the road is ❹ **Chloride**, which went bust just 20-years after it boomed in 1879. It's even more ghostlike than Winston. About the only thing left to see is the "hanging tree." Standing on Wall St in the center of town, this 200-year-old tree was used to hang criminals during the 19th century.

Backtrack to T or C for the night. Native Americans, including Geronimo, have bathed in the area's mineral-laden hot springs for centuries now, and you should too. Long said to boast therapeutic properties, the waters range in temperature from 98°F to 115°F and have a pH of 7 (neutral). Most of T or C's hotels and motels have hot mineral pools. The swankiest place to sleep and soak is the masterfully renovated 1920s-era ⑤ **Sierra Grande Lodge & Spa.** Rooms are relaxing, and the holistic spa serves everything from Reiki to massage on its menu. Grab dinner from ⑥ **Los Arcos.** The 1960s-era steakhouse is as posh as T or C gets, and serves delicious freshly caught local fish with its New York strips and tenderloins. If you've still got energy after dinner, head to popular local watering hole the ⑦ **Pine Knot Bar.** There is live Mexican music and dancing, and all the usual cocktails.

South of T or C, Hwy 152 heads west, following the austere cactus and mesquite desert of the Rio Grande Valley before winding through piñon and juniper forests, then climbing in a slow, serpentine series of hairpin turns up New Mexico's most rugged chain of mountains, the densely forested Black Range, where many a bloody battle between the United States military and Native American warriors went down.

⑧ **Hillsboro** is 17 miles west on Hwy 152, and the first in a series of almost ghost towns stretching between T or C and Silver City. Precious ore, including gold, silver and copper, was discovered in these mountains in the mid-1800s, and by the 1880s the white man had wrested the last remaining land from Geronimo's people and set mining camps up all along what is now Hwy 152. The boom didn't last long, and when the silver market crashed in 1893 so did most of these towns. Today they are in various stages of revival (or decay). Hillsboro is one of the larger remaining towns, although with a population of just 330 it's hardly big. The residents who do still call the pretty mountain village

PLANNING YOUR TRIP

The 150-mile Geronimo Trail is technically a loop, starting and ending in Truth or Consequences, but most people only tackle the first two sections described in this trip. That's because the 46 miles along triangular loop's western edge are rough packed-dirt only accessible to 4WD vehicles. If you have the right wheels, however, this is a great off-road trip through the green wilderness of Gila National Forest. From Chloride, continue west on Hwy 52 until reaching Forest Rd 150 south. Follow it all the way to Silver City.

home make their living farming or catering to tourists on the ghost-town trail – there are a few galleries and shops open on the old-fashioned main street. Hillsboro is best known for its Apple Festival on the Labor Day weekend (early September), featuring everything apple, including freshly baked pies and delicious cider. The ⑨ **Barbershop Café** is the local hang-out and serves the best booze-soaked desserts around – try the Grand Marnier cake or the bread pudding spiked with bourbon. Wash all the sugar down with a sandwich; we like the grilled veggie.

Continue west after lunch, and keep an eye out for the "dead end" sign that points to ❿ Kingston. With 100 people fewer than Hillsboro, the sign is pretty appropriate. A blink-and-miss-it community of just 30 people (compared to 7000 in its heyday), Kingston is just a small clutch of wooden buildings lining a narrow portion of the road. The place is very quiet – so quiet, in fact, it's hard to believe this was once the biggest, baddest city in New Mexico, boasting 27 bars catering to everyone from Chinese fortune seekers to Billy the Kid, Butch Cassidy and Mark Twain. The only building that looks almost exactly as good as it did during the 19th century is the beautifully restored ⓫ Percha Bank, c 1884. Complete with an enormous working vault, the bank building is now a museum and art gallery. The friendly owners create, and sell, very fine quality letter-press printing. Spending the night in a true ghost town is a hair-raising experience. There's just something special – an almost tingly feeling – about slumbering amidst all that history and hardly any people. In Kingston, stay at the atmospheric ⓬ Black Range Lodge. The main building dates to the 1880s and features thick stone walls and wooden beams on the ceiling. Rooms are cozy and warm with antiques and old quilts. A full breakfast is served in the morning and you're welcome to use the big kitchen for self-catering at night (which is good because there isn't anywhere else to eat in Kingston!).

DETOUR

The **Gila Cliff Dwellings National Monument** is just 44 miles northwest of Silver City, in the pristine Gila National Forest at the end of Hwy 15. Inhabited by native people for one generation at the end of the 13th century, the monument consists of about 40 rooms in a series of five shallow caves. Reach the ruins via a 1-mile round-trip trail 2 miles north of the visitors center on Hwy 15. Parts of the trail are steep and require ladder climbing.

It's a very slow uphill crawl around a series of hairpin bends from Kingston to the top of the Black Range, which crests at the 8228ft ⓭ Emory Pass. The view from the lookout point atop the summit makes the drive worthwhile. From here the dark, craggy peaks disappear into the umber hills of the Rio Grande Valley to the east and the sky, up here above the tree-line, seems bigger and bluer than anywhere else on the trail. Continue on towards Silver City, stopping at the ⓮ Santa Rita Chino Open Pit Copper Mine Observation Point, about 6 miles from the intersection with Hwy 180. Worked by Native Americans and Spanish and Anglo settlers, it's the oldest active mine in the Southwest. The open-pit mine is a staggering 1.5 miles wide and 1800ft deep, and produces 300 million pounds of copper annually.

⓯ Silver City, the grand-daddy of New Mexico's boom-bust-boom town success stories, is your final destination. Silver City's streets are dressed with a lovely mishmash of old brick and cast-iron Victorians and thick-walled red adobe buildings, and the place still emits a Wild West air. Billy the Kid spent some of his childhood here, and a few of his haunts can still be found mixed in with the new gourmet coffee shops, quirky galleries and Italian ice-cream parlors gracing its pretty Victorian downtown. Silver City is, especially by Southwestern New Mexican standards, a pretty happening place these days. The town attracts adventure addicts, who come to work and play in its some 15 mountain ranges, four rivers and action-packed Gila National Forest just outside its front door. It's also home to a healthy student population – Western New Mexico University is based here. Ensconced in an elegant house from 1881, the **16** Silver City Museum displays pottery, and mining and household artifacts from Silver City's Victorian heyday. Its shop has a good selection of Southwestern books and gifts.

" Silver City's streets are dressed with a lovely mishmash of old brick and cast-iron Victorians…"

Grab some food at Silver City's most popular restaurant, **17** Diane's Restaurant & Bakery, which does a romantic dinner under dim lighting. Go back in the morning for breakfast, when you should order the Hatch Benedict eggs – the house take on the original is doused with the region's beloved green chile pepper. Spend your last night on the Geronimo Trail at Silver City's best sleeping spot, the venerable **18** Palace Hotel. In a restored 1882 hostelry, it has 19 wonderful rooms kitted out with old-fashioned Territorial-era decor.

Becca Blond

TRIP INFORMATION

GETTING THERE
Truth or Consequences is located 150 miles due south of Albuquerque on I-25.

DO
Geronimo Springs Museum
Extensive place with minerals, local art and historical artifacts including prehistoric Mimbres pots. ☎ 505-894-6600; 211 Main St, Truth or Consequences; adult/student $3/1.50; ⏱ 9am-5pm Mon-Sat

Percha museum
A museum and art gallery in a carefully restored period building. ☎ 575-895-5032; www.perchabank.com; Main St, Kingston; admission free; ⏱ 10am-4pm Fri-Sun Jun-Aug

Silver City Museum
In an elegant Victorian home, the shop has a good selection of Southwestern books and gifts. ☎ 575-538-5921; www.silvercity museum.org; 312 W Broadway, Silver City; admission free; ⏱ 9:30am-4:30pm Tue-Fri, 10am-4pm Sat & Sun

EAT & SLEEP
Black Range Lodge
This mountain outpost is the perfect ghost-town sleep. ☎ 575-895-5652; www.black rangelodge.com; 119 Main St, Kingston; r $80

Barbershop Café
Delicious sandwiches and desserts are served in appealing old-fashioned environs. ☎ 575-895-5283; 200 Main St, Hillsboro; mains $5-12; ⏱ 11am-3pm Wed, Thu & Sun, to 8pm Fri & Sat

Diane's Restaurant & Bakery
Order something doused in green chile at this popular eatery. ☎ 575-538-8722; 510 N Bullard St, Silver City; mains $10-25; ⏱ 11am-2:30pm & 5-8:30pm Tue-Fri, 9am-2pm Sat & Sun

Los Arcos
The most upscale place to dine, inside or out, in town. ☎ 575-894-6200; 1400 N Date St, Truth or Consequences; mains $15-25; ⏱ 5-10pm

Palace Hotel
Rooms that vary from small (with a double bed) to two-room suites (with king- or queen-size beds) outfitted with refrigerators, microwaves, phones and TVs. ☎ 575-388-1811; www.zianet.com/palacehotel; 106 W Broadway, Silver City; r from $45

Pine Knot Bar
Come to T or C's top local hang-out for live Mexican music and dancing. ☎ 575-894-2714; 1400 E Riverside Dr, Truth or Consequences

Sierra Grand Lodge & Spa
Nonguests are charged $25 for the first person then $5 per additional person to use the pool. Rooms and suites are a mix of luxe and tranquil and have wi-fi access. ☎ 575-894-6976; www.sierragrandelodge.com; 501 McAdoo St, Truth or Consequences; r from $99

USEFUL WEBSITES
www.geronimotrail.com
www.livingghosttowns.com

LINK YOUR TRIP
www.lonelyplanet.com/trip-planner

Stargazing New Mexico

WHY GO Astronomers and romantics alike rejoice at New Mexico's night sky: a black-velvet blanket sparkling with constellations of diamonds. With little light pollution and wide open spaces, stargazing here is pretty perfect. And from B&Bs to hot mineral springs, this trip takes you to the best places to watch the stars fall.

Start your stargazing explorations in America's original sin city, ① Las Vegas, NM. At one time a true-blue outlaw town, this is where Billy the Kid and pal Vicente Silva (who once killed 40 people at one time) held court and Doc Holliday owned a saloon (although his business ultimately failed after he shot at too many customers). Today, Las Vegas is an elegant, sienna-tinted city that serves as a backdrop for many a star-studded Hollywood Western, including recent Oscar-winner *No Country for Old Men*.

But enough about silver-screen stars; you've come for stars of the night sky. Take Hwy 518 north for 13 miles to tiny Sapello and the ② Star Hill Inn, your home for two nights (the required minimum). Sitting on 200 remote acres high in the Sangre de Cristo Mountains, it is one of the state's top stargazing retreats with little light pollution, so when owner Phil Mahon introduces you to the night sky's grandeur, you really see a million stars. The eight Southwestern-style cottages are decorated with fireplaces and kitchens. Bring food. Spend day two hiking through the surrounding wilderness area or just relaxing in the high desert sunshine.

Backtrack to Las Vegas on morning three for breakfast at the ③ Super Chief Coffee Bar. Organic food is prepared to order and the coffee is the best in town. It's 250-plus miles from Las Vegas to Cloudcroft,

TIME
5 days

DISTANCE
400 miles

BEST TIME TO GO
Aug – Nov

START
Las Vegas, NM

END
Truth or Consequences, NM

your next stargazing destination. We won't lie: the first half of the drive, on Hwy 84 south, isn't all that interesting, but the scenery improves drastically after merging with Hwy 54 south. Here the road climbs through forest and over mountain passes before descending into the otherworldly-looking realm of gleaming white dunes in mysterious ❹ **White Sands National Monument**. By this point you'll be ready to stretch your legs. From the monument visitors center, drive the 16-mile scenic loop into the heart of the dazzling white sea of sand – actually not sand at all, but granulated chalky gypsum rock – stopping frequently to climb, romp, slide, roll and hike (and maybe pretend you're on another planet).

WHAT'S WITH THE NAME?

In 1950, TV game-show host Ralph Edwards wished aloud that a town somewhere in the US liked his show so much that they would name themselves after it. And, by a margin of 4 to 1, the 1294 residents of Truth or Consequences – called Hot Springs at the time – voted to change their name to match the show. That same year, NBC broadcast its first live game show ever from… (where else?) Truth or Consequences, NM to celebrate the show's 10th anniversary.

From White Sands it's a short trip to ❺ **Cloudcroft** and then a gorgeous 20-mile drive south on the Sunspot Scenic Byway (Hwy 130) to the ❻ **Sacramento Peak Observatory**, one of the world's largest solar observatories. Though it's primarily for scientists, tourists can take self-guided tours on Friday, Saturday and Sunday at 2pm June through August. Double back to Cloudcroft after touring the observatory, and grab a beer on the outside deck at ❼ **Rebecca's**, which has distant views of the dunes at White Sands. After the sun starts to set, head inside for an elegant menu covering everything from steak tenderloin to cheese enchiladas. There is more star peeping in store for the evening. Sleep at ⑧ **New Mexico Skies**, which rents high-powered stargazing equipment to guests for night-sky viewing – the place is virgin when it comes to light pollution. Ask the staff for help if you are an astronomy amateur.

The classic, rural New Mexican town of ⑨ **Socorro** is your next stop. Wander the historic downtown and check out the 17th-century ⑩ **San Miguel Mission**, three blocks north of the plaza. Then grab breakfast or lunch at the popular ⑪ **Socorro Springs Brewing Co**. The restaurant brews its own beer. Head west on Hwy 60 for 40 miles to Hwy 52 and south 4 miles

DETOUR Drive 50 miles north-west of Socorro to see New Mexico's strangest attraction, the **Lightning Field** (www.lightningfield.org). The work of sculptor Walter de Maria, it was laid out in 1977 by setting 500 stainless-steel poles in a 1 mile by 1km grid. The poles attract electricity during violent summer thunderstorms, and when lightning strikes it creates a crackling, brilliant, white strobe light and sound show. Sleep in basic digs by the field ($150 to $250 per person). It's expensive, but you're paying for the experience, which is priceless.

to visit the ⑫ **Very Large Array Radio Telescope**. If the setting looks familiar, it's because you've seen it in the Jodie Foster alien classic *Contact*. Set in a Y-shaped configuration, the National Radio Astronomy Observatory's giant telescope consists of 27 huge antenna dishes (82ft wide and weighing 240 tons apiece) sprouting from the high plains like a mother ship docking station. So what's the point, besides looking cool and being in a movie set – what is with stars and stars on this trip anyway? Well, the radio waves collected have increased humankind's understanding of the phenomena making up the surface of the sun and other planets.

When you've finished contemplating the space-time continuum, or at least tried to make contact with Mars, take the long-road to your final destination. Hwy 52 winds south from the big telescope through wild country and ghost towns before popping out on I-25 just north of ⑬ **Truth or Consequences**, New Mexico's best kooky town. End your astronomy adventure staring at the star studded sky from the 112°F-warm comfort of heavy mineral water in an outdoor tub at ⑭ **Charles Motel & Bath House**, where you can also sleep.
Becca Blond

TRIP INFORMATION

GETTING THERE
Las Vegas, NM, is located on I-25, 65 miles east of Santa Fe. Hwy 85 (Grand Ave) parallels the interstate and is the main thoroughfare.

DO

New Mexico Skies
Digs at this stargazing B&B are in simple knotty pine cottages or a family apartment. Advance reservations required. ☎ 575-687-2429; www.nmskies.com; off Hwy 82, east of Cloudcroft; 1-/2-bedroom apt from $150, 3-bedroom home from $250

Sacramento Peak Observatory
The world's largest solar observatory is used mostly by scientists, but public tours are offered three days a week in summer. ☎ 575-434-7000; Hwy 130 south of Cloudcroft; 🕐 visitors center 10am-4pm

San Miguel Mission
Originally built as a small church by the Spaniards, it was expanded into a mission in the 1620s, and remains Socorro's star historical attraction. ☎ 575-835-1620; 403 El Camino Real, Socorro; admission free

Star Hill Inn
Astronomy buffs will dig this experience-based inn, where nights are spent looking through a telescope. ☎ 505-425-5605; www.starhillinn.com; 247 Las Dispensas Rd, Sapello; cottages $170-380

Very Large Array Radio Telescope
The radio waves collected by the enormous dishes here collect data to help scientists understand the mechanics behind geophysics. VLA; www.vla.nrao.edu; Hwy 52; admission free; 🕐 8:30am-sunset

White Sands National Monument
Driving loops and hiking trails cross the 275 sq miles of stark, rolling dunes. ☎ 575-679-2599; www.nps.gov/whsa; 15 miles southwest of Hwy 82/70; admission $3; 🕐 8am-7pm Jun-Aug, to 5pm Sep-May

SLEEP & EAT

Charles Motel & Bath House
An affordable retro 1940s motor-court motel with the hottest mineral water in town. Offers spa with ayurvedic treatments, sauna, massage and holistic healing. ☎ 575-894-7154; www.charlesspa.com; 601 Broadway, Truth or Consequences; r $41-47

Rebecca's
Rebecca's runs a longstanding favorite Sunday brunch and serves the best food in Cloudcroft. ☎ 575-682-3131; 1 Corona Pl, Cloudcroft; mains $6-25; 🕐 7am-9.30pm

Socorro Springs Brewing Company
An airy place serving calzones, decent pasta dishes, homemade soups and big breakfasts. ☎ 575-838-0650; 1012 N California St, Socorro; mains $6-11; 🕐 6:30am-10pm Mon-Fri, 8am-10pm Sat & Sun; 🚼

Super Chief Coffee Bar
If you're hungry, it's worth getting off I-25 just to eat at this relatively new café serving healthy, organic fare and the best coffee in town. There's wi-fi. ☎ 505-454-1360; 514 Grand Ave, Las Vegas; mains $4-19; 🕐 6.30am-2pm

USEFUL WEBSITES
www.nmskies.org
www.taas.org

LINK YOUR TRIP

www.lonelyplanet.com/trip-planner

Day Trips from Santa Fe & Albuquerque

If Santa Fe and Albuquerque's urbaneness starts to stifle, escape. Soak in mineral-heavy hot springs sipping lithium-laced water or hike through lunarlike badlands. There are plenty of adventures within an hour's drive of both cities that help you discover exactly why this state is nicknamed the "Land of Enchantment."

CHIMAYÓ

Chimayó, a tiny adobe village sandwiched between cliffs in a sage-scented high-desert locale, is our favorite day trip from Santa Fe. It doesn't matter how many times you visit, there's something magical about the 1816 Santuario de Chimayó that keeps drawing you back. Legend has it that the dirt from the church has healing powers, and the back room is a shrine to its miracles, with canes, wheelchairs, crutches and other medical aids hanging from the wall. Kneel by the earthen pit, set up almost like an altar, and smear some of the healing dirt inside on your ailing body. Also stop by the Centinela Traditional Arts to admire (and perhaps purchase) the hand-loomed weaving of Irvin Trujillo and 20 local weavers. Trujillo is a seventh-generation weaver whose carpets are in collections at the Smithsonian in Washington, DC. The Rancho de Chimayó is where to break bread. The fabulous restaurant serves classic New Mexican cuisine, courtesy of the Jaramillo family's famed recipes, along with perfect margaritas. But it's the high-desert location and old-school ambience that makes it most appealing. **From Santa Fe take US 285/84 north to Española, then Hwy 64 (the High Rd to Taos) north to Chimayó.**

See also TRIPS 44, 47 & 49

OJO CALIENTE

Billed as America's oldest health resort, Ojo Caliente is our favorite high-desert escape. Set against a crumbly orange sandstone and baby-blue New Mexican sky backdrop, Ojo, which means 'hot eye' in Spanish, is a charmingly

339

shabby-chic family-owned resort offering five wonderful hot mineral springs. The on-site Artesian Restaurant prepares organic and local ingredients three meals a day with aplomb. The springs are considered sacred by Pueblo Indians. In an unusual trick of hydrogeology, each of the beautiful pools is fed by a different water source with different mineral contents. We love the indoor soda spring, and floating in its heavy tepid waters is as relaxing as life gets. The enclosed pool is full of steam and perfect for floating in the mist. It's meant to help relieve digestion problems. Also check out the cliff-side iron spring pool, known for its blood -leansing and immunity-boosting waters. Hit the sauna and steam room after soaking, then indulge in a spa treatment. On your way out fill up a water bottle from the lithium spring fountain – it's meant to cure depression. **Ojo Caliente is located 40 miles north of Santa Fe on Hwy 285.**

See also **TRIPS 43, 47, 51 & 53**

KASHA-KATUWE TENT ROCKS NATIONAL MONUMENT

Kasha-Katuwe Tent Rocks National Monument is a beloved weekend hiking spot for Santa Fe and Albuquerque residents and their canine companions. Conveniently located just off I-25 between the two cities, hitting the trail at Tent Rocks is a bizarre and beautiful experience taking you over smooth rock mounds and through narrow slot canyons. New Mexicans often refer to the rocks as "the Hoodoos," due to their strange light-orange, sometimes tiger striped, cone-like shape. The strange formations are the result of volcanoes in the nearby Jemez Mountains. When the ash from the spewing lava pit spread and cooled it was sculpted into the teepee-like formations and steep-sided, narrow canyons you see today. Visitors can hike up a dry riverbed through the piñon-covered desert to the formations, where sandy paths weave through the rocks and canyons. Bring lots of water – it can get hot up here. The trail ends at the edge of a sandstone cliff, looking into one of the long canyons below. You'll need a couple of hours to drive the desert dirt road to get here and to hike around a bit, but it's well worth it. **To reach the national monument, take I-25 exit 264; follow Hwy 16 west to Hwy 22.**

See also **TRIPS 38, 54 & 55**

BANDELIER NATIONAL MONUMENT

Pale and pockmarked canyon walls plunging into lush, narrow valleys would have marked Bandelier National Monument for preservation even without the beautiful and well-preserved Ancestral Puebloan Indian ruins, occupied between 1150 and 1550. Show up early on weekends to beat the crowds. More than 70 miles of trails traverse almost 33,000 acres of pine forest. Standouts include the easy 1.4-mile Main Loop Trail, which runs past petroglyphs and the Frijoles Ruins, with a worthwhile 2-mile round-trip spur out to the sky-scraping Ceremonial Cave, otherwise known as the Alcove House. (The 150ft of ladders at the Alcove House may not be suitable for smaller kids, but climbing into these actual ancient dwellings is a remarkable experience for everyone else.) The Falls Trail offers a 3-mile round-trip to the Upper Falls, and a steep and recommended 5-mile round-trip past the Lower Falls to the Rio Grande. In an unattached segment of the park 13 miles north on NM 4, 2-mile Tsankawi Trail threads along a path so ancient that it's literally worn into the mesa bedrock. **Bandelier is 42 miles from Santa Fe via Hwy 285 north to Hwy 502 west towards Los Alamos, where you'll merge onto NM 4 and continue 12 miles south to the park entrance.**

See also **TRIPS 42, 43, 49 & 52**

ESPAÑOLA

Founded by Don Juan de Oñate as the first state capitol in 1598, Española today is the anti Santa Fe. It serves up the reality of life for many rural New Mexicans without any blinders. Yet despite the hardships facing its residents, Española is also home to many proud and optimistic people – like town celebrity Monica Lovato, a champion super-flyweight boxer highly ranked by the World Boxing Council, who brings hope and a great example to kids coming up behind her. Grab a meal at the Rancho de San Juan, just north of town. This little gem features a spectacular setting for dining on New Mexican classics at two nightly sittings. Considered the number-one restaurant in New Mexico by many, Rancho de San Juan is so good, locals drive from Santa Fe just to dine here. Duck arrives at the table cooked with Chinese spices, drizzled with a blood-orange glaze and served with pineapple and rice pilaf. The town is also the headquarters for the Northern and Northwestern loops of New Mexico's new green byway, the Fiber Arts Trail. Pop into the Española Valley Fiber Arts Center for the scoop on the grass-roots art trail. You can even do a bit of shopping for hand-loomed shawls and blankets while you're here. **Espanola is 25 miles north of Santa Fe on Hwy 285.**

See also **TRIPS 37, 39, 44, 48, 50 & 51**

LOS ALAMOS

Built on long, thin mesas separated by steep canyons, Los Alamos sits in a stunning location surrounded by forest and offers a fascinating dynamic where the smartest scientists in the world coexist alongside back-to-nature hippies and society drop-outs. Los Alamos gained instant fame on July 16, 1945, when a flash in the New Mexico desert forever changed the world. In that single moment, later said to be the most important event of the 20th century, scientists released energy equal to all the bombs dropped on London by Nazi Germany. Soon afterwards, on August 6 and August 9, 1945, the cities of Hiroshima and Nagasaki were destroyed by the first atomic bombs used in warfare. You can't actually visit the Los Alamos National Laboratory, where the first atomic bomb was conceived, but you can visit the well-designed Bradbury Science Museum for the scoop on atomic history. It's one of several museums devoted to nuclear science sprinkled around the small mountain town. Your best bet for a beer and a great green-chile cheeseburger is at the Canyon Bar & Grill. You won't find any glitz or Southwestern affectations here, but the local hang-out has a long bar, a pool table, live music and dancing on Friday, and karaoke on Thursday. **Los Alamos is northwest of Santa Fe; follow Hwy 285 north to Hwy 502 west into town.**

See also **TRIPS 39, 43, 51 & 56**

LAS VEGAS

Not to be confused with its wild-n-crazy namesake in Nevada, Las Vegas is one of the loveliest towns in New Mexico. It has a strollable downtown, a shady plaza and some 900 gorgeous buildings – most of them not adobe – listed in the National Register of Historic Places. The classic Western backdrop is the perfect spot for a high-noon shootout, an ambience exploited in cowboy flicks like *Wyatt Earp* and *The Ballad of Gregorio Cortez*. Home to the Comanche people for some 10,000 years, Las Vegas was founded by Mexico in 1835 as a stop along the Santa Fe Trail and later the Santa Fe Railroad. It quickly grew into one of the biggest, baddest boomtowns in the West. Today Las Vegas retains a sienna-tinted elegance and lively social whirl, thanks in part to the city's two universities. It's also the gateway to two striking wilderness areas: the Pecos Wilderness and Las Vegas National Wildlife Refuge. Do as the locals do and head to Estella's Café for lunch. The devoted patrons treasure the homemade New Mexican fare offered by the Gonzalez family since 1950 in this time-tested favorite. **Las Vegas is about an hour east of Santa Fe on I-25.**

See also **TRIPS 2, 9, 46 & 57**

Behind the Scenes

THIS BOOK

This guidebook was commissioned in Lonely Planet's Oakland office, and produced by the following:
Product Development Manager Heather Dickson
Commissioning Editor Suki Gear
Coordinating Editor Jeanette Wall
Coordinating Cartographer Hunor Csutoros
Coordinating Layout Designer Katherine Marsh
Managing Editor Geoff Howard
Managing Cartographer Alison Lyall
Managing Layout Designers Laura Jane
Assisting Editors Sarah Bailey, Andrea Dobbin, Carly Hall, Averil Robertson
Assisting Cartographers Mick Garrett, David Kemp
Series Designer James Hardy
Cover Designers Gerilyn Attebery, Jennifer Mullins
Project Manager Eoin Dunlevy
Thanks to Imogen Bannister, Sasha Baskett, Adam Bextream, Yvonne Bischofberger, David Burnett, Owen Eszeki, Mark Germanchis, Chris Girdler, Michelle Glynn, Brice Gosnell, Martin Heng, Liz Heynes, Lauren Hunt, Ali Lemer, John Mazzocchi, Darren O'Connell, Paul Piaia, Julie Sheridan, Glenn van der Knjiff, Karla Zimmerman

THANKS

Becca Blond This book is for my best friend, Nicole Dial, who was killed when the convoy she was traveling in was ambushed on August 13, 2008, outside Kabul, Afghanistan. Nicky was a humanitarian helping Afghani children traumatized by the war. She was only 30. To Suki Gear, Heather Dickson, Brice Gosnell and Jeanette Wall: Thank you SO MUCH for your patience and compassion. To my boys, Aaron & Duke: I love you both. To my parents: Thank you for throwing me the best wedding in the world. I love you.

Aaron Anderson Thanks to Suki Gear and Jeanette Wall for being fabulous, patient editors. To my Grandma Pauline and Uncle Joe, I love you and was so happy you were able to share my wedding day. Thanks for your faith and support. To Eric Hoerske: Thanks for being my best man, brother, the dude abides. To my wife, I love you.

Jennifer Denniston Thank you to Suki Gear, Alison Lyall, Becca Blond, Jeanette Wall, and Carly Hall at Lonely Planet; to Heather Webb; the Cottonwood School community; Edward Borins, Nancy Rutland, Richard Harris and Yemane Asmerom; Marj and Wes Whitley; and to my family Rhawn, Anna and Harper, I can't imagine a road trip without you.

Lisa Dunford I'd like to thank all the friendly people I met on the road who made the trip such a delight. I so appreciate Michael Plyer and Larry Sanford's help. And I'm grateful to Tom and Tracy Thegze for paving the way. Suki, Becca and Jeanette – you're great to work with!

Josh Krist Thanks to life-partner-in-crime Hélène Goupil. Miriam Krist, welcome! Thanks to mom and Jacob Whitt; my dad, Arizona native and former gold miner; Elodie, Joelle, and Regis Goupil; all my Arizona friends, especially Tommy Fasano. Triple thanks to Didier Bruneel. Joe Vasquez, thanks for the car!

Wendy Yanagihara Many thanks to Suki Gear for sending me out and being a kick-ass editor; Dean Reese for his vast expertise; Danna and Bill Hendrix for making the rim-to-rim so fabulous; Serena Supplee (www.serenasupplee.com) for artistic insight; Matt Fahey for giving good quotes; and Jason Lemon for saving me from North Rim snows.

Sara Benson Big thanks to Suki Gear for this gig. Heaps of gratitude are due to all of the local Las Vegas folks who helped me out on my many research trips. Most of all, thanks to my road-trip buddy and poker-playing partner, Mike Connolly, Jr.

ACKNOWLEDGMENTS

Many thanks to the following for the use of their content:
   Internal photographs p11 (top) by Lisa Dunford; p22 Craig Lovell/Eagle Visions Photography/Alamy. All other photographs by Lonely Planet Images, and by Mark Newman p5, p24 (bottom); Douglas Steakley p6 (bottom), p16; Richard Cummins p7 (bottom), p11 (bottom), p18 (bottom), p22 (top), p24 (top); Holger Leue p6 (top), p18 (top); Witold Skrypczak p7 (top), p8 (bottom); Ralph Hopkins p8 (top), p20; John Elk III p9, p10, p17 (bottom); Karl Lehmann p13, p14; Ann Cecil p12; John Hay p15 (top), p15 (bottom); Christian Aslund p17 (top); Stephen Saks p19; Ray Laskowitz p21 (bottom); Eddie Brady p21 (top); Jerry Alexander p23.

SEND US YOUR FEEDBACK

Got feedback? We'd love to hear your corrections, suggestions, compliments or complaints, so feel free to use our feedback form: **lonelyplanet.com/contact**.

Note: We may edit, reproduce and incorporate your feedback comments in Lonely Planet products such as guidebooks, websites and digital products. If you send it in, then that counts as permission for us to use it. If you don't want your name acknowledged, please let us know.

To read our privacy policy, visit **lonelyplanet.com/privacy**.

Index

000 map pages
000 photograph pages